ECONOMIC DIGNITY

ECONOMIC DIGNITY

GENE SPERLING

PENGUIN PRESS | *New York* | *2020*

PENGUIN PRESS
An imprint of Penguin Random House LLC
penguinrandomhouse.com

TAKE THIS JOB AND SHOVE IT
Words and Music by DAVID ALLEN COE © 1977 (Renewed) WARNER-
TAMERLANE PUBLISHING CORP.
All Rights Reserved
Used By Permission of ALFRED MUSIC

ISBN 9781984879875 (hardcover)
ISBN 9781984879882 (ebook)

Printed in the United States of America
10   9   8   7   6   5   4   3   2   1

Designed by Nicole Laroche

Through their love and example, my parents, Doris and Larry Sperling, sought to inspire all their children and grandchildren to find their own path and purpose, think for themselves, cherish family above all, and fight for those denied justice and dignity. This book is for them.

CONTENTS

INTRODUCTION

In the fall of 2009, it was not unusual for me to get a call from a congressman or senator wanting to complain about President Barack Obama's economic policy. I was doing a stint as a senior counselor to the secretary of the Treasury—part of the special firefighting team brought in during the worst of the financial crisis. As I had previously been President Bill Clinton's White House national economic adviser and had worked in the West Wing every day of his eight years, many members of Congress knew me well—certainly well enough to feel comfortable complaining.

One call that fall got right to the point: "Gene, a few of us were talking, and we were hoping you could help convince President Obama that he should be focusing only on the economy—not health care!"

The congressman was not claiming that President Obama had not thrown his heart and soul into saving the economy from the most devastating financial crisis since the Great Depression. Clearly, he had. Nor was he asking for a dramatic second stimulus plan. This member of Congress, like many others, was already petrified about a political backlash over the false notion that too much had already been spent. What he wanted was better "optics." He wanted President Obama to demonstrate that he was focused solely on the economy— to use President Clinton's famous line—"like a laser beam." And that meant that he should stop talking about his fight for universal health care and talk only about jobs and growth.

At one level, this was just another call you get in the government that makes you want to scream in frustration. But there was something else that struck me more deeply: the unexamined assumption that guaranteeing health-care security for every American was somehow not about "the economy."

In the over two decades since I started my policy career on the 1988 presidential campaign of Massachusetts governor Michael Dukakis, I had been privileged to be on the field or at least in a good box seat for most of our national economic policy debate. I had been blessed to work for leaders truly committed to economic justice, from Mario Cuomo to Bill Clinton to Barack Obama. Yet I had also come to see that even for well-meaning policymakers, it was too easy to take your eye off the ball; to start confusing means and ends. Economic conventions and the day-to-day battles of politics can lead anyone to focus too much on particular economic metrics and political strategies and too little on how economic policy ultimately affects the happiness and sense of meaning and fulfillment in people's lives. Of course, no one means to lose their focus. And yet we can become too attached to certain policy designs, ideological tribes, or message frames, as if they were ends in themselves. People on all sides dig in to defend specific positions without remembering that their favored metrics or policy mechanisms are means to the ultimate end goals of lifting up people's lives, and should be evaluated and reevaluated based on their effectiveness in light of changing economic, technological, and political trends.

I personally have never related to any of the labels or policy camps that others have assigned to me over the years. It's easy to be accused of being a technocrat without conviction if you confess to being open to any policy or strategy that would work to enhance what matters most in the lives of the most people possible. Why should this be so? Why shouldn't our economic convictions and philosophies be centered on our end goals for lifting up all people, as opposed to fixed strategies for getting there? When we go to doctors for a serious matter, we want their end goal to be the promotion of our good health—not their commitment to a particular medicine or a defense of past prescriptions when they have better evidence of what now works best.

Keeping a clear eye on that ultimate end goal is also crucial for knowing what to prioritize when you are making policy. It requires not just knowing what is right, but what you feel will matter most in lifting up the lives of people you are there to serve. Too often, decisions about prioritization end up being compelled by the congressional calendar, polling, or current policy fads—without a deep and reflective consideration of what will be most meaningful in lifting up lives.

My way of clearing my head and avoiding this trap has always been to step away and ask a simple question: When someone is on their deathbed and looks back on all their years, what would they say mattered most in their economic life? What would make them feel pride and satisfaction instead of despair or frustration?

Those questions might not help determine the precise level of corporate taxation or what specific jobs program to favor. But it forces us to ask ourselves: What economic policies will matter most at a human level? Nobody on their deathbed is going to say that what mattered most to them was the deficit or spending as a percentage of gross domestic product (GDP). Instead, they will be thinking about how well they were able to care for their families; provide opportunity for their children; enjoy the best moments of family life; feel proud of their work; and enjoy camaraderie, autonomy, and respect in their jobs; and whether or not they had at least a fair shot to pursue their sense of ambition or purpose.

These reflections made me think more and more about the questions of dignity at stake in our debates on health-care policy. I found myself ruminating on the heartbreaking stories of parents with terribly ill children who couldn't provide the care they needed or whose family was left in economic despair and even bankruptcy because of gaps in coverage, discrimination against preexisting conditions, or arbitrary limits on care.

Perhaps because I was in a time of life where I was growing my own family, these stories hit me particularly hard. I knew that efficiency and controlling costs were more conventional "economic" issues in health care. But as a human being, I could think only about what a devastating assault these situations were on the very soul of these parents—on their dignity as human beings. They had done their part and worked hard their whole lives, and yet were unable to provide essential care when it was most needed for the children they loved more than life itself. While I had scores of economic ideas that I hoped to encourage future administrations to take on, I decided if there was ever a chance to permanently prevent these assaults on human dignity, it would be at the top of my list. In 2008, I was proud that those I advised—both Hillary Clinton and Barack Obama—placed universal health care at the heart of their campaigns, and that Obama stayed with it as president, even when polling and political considerations might have suggested otherwise. I took enormous pride in the endless hours I spent leading the Treasury team on its part of the Affordable Care Act (ACA).

And yet, after this whole personal journey, there I was holding a phone, listening to this congressman tell me that health-care security did not even make the cut as an economic issue.

That phone call solidified for me that the need for greater clarity on the ultimate goal of economic policy was not just about personal reflection. It mattered for real-world policy. When policymakers come to see "the economy" as distinct from what matters most to human fulfillment and dignity in people's economic lives, there's a problem. It impacts what gets prioritized or even recognized as a vital economic issue. In this case, it meant members of Congress believing that messaging on economic growth was a more important economic priority than ensuring that tens of millions of working Americans would not experience the heartbreak and loss of economic dignity that comes from not being able to provide health care for their loved ones.

Today we are in a moment of major reexamination of how well our existing model for modern capitalism is serving the majority of working people. Can it create paths out of poverty and reverse accelerating economic inequality, repair the hollowing out of the middle class, and cope with dramatic technological change? Such major questions rightly call for equally major new policies and structural changes. It is precisely at moments when we want to make giant strides that we should make sure we have clarity on our ultimate destination. Economic dignity should be the North Star to guide that journey.

In a 2005 book, I wrote about why "economic dignity" should be seen as one of three defining progressive values underlying our policy agenda. As I continued to explore the question of what our ultimate end goal for economic policy should be, I became more convinced that ensuring a universal level of economic dignity was more than a core value: it should be the central, organizing goal of economic policy. This is not a quest for an unreachable utopian ideal. There is no reason that we, as a nation, should not be able to guarantee a basic level of economic dignity for everyone.

The value of economic dignity reveals both the most admirable ideals and the brutal hypocrisy in our history. The protection and promotion of dignity in our economic lives is a powerful explainer of many moments in our history when the need for collective action through government policy triumphed over the call for rugged individualism and idealized free markets. On the other hand, as with American values like freedom, the brutal hypocrisy of our history regarding dignity is devastating. It is no exaggeration to say that true economic dignity has, through law and discrimination, been denied to a majority of our population for a majority of our history through systemic discrimination, violence against Native Americans, and the shame of slavery—the most extreme antithesis imaginable of respect for human dignity.

I have chosen in this book to neither ignore our shameful history on racism and sexism nor dismiss the degree to which values of economic dignity informed our nation's highest—though unrealized—economic ideals. As Martin Luther King Jr. and Thurgood Marshall masterfully showed, there can be great power in elevating cherished though unrealized American ideals as a means to force our nation to wrestle with the devastating gap between self-professed values and the harsh and discriminatory treatment of tens of millions of fellow Americans. They chose to elevate such unrealized aspirations as a means of both exposing the depth of unfulfilled promises to African Americans and making clear that their demands for racial justice represented not special pleading but a call to make progress toward realizing universal American ideals. As Pauli Murray, the remarkable civil rights pioneer who refused to give up her seat on a public bus in Petersburg, Virginia, fifteen years prior to Rosa Parks,[1] wrote in 1945: "As an American I inherit the magnificent tradition of an endless march toward freedom and toward the dignity of all mankind."[2]

Calling for economic dignity to be our ultimate end goal for economic policy carries with it the obligation to give a more complete and enduring definition of dignity than is currently used in our economic and political dialogue. Dignity has often been used in modern political debate to signify the deeper and more intrinsic human value at stake in the fight for civil rights, secure retirements, decent pay, and workers' rights. Others see dignity as a matter of when and whether a person feels demeaned or treated with respect. Each of these usages is compelling. Yet in isolation, they do not come close to creating a complete definition of what it would mean for a person to experience economic dignity—and for a nation to create a set of policies that would guarantee a basic level of economic dignity for all its people.

I have come to the firm view that a complete and enduring definition of economic dignity must rest on three integral and irreplaceable pillars. First, the economic capacity to care for family while not being deprived of fully experiencing the moments, joys, and roles that humans most value. Simply put, being able to not just put food on the table but to be at the table as well, and in your children's bedroom for story time and at the bedside for the most heartwarming and heartbreaking moments of caring for older loved ones. Second, being able to pursue purpose and potential—to have true first and second chances in your economic life to contribute and find meaning and to never feel given up on. And third, to be able to work and participate in the economy—to work, care for family, and pursue potential—with respect and not with abuse, domination, or humiliation. Economic dignity, defined by these three pillars, represents a more full, complete, and stable definition that can stand strong no matter what variation or circumstance is considered.

There is still the question of who one wants to write a book for. I considered a more academic approach, aware of the deep philosophical literature on dignity and the field of welfare economics that seeks to delve into how to measure well-being. Yet such an approach would have fit neither my experience nor my motivation. My expertise is in the realm of national economic policy, and the audience I want to reach is the concerned citizens, advocates, journalists, students, and policymakers who debate over kitchen tables, social media, and the floors of Congress. I aim for this book to be thought-provoking for those who live and breathe economic policy—but I have written with a much broader audience in mind that does not require an economics background.

In my last year as President Obama's top White House economic adviser, I chose to start each speech by reciting oft-mentioned economic statistics—from debt as a percentage of GDP to productivity indicators—but then reminding each audience that none of those metrics are end goals. I would state that each and every one of them had worth only to the degree that it helped us fulfill a deeper American value like whether we were a nation where the accident of birth did not determine the outcome of your life; whether each of us had a chance to rise; whether each of us could work, raise our families, and retire with dignity. Whether I got it exactly right then or whether I get it exactly right now in this book, I could feel in every audience the hunger for an economics defined by our most basic human values: one rooted in the clear understanding that there can be no end goal for economic policy other than what aims to lift up our happiness, fulfillment, and inner sense of dignity. That is the purpose of this book.

DEFINING DIGNITY

CHAPTER ONE

ECONOMIC METRICS AND INVISIBILITY

There is a joke about an inebriated man looking in a parking lot for his car keys one night. He keeps looking over and over again in the same spot. Finally, a helpful pedestrian tries to assist and asks, "So I take it you think you lost them in this spot?" The man replies, "No, but this is the only place where the light is shining."

This may be a bad joke, but it is not a bad metaphor for describing the error of allowing economic metrics like gross domestic product (GDP) to be viewed as the main *end* goal of economic policy. Of course, growth is important. But the focus on GDP represents the most classic economic confusion of means and ends. Indeed, any economic metric that cannot tell us whether the great majority of people are seeing their lives enhanced cannot be a rational or humane end goal for economic policy. The only logical end goal for economic policy in a democracy is that which lifts up what matters most in the lives of the people that policy is supposed to serve. Economics, by the people, of the people, and for the people.

Nobel Prize–winning economist Richard Thaler has said that a mistake in many human activities is to focus more on what can be measured than on what is most important.[1] Consider your own life. For many of us, finding a loving, supportive life partner and the happiness of our children are the highest values—even if those values are incalculable and can never be measured with precision. Yet economics in practice is unusually focused on what can be counted, measured, added, or subtracted. As a consequence, we miss a lot of what we would capture if we focused more on the end goal of economic dignity.

TWO KENNEDYS AND TWO VIEWS OF GDP

Robert F. Kennedy is known for offering an eloquent critique of what GDP does and does not measure. In 1968, he noted that

> Gross National Product counts air pollution and cigarette advertising, and ambulances to clear our highways of carnage. It counts special locks for our doors and the jails for the people who break them. It counts the destruction of the redwood and the loss of our natural wonder in chaotic sprawl. It counts napalm and counts nuclear warheads and armored cars for the police to fight the riots in our cities.[2]

He went on to note what it does not measure:

> The gross national product does not allow for the health of our children, the quality of their education or the joy of their play. It does not include the beauty of our poetry or the strength of our marriages, the intelligence of our public debate or the integrity of our public officials. . . . It measures everything, in short, except that which makes life worthwhile.[3]

This is not to dismiss the importance of economic growth. A growing economy with rising productivity is critical to how a nation can produce more goods and critical services with fewer labor hours and raise standards of living generation by generation. A growing economy can make more room for more people to move up or move in without others having to take a smaller slice of the economic pie. And there is increasing evidence of how promotion of aspects of economic dignity complement, not detract from, growth. Reducing vast inequality puts more money in the pockets of families who will spend on their basic economic security, leading to higher economic demand. Policies that ensure that all Americans have first and second chances to pursue their potential means not only more people find-ing purpose and meaning in their economic lives, but more success in ensur-ing we are producing at our national potential.

Yet economic growth by itself *should never be considered an appropriate ultimate end goal for economic policy.* Its value lies in the degree it serves as a means to lift up what is most universally treasured and precious in people's lives. In a nation that structures its markets and economic policy to lift up all of its people, a 4 percent growth rate can be a vital means to the end goal of a more just society. Yet a 4 percent growth rate is hardly an end goal for all economic policy if it is produced through mass exploitation of workers or delivers benefits to only the top one-tenth of 1 percent.

This is not a theoretical exercise: consider Norway and Saudi Arabia. Both are relatively high-wealth nations with major oil reserves. Over the past few decades, both have had multiyear GDP growth rates of 4 percent or more.[4] Yet the benefits of this strong GDP vary dramatically for each coun-try's citizens. Norway is famously egalitarian, its increased growth broadly shared. In Saudi Arabia, meanwhile, a royal family leads the government and owns the world's biggest oil company, which dominates the country's economy.[5] Changes in GDP may reflect the fortunes of the royal family but reveal little about the standard of living for the typical Saudi Arabian, espe-cially women, who lack the most basic freedoms.

Ironically, the line that is often used to justify a focus on economic growth as an end goal came from Robert Kennedy's brother John F. Kennedy. JFK's line that "a rising tide lifts all boats" is often used to promote GDP as an ul-timate end goal based on a kind of faith that a rise in growth will automati-cally lift the well-being of all people. It has also been used by some to argue that tax policies that benefit the most well-off will automatically lead to widely shared growth. This is kind of a double-water metaphor: benefits to the most well-off will trickle down and thus create a rising tide benefiting everyone. In fact, Kennedy never used the "rising tide" line to defend tax cuts or the types of market fundamentalist policies that conservatives frequently use it to advance.[6] Indeed, the first time JFK used the line as presi-dent was in Colorado on August 17, 1962, to appropriately praise congres-sional approval of a giant dam project.[7] But there is little question that JFK's rising tide line gets repeated across the political spectrum to advance the dangerously false assumption that the connection between raising the economic tide and lifting up all families is automatic. It is not. Whether all boats are being lifted in the ways that matter most to people's lives is the test for whether economic growth is working—and never to be assumed to be a by-product of GDP.

Some who seek to push GDP as the only goal that matters suggest that the question of whether all boats are in fact lifted in a rising tide is a second-order matter of "distribution." Nobel Prize–winning economist Robert E. Lucas Jr. has written, "Of the tendencies that are harmful to sound economics, the most seductive, and in my opinion the most poisonous, is to focus on questions of distribution. . . . The potential for improving the lives of poor people by finding different ways of distributing current production is nothing compared to the apparently limitless potential of increasing production."[8] The notion is that hardheaded, serious economic thinkers focus on the core end goal of economic growth, and the idea of how well it spreads benefits to the large majority of a nation's people is for those who place soft-hearted politics over hardheaded economics. I vehemently disagree. How well markets and economic policy lift up what matters most in people's lives is not a second-order issue. It is the whole ball game, the only legitimate end goal of economic policy.

BUT WHAT ABOUT BETTER ECONOMIC METRICS?

For many years, I bought into the notion that the way to get beyond GDP as the end goal of the economic policy world was simply to push our focus toward other economic metrics that were better proxies for shared growth and shared prosperity. Measures like the Gini coefficient, median income, unemployment rates, and job growth paint a more accurate picture of whether a rising tide is in fact lifting all boats than examining GDP or the value of the stock market. Yet even those metrics are still means to larger economic ends—and have shortcomings when they are considered ends in themselves.

Consider the Gini coefficient, which is named after an Italian statistics whiz named Corrado Gini (I promise it is not as complicated as it sounds). The Gini coefficient measures how much inequality there is in an economy, with a measure between 0 and 1. If a country had a 1, it would mean that one person controlled all of a nation's income. If it was 0, it would mean that income was perfectly equal among all its citizens. If the number is moving toward 0, it means the nation is experiencing less economic inequality.

While there are few economic goals as important as reducing economic inequality, even a measure like reducing the Gini coefficient cannot be seen as an ultimate end goal in itself. For example, imagine if the United States implemented a set of policies that reduced the income of the very richest Americans by 30 percent while reducing the income of everyone else by 20 percent. The Gini coefficient would have gotten better, but no one would likely be celebrating. A version of this actually happened: the World Bank estimates that the United States' Gini coefficient declined from 2007 to 2010 during the severe economic hardship of the Great Recession.[9] The point here is that even a metric that measures something as unobjectionably good as reducing inequality is still not an ultimate end goal in itself, if it is not in the context of serving a larger end goal of lifting up people's lives and well-being while reducing economic inequality.

Median income is certainly more informative to our economic goals than average income. To ruthlessly steal a metaphor from my friend and fellow short man Robert Reich, telling people what average income is can be like saying that LeBron James and I are on average six feet tall (I am five foot five). Or like saying that when Bill Gates walks into a bar, the average income inside immediately becomes astronomical. Median income avoids this problem: it tells us whether the typical American is making more or less income. As painfully slow income growth over the last several decades has been one of the great drivers of economic inequality and insecurity for working families, sustained and robust increases in median income would clearly be a critical ingredient to more shared prosperity. And yet even seeing median income alone as an economic end goal can blind policymakers to other economic dignity pains. Median income can easily rise for a few years, even as Americans experience greater insecurity over health and retirement security and pessimism over the prospects for their children—not to mention rising health care, childcare, and higher-education costs that for many families can swamp an increase in wages. A singular focus on even median income can make invisible much of the anxiety, economic fear, abuse at work, and economic disillusionment that has been part of the recent angst with status quo politics in the United States and across much of the world.

None of this is to suggest we should give up on economic metrics. Far from it. The economics profession should do everything in its power to design economic indicators that paint a more refined and accurate picture of whether the quality of most people's lives is improving. There has been progress. Official unemployment statistics now include a broader measure with a riveting name, the "U-6." While that name may sound like a rock band or military plane, it provides a much better economic picture of not just who is unemployed, but who is struggling due to working only part-time, against their will, or has given up looking for a job because they are so discouraged. There also is a better poverty metric. The relatively new Supplemental Poverty Measure gives a more accurate picture of economic hardship by reflecting out-of-pocket health-care spending, local living costs, and whether low-income people benefited from policies like the earned income tax credit (EITC).[10] The Commission on the Measurement of Economic Performance and Social Progress, which was called for in 2008 by French president Nicolas Sarkozy and is led by noted economists Amartya Sen, Joseph Stiglitz, and Jean-Paul Fitoussi, was a search for better economic measurements of human well-being.[11] Heather Boushey, head of the Washington Center for Equitable Growth, has made great progress in promoting an important new measurement of GDP—GDP 2.0—that aims to tell us how much growth is going to people at the bottom, middle, and top of the income ladder. Likewise, it could be worthwhile to create an Economic Dignity Index that seeks to paint a comprehensive picture of how well people in our nation experience a comprehensive sense of economic dignity in their lives.[12]

Yet we should also be under no illusions. As Stiglitz and his coauthors rightly note, "there is no simple way of representing every aspect of well-being in a single number in the way GDP describes market economic output."[13] Any single metric makes it too easy to make too many people and too many types of economic pain invisible to policymakers.

When I was the national economic adviser under President Clinton, I can remember during the boom of the late 1990s that the classic economic metrics—GDP, jobs, poverty, median income—were all clicking so well. I asked our star economic staffer and future Office of Management and Budget director Peter Orszag to look through every possible economic metric to see if we could spot any weaknesses in the economy. It turned up a curious weakness: personal bankruptcies, which ended up being explained in a significant way by the devastating cycle stemming from health-care costs, even in a roaring economy. So yes, the review of all economic metrics was of course worthwhile. But it would have been smart as well to ask the entire staff to consider, even in a strong economy, what were the worst types of economic pain, despair, and domination that existed in our economy even if they were not showing up in any metric? That type of inquiry avoids the unfortunate tendency in the economics profession to dignify an issue as "economic" only when it shows up in a traditional economic metric—a habit that allows too much economic pain to be invisible. Too often, important issues such as paid family leave, workplace sexual harassment, or workers struggling with addiction are classified as an "economic issue" only when they appear in a quantifiable metric like workforce participation numbers. But why?

If, for example, the need to support family or to pursue economic potential leads millions to experience harmful abuse or harassment at work, or compromises their capacity to care for their children or other loved ones, why should that not be seen as a major economic issue—whether or not it shows up in a traditional economic metric? Economic dignity will never be moneyball.

Painful as it is to consider, it took a political and media focus on the "gig economy" to train national economic attention on the number of people who are considered independent contractors and lack true economic security or worker protections. It was never a first-tier economic issue before the obsession with Uber drivers. Call it the invisibility of the "pre-gig workers." It should not have required the experience of wealthier Americans using the services of Uber drivers for the national economic dialogue to focus on the fact that millions and millions of workers—such as taxi drivers, domestic workers, and contract construction workers—have long faced the same economic insecurity and lack of protections. As UberX was launching in 2012, of the nearly two million in-home workers like housekeepers, childcare workers, and direct-care aides—overwhelmingly women and a majority people of color—only 12 percent received health insurance from their job, and only 7 percent received a pension plan.[14] According to a survey by the National Domestic Workers Alliance, fewer than 2 percent of domestic workers in 2011 received retirement or pension benefits from their primary employer, and only 4 percent received employer-provided health insurance; 65 percent of domestic workers did not have any health insurance.[15] Even today, few realize that before the ride-sharing revolution, the taxi drivers that people used for generations rarely had health-care coverage or qualified for unemployment insurance or any help during downturns and recessions.[16] For example, a 2007 study of New York City cabdrivers found they were generally classified as independent contractors—just as Uber and Lyft drivers are now—and did not qualify for overtime pay despite typically working more than seventy hours a week. A large majority lacked health insurance, despite substantial risk of on-the-job injuries.[17] These facts may not have been easily captured in traditional job growth statistics or GDP measurements, but they mattered to people's lives.

Here's another example: neither GDP nor job volume nor median income captures the economic pain felt by millions of working women suffering sexual harassment or sexual violence. Beyond the most high-profile cases that helped spark the #MeToo movement, there's an epidemic of sexual harassment plaguing female farmworkers;[18] more than 90 percent of women in the restaurant industry have faced unwanted sexual advances at work;[19] and according to one state study, more than one in ten home care workers have faced sexual aggression at work.[20]

Median income statistics do not capture the severe income volatility so many workers face, the nearly half of Americans with annual swings in their income of 25 percent or greater,[21] or the pervasive economic stress faced by the more than 40 percent of American adults who wouldn't be able to pay a $400 emergency expense.[22] Even these economic metrics do not encompass the disillusionment of the half of Americans who do not think their children will be better off than they were.[23]

YOU KNOW IT WHEN YOU SEE IT?

I am not naive about the risks of increasing our focus on economic measures that rely on some qualitative judgment. Even the best definition of economic dignity as the ultimate goal of economic policy will never have the precision of a specific metric. There is a risk that some will try to define it as Supreme Court Justice Potter Stewart infamously defined pornography—"I know it when I see it"—in his opinion in *Jacobellis v. State of Ohio* in 1964.[24] But this risk is more problematic when one is sloganeering with a simple word alone—freedom or liberty or dignity. That is not what I am recommending here. My goal in doing a full book is to develop a deeper definition of economic dignity that can be analyzed, critiqued, debated, and hopefully deployed in shaping and prioritizing policy choices. The focus on economic dignity, as it is defined here, will certainly draw strong disagreement in some corners, but it at least forces a debate on end goals and an in-depth discussion of what the promotion of economic dignity should mean that goes far beyond "I know it when I see it." Such a qualitative goal in no way minimizes the obligation to engage in rigorous analytical and evidence-based policy processes to address our top economic priorities or to exercise sound economic management. It simply forces us to ask what matters most in the lives of the people we should be serving in determining those priorities.

It also prevents us from confusing metrics that are means to ends with those end goals themselves. I wish I had a dollar for every time someone said disparagingly, "I can't believe people are so unhappy when the numbers are so good"—as if the numbers were the end goal that should dictate how people measure their happiness, as opposed to, well, their happiness. This view was exemplified by the use of the phrase "economic hypochondriacs," coined by columnist George Will in 2006 and trumpeted by the American Enterprise Institute (AEI).[25] The term mocks people who "see economic sickness" amid decent economic metrics and "record high" stock performance. The attitude expressed by those using this term implies that a worker should rely on broad-based economic metrics—rather than their expertise on their own individual economic condition—to be the ultimate judge of their economic happiness.

Economic dignity will never have the precision of an economic metric. And yet, a focus on it will reduce the risk that economic pain and matters of dignity, happiness, and fulfillment that do not fit neatly into traditional metrics and measurements will be invisible. It forces policymakers to ask the right questions, to go outside the comfort zone of numerical measurement to the hearts and minds of people. It is not precise, but then, it may lead us to be more often approximately right than precisely wrong. It is better to search for and try to find the true keys to what matters most to people's economic lives, even if they are not where the light is shining, and we have to look a little harder.

CHAPTER TWO

DEFINING DIGNITY:
NEGATIVE AND POSITIVE

Few terms have the intuitive power of the word "dignity." Yet as often as it is invoked, there is little clarity on its exact meaning in our national dialogue.

One hears the word used in a variety of different contexts. If, in a difficult situation, you "can keep your head when all about you are losing theirs," in Rudyard Kipling's words, it may be noted that you handled yourself with dignity.[1] Then there is the Morgan Freeman test. If you tend to look or speak like many of the characters that Morgan Freeman has played in movies—gray hair, a distinguished demeanor, exuding deep wisdom and a measured but purposeful manner—you are likely to be seen as particularly "dignified." This might indeed be a relic of the usages of "dignity" from centuries ago, when "dignity," as Harvard philosopher Michael Rosen explains, "originated as a concept that denoted high social status and the honors and respectful treatment that are due to someone who occupied that position."[2]

Over time, perhaps as the ideal that all people are "created equal, that they are endowed by their Creator with certain unalienable Rights," became professed to be "self-evident,"[3] the meaning of dignity became tied to the notion of equality. The concept of dignity has gone from being a trait of the elevated to something universal, intrinsic, and equal in all people by virtue of their common humanity. Rosen, describing this "expanding circle" of who is seen as possessing equal worth as humans, writes that "'dignity' goes from being a matter of elevated status of a few persons in a particular society to being a feature of human beings in general, closely connected with their capacity for self-determination."[4]

Our modern definition of dignity rests on the notion that within each of us is a universal value—something precious, immeasurable, and inherent to our common humanity—and a fierce desire for that to be respected and defended. Immanuel Kant's famous description of dignity is that people should never be treated as just means to an end but as ends in themselves. Kant's view is, as philosopher Michael Sandel describes, that all humans have "an absolute value, an intrinsic value."[5] When that most intrinsic value in all of us is not recognized and protected, dignity is denied.[6]

In our national economic dialogue, the concept of dignity is rarely defined in depth and largely assumed to be intuitively understood. Its most common usage is in expressing the notion that beyond the dollars-and-cents value of a specific economic cause, there is a higher, more intrinsic human value at stake. Think of the long-running Mastercard "Priceless" commercial, launched in 1997. A host of products and services are enumerated—a football game, plane fare, hotel costs—before the ad closes with "memories with your brother," which the Mastercard philosophers deem "priceless." While it is doubtful that the marketing heads for the Mastercard "Priceless" campaign were cribbing from Kant's 1785 *Groundwork of the Metaphysics of Morals*, it is worth noting that in his "Kingdom of ends," part of his definition of the word "dignity" is the notion of those aspects of life that had no comparable value and were thus priceless.[7]

The fact that dignity is seldom defined extensively—that dignity may have a "know it when you see it" quality—should not be seen as diminishing its power. Just the opposite. It is instead evidence of its intuitive universality. Those who have been the most effective advocates for civil rights, labor rights, and economic justice have understood that invoking dignity is an effective means to communicate a higher and deeper human value at stake in their cause.

When Martin Luther King Jr., Bayard Rustin, and A. Philip Randolph called for outlawing employment discrimination, they evoked the "quest for respect and dignity" of parents no longer being denied the capacity and pride of being able to provide for and care for their family.[8] When King went to

Memphis in his final days to advocate for striking sanitation workers, he not only spoke his most famous words on dignity, but was greeted with countless signs saying I AM A MAN, understood as an assertion of inherent dignity. The great union leaders, from Samuel Gompers to Cesar Chavez, often spoke of their collective bargaining gains as not only about wages and benefits but also about having their full dignity and humanity appreciated and recognized.[9] "All my life, I have been driven by one dream, one goal, one vision," Chavez stated, essentially paraphrasing Kant, "[to] overthrow a farm labor system in this nation which treats farm workers as if they were not important human beings. . . . Farm workers are not agriculture impediments . . . to be used and discarded."[10] Leading figures in the women's rights movement, too, have often invoked the concept of dignity in battling against second-class citizenship and laws and norms allowing men to have power over women's lives. At the Seneca Falls Convention in 1848, Elizabeth Cady Stanton declared, "There can be no true dignity or independence where there is subordination to the absolute will of another, no happiness without freedom."[11]

Scores of leaders, from Franklin Roosevelt to National Domestic Workers Alliance head Ai-jen Poo, have defined the end goal of their policies for retirement security as in pursuit of the higher value of dignity after a lifetime of work and contribution.[12] Vice President Joe Biden has for decades retold the story of his father telling him to always remember that "a job is about a lot more than a paycheck. It's about your dignity. It's about respect. It's about being able to look your kid in the eye and say, 'Honey, it's going to be okay.'"[13] Ohio senator Sherrod Brown has used the "dignity of work" as his mantra and policy frame, including during his listening tour when he contemplated running for president in 2019.[14] It was a common theme of New Jersey senator Cory Booker in his presidential campaign as well. Advocates of job guarantees like Darrick Hamilton, and Rustin and Randolph before him, often point to "dignity" as a basis for ensuring that Americans can always provide for themselves and others through work.[15]

Yet for all its invocations and all its intuitive power, the notion of economic dignity is rarely defined in any comprehensive or rigorous way—and certainly not with the depth that allows it to serve as a clear end goal and organizing principle for national economic policy. This book seeks to change that.

To be clear, my goal is not to decipher the most perfect definition of dignity from philosophical texts and then use that meaning as an inflexible guide to our economic policy debates. Instead, I intend to explore what in our economic lives, even if immeasurable, is most fundamental to our sense of dignity, fulfillment, and value as people who work, love, and seek purpose in our lives. It is this inquiry, this deeper meaning of economic dignity, that should be our ultimate goal for economic policy.

So, let me now turn to a more in-depth definition of economic dignity, first by reckoning with its history as an American ideal.

HISTORICAL ROOTS

The protection of individual dignity has been an American ideal since our founding, even in the face of its blatant and categorical denial to African Americans and many others. Alexander Hamilton opens *The Federalist Papers* with the argument that the adoption of the Constitution "is the safest course for your liberty, your dignity, and your happiness."[16] Swedish philosopher Gunnar Myrdal's book *An American Dilemma* identifies "the essential dignity of the individual" as integral to "the essential meaning of the nation's early struggle for independence."[17]

We can better understand the evolution of economic dignity in our history by seeing it as divided into two broad categories: "positive" and "negative" dignity. This division draws inspiration from Isaiah Berlin's classic 1958 lecture on negative and positive liberty.[18] Berlin defines negative freedom or liberty as essentially freedom *from* coercion or interference—particularly by the government. In his words, this means a "frontier [that] must be drawn between the area of private life and that of public authority." Private life, then, forms a sphere of a "certain minimum area of personal freedom which must on no account be violated."[19]

The United States Bill of Rights strongly embodies a sense of negative dignity. Its safeguards against state coercion to limit free expression and religious worship, the basic rights of due process, and prohibitions on inhumane punishment and involuntary quartering of soldiers represent a commitment to the protection of a sphere of human dignity that cannot be trampled on by government—even in the case of national security or criminal activity. Justice William J. Brennan Jr. defined due process as "requir[ing] fidelity to . . . the essential dignity and worth of each individual," essentially "commanding [government officials] to treat citizens not as subjects but as fellow human beings."[20] Similarly, the Eighth Amendment's prohibition of "cruel and unusual punishment" reflects a devotion to individual dignity even in the case where the government has been permitted to deny citizens their freedom due to a criminal conviction. Chief Justice Earl Warren writes that "the basic concept underlying the Eighth Amendment is nothing less than the dignity of man."[21] Brennan wrote in a different case that the Eighth Amendment represents the notion that "even the vilest criminal remains a human being possessed of common human dignity."[22] The same is true for the Geneva Conventions, which explicitly forbids "outrages upon personal dignity, in particular, humiliating and degrading treatment" even among prisoners of war who are being denied freedom for engaging in violence against the government holding them.[23]

Perhaps no American jurist focused on dignity as the core of the Constitution more than Brennan. He defined the Constitution as a "sparkling vision of the supremacy of the human dignity of every individual."[24] While Brennan often spoke in terms of negative dignity—or as he described it, "the ideal of libertarian dignity protected through law"[25]—he also saw the need for its application to those Americans who "live entire lives without any real prospect of the dignity and autonomy that ownership of real property could confer."[26] From "its founding," Brennan states, "the Nation's basic commitment has been to foster the dignity and well-being of all persons within its borders."[27] To Brennan, this requires a recognition that "forces not within the control of the poor contribute to their poverty."[28]

Like Brennan, Justice Anthony Kennedy found "dignity" at the core of the Constitution, specifically in his decisions to defend the constitutional right to privacy and to gradually extend rights to same-sex couples. Starting with a joint opinion on the right to terminate a pregnancy, Kennedy found that "these matters, involving the most intimate and personal choices a person may make in a lifetime, choices central to personal dignity and autonomy, are central to the liberty protected by the Fourteenth Amendment."[29]

In *United States v. Windsor*, the case striking down the federal Defense of Marriage Act, Kennedy used the words "dignity" or "indignity" ten times. The *Obergefell v. Hodges* decision legalizing marriage equality ends by stating that those who seek to marry same-sex partners are asking only for an "equal dignity" granted to them by the Fourteenth Amendment.[30]

PROTECTING NEGATIVE DIGNITY IN THE PRIVATE ECONOMY

Like negative political dignity, negative economic dignity requires protection from government infringements: from slavery and segregation to "taxation without representation" to archaic sex discrimination statutes to policies that criminalize poverty. There will always be a need to prevent state power from trampling on the economic dignity of all people, especially those with the least power and most vulnerability.

As the United States entered the industrial era, even those white and male Americans who had not suffered slavery or harsh discrimination began to recognize that for negative dignity to have any true meaning in their lives, there must be a sphere of dignity that cannot be infringed upon, traded, or abused in the economy—not just by government, but by *private* power.

Many of the initial legislative achievements of the Progressive Era at the turn of the twentieth century emanated from a collective recognition of the need for protections of negative dignity in the private economy. The lives of family farmers and small artisans in much of the nation's first century could be painful, strenuous, and economically uncertain. For millions, however, this work offered the capacity to engage economically with a degree of autonomy, voice, and control over their work lives that represented respect and dignity. The gradual shift to the industrial era—with large numbers working for bosses in large enterprises—meant a loss of the dignity and respect that millions previously felt through their capacity to control their work lives.

Worse, for millions of workers that sense of autonomy was replaced by a sense of domination and relative powerlessness when it came to wages, hours, and working conditions. When the Supreme Court—in what is known as the Lochner era in the early twentieth century—struck down some of the first laws designed to afford basic protections against abusive hours and labor practices, they argued such laws offended the defining characteristic of American labor markets: the equal freedom of all to enter into labor contracts. For millions of workers in this era, however, they found the defining characteristic of labor markets to be the twin realities of economic desperation and powerlessness.

Millions of workers discovered that there was neither a legal nor a moral floor to protect them from being brutally exploited by employers. The initial efforts to establish a minimum wage, pass child labor prohibitions, unionize, and limit hours—often twelve hours a day, six days a week for adults and their children—can all be seen as a growing recognition of that reality. In a world of economic desperation and powerlessness to stand up to their employers, the notion of "freedom to contract" had to be buffered by limits on the degree any employer could deny a person's basic dignity in pursuing their economic ends.

Between 1910 and 1915, eleven states passed minimum wage laws[31] to improve workers' financial security and ensure that they would not be entirely at the mercy of employers. Felix Frankfurter, who would go on to become a Supreme Court justice, defended Oregon's minimum wage laws in court against claims that they violated workers' "freedom of contract." He highlighted how economic desperation destroyed any hope of liberty for workers:

> The "liberty of contract" which the present [minimum wage] legislation would destroy is only the "liberty" of an employer to abuse and the "liberty" of an employee to be abused. True freedom of contract is established, rather than impaired, by such restrictions. Their very purpose is to assure the parties an equal basis for bargaining, so that they may be free to bargain on the merits, and not under the compulsion of a crippling necessity. With no margin or the margin of but a single meal between starvation there can be no true liberty of contract.[32]

During the Progressive Era, many jurisdictions came to realize the merits of regulations that prevented "the compulsion of a crippling necessity" from forcing vulnerable people into dangerous or exploitative situations. In 1899, only five states had any child labor laws that set age limits for employment across all occupations, but by 1909, twenty states had passed such legislation, with a median minimum age of fourteen years old.[33] In 1916, Woodrow Wilson signed the first federal child labor law, which prohibited children under the age of fourteen from working in factories, workshops, and canneries, and those under age sixteen from working in mines and quarries.[34] In the effort to limit sweatshop hours, fifteen states "had statutorily limited miners' workdays to eight hours by 1921."[35]

The Supreme Court finally upheld legislation that placed limits on the right to contract, driven by the unavoidable realities of economic desperation and economic power during the Great Depression. In the New Deal years, the Supreme Court reversed its 1923 decision to strike down minimum wage laws. In 1937, in *West Coast Hotel Company v. Parrish*, Chief Justice Charles Evan Hughes explicitly recognized the potential loss of economic dignity for vulnerable workers—particularly women—because "bargaining power is relatively weak, and . . . they are the ready victims of those who would take advantage of their necessitous circumstances."[36]

The Supreme Court's decisions to uphold collective bargaining laws in this same period represented a clear rejection of the formalistic view of an individual employee and an individual company as engaging in equal freedom to contract. Instead, the Supreme Court recognized that without the freedom to organize, "workers often had to accept employment on whatever terms employers dictated" due to the "bargaining power imbalance workers faced," as Justice Ruth Bader Ginsburg wrote in her recent dissent in *Epic Systems Corp. v. Lewis.*[37]

TEDDY ROOSEVELT AND THE PROTECTION OF NEGATIVE DIGNITY

The American revolution in favor of economic dignity can be seen in the evolution of one of the Progressive Era's most consequential presidents: Teddy Roosevelt. When Roosevelt began his political career in Republican politics, he ascribed to the laissez-faire—literally, "let [them] do"—theory of political economy, which holds that there should be limited, if any, government interference with markets. Roosevelt absorbed this attitude from the people he grew up around and "the books [he] read at home and the books [he] studied at Harvard."[38] Reflecting years later on the influence of these texts, Roosevelt wrote, "there was almost no teaching of the need for collective action, and of the fact that in addition to, not as a substitute for, individual responsibility, there is a collective responsibility."[39]

Roosevelt's shift in worldview was driven not by a new or abstract economic theory but by his late-night inspections as a New York State assemblyman and later New York City police commissioner.[40] When the state legislature was considering a bill that would prohibit cigar making in crowded tenement buildings, Roosevelt was initially skeptical, as the bill went against the grain of laissez-faire principles.[41] But he decided to see for himself the tenements where cigar makers worked. There he saw the humiliating and degrading conditions that economically desperate workers seeking to care for their families were forced to "choose" in the face of unrestrained economic power. Decades later, Roosevelt still remembered the "foul" conditions men, women, and children suffered while they worked "by day and far on into the evening and they slept and ate there."[42] Seeing it with his own eyes convinced him that cigar making in tenements was "an evil thing from every standpoint, social, industrial and hygienic."[43] Roosevelt ultimately championed the bill's passage.

His first "intimate exposure to the hardships confronting the city's poor," writes historian Doris Kearns Goodwin, spurred Roosevelt's "marked change" and the "loosening [of] the 'steel chain' of conservative opposition to government intervention in the economic and social processes that had been his birthright."[44]

Serving as police commissioner further pushed Roosevelt toward Progressivism. He joined muckraker Jacob Riis on many midnight inspections of tenement buildings. Roosevelt wrote that the inspections "gave [him] personal insight into some of the problems of city life. It is one thing to listen in perfunctory fashion to tales of overcrowded tenements, and it is quite another actually to see what that overcrowding means, some hot summer night."[45] Roosevelt saw that those who held economic power felt no compunction or moral constraint about completely dominating and humiliating those on the bottom of the industrial economy. He later wrote that "we must protect the crushable elements at the base of our present industrial structure" and "industry, therefore, must submit to such public regulation as will make it a means of life and health, not of death or inefficiency."[46]

Roosevelt also came to realize how "wealthy individuals" and their "expensive lawyers" would use the Constitution "to cloak their opposition to vitally necessary movements for industrial fair play and decency."[47] By the end of his tenure as police commissioner, Roosevelt "was becoming a strong believer in labor unions, a strong believer in the rights of labor," and less sympathetic to those who stood in the way of their progress.[48] In the words of political scientist George Ruiz, Roosevelt went on to "[become] the first modern president to publicly acknowledge the fundamental role played by organized labor in achieving a measure of human dignity for America's working class."[49]

What distinguishes Roosevelt from so many ingrained in privilege and laissez-faire ideology—including many conservatives today who profess to care about the dignity of work—was his willingness to adjust his worldview to fit the actual struggles of working families, as opposed to simply refusing to acknowledge any economic realities or necessary solutions that contradicted his ideological vision. Roosevelt's personal evolution from a traditional pro-business Republican to a progressive champion was unquestionably impacted by his own exposure to what economic desperation and the denial of economic dignity meant in reality for workers and families in the face of unregulated economic power. As governor of New York and as president, Roosevelt pushed for labor protections, antitrust laws, and other progressive measures. The former laissez-faire adherent had come to realize that "it is only by a slow and patient inward transformation such as these laws aid in bringing about that men are really helped upward in their struggle for a higher and a fuller life."[50]

These transformations in the hearts and minds of leaders like Teddy Roosevelt, as well as in the makeup of the Supreme Court, reflected a striking shift in the way the United States saw the protection of negative economic dignity. No longer were our laws starting from the default assumption of idealized markets where there were free, equal, and noncoercive job and market choices—even if a worker was accepting sweatshop conditions or putting a child to work in a factory. This new recognition also extended to small businesses that faced abuse or domination from bigger companies with overwhelming economic power. Many entrepreneurs and small suppliers could only watch as the American ideal of fair competition was subverted by the crooked practices of enormous trusts and monopolies, until the Progressive Era saw the passage of three pivotal antitrust laws: the Sherman Act of 1890, the Clayton Act of 1914, and the Federal Trade Commission Act of 1914.

From America's founding, we have recognized that individual rights serve as a constraint on government power, even in its pursuit of appropriate objectives like efficient law enforcement. You can't torture people or pull them out of their homes in warrantless searches, even if one could prove it would be an efficient means of law enforcement. The expansion of protections of negative economic dignity meant that in the private sector, even in the legitimate pursuit of profits or market share, there was a wider sphere of dignity that also could not be trampled on for any reason—a limit on the degree workers could be seen only as means to the economic ends of others.

FDR AND THE PROMOTION OF POSITIVE DIGNITY

If negative dignity involves protection *from* government and market abuse, positive dignity requires the affirmative use of public resources to ensure the basic elements of economic security and economic opportunity that are integral to dignity. And as Teddy Roosevelt championed negative dignity, it took Franklin Roosevelt and the New Deal for the passage of major legislation that served as a leap forward in the promotion of *positive* economic dignity.

The ultimate example of this is FDR's most lasting New Deal achievement: Social Security. It was premised not just on macroeconomic stabilization, or even on just reducing elderly poverty, but fundamentally on the notion that it is an assault on dignity for a person to have worked hard their whole life only to experience humiliating economic desperation in old age. Poverty in old age reflects a broken compact. In speaking of the goal of his new Social Security program, FDR said, "our old-age pension system . . . must be given in a manner that will respect the dignity of the life of service and labor which our aged citizens have given to the nation."[51] The new embrace of positive economic dignity was reflected in the relatively rapid adoption of a spate of state and federal legislation. Wisconsin was the first state to pass an unemployment insurance law, in 1932, after a struggle lasting more than twenty years.[52] The passage of the Social Security Act of 1935 spurred the adoption of unemployment insurance across the country, with forty-three states passing laws after the Social Security Act was signed into law.[53]

The New Dealers understood that to make dignity real it had to apply to "the world of the individual person; the neighborhood he lives in; the school or college he attends; the factory, farm or office where he works," as Eleanor Roosevelt said about human rights more broadly. "Such are the places where every man, woman, and child seeks equal justice, equal opportunity, equal dignity without discrimination. Unless these rights have meaning there, they have little meaning anywhere."[54]

The center of gravity in progressive economic policy since the New Deal has been the effort to fully realize the social compact on economic dignity. FDR himself acknowledged the remaining holes in the New Deal in his final State of the Union in 1944—often referred to as his Second Bill of Rights speech. He argued that the negative freedom and political rights guaranteed in the Bill of Rights had "proved inadequate to assure us equality in the pursuit of happiness."[55] FDR enumerated rights to education, health care, social insurance, housing, and a living wage, among others. "True individual freedom cannot exist without economic security and independence,"[56] he said. He evoked Thomas Jefferson to say that the need for "economic truths" is now "self-evident," and a "second Bill of Rights" is needed "under which a new basis of security and prosperity can be established for all regardless of station, race or creed," and that once the war was won, the nation should focus on "new goals of human happiness and well-being."[57]

Later in the twentieth century, the cause of economic dignity was greatly advanced by Martin Luther King Jr. and other leaders in the civil rights movement. Many of King's words spoke to a form of negative dignity—the protection of civil rights from coercive government and private power. Yet King also recognized, as he wrote in *Why We Can't Wait*, that "equality meant dignity and dignity demanded a job that was secure and a paycheck that lasts throughout the week."[58]

Bayard Rustin, a key behind-the-scenes leader of the civil rights movement and the mastermind of the 1963 March on Washington, sought to build the case for positive economic dignity as integral to the larger fight for economic justice. Reflecting on King after his assassination in 1968, Rustin—a gay black man who dealt with the pain of exclusion over his sexual identity even within the leadership of the civil rights movement—wrote: "Dignity and self-respect are not abstract virtues that can be cultivated in a vacuum. They are related to one's job, education, residence, mobility, family responsibilities, and other circumstances that are determined by one's economic and social status in the society."[59] This was no offhand comment. Rustin as much as anyone sought to merge civil rights and labor rights, himself working for both the civil rights and union movements. He lauded his mentor, A. Philip Randolph, for understanding that "social and political freedom must be rooted in economic freedom," for insisting "that economic security is the precondition for pride and dignity," and for advocating for a coalition between the civil rights movement and the labor movement. "Today," wrote Rustin, "there are two million black trade unionists in America who have attained economic dignity, job security, and protection against racial discrimination."[60]

When Lyndon Johnson put forward his Great Society agenda in the 1960s, he specifically invoked the goal of economic dignity. Johnson stated that the core promises of equality and democracy were

a promise to every citizen that he shall share in the dignity of man. This dignity cannot be found in a man's possessions; it cannot be found in his power, or in his position. It really rests on his right to be treated as a man equal in opportunity to all others. It says that he shall share in freedom, he shall choose his leaders, educate his children, and provide for his family according to his ability and his merits as a human being.[61]

While there has been progress since the Great Society—in, for example, the Children's Health Insurance Program, the Affordable Care Act, expansions of Medicaid, and the creation of and major increases in the earned income tax credit that have lifted millions out of poverty—we've also seen deterioration on many fronts: increasing polarization in the workforce, accelerating wealth and income inequality, the hollowing out of the middle class, and devastating deficiencies of the employer-based benefit model. These trends have all rightly led to a growing push for more sweeping policies that would close the positive dignity gap. In a moment when the very capacity of modern capitalism to provide economic security for the majority of workers and prevent growing inequality and winner-take-all results is being seriously questioned, the completion of this positive economic dignity agenda is perhaps the work of our time.

THE THREE PILLARS OF ECONOMIC DIGNITY

INTRODUCTION TO
THE THREE PILLARS

What constitutes economic dignity? One might assume that the answer lies in creating the right list of goods and services we all need to achieve a life of economic dignity.

FDR's Second Bill of Rights was one such list, and it certainly informs this book. There have been many others, including Truman's Fair Deal and even Huey Long's "Share Our Wealth" plan, a powerful populist list that came with a theme song—"Every Man a King"—which Long cowrote and sang himself.

I chose not to emulate Long and compose and perform my own theme song, and not just to spare my teen daughter the embarrassment. Nor did I opt against a list of goods and services in order to downplay the importance of so many critical essential policies—health care, housing, a living wage, retirement security—all essential to economic dignity. I chose to avoid a list-making exercise because I believe it is more instructive to force oneself to first ask what are the most overarching human needs that any such list would aim to fill. That requires us to look beyond specific material requirements, however essential, to examine the deeper notions of purpose and joy, and the desire for meaning and respect.

This forces us to continually reexamine how a changing economic and social landscape impacts what is required to achieve economic dignity for each generation, much like understanding the enduring values expressed in the Constitution helps courts apply it to modern circumstances that the founders could not have imagined. The specific needs of economic dignity do change over time. As powerful as FDR's Second Bill of Rights is, and as radical as it might have been in its day, it excludes many of what we might think today are the essential aspects of economic dignity—such as childcare, paid leave, and affordable college education. A deeper understanding of the basic human needs of economic dignity can help us and future generations to design, refine, and evolve our policy lists to ensure we are fully meeting our end goal of economic dignity under new and changing circumstances.

When I reviewed the variety of historical invocations of economic dignity in our past, I did not find that the definitions or usages missed the mark. Instead, what was missing was a more complete definition that encompassed what full economic dignity would require. I cannot claim to have developed a scientific or historically certain definition. All I can offer is that from my research, life experience, professional work, readings, and observations, I came to the view that the goal of economic dignity has to rest on three essential pillars. These are, I believe, rooted in the better angels of American ideals and worthy of serving as our economic North Star going forward.

These essential pillars are:

- The ability to care for family without economic deprivation or desperation denying us the most meaningful moments and joys in our most important loving relationships;
- The capacity to pursue potential and a sense of purpose and meaning; and
- The ability to contribute and participate in the economy with respect, free from domination or humiliation.

These pillars are each essential and interdependent. The capacity to care for family, as we will discuss, should never simply be seen in terms of material provision, no matter how essential. If economic deprivation or facets of work life require such extreme effort or sacrifice that people are denied the capacity to experience the most meaningful and joyful moments of family and personal life, then we cannot say that the pillar of caring for family has been satisfied.

There will, of course, be important intersections between our need to care for family and our desire to pursue purpose and potential in all aspects of our lives. Certainly, for millions of workers, caring for family is a critical element of the sense of purpose and meaning in their lives. My late father was a talented lawyer who drew a strong sense of purpose from his work, taking great pride in defending those with disabilities and in several prominent civil rights victories, including winning one of the first constitutional cases giving girls the right to play high school sports prior to Title IX. Yet, as he got older, he took a pass on what he had always said was a dream of becoming a judge. When my family pressed him on why he was giving up his dream, he was as serene as he was certain. Working as a lawyer allowed him to support the three remarkable nonprofits my mother and younger brother Rick had founded (including the Mosaic Youth Theatre in Detroit and the Family Learning Institute) and to be a backup for his kids when they pursued public service and scientific research. He was insistent: contrary to what he had imagined as a younger man, he was now certain that he achieved a greater sense of meaning and purpose by supporting the public-minded efforts of his family—and continuing to defend those with disabilities—than he would wearing a judicial robe.

These types of trade-offs are made every day by people at different times of their lives and are consistent with a life with economic dignity. The challenge for policymakers is not to dictate the exact right work-life balance for each person, but to create an economy that allows people to both care for family and pursue purpose—and make the trade-offs that best match their happiness and sense of meaning. My father was fortunate enough to have the opportunities and economic capacity to make such choices for himself. Tens of millions of Americans do not. Many never fully get the chance to pursue their potential or sense of purpose and find their only means to provide financially for their family is by working excessive hours and enduring mistreatment on the job and inadequate pay that leaves them constantly on the edge. Such sacrifice can be admirable, but an economic dignity test should aim higher. It should aspire to allow all people to both care for family and choose their path for purpose—the freedom to choose the right balance.

Finally, it is essential to understand that without the third pillar—the capacity to contribute with respect, and not domination and humiliation—the entire structure of economic dignity fails. The desperation to satisfy the first two pillars can, and very often has, forced millions of Americans to work under conditions of abuse, exploitation, humiliation, and domination that are the antithesis of dignity. Without a strong sphere of economic dignity that can never be trampled on, the desperate pursuit of the first two pillars of economic dignity can ensure the demise of the whole idea.

I was once asked by Josh Barro on the KCRW show *Left, Right & Center* whether the problem with people like me and our fellow guest, Roosevelt Institute president Felicia Wong, was that when we pushed for notions like positive dignity or positive freedom, we "lacked a limiting principle." Who among us truly has all our wants fulfilled? My response then and now is that an economic dignity compact is not a "fulfill your wildest dreams guarantee." It does not free us of want, or mean we can pursue our potential and purpose if we define that as taking Roger Federer to the fifth set, buying the perfect house, winning an Oscar, or even being assured of the talent, luck, connections, and timing that get us the next promotion, our dream home, or the career we most aspire to. These are individual goals based on the type of recognition, wealth, and power that are by definition available to only a few. The pillars of economic dignity—the capacity to work with respect, to find purpose, and to care for family and enjoy its most meaningful and joyful moments—can, on the other hand, be experienced by everyone. Achieving these goals for all does not need to be a zero-sum equation. They are achievable universal goals. The issue is only our commitment as a nation to make it possible.

CHAPTER THREE

IT STARTS WITH FAMILY (AND THE EQUALITY OF THE BEST THINGS IN LIFE)

While there is little question that one of the top economic challenges of our era is reducing income and wealth inequality, this first pillar of economic dignity focuses on a different type of equality. The idea that for all the advantages that wealth and privilege may bring, the greatest joys in life—including the love and support of a spouse or partner, the miracle of the birth of a child or bringing home an adopted child, the deep longing to provide care and comfort to parents and grandparents as they age, the warmth of those we choose as family, including lifelong friends who are there at every stage—can be available to all. The capacity to care for family—to enjoy and experience its most meaningful moments—ought to be life's equalizer; this is the aspect of life that is most important to many, if not most, people, and not ultimately dependent on great wealth and status.

And yet here is the obvious rub: while there is a certain truth to the old Sam Cooke song that the best things in life are free, we know that tens of millions of Americans are regularly and unnecessarily denied these fundamental joys of love and caring due to economic deprivation. These joys are denied or constrained due to poverty, extreme work hours, low wages, lack of health care, health problems caused by environmental degradation, predatory market practices, abusive work experiences (like being fired for taking a day off to care for a sick child), and lack of affordable housing. While these denials are felt most harshly and regularly by those in poverty, these deprivations of the most meaningful and joyful moments of family are often felt throughout the middle class as well. They are felt every day when working families struggle with economic emergencies; fear they will lose their homes as they look for new jobs after being laid off; endure financial challenges from the cost of treating mental illness, disability, or addiction; have resources too scarce to take leave from work to be there for a new or ill child or an aging parent; and in some cases, even feel forced to put on hold their desire to start or expand a family.[1]

I should also clarify: while I put the capacity to care and be there for family as one of three critical, fundamental pillars for economic dignity, my definition of "family" is not limited to any traditional notions or norms. It has no limits other than those one considers their most loving relationships in life. As someone who has had fatherlike relationships with two godchildren (Derick and Samantha) for twenty-eight years—in addition to being a father to a twenty-five-year-old son (Miles) and fourteen-year-old daughter (Nina)—I believe, like my parents did, that family is who you choose.

1. BEING THERE FOR FAMILY AT LIFE'S MOST CHERISHED MOMENTS

Being there for the most priceless moments of family life—from the first months of a child's life to the last days of a parent's—should not be considered a labor market perk for the few based on their market value or negotiating power. It should be part of a basic sphere of economic dignity that is protected for all. Among developed countries, the United States falls the most woefully short in this area.

The issue of comprehensive paid family leave for the care of new babies and adopted children, medical emergencies, or ill loved ones does not always get top-tier billing in the current political atmosphere. Indeed, only two of the twenty candidates mentioned it in the first four nights of Democratic presidential debates in 2019—John Delaney and Senator Kirsten Gillibrand, the lead Senate advocate for the gold-standard Family and Medical Insurance Leave Act on comprehensive paid leave. Yet the capacity to take time off to be with a newborn or adopted child or a parent in their final days must be a universal requirement of basic economic dignity.

Consider just the issue of paid leave for a new baby or adopted child. In every Organisation for Economic Cooperation and Development (OECD) country other than the United States, there is guaranteed paid leave for new mothers of an average of four and a half months. Some, like the United Kingdom, offer nine months of such leave. Several countries guarantee months of paid leave reserved for new fathers as well.[2] Not so in the United States.

What is stunning is not just what an exception the United States is, but how dramatic the consequences of this exception are. While it is disgraceful that we fail to provide universal health-care coverage, 91 percent of Americans do have some health insurance.[3] Yet 84 percent of all Americans (in the private sector) do *not* have paid family leave.[4] Poignantly, fewer than 10 percent of those who get paid to take care of other people have any paid leave to take time off for the birth or adoption of their own children.[5]

The results are shocking and disturbing: Nearly one in eight new moms in the United States are economically forced to go back to work within one week of childbirth.[6] And nearly one in four new moms must return to work within two weeks. American fathers also suffer from lack of parental leave; the vast majority of fathers take two weeks of leave or less.[7]

Journalist Sharon Lerner documents what having to rush back to work out of economic necessity looks like. Lerner tells the stories of mothers forced by financial hardship to return to often difficult, long jobs after only short periods of leave. One was Natasha Long, who, after the birth of her third child, started twelve-hour (6 a.m. to 6 p.m.) shifts, four to five days a week, at ACCO Office Supplies in Booneville, Mississippi. Long had been ordered to bed rest for many weeks at the end of her difficult pregnancy. She had a different employer, a dollar store, during her pregnancy that had not fired her but had not paid her either, resulting in debts piling up even before the birth. Because she needed an income, she quickly returned to work at a new job at ACCO, but there, she struggled with depression and a lack of privacy, as her factory had no lactation room. Lerner writes:

When she was on breaks, she had to run out to her truck. She sat in the cab, worried that someone might see her, and pumped, while tears rolled down her face and over the plastic suction cups attached to her breasts. Long cried because she wanted to be holding her baby rather than sitting in the parking lot of a factory in her old Yukon Denali.[8]

Long suffered from headaches and worried her depression might be used against her by child welfare authorities to claim she was an unfit mother, not equipped to keep her kids.

The sad truth is that while the federal Family and Medical Leave Act (FMLA) was a huge step forward in 1993 for guaranteeing that parents could not be fired for taking unpaid leave, an estimated 40 percent of all workers are not covered by FMLA.[9] This wholly avoidable gap leads to over a quarter of all workers being fired or forced to quit their jobs when they take leave.[10] For lower-income families, taking unpaid leave is too often both unafford-able and necessary, leading to disastrous declines in their economic situations. Long worked twelve-hour shifts because of the debt she was forced to assume when she took unpaid leave during her difficult pregnancy.

Nation reporter Bryce Covert describes the efforts of Sonya Underwood, a hospital worker in Atlanta, Georgia, to hoard paid time off and take out disability insurance to cover her lost income from taking unpaid leave for the birth of her child. The doctors found cervical complications and her child arrived at twenty-six weeks. Her insurance and savings all ran out, forcing her to go back to work while her son remained in the NICU. Things only got worse. When she finally brought her baby boy home, she lost her job and car—as she failed to find any type of affordable care for such a medically fragile baby.[11]

While we accept that in a capitalist society a person's market value will impact their income, luxury vacations, and the size of their homes, do we really think from a dignity perspective that the capacity to take some weeks off after the birth of a child should be determined by a person's economic power in labor markets?

Consider bereavement leave—paid time off when one suffers the death of a loved one, including a spouse or a child. This is the greatest grief of all.

More often than not, a worker affected by such a loss is dealing with both their own immense sorrow and the grief of other loved ones who need comfort. One would think all would agree that paid time off in such tragic instances would be part of a basic guarantee of economic dignity not subject to one's economic station or status. And yet while four in five executives have some form of paid bereavement leave, only one in five of those in the lower decile of wages do. Indeed, it is common for companies to explicitly grant bereavement leave to their executives and not to the majority of their workers. In low-wage industries, the access to bereavement leave is astonishingly limited: just 16 percent in food and accommodation services, for example. In higher-wage industries, like finance and insurance, 88 percent of workers have access to bereavement leave.[12]

Again, we as a nation have to ask whether a worker's rank in a company or economic station in life should be the fundamental determinant of whether the person has the economic capacity to take time off to grieve and comfort loved ones when the most painful moments in family life occur. Whether or not comprehensive paid family and bereavement leave is always treated like a top-tier political issue, its absence leaves a major and troubling gap in an economic dignity compact.

2. PUTTING FOOD ON THE TABLE— AND TO BE AT THE TABLE

The issue of universal paid family leave is only a symptom of a bigger issue: whether what is necessary to put food on the table requires being too often absent from both the literal and figurative table oneself. For many who have the benefit of economic means, the balance between the first pillar—caring for family—and the second pillar—pursuit of potential and purpose—is an issue of choice and work/life balance. I, like many others, have chosen very different balances at different points in my life. During the Clinton administration—before I was married—I was known as a notorious workaholic in the White House, regularly working hundred-hour weeks, while going to great lengths to spend regular time with Derick and Samantha. My work life in the Obama administration—especially during the first six months of the financial crisis—was no picnic either. But like many people, I made different decisions based on my age and my children, Miles and Nina, at home. Rather than being the last one turning off the lights every night in the West Wing, every day was a sprint to get home in time to put my young daughter to sleep, and every weekend was an effort to at least work from home when possible. In my post–White House life, wonderfully, I have been able to arrange my schedule in order to take my daughter home from school the vast majority of days for the last six years.

For those of us with economic means, these major life choices are personal and context-specific, and often shift depending on the seasons of one's life. For tens of millions of Americans, however, the number and schedule of work hours is a matter of necessity, not personal choice.

When parents are forced to work three jobs to provide for their family, we are not meeting the first pillar of economic dignity. Spending time with family is the most common source of meaning for adult Americans: seven in ten adults say that it provides a "great deal of meaning and fulfillment" in their lives, surpassing even religious faith or career.[13] For parents, time spent with their children is the leading activity that brings them meaning and happiness.[14] An economic dignity goal must mean structuring our wage, benefits, and workers' rights policies so that providing food and other basic provisions of economic security is not so all-consuming that it prevents a parent from being there for both the exceptional and ordinary moments of child raising or caring for older relatives.

Martin Luther King spoke of employment discrimination as creating a cycle whereby black workers are forced to work such excessive hours—often caring for other people's children—that they are left "unable to be with our children and give them the time and the attention that they need."[15] In the case of Natasha Long, she not only works 6 a.m. to 6 p.m. shifts, but she has to drive one hour each way to and from work. She is up at four o'clock and returns past seven o'clock as her kids, whom she could not see in the morning, are on their way to bed.[16] Variations on this story are played out in millions of families across the nation. Unpredictable, grueling work schedules are on the rise. One in five employees works sixty hours a week or more.[17] Low-wage workers feel the strain of unpredictable, irregular schedules at astonishing rates: half have to do back-to-back closing and opening shifts that are separated by less than eleven hours, and seven in ten workers are required by their employer to keep their schedules "open and available," making it virtually impossible to plan life and manage time for family obligations.[18] Eight in ten low-wage workers, in fact, have little input into their schedules and a large majority have less than two weeks' notice on what their schedules are, which infringes on the sense of respect that comes in having some degree of voice and say over basic elements of one's economic and family life.[19]

What does this say about how we should best ensure a capacity to care for family with economic dignity? It means that when we design policies that determine the minimum income and benefits any working family should have, it should be devised with the understanding of what it truly means to both put food *on* the table and be *at* the table—and at the PTA meeting, at the bedside of ill loved ones, and at bedtime for children. What truly constitutes an economic dignity wage cannot just be the total income of the family or household regardless of how many hours are worked or a job's impact on our capacity to experience the most universally treasured aspects of family life.

3. DIGNITY FROM THE EYES OF LOVED ONES

We document economic reality through statistics about individual people as if they were atomized—how many people have jobs, have health care, are going to college. Most of us, however, experience much of our sense of economic dignity through our relationships, including our economic capacity to care for loved ones. There is no pain like feeling you have failed in this responsibility.

After the financial crisis, I helped lead the fight in the Obama White House for three more years of extended emergency unemployment relief in 2011, 2012, and 2013. Some labor market economists focused only on whether such benefits might reduce the incentive of some unemployed workers to take a new but suboptimal job. These are reasonable factors to weigh when designing unemployment insurance policies. But those were also years where stories abounded of working parents falling into extreme financial hardship, sometimes leading to eviction or foreclosure, with those outcomes then driving parents to despair, addiction, or worse. When weighing an economic policy decision like extending unemployment benefits in a weak economy, should it be improper to also weigh the devastating loss of economic dignity some working parents may suffer from feeling they failed the loved ones who relied on them the most?

If a child is unable to access proper medical treatment, it may only be recorded in statistics about coverage and health care. But beneath those statistics is likely the deep loss of dignity for parents who find that despite their hard work and best efforts, they are not able to provide the care and opportunity their children need without bankrupting their family. That's why universal health care is such a powerful dignity issue. A searing tweet thread by Andrew Kimmel, a documentary and television producer, told of how his once thriving father had endured immense economic challenges because of Kimmel's sister's mental illness. Kimmel described the downward cycle his father experienced dealing with his sister's and his own health while losing his capacity to provide for his family. Kimmel's father took his own life. Kimmel said of his father, "His last words to paramedics were 'I failed my family.'"

In 2019, journalist Sarah Kliff wrote about Texas resident Lindsay Clark, who could not afford insurance for her two children. Clark's family income was too high to qualify for Medicaid in Texas, a state that has not expanded Medicaid under the ACA and has very limited eligibility with over 700,000 people living below the poverty line and still ineligible for Medicaid.[20] Clark actually waited in the ER parking lot to see if her two-year-old daughter went into a potentially deadly seizure from possible poisoning, avoiding the emergency room for fear that it would be financially ruinous. After the story ran, Kliff heard from many other parents who had faced the same terrible dilemma and done the same harrowing thing.[21]

Every year thousands of families with children suffering from severe mental illness are forced to give them up to the foster care system so that they can get state-funded medical treatment. One such family is Toni and Jim Hoy of Illinois, whose adopted son, Daniel, began to have frequent psychiatric episodes requiring hospitalization at ten years old. The episodes turned violent and threatened the safety of their other children, making the need for treatment unquestionable to the family's well-being.[22] Neither private insurance nor Medicaid would cover the $100,000 yearly cost of the residential treatment Daniel needed, so two years later, out of options, they took twelve-year-old Daniel into a hospital and told the staff they were abandoning him. The Hoys were initially charged with child neglect, but Daniel was then able to get the care he needed—as a teenager in the custody of the child welfare system.[23] A 2003 report surveying nineteen states found that just those states had over 12,700 cases of this type of act in 2001 alone, likely a severe undercount of the number nationally.[24] These are the pains that RFK referred to as "the breaking of a man's spirit."[25]

Too many parents—often lower-income, racial minority parents—also feel powerless to protect their children's health when they are disadvantaged by limited economic choices and political power to combat environmental hazards in their communities and homes. The experiences of parents in Flint, Michigan, may be the most egregious but are, in fact, only one painful example. Across the country, African American kids are nearly three times more likely than white children to get lead poisoning.[26] African Americans, Hispanic Americans, and Asian Americans are exposed to air with 21 to 43 percent more pollution from cars, trucks, and buses than white Americans, leading to higher rates of asthma and other negative complications among children.[27] Incalculable studies have found that non-white Americans and communities with high concentrations of non-whites tend to be burdened by more pollutants and are more likely to have high-polluting facilities geographically located in their residential communities.[28] From Houston to the central valley of California, African American and Hispanic communities face disproportionate harm from drought, localized flooding, and wildfires. Marvin Gaye had it right nearly fifty years ago in his environmental anthem "Mercy Mercy Me (The Ecology)": "Poison is the wind that blows from the north and south and east."[29] When a parent is forced to raise their child where this poison disproportionately blows, in spaces that expose them to known physical or cognitive harm, or even death, it offends a basic sense of dignity.

These strains to the capacity of parents to truly care for family are challenges that are not confined to those with low incomes. For example, as I will discuss in future chapters, we fail miserably to economically support the inspired efforts of loving parents—both middle class and lower income—to ensure that their children with physical or intellectual disabilities have every opportunity to contribute, pursue purpose and potential, and live with as much independence as possible.

4. OPPORTUNITY FOR FAMILY AND ACCELERATING INEQUALITY

We live in a time of accelerating inequality, and as Alan Krueger showed, in the United States this correlates with lower intergenerational mobility. He refers to this as the Great Gatsby Curve.[30] As we've become more unequal, children from lower-income families are less likely to earn more than their parents did. We still revere the American Dream, but now, as economist Raj Chetty said, "it's basically a coin flip as to whether you'll do better than your parents."[31]

Much of the pursuit for universal economic dignity centers on achieving a basic standard or floor for everyone in vital areas of caring for family. As long as a pregnant person can deliver their baby safely and affordably, the fact that some who are wealthy go to the hospital in chauffeured limousines or have doctors perform the birth at their mansions does not in and of itself make other people's childbirths less safe or less dignified. But part of the troubling trend in accelerating inequality is that components of inequality feed on themselves, giving those with resources and connections an ever greater momentum to compound their gains for themselves and their children at the expense of the economic mobility and dignity of others. When those same upper-income Americans can marshal every possible advantage for their children—including extra tutoring, choice of the most rigorous educational programs and schools, college advising, internships, and all-out mobilization to gain admission to elite colleges—one cannot say their deployment of economic privilege and wealth is a victimless crime. The amount that parents in the top income quintiles spend on educational enrichment, like SAT prep, private tutors, music lessons, and technological equipment, has ballooned to seven times more than what is spent by those in the bottom.[32] These advantages can lead people to question whether their children have real first chances or whether the system is rigged against them as the economic advantages of the privileged add on, compound, and accelerate at the expense of opportunities for those less economically well positioned.

Even if arrests of several celebrities and prominent financiers deter blatantly fraudulent efforts to gain admission to elite colleges, it likely flies in the face of human nature to think that well-off parents are going to restrain themselves from doing everything that is legal and ethical to help their children succeed. The more realistic and effective course is to have rules that limit such advantages—like no legacy or fund-raising advantages for college admissions—and to have affirmative policies that level the playing field, such as more public assistance to provide top-quality SAT preparation, substantive summer activities for lower-income children, college advisory help, internships, mentors, and high-quality after-school programs for those with less economic advantage.

Life's greatest equality could be and should be the capacity for all of us to experience the greatest and most universal joys and moments of meaning with our families and in our loving relationships. Perhaps no economic metric perfectly measures that aspiration. But this is one goal that does not require better measurement. It just requires our collective heart and will.

CHAPTER FOUR

THE PURSUIT OF POTENTIAL AND PURPOSE

When philosopher Martha Nussbaum posed the question "What does a life worthy of human dignity require?" she noted that the "notion of dignity is closely related to the idea of active striving."[1] As with the most famous line in the Declaration of Independence regarding happiness, it is the capacity to *pursue* potential and purpose—not its guarantee—that is integral to economic dignity. Indeed, all aspects of the American political landscape praise the distinctive ideal that in the United States the accident of your birth shall not determine the outcome of your life: that regardless of race, religion, or economic station everyone should have the ability to pursue their potential, to be afforded real first and second chances, and to never feel given up on. Unfortunately, the gap between this ideal and the reality for millions of our citizens is a particularly wide chasm.

This is an indefensible gap on both economic dignity and economic growth grounds. Ensuring everyone continually has the capacity to contribute in the economy and society is a recipe for both expanding a sense of value and worth for individuals and maximizing national potential. While the notion of active striving is closely related to pursuit of potential, the opportunity to contribute and make a difference is closely related to the pursuit of purpose and the fulfillment of a basic human need integral to dignity.

Just over a half century ago, Robert F. Kennedy called for a recognition that "even if we act to erase material poverty, there is another greater task, it is to confront the poverty of satisfaction—purpose and dignity—that afflicts us all."[2] In a speech later that year just before his death, RFK added, "Those who live with us are our brothers . . . [and] share with us the same short movement of life . . . [and] they seek—as we do—nothing but the chance to live out their lives in purpose and happiness, winning what satisfaction and fulfillment they can."[3]

FIRST CHANCES

Since the establishment of the new republic, no economic notion has been more idealized in the American story than the idea that one's life should not be predetermined by the economic station of one's birth.

James Truslow Adams, an early twentieth-century historian, highlighted this value when he laid early claim to the term "American Dream" in 1931. Adams wrote that part of what distinguished the American Dream from the understandings of the "European upper classes" was the "dream of a social order in which each man and each woman shall be able to attain to the fullest stature of which they are innately capable, and be recognized by others for what they are, regardless of the fortuitous circumstances of birth or position." Adams went on to define the heart of that dream as "being able to grow to fullest development as man and woman, unhampered by the barriers which had slowly been erected in older civilizations, unrepressed by social orders which had developed for the benefit of classes rather than for the simple human being of any and every class."[4]

Of course, there is reason to discount the ideal of true first chances in light of the immense hypocrisy at our founding of excluding nearly everyone but white men from any semblance of this ideal. Throughout most of our history, the majority of people residing on U.S. soil were denied by the accident of birth their capacity to pursue their potential by laws, policies, and discriminatory social norms. Yet as legal scholar Ganesh Sitaraman writes in *The Crisis of the Middle-Class Constitution*, there is still worth in understanding the values that were upheld for those considered "within the political community" even as one recognizes the brutality of those excluded from that "political community."[5] Doing so creates the power to define—as Martin Luther King, Frederick Douglass, and Thurgood Marshall so effectively did—the claims of those excluded or newly included in terms of asking only for equal application of cherished American values. A central theme of Martin Luther King's "I Have a Dream" speech was to elevate the ideals of American equality of all people, and then to define those ideals as a "promissory note to which every American was to fall heir . . . black . . . as well as white."

In fact, there are few founding values so revered from all sides even today, from former House of Representatives Speaker Paul Ryan, who said the United States was founded on the idea that "the condition of your birth does not determine the outcome of your life,"[6] to President Obama, who in his 2014 State of the Union address declared, "I believe, that here in America, our success should depend not on accident of birth, but the strength of our work ethic and the scope of our dreams. That's what drew our forebears here. It's how the daughter of a factory worker is CEO of America's largest automaker; how the son of a barkeeper is Speaker of the House; how the son of a single mom can be President of the greatest nation on Earth."[7]

But beneath these statements lie deep divisions. Some see the goal of true first chances as achieved simply by the absence of formal legal barriers. Others rightly ask whether in reality the accident of birth ends up being overwhelmingly determinative of the economic outcomes and opportunities in one's life. Taking economic dignity seriously means ensuring first chances in fact, not just theory.

Suppose that the U.S. Congress was to pass a law stating that only 3.2 percent of poor children could go on to graduate from a four-year college, but 60 percent of affluent kids could. Most Americans would find such a law outrageous and contrary to our values. Yet what does it say when this is in fact our current reality and there is so little outrage?[8] How can so many people across the political spectrum laud and elevate the value of being a nation where your economic life is not determined by the accident of your birth, when it is devastatingly clear that for so many this is the case? How can even the most libertarian market fundamentalists claim that the lack of more equal educational and economic attainment is a matter of individual failing, when the evidence suggests the odds are so deeply stacked against tens of millions by the time they are in the crib? These facts should be seen as an all-out assault on this most central economic ideal. It should be a mark of shame and a call to action. It should compel us to recognize and address the roots and dynamics of cumulative economic disadvantage and, for many, the impacts of past and present racial discrimination that work to repudiate our ideal of true first chances for all.

Consider a few stark realities.

If a child is poor at birth, there is a strong possibility that child will remain poor for most of their childhood. Nearly 70 percent of black children and about half of all children born into poverty remain impoverished for most of their childhoods.[9] As an exhaustive review by the National Academy of Sciences summarized, "The weight of the causal evidence indicates that income poverty itself causes negative child outcomes, especially when it begins in early childhood and/or persists throughout a large share of a child's life."[10] Children born poor are three times as likely to not earn a high school diploma.[11] This is not due to a lack of ambition. Like kids from high-income families, a majority of high school sophomores who were born into low-income families plan to earn at least a bachelor's degree,[12] but only 14 percent do so, compared with 60 percent of more affluent children.[13] In their late twenties, the kids who were born in poverty are more than five times as likely to be poor.[14] In their early thirties, boys born to the poorest 10 percent of families are more than twenty times as likely to be incarcerated as children born to families in the wealthiest 10 percent.[15]

Judging the existence of first chances only through the lens of whether there are current legal barriers to upward mobility does not allow one to see the real barriers so many face. It can blind us to the reality that current and historic racism can have negative multiplier effects with each generation. If a black child is born into a low-income family, they are four times less likely to reach the top income quintile in their midthirties than a white child who was also born into a low-income household.[16] In 99 percent of neighborhoods measured by the Census, black boys are less likely to earn more than their parents than white boys who grew up in the same neighborhood, even in wealthy households.[17] Sociologists Alexandra Killewald and Brielle Bryan argue that "decades of discrimination and segregation give white and non-white young adults very different sets of childhood experiences and parental resources" that play out in vastly different ways, critically shaping the ability to accumulate wealth throughout life.[18] For instance, if one's grandparents have wealth stemming from their access to homeownership early in their lives, this gives their children and grandchildren a greater ability to invest in themselves during their lives. This means that the historical roots of racist housing policy have very real implications for the present, undermining the promise of true first chances.[19]

Internationally, when we look at the connection between how children in adulthood fare compared with their parents in terms of education and income, the tightness of this relationship in the United States is comparable to what is seen in some developing countries, where opportunity is often presumed to be limited to family wealth and status.[20]

Is this the American Dream we praise? These statistics reflect the reality that the accident of birth too often plays a devastating role in denying the economic dignity that comes from, to use the words of Nobel Prize–winning economist Amartya Sen, "a life of genuine choice with serious options."[21]

SECOND CHANCES

A commitment to second chances is equally ingrained in our country's roots. This is a commitment that the accidents of life and bad luck should not cut off a person's intrinsic chance to contribute, find purpose, and pursue potential. We have uniquely romanticized in the United States the capacity of people who stumbled or fell on hard times to move to America or move west, plot their own land, even chase gold in the pursuit of their dreams. Americans revere the stories of entrepreneurs who failed repeatedly before striking it big. "This American continent," as FDR stated, "is to be a place of the second chance."[22] George W. Bush also revered this country as "the land of second chance," where "the gates of the prison open," and "the path ahead should lead to a better life."[23]

This value is not just folklore. It is evident in our country's early rejection of debt prisons. Richard Johnson, who later became vice president of the United States under Martin Van Buren, was a fierce advocate in the 1820s for abolishing debt prisons. As a Kentucky senator, he centered his arguments on the importance of protecting a sphere of dignity from being crushed at the discretion of creditors. Debt prison law, he charged, "gives to the creditor this sovereign power over his person, a power too sacred to be abridged by his own act, to lodge him in prison at discretion." It was one thing, Johnson argued, to "strip the debtor of everything that can benefit the creditor," but "do not take that which will degrade the man . . . inflict the keenest wound upon the whole family." Instead, Johnson argued, "the law should carefully avoid giving one citizen a control over the personal liberty of another." It should not cast him in a debt prison where "his prospects are blasted, and his hopes are withered."[24]

As economist Bradley Hansen writes, "Many people came to believe that the forces that brought people to insolvency were often beyond their control and that to give them a fresh start was not only fair but in the best interest of society. Burdened with debts they had no hope of paying they had no incentive to be productive, creditors would take anything they earned. Freed from these debts they could once again become productive members of society."[25]

The movement to end debt prisons spread through the United States at both the federal and state levels decades before other nations. New York had instituted partial repeal of debt prisons by 1818, and full abolishment there and in Maine and Tennessee followed by 1831. As historian Jill Lepore notes, it was a "wonder, really, that Americans managed to get rid of [debt prisons]; at the time, debtors were imprisoned in every country in Europe except Portugal."[26]

For the same reasons, beginning in the 1800s, the United States repeatedly returned to the issue of personal bankruptcy laws, not just to avoid the chaos of a creditor rush, but to provide people with a "fresh start." Historian Edward Balleisen notes that "the legal treatment of bankruptcy in the United States astonished European visitors such as Alexis de Tocqueville."[27] In *Democracy in America*, Tocqueville noted that a critical part of the American economic story was its lack of a punitive or degrading attitude to those who tried and failed on a commercial enterprise. Tocqueville celebrates the United States as a place where "fortunes are lost and regained without difficulty," noting that America does not "disgrace" those who take risks in new commercial enterprise and fail. "Hence," says Tocqueville, "arises the strange indulgence which is shown to bankrupts in the United States; their honor does not suffer by such an accident. In this respect the Americans differ, not only from the nations of Europe, but from all the commercial nations of our time."[28]

DENIALS OF SECOND CHANCES:
OUR WEAK ECONOMIC COMPACT

Our history holds the utmost reverence for second chances, but today the United States stands out among almost all industrialized nations in the failure of its policies to ensure second chances. We revere the Silicon Valley entrepreneur who hits big on their third or fourth chance, but for those who happen to work in the wrong industry at the wrong time, whose factories close and whose communities wither, who struggle with long-term unemployment, or who at some point enter our criminal justice system, the American promise of limitless potential and second chances feels distant, if not pathetic.

The United States spends less as a percentage of GDP than any other OECD country except Mexico on programs to help those who are unemployed or at risk of losing a job to make transitions to new jobs. In 2015, the United States spent 0.1 percent of GDP; Denmark spent twenty times more, and Sweden spent twelve times more.[29] During the first year out of work, the United States offers the least generous unemployment benefits of any country in the OECD.[30] Two out of three families with a displaced worker in America experience poverty.[31]

DENIALS OF SECOND CHANCES:
THE ISSUE OF LONG-TERM UNEMPLOYMENT

The United States tolerates devastating discrimination against the long-term unemployed most in need of second chances. These impacts are cumulative and accelerating. Once a worker has experienced a certain length of unemployment, a negative cycle sets in: difficulty getting interviews can lead to depression as well as declines in self-esteem and even physical health—a downward spiral for once-thriving workers. The result can lead to a deep assault on economic dignity.

Economists often pay close attention to permanent loss of earning power from a major event, such as a recession or losing a job, even after the event is no longer present—a phenomenon known as hysteresis. When it comes to being displaced from work for a long period of time, the harm from an economic dignity perspective is broader and deeper. Simply put, when people go through short-term unemployment, they go through real economic stress and temporary hardship, but most recover. Those who are involuntarily unemployed for long periods may lose their house, their spouse, their confidence, and their self-worth, and many never fully recover. A review of four thousand studies on work found that unemployment over time has a worse impact on emotional health than the death of a spouse or divorce.[32] Nearly four in ten of the long-term unemployed report strained family relations and a loss of self-respect and are significantly more likely to say they sought professional help for depression.[33] The impacts of long-term unemployment reverberate through families across generations. The future job prospects[33] of children are negatively affected by the damage—financial and psychological—of parental job loss.[34] Children of the long-term unemployed are 15 percent more likely to repeat a grade,[35] and when they grow up, they are more likely to report lower life satisfaction.[36] Across entire communities with high rates of long-term unemployment, suicide rates have been found to go up.[37]

The long-term unemployed face a vicious discriminatory cycle. This was seen when researchers sent out nearly identical résumés to employers, except that one of the two résumés showed long-term unemployment. The long-term unemployed applicant needed to send out three and a half times as many résumés on average to get in front of a potential employer. The study found the bias was so significant that even when they also changed the applicant's work experience, the long-term unemployed person with relevant experience was less likely to be interviewed than a recently unemployed person with no relevant experience.[38] Another study found that when the only difference in otherwise identical résumés was whether the applicant had been unemployed for one month versus eight months, the résumé with the longer period of unemployment received 45 percent fewer callbacks.[39] They also found that the negative ratio of long-term unemployment to employer callback was *stronger* in cities with lower unemployment, indicating that those caught in joblessness over an extended period of time may never be able to catch up even with a strong local economy.

Sometimes the discrimination is intentional, while other times it is based on seemingly neutral criteria like credit scores, which can signify nothing more than unemployment—not any form of irresponsible behavior. Journalist Annie Lowrey wrote about one long-term unemployed woman, Jenner Barrington-Ward, a fifty-three-year-old college graduate who worked steadily for three decades, and over the course of five years slid from a comfortable middle-class life to being "broke and homeless" after being laid off. "I've also been told point-blank to my face, 'We don't hire the unemployed.' And the two times I got real interest from a prospective employer, the credit check ended it immediately."[40]

The implications are devastating for second chances. If a person fails to get a job within a few months, employers make it harder for them to ever get a job again, and the unemployed person often sinks into isolation and depression. Once people do find a job, their wages are lower than those of continually employed workers for up to twenty years after the initial employment loss.[41] A study by economist Daniel S. Hamermesh found that workers who were unemployed for six months or more made 5 to 15 percent less than similar workers when they regained employment.[42] As former Federal Reserve chairman Ben Bernanke noted in 2012, this means that over time, "the long-term unemployed will see their skills and labor force attachment atrophy further, possibly converting a cyclical problem into a structural one."[43]

In my last full year as President Obama's national economic adviser, I spearheaded his effort to get private sector commitments to stop the devastating discrimination against the long-term unemployed. With President

Obama's blessing, I spoke at the Business Council Executive Committee to ask if we could work to create a compact against discrimination versus the unemployed. Several business leaders told me there was no way their firms used screening that would hurt the unemployed, but within hours they called me to say that they were wrong and wanted to be involved with fixing it. Many didn't realize that employment status was a negative screening criterion or that other criteria—like a sudden drop in credit scores—would de facto penalize the long-term unemployed. About three hundred businesses— including twenty Fortune 50 companies—signed a pledge to take active measures not to weed out the long-term unemployed during their hiring processes. Yet many major companies never signed up. And in the negotiations on the pledge, to my great frustration, we were not able to include an explicit ban on the use of credit scores. I found this maddening, as it could not be more clear that screening workers for falls in credit scores during a major recession was like refusing an emergency flood loan to homeowners because their house was wet. A voluntary pledge was clearly going to be only a small step forward.[44]

THE WORST BETRAYAL OF SECOND CHANCES: OUR CRIMINAL JUSTICE SYSTEM

The American criminal justice system stands out as the greatest offender of failing to realize our idealized promise of second chances. The United States imprisons far more people than any other nation, imprisons far too many people for long periods for minor offenses, and has racial disparities in countless metrics. Black men receive federal sentences that are 20 percent longer for the same crimes as white men.[45] In five states, African Americans are incarcerated at rates of ten times or more than whites.[46] The United States has also erected a multifaceted, counterproductive system of barriers preventing people convicted of crimes from ever getting a viable second chance. This is seen in the way the system makes it very difficult for incarcerated individuals to set themselves up for employment success when they are released. These barriers to employment are cruel and illogical. Finding a steady job relatively quickly after reentry is one of the most effective ways of helping people avoid returning to prison.[47]

Consider the following barriers to a second chance, no less a fresh start.

First, the criminal justice system does a very poor job at helping inmates maintain ties to their social support networks that for most are critical to having a real second chance when they reenter society. Low-income families of incarcerated individuals—many trying to economically survive with the loss of their primary breadwinner—are left with no option but to pay exorbitant costs, as high as $400 to $500 per month, for phone calls and emails to stay in touch with their incarcerated family member.[48] With so many who are incarcerated sent to prisons far from their support networks, fewer than one in three incarcerated people receive a visit from a loved one in any given month.[49] From an economic dignity perspective, why does the system make it so hard for incarcerated people to maintain or build relationships with loved ones while in prison?

Second, while we know that some form of higher education is increasingly necessary to get a good-quality job in the economy that returning individuals enter, we do a terrible job of making quality postsecondary education available to people while they are behind bars. A major part of why there are so few higher education opportunities offered in prisons is that people incarcerated in federal and state prisons are banned from receiving Pell Grants. While 64 percent of incarcerated individuals have attained a high school diploma or equivalent, in 2014, only 9 percent completed any type of postsecondary education program while in prison. Nearly six in ten people behind bars do not earn any education credentials while in prison.[50] This is not only a harm to the economic dignity of the individuals but also irrational for governments, given both workforce needs and that the best available evidence finds that incarcerated individuals who participate in postsecondary education are 48 percent less likely to recidivate.[51]

Third, we allow a set of discriminatory employment measures to block the path to getting a job for the more than 650,000 people who reenter society from prison each year.[52] In addition to the controversial commonplace practice of requiring those with criminal records to check the box on job applications, when individuals gain skills in prison that could set them up for good-quality jobs post-release, they are barred due to an array of occupational licensing restrictions. In California, incarcerated individuals recently made up half or more of the firefighters who fought historic wildfires while being paid less than $2 per hour.[53] Yet when these individuals—who no doubt saved lives and gained experience battling blazes—reenter society, they are effectively blocked from being able to serve as firefighters due to licensing restrictions.[54] Regardless of whether someone gained the relevant skills in prison, a real second chance means not being banned from accessing one in four jobs that require an occupational license. There is also a vicious cycle in housing. An inability to have shelter and a permanent address can make interviewing for jobs very difficult while the obstacles to finding employment no doubt contribute to the painful reality that the formerly incarcerated are roughly ten times more likely to experience homelessness than the general population.[55]

Fourth, when individuals become involved in the criminal justice system—whether they are convicted or just arrested—the record can trail them for the rest of their lives, unless they can have the record sealed or expunged. While at least thirty-six states have some kind of legal mechanism to clear some criminal records,[56] these remedies often do not end up being accessed for a number of reasons, including that the person may be unaware or not have the correct information to navigate the cumbersome process or may be required to pay a fee of hundreds of dollars. One study of Michigan criminal convictions found that only 6.5 percent of eligible records had applications for expungement after five years of being eligible![57]

Finally, as I will discuss below, the increasingly common use of fines and fees imposed on people who become involved in the criminal justice system is a major barrier to the prospect of starting anew.

Fortunately, there is some progress. There is growing bipartisan support for the critically important policy of restoring the Pell Grant for those in prison. There has also been some momentum at the state level to fund in-prison college programs.[58] It will be critical to the success of such programs to ensure rigorous quality and antipredator requirements and that individuals can easily continue and transfer credits toward completing degrees when they are released. And "fair chance" licensing reforms have been gaining bipartisan momentum at the state level, too, with at least nine states passing reforms to ease irrational barriers to occupational licenses in 2019.[59] In the past two years, more than twenty states expanded access to record-clearing remedies to give more people a shot at a second chance,[60] and Pennsylvania even made the process much more straightforward, enacting legislation to automatically seal the records of some thirty million criminal cases.[61]

THE NEW DEBT PRISONS

Whereas once the United States led the way in banning debt prisons, today we are seeing the rise of actual and virtual debt prisons through the practice of fines and fees in the criminal justice system.

This practice emerged as a by-product of state and local finances. Toward the end of the twentieth century, in tandem with mounting costs to fund the ballooning criminal justice system, governments began requiring more of the costs to be paid by defendants through fines and fees.[62] At least one estimate places the amount that state and local governments collect each year at $15 billion, with some counties relying on fines and fees for as much as half of their policing and judicial expenditures.[63] Punitive fines and fees are also used disproportionately in jurisdictions with higher shares of black residents.[64] Indeed, in Ferguson, Missouri, the Department of Justice found that court fees and fines constituted a major source of city revenue.[65]

The number of people affected by such fees is dramatic. In 2004, the latest year that the federal government surveyed incarcerated individuals on this topic, two-thirds of inmates reported that they were ordered to pay various fines or fees, compared with 25 percent in 1991.[66] In 2014, sociologist Alexes Harris estimated that the share of returning individuals with these costs was 80 to 85 percent.[67]

Many of the most common fees are for things that most Americans probably believe are guaranteed by law to indigent defendants. For example, in 2014, at least forty-three states and Washington, DC, allowed courts to bill defendants for a public defender. Many states also charge for a jury.[68] Fees for probation services are common, too. In 2014, forty-four states used the practice of charging released individuals for their own court-imposed probation and parole,[69] in some cases in connection with for-profit probation service providers. There are also fees that are tacked on essentially if you're poor: interest rates as high as 12 percent,[70] late fees, fees for setting up a payment plan, even paying for collection.[71] Ten million people collectively owe over $50 billion as a result of their engagement with the criminal justice system.[72]

These fines and fees operate as modern-day debt prisons. They force untold numbers of Americans to go to prison for nothing more than being too poor to pay debts to the criminal justice system—a criminalization of poverty. For millions more, these fines and fees create virtual debt prisons: economic barriers that make it nearly impossible for someone engaged with the criminal justice system to make the escape from debt that is needed for a true second chance and fresh start. These practices are as irrational as they are cruel and contrary to our ideals of giving people second chances. In some jurisdictions, governments set these fines and fees knowing that much of the criminal justice debt will never be collected[73] and then are willing to re-incarcerate people at costs to taxpayers that are frequently higher than the individual's outstanding debt.

ACTUAL PRISON FOR DEBT

The number of Americans who experience jail or prison simply for criminal justice debt is a national scandal. One case in point: An NPR investigation told of a homeless man named Tom Barrett arrested for stealing a can of beer. In an example of the downward spiral caused by such fees, his inability to pay a $50 public defender fee led him to proceed alone, and he was eventually ordered to pay $400 a month for for-profit probation services, an electronic ankle monitor, and other fees. Because he failed to pay, Barrett was sent to jail with a twelve-month sentence.[74]

Mr. Barrett's case is not an isolated incident. Failure to pay these kinds of fines and fees is a major cause of re-incarceration. While the U.S. Supreme Court ruled in *Bearden v. Georgia* in 1983 that it is unconstitutional to incarcerate people simply because of their inability to pay fines and fees that courts impose,[75] that ruling is not holding up in the real lives of people across this country. Even in 2004, a study found that twenty-one thousand people returned to prison because their parole or probation had been revoked because they failed to meet the financial conditions of their release.[76] A study in Rhode Island found that between 2005 and 2007 nearly one in five of all incarcerated people were imprisoned for failure to pay a court debt.[77] In Ferguson, Missouri, missed payments or court dates often resulted in jail time for the predominantly poor African American population disproportionately targeted by police.[78] On any given day in the United States, close to half a million people are incarcerated but not convicted of a crime.[79] Those who remain incarcerated are there because they cannot afford to post bail. If they use bail bondsmen to get out of jail, they likely incur high interest rates on the loans that can take years to pay back. In many states, offenders may opt to stay in prison instead of paying fees that come with parole supervision or other fees.[80]

It is a cruel irony that the nation that first shunned debt prisons has recreated them through the use of fines and fees that effectively criminalize poverty and imprison low-income Americans—disproportionately people of color—in endless debt and the denial of true second chances.

VIRTUAL DEBT PRISONS

The impact of such criminal justice debt on creating virtual prisons—barriers to a true second chance—is even more widespread. In 2011, approximately 20 percent of Philadelphia city residents had unmet criminal justice debt, with a median debt of $4,500.[81] In Alabama, more than half the individuals with felony convictions had a bill of $5,000 or more in sanctions.[82] Across all reintegrated individuals in the United States, nearly half report having zero earnings in the first year after reentering society.[83] Simply put, such debt can serve as a major block for anyone leaving prison to get housing or a job, or provide for themselves and their families with any form of dignity. These debts hold back a population who we know are among the most disadvantaged economically in society from having true second chances. It not only increases the risk of reincarceration, but robs those leaving the criminal justice system of the funds they need to gain access to housing, care for their children, and to set up a new shot at life, even after they supposedly served their debt to society.

Ironically, the system of fees and fines works to block those reentering the economy from getting the jobs they need to repay the criminal justice debts. Outstanding debt from these fines and fees can prevent many from having a driver's license, a necessity for many Americans to find and maintain a job; plus, many jobs outright require a driver's license. The vast majority of states allow for the suspension of licenses for unpaid court debt and traffic fines,[84] and a survey of fifteen states found that eight of those states take away driver's licenses when individuals fail to pay monetary sanctions,[85] a direct roadblock to maintaining employment to provide for self and family. Some feel they have no choice and drive to work on a license suspended due to criminal justice debt at the risk of further incarceration.

Fines and fees also play a role in determining who has a fresh start by being able to clear or seal a criminal record. While a sizable share of states have recently taken action to make it easier for more people with criminal or arrest records to petition to have their records cleared, associated fees may still be prohibitively costly. An obvious way to expand access to the fresh starts afforded by record clearing is for jurisdictions to automatically seal or expunge records on certain conditions. In describing the decision to automatically expunge marijuana convictions, former San Francisco district attorney George Gascón aptly said, "It's a way to get people out of the paper prison they get sucked into once they have an arrest record or conviction. . . . When you remove the ability for people to participate fully in their community—employment, housing, education, other activities—you marginalize them until they're left with no hope."[86]

HOPE, FIRST AND SECOND CHANCES, AND DEATHS OF DESPAIR

We also can see a failure to ensure first and second chances in the disturbing rise of deaths due to drug and alcohol poisoning, suicide, chronic liver diseases, and cirrhosis. Princeton economists Anne Case and Angus Deaton famously found that roughly since the turn of the century, midlife (ages forty-five to fifty-four) mortality among white non-Hispanic men and women without any college education skyrocketed, largely as a result of an increase of deaths of despair.[87] This trend has been so severe that overall life expectancy at birth in the United States actually declined for three straight years, in what has been the longest downturn in a century, since World War I and the Spanish flu epidemic.[88]

While, to be sure, the rise of opioid addiction and suicide has multifaceted explanations,[89] loss of a sense of purpose and the capacity to care for family—through our failure to provide true first and second economic chances—should not be ruled out as a partial cause either. Whites with low levels of education—a group that has suffered from deaths of despair at high rates, though far from the only demographic to be affected—report a lack of hope and optimism, and low satisfaction in life, even when compared with other demographic groups that are objectively worse off economically.[90] As economists Carol Graham and Sergio Pinto note, "Lack of hope for the future stands out as the most important sign of vulnerability to deaths of despair," and the declining life expectancy of less-educated whites due to suicides and opioids is only the most recent "marker of this desperation."[91] Economists Eleanor Krause and Isabel Sawhill found that in the ten counties with the highest rates of deaths of despair, the male labor force participation rate (those who are working or looking for work) was only 73 percent—compared with 88 percent nationally at that time in 2014.[92] Alan Krueger found that prime-age men who are out of the labor force, about half of whom take medication for pain on a daily basis, report having low levels of emotional well-being and find little meaning from their daily activities.[93]

While the rise in mortality rates of low-educated white Americans is a critical development that deserves national attention, no one should see the tragedy of deaths of despair as new or limited to any racial group. African American men have for generations, and still do have, lower life expectancy than white men.[94] Recent research found that by 2014, midlife mortality was increasing across all racial groups, again largely caused by deaths of despair.[95] Within fifty-six cities in the United States, there are life expectancy gaps between neighborhoods—separated by just a few miles—of twenty to thirty years, with the largest gaps where we see the highest rates of racial segregation.[96] African American, Native American, and Alaskan Native women die from pregnancy-related causes at rates that are about three times higher than those of white women.[97] A major contributor is thought to be the severe impact of chronic stress stemming from a host of societal disadvantages and discrimination that takes a toll on minority women's bodies—what public health scholar Arline Geronimus calls "weathering."[98] Shorter lives due to worse-quality health care, exposure to gun violence, and intergenerational poverty, or factors that stem from structural race-related inequities, are every bit as worthy of the label of deaths of despair.

Issues of income inequality and lack of first and second chances are life-and-death issues. At midlife, those in the top 10 percent have a life expectancy of thirteen to fourteen years greater than those in the bottom 10 percent.[99] It is crucial that we explore the relationship of this second pillar of economic dignity—the capacity to pursue potential and purpose—and the pain that leads to deaths of despair.

EVERYONE BENEFITS FROM A NATIONAL EFFORT TO ENSURE TRUE CHANCES

We may initially think of a minority teen who has experienced multiple layers of discrimination and economic disadvantage and a fifty-five-year-old laid-off white male who has turned to opioids and stopped looking for work in a rural town as far apart on the political landscape. Yet while the conditions each faces and the policy solutions each requires may be distinct, they are linked by a common dignity hit: a feeling of being forgotten and abandoned with a scarcity of realistic avenues available to contribute meaningfully or pursue their full promise. A true commitment to economic dignity must recognize and address the different barriers individuals face—whether the cumulative economic disadvantages from racism and child poverty or the vicious negative cycles of economic decline in more isolated rural parts of our nation. And yet it is also critical to see these sometimes distinctive policies as part of a more unifying national commitment: to make real our values in allowing everyone to have true first and second chances at finding purpose, making a difference, and pursuing potential.

CHAPTER FIVE

ECONOMIC RESPECT: FREEDOM FROM DOMINATION AND HUMILIATION

Without the third pillar—being able to work and contribute economically with respect, not domination or humiliation—the foundation for economic dignity can collapse. Why? Because the need, and even desperation, to care for family and find purpose can be so immense that the pursuit of these vital ingredients of economic dignity can force people who lack viable options into conditions of exploitation and humiliation. To prevent this, and to guarantee economic dignity for all, requires legally protecting certain "spheres of dignity" that can never be traded, trampled, or compromised by government or market players in pursuit of profits or other economic goals.

As discussed earlier, these spheres of dignity were not protected for African Americans—most notably and brutally in the form of slavery, but also through economic cruelty and humiliation in the post-Reconstruction and Jim Crow era. For those who were not categorically denied economic rights due to race or gender, the need for such protections of economic dignity became most acute as the nation entered the industrial era in the nineteenth century. Before that, for those allowed some semblance of first-class citizenship, the U.S. economy offered a break from the domination and humiliation of the feudal lord/serf system of old Europe. Self-employment was a widely available option. The notion of working with respect in the sense of control and economic autonomy was deeply entwined with early American ideals.

The movement from a rural, agricultural economy to a more heavily urban, mass-production economy brought about a change in the nature of work for millions of Americans. The number of self-employed workers declined dramatically, with more workers having bosses and growing firms creating an unprecedented number of ranks within their hierarchies. By the 1870s, the number of wage workers exceeded the self-employed, excluding farmers;[1] the fraction of free workers who were self-employed fell from 83 percent in 1800 to only 22 percent of workers in 1910.[2]

Rather than having masters working side by side with journeymen and apprentices in small workshops where workers might still have felt a sense of respect and hope of increased responsibility, a new type of boss emerged: direct employers in an unregulated labor market with immense power over workers' wages, hours, and conditions. For millions, the capacity to work with respect, voice, and some control was replaced by a sense of economic domination. Free workers, like apprentices and journeymen, were no longer positioned with much of a chance to work toward owning an autonomous enterprise within a few years.[3] As philosopher Elizabeth Anderson writes, "Economies of scale overwhelmed the economy of small proprietors. . . . The Industrial Revolution also altered the nature of work and the relations between owners and workers in manufacturing, widening the gulf between the two."[4]

What shook even the idealized notion of American economic values was the lack of any protections against employers using brute power differentials to exploit workers' desperation. There was no protected sphere of dignity in the employment relationship. Increasingly, people began to question whether there was a missing link to the promise of our Constitution. What good was a system of rights that protected negative dignity against the government if private employers could dominate, humiliate, and exploit an employee with unrestrained power in the long hours and years at work that defined so much of a person's life?

UNCHECKED ECONOMIC DOMINATION AND THE PROGRESSIVE ERA

The Progressive Era saw innumerable battles to create a sphere of protected economic dignity in the workplace and in the larger economy at the end of the 1800s and into the early 1900s. Many of these struggles continue in some form today. Many such battles are worthy of detailed books in themselves. Yet a strong sense of these battles against economic domination and humiliation, both then and now, can be told through highlighting the fierce leadership of many female advocates and organizers—some of whom have been historically overlooked or underappreciated.

FLORENCE KELLEY: COMBATING CHILD LABOR AND SWEATSHOP CONDITIONS

Perhaps no practice epitomizes the need for legal restraints on the private sector more than child labor. Such forced labor robs children of childhoods and opportunities to develop through education. It also robs parents in positions of extreme economic desperation of the capacity to truly care for family. Labor rights activist Florence Kelley (1859–1932) devoted her life to documenting and fighting against degrading conditions in factories and sweatshops, and especially the scourge of child labor outside of family farms, which became more prevalent at the end of the nineteenth century with industrialization.[5] In 1870, about one out of every eight children was employed,[6] and this rate rose to one in five by 1900.[7] Child workers were exposed to shockingly dangerous situations, suffering injuries ranging from a lost finger or hand in twine factories to blindness or death in torpedo factories.[8] Children typically experienced more harm in the same working conditions than adults did. Children under sixteen who worked in the mines were more than three times as likely to be killed there. Among slate pickers, 75 percent of those killed were children.[9]

While living and working at Hull House in Chicago, which hosted social and educational programs for the surrounding working-class community, Kelley was appointed by the Illinois Bureau of Labor Statistics to investigate sweatshop conditions. "The sweating system," as it was called, was a series of subcontracted workspaces that grew out of the terrible conditions in factories in Chicago's garment industry.[10] They were overcrowded, dimly lit, often windowless rooms in run-down buildings where women and children as young as three or four worked to produce garments and toys, paid for by the piece, forcing them to continually work at a rapid pace. Diseases like smallpox and tuberculosis were rampant.[11] The outsourcing of work to laborers in tenement houses allowed manufacturers to pay workers the cheapest prices possible, as subcontractors "underbid each other to obtain work," and did not organize against the manufacturers.[12] Factory owners could avoid any responsibility for overseeing compliance with sanitary or safety ordinances. In describing the subcontracted sweatshops, Kelley wrote, "If an inspector orders sanitary changes to be made within a week, the sweater may prefer to disappear before the close of the week and open another shop in another place. Such easy evasion of the authorities places the sweater almost beyond official control, and many of them overcrowd their shops, overwork their employees, hire small children, keep their shops unclean, and their sanitary arrangements foul."[13]

The horrific conditions detailed in Kelley's groundbreaking investigative reports were the catalyst for the Illinois legislature's passing a law in 1893 that prohibited child labor under the age of fourteen in factories, workshops, or manufacturing establishments, mandated safety standards in factories, limited work hours for women and children, and banned subcontracted sweatshops.[14] Based on her illuminating investigations, Kelley forcefully argued that child labor was a direct consequence of families' desperation amid the lower wages of "the epoch of industrial instability."[15] Adults could no longer provide sufficiently for the survival of their families, leading to the need for child labor—and the deprivation of children's education—to supplement the household income. Kelley wrote, "Child labor comes of poverty and breeds low wages."[16] In 1899, only five states (Connecticut, Illinois, Massachusetts, New York, and Ohio) set age limits for employment across all occupations.[17] By 1909, twenty states had passed such legislation. The median minimum age was fourteen years old.[18] By 1920, 9 percent of children still worked, down from 18 percent in 1910.[19] In 1938, Congress passed a child labor law as part of the Fair Labor Standards Act (FLSA) that limited legal child labor to children sixteen and older, with lower ages allowed for work on farms. For hazardous occupations, the minimum age was eighteen.[20]

MOTHER JONES AND THE FIGHT AGAINST VIRTUAL INVOLUNTARY SERVITUDE

When the Thirteenth Amendment's prohibition against slavery and involuntary servitude was passed on January 31, 1865, Mary Harris Jones was a teacher, dressmaker, and mother of four. Few could have imagined that she would become a take-no-prisoners union organizer who took on the virtual involuntary servitude of mine workers employed by the big coal companies. Not long after, however, Jones lost all four of her children to yellow fever. And then she lost her home and dressmaking shop to the Great Chicago Fire of 1871. From there, she found a new purpose: organizing for the Knights of Labor and the United Mine Workers union, adopting the title "Mother" along the way.

The coal mines of America in the late nineteenth and early twentieth centuries exemplified a domination of labor that bordered on involuntary servitude. Workdays ranged from ten to twelve hours. Conditions in the mines meant deaths, and serious injuries of mine workers were far from uncommon. A typical feature of company towns—rapidly built villages around mines erected by firms in extractive industries—was that the company owned all the services and infrastructure in the town, forcing workers to subsist in employer-owned housing and rely on employer-owned stores. The management of coal mines often paid the workers on slips of paper that were redeemable only at the company-owned store.[21] Without competition, the companies were free to charge for housing and food at prices that far exceeded workers' compensation, leaving workers in debt, and then forcing them to pay off the debts before being permitted to leave the town; often they were blocked from leaving by armed guards.[22] Labor rights activists of the time battled private armies and sheriffs who protected the interests of coal companies.

Mother Jones traveled the country organizing miners and workers in the railroad, textile, garment, steel, and trolley car industries to harness their collective leverage to demand conditions that were less exploitative and dominating.[23] Her activism was not limited to male workers: she organized young women in Milwaukee breweries who toiled under horrendous work conditions and where sexual harassment was rampant. She convinced the United Mine Workers to boycott several breweries that refused to change the conditions. Mother Jones wrote of the bottle washers' conditions: "Condemned for life, to slave daily in the washroom in wet shoes and wet clothes, surrounded with foul-mouthed, brutal foremen. . . . And their crime? Involuntary poverty."[24]

One of Mother Jones's central causes was organizing coal miners in West Virginia, which at the turn of the last century had the highest death rate of any mining state, five times higher than in European countries. Approximately 94 percent of the miners lived in company-owned towns, and they were paid the lowest rates in the industry.[25] In describing why she once went to organize miners in West Virginia, she recalled, "When I heard of the coal company's efforts to kill the union officers, I decided I myself must go to Kelly Creek and rouse those slaves."[26]

Mother Jones and other union leaders fought private armies, on-the-take sheriffs, and the fear of retaliation and starvation that made many workers hesitant to demand better treatment. But during Mother Jones's era, union membership surged, illustrating the hunger among workers to bond together to have more leverage against employers than they could ever have individually. In 1897, 447,000 people were union members. By 1930, the year Mother Jones died, over three million Americans were union members. By 1940, the number of union members had more than doubled, to over seven million.[27]

These organizing gains took place well into the twentieth century, even while the U.S. Supreme Court still held on to the idea that regardless of how much workers faced domination and degradation at work, experiencing such treatment was a matter of workers' freedom of choice to contract out their labor. The election of FDR and pivotal Supreme Court rulings such as *NLRB v. Jones & Laughlin Steel* in 1937 eventually changed the playing field.

The Supreme Court held that workers have a "fundamental right" to organize and select representatives of their own choosing for collective bargaining, and that the right to contract must take into account the realities of economic desperation that stem from inherent power imbalances in labor markets. This was a recognition of the reality that without legal protection to band together without retaliation, workers lacked the capacity to not only prevent domination and humiliation, but work with the sense of respect that comes from having their voices expressed in the decisions impacting basic matters of their labor.[28]

Unfortunately, today, we still too frequently encounter examples of mining companies overlooking safety at the expense of workers' lives, as evidenced by a 2019 federal audit that found "no evidence that more than $1 billion in mine safety penalties over eighteen years deterred unsafe mining practices."[29]

FRANCES PERKINS: RAISING SAFETY STANDARDS IN THE WORKPLACE

While Frances Perkins may always be best known as the United States' first female cabinet secretary and a central figure in crafting policies for the New Deal, some of her earliest victories concerned protecting workers from grossly unsafe working conditions. Her activism on worker safety took a turn when she was having tea with friends in New York's Washington Square one spring afternoon in 1911, a full two decades before the start of the New Deal.[30] At the time, Perkins, then just thirty years old, was deeply engrossed in the fight for workers' rights through her role leading the New York office of the National Consumers League.

On that day, Perkins heard commotion and cries for help coming from the Triangle Shirtwaist Factory and ran to the scene, where she witnessed the "horrifying spectacle"[31] of more than fifty young female workers forced to jump to their deaths from the burning building.[32] The women, Perkins recalled watching, "had been holding on until that time, standing in the windowsills, being crowded by others behind them, the fire pressing closer and closer, the smoke closer and closer."[33] The ninth-floor exits had been closed by management seeking to prevent theft, keep out union organizers, and prevent walkouts. The city's fire brigade ladders were too short to reach the floors where the factory was contained, and many of those who reached the fire escape died as it collapsed under the heat and the weight of workers trying to flee.[34] It was one of the deadliest industrial disasters in New York City's history.

The Triangle Shirtwaist disaster could in no way be described as an unforeseeable accident or misfortune. The workers in New York City's garment industry had long tried to focus attention on the risk these dangerous conditions created. Not even two years before the fire, in the biggest female-led strike up to that point, known as the Uprising of the Twenty Thousand, a majority of the city's thirty thousand garment workers walked out in protest of unsafe working conditions, pay, hours, and lack of union rights as well as protections against indignities like sexual harassment. At the end of the strike, 85 percent of the city's shirtwaist workers had joined the International Ladies' Garment Workers' Union (ILGWU),[35] but the Triangle Shirtwaist Factory remained anti-union.[36] At the time, New York, like most states, had new factory safety laws on the books, but they were rarely enforced, with "standards for fire drills, fire escapes, and sprinkler systems [in New York] . . . followed 'only where practicable.'"[37] The Fire Department of the City of New York had cited the Triangle Shirtwaist Factory multiple times for failing to provide sufficient fire escapes, yet had taken no meaningful action against the owners.[38]

Following the tragic fire, a citizens' Committee on Safety was established to spur workplace safety legislation. Former president Theodore Roosevelt endorsed Frances Perkins to lead it.[39]

Perkins's service led to sweeping changes to labor rules and public safety codes. The reforms and investigations would go beyond workplace safety to address low wages, long hours, unsanitary conditions, and child labor, with the adoption of thirty-six new laws at the city and state levels that eventually served as models for other states and for the New Deal's labor laws in the 1930s.[40] Perkins later said that the legislation in New York was a "turning point" in "American political attitudes and policies towards social responsibility," and described the Triangle Shirtwaist Factory fire as "the day the New Deal was born."[41]

Later, in her role as secretary of labor, Perkins led the agency to create the Bureau of Labor Standards in 1934, the first permanent federal agency established primarily to promote safety and health for workers. This was the predecessor of the Occupational Safety and Health Administration (OSHA), which was created in 1971.

IDA TARBELL: SMALL BUSINESSES UP AGAINST A MONOPOLY

Another way economic domination can undercut a basic sphere of dignity is when entrepreneurs and small business owners are crushed under brutally unfair, unchecked monopolistic practices. To be clear, there is nothing wrong in a free-market economy with any company being outcompeted by a rival that makes a better widget, or the same widget at a better price. Yet a basic underpinning of economic freedom has long been that competition between sellers of goods and services is driven by price, quality, and fair opportunities—not by arbitrary, brute power.

Ida Tarbell was a fourteen-year-old eyewitness to the ruin that took over her once prosperous hometown in the oil-rich region of western Pennsylvania in the early 1870s when it received "a blow between the eyes"[42] when small business owners like Tarbell's father found themselves victimized by Standard Oil's brute monopolistic practices. The power amassed in John D. Rockefeller's oil business came from collusion with major railroads to keep competitors' prices artificially high, among other tactics.[43] The price-fixing alliance afforded Rockefeller and other larger refineries not only lower freight prices but also the power to force small refineries to sell their businesses to him at a loss.[44] If they refused to sell, Rockefeller assured them that there was little to no chance of their business surviving.[45] When my wife—a TV writer—wrote for Netflix's *Narcos*, the first line she told me from her research of Colombian drug lord Pablo Escobar was how he offered a "choice" to the elected officials he wanted to bribe: *¿Plata o plomo?* Silver or lead? This money-or-a-bullet coercion was experienced by small oil refiners who felt "entirely at the mercy" of Standard Oil's monopoly power.[46]

Tarbell's motivation to take down Rockefeller was no doubt inspired in part by the devastating harm to small business owners from his brute oil monopoly that she saw up close. Her father's business partner shot himself following his economic ruin, leaving her father with so much debt that he was forced to do what he considered "unsound and humiliating—mortgage our home."[47] When he was given the silver-or-lead choice by Rockefeller, Tarbell's father refused because, as she wrote later, for him "dignity and success lay in being your own master." An economy where such men could be forced by arbitrary economic power to be "hired men . . . taking orders, even orders as to what to say, for whom to vote [was] . . . to his way of thinking . . . a failure for an American."[48] In 1904, Tarbell published a multi-installment, widely read exposé on the unscrupulous tactics and unethical practices Rockefeller and Standard Oil deployed in building their monopoly and crushing competitors. The attention the piece garnered was seen as the event that gave Teddy Roosevelt the final impetus to pull the trigger on bringing the Northern Securities Trust case that led to the breakup of Standard Oil into thirty-four independent companies.[49]

ONGOING BATTLES AGAINST ECONOMIC DOMINATION

The United States has moved beyond the worst acts of economic domination seen in the Industrial Revolution, but the imperative to ensure negative economic dignity remains an ongoing struggle, with both new challenges and new versions of old challenges.

FIGHTING FOR THE EXCLUDED: DOROTHY BOLDEN, AI-JEN POO, DOLORES HUERTA, AND MARY KAY HENRY

Even with significant remaining safety problems, such as the persistent high prevalence of black lung disease among coal miners, Mother Jones's mission to see mine workers largely unionized and protected by federal law came to fruition following her death in 1930. But the New Deal–era victories for labor rights left gaping holes, the consequences of which still leave millions of workers unprotected today. Dolores Huerta, Dorothy Bolden, and Ai-jen Poo are some of the leading figures who have fought to correct the purposeful exclusion of domestic workers and farmworkers. Numerous factors compound the vulnerability of these workers to abuses: they are often racial and ethnic minorities; large numbers lack work authorization; the workforces are extremely low paid, with little savings to fall back on; most have low levels of education; and many have limited English proficiency. Domestic workers by definition work in isolation behind closed doors in private homes, and farmworkers face their own unique challenges that make it hard to execute collective bargaining. Many of these workers believe they have few labor market options and little or no recourse to wage theft, on-the-job injuries, and verbal, sexual, and racial harassment.

Both farmworkers and domestic workers were excluded from critical New Deal legislation. These exclusionary laws included the National Labor Relations Act (NLRA) of 1935, which guaranteed the right to form a union and to collective bargaining; the Social Security Act of 1935, which established not just an old-age pension but unemployment insurance and workers' compensation; and the Fair Labor Standards Act of 1938, which enacted protections such as overtime rules, minimum wage, and limits on child labor. Later, these workers were also excluded, either de facto or de jure, from the Occupational Safety and Health Act protections, despite working in physically intensive jobs, and despite numerous federal antidiscrimination laws. The New Deal–era exclusions were hardly accidental. They were the result of the insistence by Southern congressmen on maintaining a system of domination of black laborers,[50] who were mostly employed in farm labor or domestic work in the Southern states.[51] A New York congressman who opposed the exclusions in the 1930s proclaimed that it would guarantee "a continuance of virtual slavery."[52]

Domestic workers bonded together to fight domination and abusive treatment long before their exclusion from the New Deal legislation. In 1881, approximately three thousand black laundresses in Atlanta participated in a strike that ultimately led to higher wages and a recognition that organized black domestic workers could indeed exert leverage through their collective strength.[53] Decades later in Atlanta, a domestic worker named Dorothy Bolden took up the torch again in the heart of the civil rights movement. Recognizing the immense need for bettering the conditions and wages of domestic workers, mostly black women, alongside fighting for legal equality, Bolden initially approached Martin Luther King to help organize household workers. King encouraged her to take the lead. Bolden then deployed some of the most creative organizing tactics of the civil rights era. Like domestic workers today, these workers were isolated from one another. Bolden recognized the one place where the potential for convening was possible: the bus to and from work. She handed out flyers at transfer hubs that the vast majority of domestic workers relied on to get to work and convened meetings on city buses. The buses became places where these workers could share stories of abuse, learn about rights, and exchange information about wages and workload as a critical, empowering first step to demanding improved conditions. Bolden saw her advocacy and organizing as also complementing the larger work of the civil rights movement, including the desegregation of schools. While Constance Motley was working hand in hand with Thurgood Marshall and the NAACP Legal Defense Fund to convince the Supreme Court and the white political power structure that segregation was an assault on first-class citizenship and basic dignity, Bolden saw raising the wages of black household workers as critical in that fight because "we couldn't be going to integrate schools out there barefooted."[54]

Shortly after Martin Luther King's assassination in 1968, Bolden and others formed the National Domestic Workers Union of America (NDWUA), an education and advocacy organization committed to improving conditions for domestic workers that at its height served over ten thousand members nationally.[55] Bolden led the NDWUA for twenty-eight years.[56] As Ai-jen Poo, the head of the National Domestic Workers Alliance (NDWA), notes, the organization represented "the first time there was ever a voice [for domestic workers] that was powerful in terms of raising standards for the work force and improving wages."[57]

Today, Ai-jen Poo has launched and run the NDWA to carry on Bolden's efforts in organizing domestic workers around the country to fight back against the exclusions of household workers from our country's labor protections. More than eighty years after the passage of the FLSA and NLRA, domestic workers are still excluded from numerous basic labor protections, including the right to form a union and bargain collectively, overtime for live-in domestic workers who are routinely asked to work outside of agreed-upon hours, OSHA safeguards and workers' compensation despite high rates of on-the-job injuries, and antidiscrimination protections.[58] In tandem with vital workplace exclusions, "hidden behind closed doors, in many ways this work is almost defined by invisibility," notes Ai-jen Poo.[59] Nearly every domestic worker lacks a written contract with their employer. Many live paycheck to paycheck, and experiences of wage violations are common (almost one-quarter of all domestic workers and nearly seven out of ten live-in domestic workers were paid less than the minimum wage; one in ten said they were not paid what they were owed in the previous year).[60] Hardly any domestic workers are covered by unemployment insurance, and there are no requirements for notice of termination. I will never forget the deep hurt experienced by a woman my family was extremely close to when she came back to work a couple of days late from the Philippines because her father's health had taken a turn for the worse and he was near death. When she came to the door of the home where she had lovingly cared for the children for years, she found that her employer had, in a fit of rage, gathered all her belongings and put them in trash bags that were waiting for her at the door of the house. Bolden, too, experienced gross mistreatment. In 1940, her employer had her arrested. The crime? Not agreeing to stay beyond her shift to do dishes.[61]

Poo, like Bolden before her, sought not only to build up legal protections for household workers but also to raise to the fore the principle that these workers deserve respect and dignity for their roles in providing incalculably valuable care for people. Bolden declared, "A domestic worker is a counselor, a doctor, and a nurse."[62] Poo defines domestic work as "the work that makes all other work possible." As I will discuss in Chapter Fifteen on worker power, NDWA's organizing is winning legislative battles to bring protections to domestic workers: at least nine states and Seattle have passed Domestic Workers' Bills of Rights that extend labor protections for the first time to domestic workers—but there remains a long way to go.[63]

Like domestic workers, farmworkers have struggled due to their exclusion from basic legal protections. Despite hard-fought organizing efforts over several decades, many farmworkers across the United States still experience some of the most egregious violations of economic dignity. Over the last half century, the struggles of farmworkers—the pains, the gains, and the remaining distance that still needs to be traveled—can be seen through the life's work of activist Dolores Huerta. As a young woman in the 1950s and '60s, Huerta saw up close the plight of farmworkers—working hard while living in poverty, their children going to school hungry, rampant sexual abuse, living in dilapidated shacks, and sleeping on floors—which rivaled conditions that had shocked Teddy Roosevelt and Florence Kelley decades earlier. Huerta founded the Agricultural Workers Association, and later, with Cesar Chavez, led the United Farm Workers (UFW), which became the nation's largest farmworkers' union. In protest of low pay, dangerous working conditions, denial of drinking water and bathrooms in the fields, and exposure to pesticides that could cause shocking bodily disfigurement, Huerta organized, along with Chavez and Larry Itliong, an international boycott of grapes from Delano, California, and stores that sold them. Under pressure from the consumer boycott, in 1970, twenty-six grape growers—35 percent of grape growers in the industry—signed contracts with the UFW.[64] These contracts were the first major union-negotiated contracts for farmworkers in the United States. The national attention garnered by this strike also led to California's 1975 Agricultural Labor Relations Act (ALRA), which historically extended the right to collective bargaining without retaliation to agriculture workers.

Despite the grape strike and other hard-fought organizing efforts over several decades, many farmworkers across the United States still experience egregious violations of dignity. These include deplorable, inhumane living conditions in facilities often provided by employers that grossly fail to meet state-mandated quality standards, and poverty-level income for backbreaking work. Farmworkers are still ineligible for overtime pay, and those who work on small farms are not even protected by the federal minimum wage. Many experience wage theft. Many are denied water breaks while working at breakneck pace under the hot sun without shade. Others are exposed to harmful pesticides that cause short- and long-term health effects made even worse by very low access to health care. Still, at a federal level and in most states, farmworkers are excluded from the right to form a union. And since large numbers of farmworkers are undocumented immigrants, they have particularly little leverage in combating abuses by growers and foremen. Although farmworkers do not work in isolation like domestic workers, the work is seasonal, making it difficult to enact robust campaigns to collectively leverage for better conditions.[65]

The lingering exclusions of farmworkers and domestic workers from basic dignity protections mean that these workers are still paying the price of Jim Crow–era legislative battles.

Mother Jones's fight for workers to be able to bond together to exert collective leverage is a fight that continues today, and indeed, the right to form unions is one of the most consequential and pervasive remaining issues of exclusion from labor laws. Mary Kay Henry, president of the Service Employees International Union (SEIU), has pointed out that up to 45 percent of all workers are still legally excluded from the right to form a union.[66] As will be discussed in the chapter on worker power, the successes of the Fight for $15 grassroots movement, with leadership from Henry, the AFL-CIO, and others, is part of a larger movement to expand not only eligibility to form a union but to negotiate at a broader sectorwide level that can make collective bargaining both more accessible and more powerful for workers.

#METOO: ECONOMIC DOMINATION, HUMILIATION, AND ABUSE AT WORK

The #MeToo movement calls out sexual mistreatment and abuse that goes beyond the workplace. Yet the national discussion it fuels on the depth and breadth of sexual harassment that takes place in the workforce speaks to how economic pain can be invisible when we see economics as only about what shows up in metrics, like GDP or job growth, as opposed to what matters most for economic dignity. If our end goal is economic dignity based on the prevention of domination and humiliation, then sexual harassment at work must be seen as a tier-one economic issue.

Much of the initial #MeToo media attention focused on the sexual harassment of more well-off men and women in professional jobs, including actors and journalists. But advocates of low-income workers rightly chided the media to not let such high-profile cases sweep all attention away from the abuses that happen regularly to working women with less income, profile, and power.

Power dynamics inherent in labor markets mean that nearly any class of worker can experience sexual harassment and violence on the job, whether a home care worker or, as we saw with allegations concerning Harvey Weinstein, a famous actress. Yet the degree that job-related sexual mistreatment is crushing for women in both professional and lower-paid service jobs is powerful evidence of how essential the protection against domination and humiliation is for economic dignity across the income and work spectrum. Entire career paths are opened or closed by networks, by mentors, by whispering that a person either has that special something or is to be avoided. A person can be denied access to participate in projects that are critical opportunities for advancement. In academic sciences, engineering, and medicine, a study found that some female victims of sexual harassment felt forced to give up tenured positions and some left their fields entirely.[67] Those whose careers are tied to a specific city or closely knit industry can feel that even the clear establishment of a sexual harassment claim against a powerful colleague or boss can, in the long term, lead to subtle but devastating retaliation that will set back their pursuit of potential. Anonymously, a formerly prominent television personality described the experience of retaliation after suing a large corporation for sexual harassment: "On your deathbed, you will probably feel that you have done the moral thing by speaking up, but in the years you are alive, you are very cognizant of the toll your decision to come forward has taken on your life and your career path."[68] Some of the most high-profile victims who have shared their stories in the #MeToo movement discussed not only the pain of sexual abuse but the pain that comes from being denied the opportunity to pursue potential and purpose out of the need to avoid sexual abuse.

In low-wage workforces, the vulnerability to workplace sexual harassment can be exceptionally high, with jobs a matter of economic survival, and even fewer avenues for recourse.[69] The janitorial services industry exemplifies some of the structural issues that can make low-wage workforces particularly vulnerable to unchecked abuses.[70] Workers are often subcontracted, and with high shares of immigrants who may not be legally authorized to work in the United States, employers can exploit their fear of being deported as a matter of retaliation. These are factors that abusers exploit, making janitorial workers particularly vulnerable to unchecked abuse as they seek to care for family and pursue potential. Some of the elements that create this grave situation are that the employees—often female—work in isolation without coworkers, which means there are less likely to be witnesses to abuse.[71]

A *Frontline* investigative report, "Rape on the Nightshift," brought to light the case of pervasive sexual harassment and sexual violence in the country's largest janitorial services company, ABM, which had at least forty-two separate lawsuits over two decades that involved janitors saying they were sexually harassed, assaulted, or raped at work.[72] Even after the government imposed reform requirements on ABM following multiple federal suits related to sexual harassment, there were more lawsuits in which female janitors said they told the company about sexual harassment or assault they experienced on the job but were ignored. In one case, a serial rapist (with a criminal record for rape) was employed by ABM as a supervisor. He sexually harassed and assaulted multiple janitors, and despite there even being a witness who reported it to the company, ABM still let him return to oversee janitors, at least one of whom he later raped.[73] Since 2002, the company has paid out over $150 million in penalties related to numerous labor code violations, including wage theft and sexual harassment.[74]

The problem is hardly limited to ABM. A majority of janitorial workers surveyed in California said they had experienced or witnessed sexual harassment or assault at work.[75] Advocates also raised issues for women working late nights, often isolated, alone, and with poor lighting in parking lots. These findings led the Ya Basta! Coalition, the SEIU–United Service Workers West with leadership from David Huerta, and the California Service Employees International Union (SEIU), then headed by Laphonza Butler, to organize for a state law that now mandates sexual harassment prevention training and increases accountability to protect janitorial workers. When some of the janitorial workers organized a weeklong hunger strike outside the state capital as part of their advocacy, Dolores Huerta, in her eighties, joined the gathering to show support.

As Saru Jayaraman, advocate and organizer for restaurant workers, notes, "You can know you have rights, and know you're being harassed, but if you have no power on the job to do anything about it, it really makes no difference."[76] For many of these workers, their grit and determination to care for their family will not allow them to show up in our economic statistics as discouraged workers or those who dropped out of the workforce. But as an economic dignity goal of ensuring all can care for family without abuse and humiliation, it is an urgent economic issue.

WORKERS AS MEANS, NOT ENDS

During my experiences as executive director for the Center for Universal Education and in the Clinton administration, working to fight abusive child labor, I heard stories from and saw with my own eyes children in poor nations who spent their days in dreary and repetitive work—such as sitting on the floor for hours and hours without a break assembling bracelets or carrying bricks—instead of learning in a classroom. Yes, child labor is now mostly banned in the United States—and one hopes more and more of the world. But that same willingness to force people, often those doing repetitive tasks, to work in harsh and inhuman conditions at breakneck speeds is alive and well in the United States. Even with the labor protections gained since the days of Florence Kelley and the bans on subcontracted sweatshops, there remains a disturbing willingness—and legal space—for employers to treat workers as if they are merely means to profits through maximum efficiency. The aggressive, unchecked drive to treat workers only as a means to the end of greater profits—and not as ends in themselves—can be seen in many worksites, from poultry farms to high-tech retail warehouses.

CHICKEN AND DIAPERS

Multiple companies have been cited for unsafe and humiliating conditions that lead to workers being forced to skip bathroom breaks or wear diapers in the struggle to keep up with the high-paced monotony of processing lines. This situation is far from uncommon in poultry processing plants, where the work is often dangerous. It requires employees to use scissors and knives in close quarters to skin, cut, debone, and pack chickens at fast speeds.[77] Workers earn on average $25,000 per year.[78] Oxfam researchers found that poultry workers were routinely denied bathroom breaks at the country's four largest companies, which collectively employ over one hundred thousand poultry processing workers and control almost 60 percent of the market. Many workers reported urinating or defecating on themselves or seeing coworkers do so because they were afraid to leave their workstation or had to wait too long. To cope, many workers reported wearing diapers and restricting liquid intake.[79]

Dolores, who worked at a Simmons plant in Arkansas, said she was denied permission to use the bathroom "many, many times." Her supervisor mocked workers' requests. "He said, 'Ah, but why? I told you . . . that you shouldn't drink so much water and eat so much food so that you don't need to ask to use the bathroom." She began wearing a sanitary napkin, but because it would fill up with urine too quickly, she resorted to diapers: "I had to wear Pampers." She said she felt like she had "no worth, no right to repeal or to speak up." She decided just to endure the situation. "It made me feel ashamed."[80] Another worker, Bacilio, recalled an instance where he worked next to a woman who was eight months pregnant yet was denied a bathroom break. "An hour passed, then two. She asked again. The supervisor said, 'Sorry, lady, but no one can cover for you. Hold it awhile more.' Finally, the woman wet her pants and began to cry."[81]

Two major issues facilitate these deplorable work conditions. First, supervisors—under pressure to meet production goals—have significant discretion in deciding when employees can use the restroom, as opposed to guaranteeing breaks. This creates conditions ripe for abuse: while denying breaks, supervisors regularly mock, threaten, and even extort workers. Second, there are weak protections against outrageous production line speeds. Over the vigorous opposition of organizations like the National Employment Law Project (NELP), United Food and Commercial Workers International Union, and Oxfam America, the Trump administration recently allowed poultry processors to apply for a waiver that would enable them to increase their already grueling processing speeds from 140 birds per minute up to 175 birds per minute.[82] Even under the lower rate of 140 birds per minute, the punishing speed puts enormous pressure on employees to stop taking breaks, and some managers frequently delay or deny bathroom breaks.[83] Moreover, poultry workers "suffer serious injuries at double the rate of private industry [and] . . . are more than six times as likely to have a work-related illness."[84] Even before this waiver, NELP found that some of the top poultry and meat processing companies were among the nation's worst in terms of serious injuries, including workers requiring amputations.[85]

"ELECTRONIC WHIPS"

The willingness of employers to see workers as means only to hypereffi-ciency is certainly not relegated to the poultry industry. Technological ad-vances are allowing employers to monitor workers' movements with greater ease and reach, amounting to what some call an "electronic whip."

Another occupation where the technological tools for ever greater super-vision meet with management's demands for hyperefficient quotas and pro-duction speeds is Amazon warehouse jobs.[86] In early 2019, an employee told the *Guardian* that "pickers" were expected to grab four hundred items per hour, or one item every seven seconds.[87] Warehouse workers spend ten-hour shifts standing on their feet the whole time.[88] Every task is monitored inside the warehouse, and numerous former workers report that if associates were off task for an hour or for shorter periods several times, they would be im-mediately terminated.[89] The demanding quotas under high-stress condi-tions have reportedly led some workers to urinate in trash cans for fear of missing their targets.[90] Amazon has even patented a wristband that it could in the future use to track employees' every move and let their supervi-sors know if and when they move an inch that is not in the aim of packing boxes.[91]

Founding president of the American Federation of Labor Samuel Gom-pers in 1904 said, "We don't love to work only. The mule works, too."[92] Echo-ing that line, Rashad Long, a former picker at the Staten Island Amazon warehouse, said, "We are not robots. We are human beings. We cannot come into work after only four hours of sleep and be expected to be fully energized and ready to work. That's impossible. I feel like all the company cares about is getting their products out to the customers as quickly as humanly possi-ble, no matter what that means for us workers in the end."[93]

Sociologist Matthew Desmond traces the origins of hyper-microefficient quota-oriented management to the ultimate degradation and treatment of people as only means to an end: slavery and its use in the production of cotton. Prior to the mass movement from farms to factories in the second half of the nineteenth century, the invention of the cotton gin—and its opportunities to benefit from economies of scale—led to the use of a rigid oversight system that took the tracking of enslaved people's every movement and the accounting of each daily workload to a greater extreme than before. In a piece for the *New York Times Magazine*'s 1619 Project, Desmond writes, "Like today's titans of industry, planters understood that their profits climbed when they extracted maximum effort out of each worker. So they paid close attention to inputs and outputs by developing precise systems of record-keeping. Meticulous bookkeepers and overseers were just as important to the productivity of a slave-labor camp as field hands." One plantation owner developed a "one-stop-shop accounting manual, complete with rows and columns that tracked per-worker productivity." Desmond sees a direct relation to aspects of work life today:

Modern-day workers are subjected to a wide variety of surveillance strategies, from drug tests and closed-circuit video monitoring to tracking apps and even devices that sense heat and motion. . . . But it's only the technology that's new. The core impulse behind that technology pervaded plantations, which sought innermost control over the bodies of their enslaved work force.[94]

FINANCIAL DOMINATION: FROM IDA TARBELL TO ELIZABETH WARREN AND THE CONSUMER FINANCIAL PROTECTION BUREAU

Ensuring that Americans can participate in the economy without domination and humiliation should never be an issue limited only to people in their roles as workers. How people are treated in their roles as small business owners or as consumers trying to care for or invest in their family's well-being and future will always be an essential component of economic dignity.

Essential to our current economic conversation is the question of whether our antitrust laws allow major tech giants and firms in other industries with deep economic concentration to wield arbitrary, brute power against smaller businesses, start-up competitors, and suppliers. In this way, Lina Khan's profound 2017 piece "Amazon's Antitrust Paradox" in the *Yale Law Journal*—which questioned the current focus on consumer price at the expense of issues of abusive power over competitors[95]—carries forward the work of Ida Tarbell, as I will discuss further in my chapter on structuring markets for economic dignity.

It is also essential to an economic dignity framework to understand the degree that abusive and predatory financial transactions can impact the capacity to care for family and pursue potential as deeply as abuses at work.

Of course, a toy that malfunctions or poor treatment by an airline or a canceled appointment by an internet provider, while infuriating, doesn't rise to the level of an assault on economic dignity. There are, however, critical financial transactions—buying or refinancing a home, combating negative treatment from landlords, taking on huge costs for some form of higher education or training, engaging with health-care providers, or making nursing home arrangements—that can have impacts as devastating on economic dignity as horrendous abuses at work do.

For example, payday lending, predatory for-profit schools (which I discuss in Chapter Seven), and renting a home can have dramatic life impacts that can deeply affect the capacity to care for family or pursue potential. Annie Waldman at ProPublica brought to light the case of a former foster care youth with learning disabilities who was misled into taking out $6,000 in student loans, for a program that she would not complete, which was sent to collections, ultimately destroying her credit score and then preventing her from being able to get affordable housing for herself and her two-year-old child.[96] In a class-action suit against ITT Technical Institute, 473 students submitted statements that detailed how the debt they accumulated while there prevented them from achieving life goals ranging from getting a better education to having children.[97] Abusive payday lending is another example. Millions of workers simply do not earn enough or see such fluctuations in their wages that an unexpected expense of several hundred dollars—say, to repair a car that is needed to keep a job or to fix a hot-water heater—can leave an individual with no other options but to take out an abusive payday loan with effective interest rates that average nearly 400 percent.[98] That can lead to an inescapable debt trap that leads to major life setbacks. Landlord exploitation can similarly lead to catastrophic consequences for families. Abuse by landlords of vulnerable families can be among the most devastating assaults on economic dignity imaginable.[99]

This is why the existence of a permanent federal agency, the Consumer Financial Protection Bureau (CFPB), signed into law by President Obama in 2011 and spearheaded by two decades of advocacy by Elizabeth Warren against predatory financial behavior, is so critical. The creation of the CFPB should be seen not as a short-term response to the financial crisis but as filling a crucial structural gap in our economic landscape for protecting economic dignity. While protecting against financial power and abuse is important in and of itself—for example, in preventing large-scale fraud that costs millions of people relatively small amounts—major abuses in lending, housing, and education can have devastating effects on people's capacity to care for family and pursue their dreams.

GOVERNMENTS, MARKETS, AND CHANGE

CHAPTER SIX

ECONOMIC DIGNITY: GOVERNMENT'S RESPONSIBILITY

An economic dignity goal requires all of us to make the ultimate test for economic policy its real impact on the lives of people. Preset ideological preferences for government or markets should take a back seat to a commitment to use whatever combination of policy tools is most effective in filling dignity gaps and lifting up well-being. As we have discussed, Teddy Roosevelt's position as one of our greatest American presidents is specifically due to his willingness as a Republican president to put recognition of real-life dignity gaps and solutions for economic dignity above any preset ideological commitment to free markets, laissez-faire economics, and minimal government. He stood ready to use government action when it was the clear solution to ensure people did not experience domination and despair in the workplace and marketplace. His view reflected a crucial understanding: while there can be a mix of government and market mechanisms to achieve different economic goals, it is the responsibility of government to ensure that those policies work in fact to promote economic dignity for all.

Unfortunately, even when those on the conservative side at times seek to elevate dignity as an important goal, there is little to no willingness to think outside a self-imposed ideological box of minimalist government. Unlike Teddy Roosevelt, today's conservatives are less willing to even acknowledge clear, real-life denials of economic dignity if their recognition would require an acknowledgment of the failure of markets or the need for a larger government role.

Indeed, major conservative think tanks even go so far as to refer to smaller government not as a means to their policy ends but as an end in itself. For example, the Heritage Foundation, the Cato Institute, and Americans for Tax Reform frame "limited government" or "limited government ideals" as defining values and end goals.[1] Rather than an open-ended, thorough, data-driven inquiry into the causes of economic insecurity, lack of opportunity, or gaps in economic dignity—or a rigorous examination of what combination of government and markets can best promote the end values of freedom, dignity, and personal fulfillment—the answer is preordained: less government.

For some of its proponents, this fidelity may reflect evidence of social Darwinist end goals or a refusal to address racial injustice. Yet even if one takes a more generous view, this ideological straitjacket ends up handcuffing conservatives from reaching for a more serious economic dignity agenda that actually focuses on their own stated values of self-reliance, innovation, competition, and entrepreneurship.

A. COMPACT OF CONTRIBUTION OR PUNITIVE TEST?

There is no area where conservatives pay more lip service to dignity than the issues of work, carrying one's share of the load, and self-sufficiency. Yet, when it comes to policy, these stated values do not translate into a true compact of contribution: one where such policymakers take a hard look at the barriers people face and what measures could best support everyone who can to experience the dignity of work, contribution, and pursuit of purpose. Instead, the rhetoric of self-reliance and work are used to justify often arbitrary and punitive tests designed to exclude those deemed unworthy of government assistance.

This frame has too often reflected or promoted social Darwinism or the fostering of stereotypes that encourage racial resentment. This was foundational to Ronald Reagan's ugly trope of the so-called welfare queen.[2] Yet even when it avoids these darker subthemes, this frame subverts an open analysis of what policies would be most effective in enabling more Americans to do their part and work and contribute to their family and community in some way. Instead, such conservative thinkers force the entire frame for policies on work as a simplistic and binary choice between self-reliance and what they define as dignity-defying dependency. Every work and economic security issue is essentially framed as a single hypothetical transaction, imagining a person choosing between a desperate search for any type of job and destructive reliance on government assistance. If economic dignity is just an all-or-nothing choice between self-reliance and policies that create dependency, then no matter what the economic challenges a person faces, the answer to every question is the same: less government.

This frame is embraced across the conservative spectrum. It is entrenched in the current mainstream conservative movement, as seen in former Speaker of the House Paul Ryan's concern that the safety net is "a hammock that lulls able-bodied people to lives of dependency and complacency, that drains them of their will and their incentive to make the most of their lives."[3] And while Trump may be at loggerheads with conservative market fundamentalism in the area of trade, when it comes to programs that benefit the less fortunate, he clings tightly to this orthodoxy while stressing its worst divisive racial undertones. His administration's use of this simplistic transactional approach is perhaps best exemplified by the Trump administration's Council of Economic Advisers' July 2018 report on work requirements and the safety net.[4] The report sets self-sufficiency as the main goal of economic policy and then analyzes it on two dimensions: "receipt of benefits from Medicaid, SNAP [Supplemental Nutrition Assistance Program], housing assistance or TANF [Temporary Assistance for Needy Families] at some point during the year" and "whether non-disabled working-age recipients work."[5] In other words, any receipt of government benefits is harmful because it detracts from self-sufficiency. This view is not just a messaging frame. For example, even as this book was being finalized in late 2019, the Trump administration decided to use arbitrary work requirements to deny nearly 700,000 people basic food relief and to propose burdensome additional reviews for Social Security Disability Insurance (SSDI) that will lead to thousands of people losing their benefits.[6]

To be clear, we should favor a compact of contribution in which we do everything possible to help every person work and contribute to the best of their capacity. And yes, it makes sense to ensure that our policies create incentives that reward work and do not lead to unintended consequences that deter individuals from contributing and pursuing purpose and potential. Yet there is a major difference between a punitive approach and a more compassionate compact of contribution. The punitive model makes the primary lens through which we design our economic security policies the fear that vast numbers of Americans are actively looking for ways to cheat, not carry their load or contribute. This punitive model posits that the best solution to dignity gaps is to push for stricter, one-size-fits-all tests to ensure against their fears of dependency. By contrast, a compact of contribution recognizes that most people want to work and contribute, and seeks to address the complexities and barriers people with challenges like poverty, depression, disability, pain, and long-term unemployment face that might make it harder to contribute. And it reflects the reality-based understanding that the consistent availability of a helping hand will encourage work and contribution more than punitive cutoffs. A true compact of contribution will be a better remedy for declines in labor market participation than the punitive approach.

For all the conservative hand-wringing about lazy recipients of government benefits—or Fox News harangues when they find a surfer using SNAP to buy lobster[7]—the facts simply do not support the notion that benefits lull would-be workers into complacency or dependency. The vast number of Americans who receive benefits have an undeniable history of work effort.

Consider the Supplemental Nutrition Assistance Program (formerly known as the Food Stamp Program). More than half of SNAP recipients without a disability work in the typical month they receive benefits.[8] And only about 4 percent of households that worked in the year before starting to receive benefits did not work in the following year.[9] Far from subsidizing indulgence, SNAP benefits average just $1.40 per person per meal—an amount that is, if anything, inadequate and contributes to hunger and food insecurity.[10] Recipients are not freeloaders; they are people like Michelle Piche-Lichtman of Milwaukee, who says SNAP was a "lifesaver" when she was working three jobs and barely making ends meet; Norm Coleman, a disabled air force veteran who lives in Milwaukee; and Darla Feeback, a Tulsa mother of two children who works as a SNAP outreach specialist at a food bank.[11] Ms. Feeback says SNAP benefits helped her keep food on the table and get back on her feet after her family lost their house in a fire, and that the benefits are a "huge investment to my kids' future."[12]

Or consider Medicaid. If Medicaid discouraged people from working and self-reliance, one would expect to see those states that took advantage of the Affordable Care Act's Medicaid expansion to see some reduction in work effort. But it turns out there is no discernible effect, undercutting the idea that providing access to health insurance coverage fosters complacency.[13] Indeed, research finds states that expand Medicaid actually see increases in employment for people with disabilities.[14] Punitive, burdensome work requirements that Republicans have put forward for Medicaid and SNAP are much less likely to encourage work than to kick off eligible recipients through confusion, bureaucratic complexity, or difficulty proving work history.[15]

To listen to conservatives who vilify Social Security Disability Insurance (SSDI), you would think that it is a just-pass-Go handout for those who fake a disability to get a check. Not so.[16] SSDI requires a substantial work history— having worked at least five of the last ten years. The typical recipient has worked for twenty-two years before receiving benefits.[17] Twenty-two years. It also has a stringent application process; more than half of applicants are ultimately denied SSDI benefits, and 10,000 people a year die waiting to get approved for benefits.[18] Research on those who barely lose their appeals seeking SSDI, and therefore do not receive benefits, shows that the vast majority do not then go out and get jobs—undercutting the core premise that but for SSDI, such workers would be economically self-sufficient or at least holding down gainful employment. Even accepting the very worst assumptions, SSDI has been found to account for at most one-fifteenth of the recent decline in male labor force participation for workers ages twenty-five to fifty-four.[19] While conservatives like Rand Paul belittle those who go on SSDI for disabilities such as mental illness or musculoskeletal issues as being "either anxious or their back hurts,"[20] in reality most SSDI recipients are like Jeanetta Smith. Ms. Smith is a fifty-one-year-old SSDI recipient who lives in Robbins, Tennessee, and worked for twenty-five years, first in a textile factory, then after the factory closed down as a certified nursing assistant at a nursing home. As Dylan Matthews writes in *Vox*, the back problems that Ms. Smith developed from lifting and carrying elderly patients every day forced her to leave her job; her doctor says she can't lift anymore or she will become paralyzed, and she also has heart issues and a pacemaker. Ms. Smith wishes she could still work. She says, "I love old people, I'd absolutely love it. If I could stand it with my back, I'd be right back on it."[21]

The data and these examples support an undeniable conclusion: for most, the availability of social insurance and disability programs are lifelines that come amid a lifetime of work to prevent a single setback from leading to a downward cycle of desperation at the expense of basic dignity—not an economic drug that lulls them into dependency. The largest gaps in a compact of contribution are policy failures to provide adequate support when people face a major dislocation, cumulative economic disadvantage, disability, pain and addiction, long-term unemployment, depression, economic disruption, or challenges reentering society after involvement with the criminal justice system. A more active, supportive, and compassionate compact of contribution will be both pro-dignity and pro-growth: it will help more people to work and add value while gaining the dignity that comes with making a difference and finding purpose in one's economic life.

B. MISSING WHERE MORE GOVERNMENT WOULD PROMOTE SELF-SUFFICIENCY

There is, of course, wisdom in the saying "Give a person a fish and you feed them for a day; teach a person to fish and you feed them for a lifetime."

But there's no wisdom in refusing to acknowledge that some people, at different points in their lives and facing various barriers, may need a period of substantial assistance to learn how to fish. If one was really serious about people being able to contribute and carry their part of the load, they would realize there are times that more government support will help them to do so.

Consider the following challenges that can reduce self-sufficiency and self-reliance: (1) lack of employability due to lack of education or experience, a criminal record, or long-term unemployment; (2) a disability that reduces employability or creates a fear of losing health coverage if trying to experiment with work; and (3) addiction or mental illness. In all these cases, a key obstacle to people getting on their feet and being empowered is the need for intense and comprehensive support—even if only for a relatively short period of time. Simply put: if you look at what is truly needed to promote long-term self-sufficiency, the answer is often *more—not less*—government support at critical transitional times in Americans' economic lives. The research shows that intensive skills-building programs with comprehensive support—often called "wraparound" services –promote long-term self-sufficiency. In a comprehensive review, the Georgetown Law Center on Poverty and Inequality analyzed forty years of evidence of subsidized employment programs, including many that targeted hard-to-employ populations, and found that intensive wraparound services, like skill building and counseling, are a critical element of programs with positive long-term effects for disadvantaged groups.[22] Crucially, these supports are generally needed only at key transitional points in someone's life—not as permanent support.

Of course, the private sector can and should do more. Truly tight labor markets that lead to very low unemployment encourage companies to invest more in hard-to-employ workers and provide a stronger incentive to give additional training related to the specific job being filled. But it would be foolish to not recognize there are limits. It is well established in economics literature that companies underinvest in skills enhancements for workers because they have no assurance of receiving the benefits of their investment.[23] And when workers are being let go, companies have no economic incentive to provide counseling or to help them build skills that will be captured by their next employer.

But this does not have to be the case. In Sweden, for example, companies pay to fund job security councils that provide serious transitional skill enhancement, income support, and counseling—as frequently as once a week—as early as possible once layoffs are announced.[24] The support is effective: over 85 percent of Swedish workers who lose their job find a new one within a year, which is the highest rate among advanced economies.[25] Companies provide this support not because economic logic is reversed in Europe, or even out of pure corporate citizenship, but because the policy is imposed on them through labor contracts driven by the strength of Sweden's unions. With less than 10 percent of private sector workers in unions in the United States, government intervention is even more critical to both bolster unions and provide transitional jobs and opportunities to develop skills, as discussed further in later chapters.[26]

A lack of intensive government investment is a primary reason that while more than two-thirds of people with disabilities believe they can work,[27] only about 40 percent are currently in the labor force.[28] Our lack of policies to remove barriers to work for people with disabilities is nothing short of a national disgrace, and prevents many with disabilities from being able to contribute to the best of their abilities and to pursue their purpose. It is through more, not less, government investment that the conservative's stated goal of greater self-reliance and independence can be enhanced for so many of these Americans. The investment in expertise or the medical equipment needed for helping workers with specific intellectual or physical disabilities might be too much for individual employers—especially smaller ones. Government, on the other hand, can more effectively support more people with disabilities, contributing to and enhancing their independence through greater funding of accessible transportation, affordable and accessible housing, equipment necessary for work, and vocational rehabilitation and nonprofits with expertise in onboarding workers with disabilities.[29]

The list goes on. Helping workers overcome opioid addiction, providing intensive assistance for those leaving the criminal justice system, and ensuring that the cost of childcare is not an overwhelming de facto tax on work are all situations in which more intensive government help is essential for increasing self-sufficiency. The United States is an outlier in the OECD for its lack of universal paid leave and uniquely expensive childcare, both of which create barriers to work, as discussed elsewhere in this book. Unfortunately, conservatives miss these potential solutions—and ways to further their stated goal of self-sufficiency—because their market fundamentalism prevents them from even considering policy options that would require some increase in government involvement.

C. MISSING WHERE MORE GOVERNMENT WOULD ENCOURAGE RISK-TAKING AND ENTREPRENEURSHIP

The ideological commitment to less government also prevents conservatives from seeing those situations where more government can mean more risk-taking, more entrepreneurship, and more market innovation. Properly designed, stronger social insurance can inspire—not dull—innovation and entrepreneurial spirit.

At a private American Enterprise Institute conference, I was once put on a panel on the Affordable Care Act (ACA) with five senior Republican members of Congress. As I was outnumbered, I was offered more time and the chance to go last. I responded that I did not need more time but wanted to go first. With apologies to the poet Elizabeth Barrett Browning, I started by saying that as for why those who love entrepreneurship and risk-taking should love the ACA, "let me count the ways." Number one was that pre-ACA, those who had employer-provided health insurance and had a family member with heart disease, a serious disability, or cancer were denied the treasured freedom and liberty to leave their jobs to start their own business. Why? Because for those workers, if they had to get new health insurance once it was clear a family member had a serious preexisting condition, they would have been shut out of health insurance or faced obscenely high prices. This fear of losing health care for those with preexisting conditions is known as entrepreneurship lock. As I have long argued, it is a major barrier to starting new businesses.[30] This is a simple and obvious case of greater government regulation of insurance increasing actual—as opposed to idealized—liberty and freedom. Requiring insurers to cover people with preexisting conditions was estimated to lead to 1.5 million more Americans being self-employed, according to research by the Urban Institute and Georgetown University's Center on Health Insurance Reforms.[31] This reality is almost never recognized by conservative limited government purists, because it defies their frame of more government equaling less self-reliance.

Today, we see the same realities with excessive student debt. The fixed payments many face deter them not only from taking lower-income public service jobs but also from rolling the dice on entrepreneurship and start-ups where steady paychecks are not guaranteed. One economic analysis finds that $10,000 in student loan debt leads to a 7 percent decline in likelihood of starting a business.[32] The authors conclude that "student debt is negatively related to the propensity to start a firm, particularly larger and more successful ventures."[33] Government policies that make college more affordable or ease student debt burdens could therefore be a boon to entrepreneurship.

D. MISSING WHEN MORE GOVERNMENT MEANS MORE INNOVATION

Conservatives presume that higher government spending is the antithesis of innovation. In fact, increased government provisions of economic security reduce burdens on companies so they can focus on innovation and growth, as opposed to managing health and retirement benefits. Does the private sector find it antibusiness that college funding is provided by the government as opposed to the employer community? Of course not. And robust government benefits and protections need not be an obstacle to innovation. As Alana Semuels points out in the *Atlantic*, Sweden has a larger public sector and safety net than the United States, yet has twenty start-ups lasting three years or longer per one thousand employees, as opposed to only five per one thousand in the United States.[34] Despite the large Swedish public sector, Stockholm has the second-highest number of billion-dollar tech companies per capita in the world—second only to Silicon Valley.[35]

Government can also spur innovation directly by funding research and development when the private sector otherwise might not.[36] Government demand for research or goods in areas where the benefits are hard for a single company to capture have been behind some of the greatest American stories in innovation, from computer networking to GPS to vaccines and cancer treatments.[37] As MIT economists Jonathan Gruber and Simon Johnson recognize in their Jump-Starting America project, "Modern private enterprise is most effective when government provides strong underlying support for science and for the commercialization of inventions."[38] They note that "almost every major innovation in [the post–World War II] era relied in an important way on federal government support," yet the government is now "spending at least $250 billion per year *less* than we did during the post-war boom," the result being lower productivity growth and fewer good jobs.[39] A recent study found that starting in the 2010s, almost one-third of all patented U.S. inventions relied on federally funded science.[40]

Similarly, Dani Rodrik and Charles Sabel argue that the U.S. Defense Advanced Research Projects Agency (DARPA) and its offspring, the Advanced Research Projects Agency–Energy (ARPA-E), are "successful examples" of public investment spurring innovation.[41] DARPA and ARPA-E invest in "blue sky" research addressing challenges "at the far frontier of science and technology" where there is "underinvestment, from the standpoint of society as a whole, in research and technology" because "there may well be no solution" and "even when the search is successful it is unlikely that the daring pioneer can appropriate the returns from the discovery."[42] In other words, government is best positioned to lead innovation in these spaces because of the high risks associated with the investments and limited or diffuse profit potential.

Each of these experts sees a bigger government role as not only increasing the likelihood of game-changing breakthroughs but also as a pathway to dramatically increasing high-quality jobs. After all, DARPA-funded research formed the basis for the internet and contributed to the development of the personal computer, speech recognition software, and even Google.[43] Nonetheless, outside some support for the National Institutes of Health, conservatives rarely support such research, and the Trump administration has consistently proposed eliminating ARPA-E altogether.

E. MISSING THE LAWS OF HEALTH-CARE ECONOMICS

There is no debate that reveals the inability of a "less government" dogma to support economic dignity more clearly than health care. There is no shortage of honorable debate on health care, but there is one truth that is not subject to dispute: if your end goal is less and less government, then there is no way to make serious progress on increasing economic dignity through greater health security. The unavoidable reality is that without significant government involvement in terms of mandates, regulations against health discrimination, and subsidies or direct provision of health care, there is no way—*none*—to achieve affordable health care for all and protect people with preexisting conditions. This isn't an ideological contention. It's the reality of health-care economics. In the past, think tanks like Heritage and American Enterprise Institute essentially admitted to this truth by supporting mandates.[44] Mitt Romney even agreed to sign a mandate into law as governor of Massachusetts.[45] Yet today, only privately have I heard conservative colleagues admit this undeniable truth that without some form of greater government involvement, major gains on health coverage and security are not possible. What else can they say? Rejecting these laws of health-market dynamics is as fruitless as denying the laws of thermodynamics.

Consider why. Any health insurance company would be driven out of business if people were allowed to buy insurance—to pay premiums—only when they knew they were ill and needed large health-care expenditures. This is the issue of insurance death spirals. It is 100 percent clear. On the flip side, if insurance companies have no regulations on who they can take and what prices they can charge, they will have a clear profit motive to allow only those who are most likely to be healthy to obtain coverage—so they pay out the least for the premiums they take in—and keep out or charge excessive prices to those who are sick or seem most likely to be. That also is 100 percent clear. There is no possibility—*zero*—that a totally unregulated health system will lead to those who are sick or likely to be sick not being locked out or facing excessive costs. These are the basic and irrefutable laws of health-care economics.

Thus, if you believe in market-oriented health care and want universal coverage, you have no choice but to support what Jonathan Gruber describes as the three-legged stool of (1) "prevent[ing] insurers from denying coverage or raising premiums based on preexisting conditions," (2) "requir[ing] that everyone buy insurance," and (3) providing "subsidies to make that insurance affordable."[46] There is room to modulate between the second and third legs: if, for example, you spent enough money subsidizing health care, you might get everyone to buy insurance by making it so cheap. But you cannot avoid some version of the three-legged government stool.

The other option is to eliminate the market and have the government cover health care through taxing and direct provision. Government can expand the use of taxes to fund government-provided health care, just as we do through general taxes for those who qualify for Medicaid or Medicare Part B and D, and payroll taxes to fund Medicare Part A.

That is it. There is no other way. If you do not support a form of government involvement in health care, you are opposed to affordable universal health care. Period. End of story. The sad truth is that since the fleeting moment in 1993 when Republican senators John Chafee, Dave Durenberger, and John Danforth flirted with an alternative plan to the proposed Clinton Health Security Act, there has not been a serious effort by conservatives to even put forward a national program to deal with the dignity gaps millions of working families deal with due to illness, disability, and lack of affordable health care.

Today, it is not just that progressives support more robust health security coverage plans. Republicans could not even devise or present to the nation a "repeal and replace" plan that effectively maintained the Affordable Care Act's coverage gains and protections for people with preexisting conditions without running counter to their less-government straitjacket when they controlled all three branches of government. And that means that the constant attacks from the right on any government involvement in health care is camouflaging a hard truth: a battle against any serious government involvement in health care is one and the same as an all-out effort to oppose any effort toward the universal health-care security that is essential to economic dignity.

AN ERA OF BIG GOVERNMENT RESPONSIBILITY IS NEEDED—BUT NOT GOVERNMENT ONLY

So what is the right approach to government and economic dignity? It is not, to me, simply to counter a less-government-is-always-better approach with an automatic preference for government-only approaches. That, too, would put the means of policy first as opposed to keeping our focus on economic dignity as our end goal. Our focus should, instead, exhibit an openness to reflection and analysis of any combination of government and markets that best serves our goal for economic dignity.

This perspective does not, to be clear, reflect a neutrality about the role of government. Far from it. An end goal of economic dignity indeed compels an era of bigger government responsibility. Yet government *responsibility* is different from an insistence on government-*only* delivery of services or goods. The era of bigger government responsibility is the obligation to ensure that an economic dignity compact is real in the lives of ordinary Americans. If our policy—or lack of policy—has led to or allowed gaping economic dignity gaps, then there is a responsibility to fix them, to make things work. It is an invitation to be open to more expansive government policies—to not be constrained by worship of market fundamentalism and small-government libertarianism, especially when they have come up short—but it is still a perspective that keeps our eyes on the end goal, on what works. It is consistent with FDR's famous exhortation to policymakers, from a 1932 commencement speech, to focus with force on the end economic goal and to engage in continuous "bold, persistent experimentation" to achieve that end without limiting the range of measures for potential experimentation and ultimate success.[47]

A. HEALTH CARE TAKE TWO

Consider health care again. In the debate over Medicare for All, Howard Schultz calls a single-payer plan that covers all people not just suboptimal from his perspective but "not American."[48] On the other side, some single-payer supporters make statements like "nothing less will do."[49] To be clear, the issue here is not the vigor with which different sides press that their solution is the best answer to our health-care needs. The issue is when the debate starts to turn to the means as the end goal in and of itself. The end goal from an economic dignity perspective must be affordable health care as a right for all. If that is our end goal, we should neither disparage a government solution that achieves this as "not American" nor close our minds to other means to achieve this aspiration because they combine a robust public option with some choice for employer-provided coverage.

An economic dignity test separates our end goal—universal health security as a right—from the analytical question of what is the best or most realistic way to meet it. Those whose orientation is toward market solutions should not take off the table the respectable arguments that a single-payer plan can substantially reduce administrative and marketing costs and reduce the burden on private sector companies in hiring as well as coordinating employee health benefits. Likewise, while advocates for single payer may have a deep conviction that their solution will be the most effective, that conviction should not shut down consideration of whether a major public option could be as effective or a more politically viable means to the same end goal.

In short, a true economic dignity compact requires both a stronger government guarantee and an openness to honorable debate about what the best combination of market and government-based solutions is to get there. An economic dignity compact means *government bears the ultimate responsibility* to ensure that those who do their part are not denied economic dignity by accidents of birth, accidents of the economy, or bad luck. A government responsibility requirement is a put-up-or-shut-up test. It maintains openness to evaluating different mixes of market and government policy options, but not to accepting failure. A failure of a more market-based approach is not a per se rationale for moving to a government-only option, but it creates an imperative to provide some fix or, in FDR's words, to "try something."[50]

While I do not pretend to have magical solutions to heal the breach in our divided nation, an agreement on end goals, and then a willingness to consider different vehicles to reach them—with an insistence on results—would be a move in the right direction. When more conservatives focused on the human question of whether someone with a child who had a preexisting condition should be able to be denied health coverage or face spikes in costs— as opposed to just hearing it described by Fox News as part of an Obama, socialist agenda—progressives and conservatives alike started to tell pollsters they were overwhelmingly for it. When some democratic socialists call only for the means of large government programs, there is division even among progressives. But the definition of democratic socialism given by Alexandria Ocasio-Cortez—that it means ensuring "basic levels of dignity so that no person in America is too poor to live"[51]—is the type of focus on a desired end goal for lifting human well-being that can help people unify around shared aspirations, and certainly is consistent with this book's call for an economic dignity compact.

B. PUBLIC OPTIONS AND GOVERNMENT
GUARANTEE OF ECONOMIC DIGNITY

A promising framework that will often meet the test of ensuring a government guarantee of economic dignity without dictating only government-delivered solutions is the public option. A public option is one way in which policymakers both allow competition and bold experimentation and ensure that people will not fall through the cracks of market-based policies. The government option ensures universal, affordable access, but it does not automatically eliminate the private sector role; that would occur only if the experience led consumers to overwhelmingly favor the government option when both were available.

Although the public option concept is most commonly associated with health care, where progressives have long pushed for a universally available public health insurance plan, public options are gaining renewed and well-deserved attention across policy areas. The Roosevelt Institute has been a leading think tank promoting public options. In a major report by William Darity Jr., Darrick Hamilton, and Rakeen Mabud, the Roosevelt Institute embraced public options as a means to ensure "the provision of these goods and services" that are necessary "for achieving a baseline level of human dignity."[52] Although public options increase government's responsibility and role, the authors are careful to distinguish between a public option and a public takeover: "To be clear, we are not calling for a comprehensive public takeover of all productive activities in the United States. We are, however, calling for the public sector to competitively provide goods, services, and economic opportunities in sectors that are indispensable to the pursuit and attainment of human decency with healthy and fulfilling lives."[53] They note that market forces can be very effective in innovation and provision of goods and services, but "private firms alone have never delivered goods in the necessary quantity, quality, or access to achieve . . . fundamental economic rights."[54] Roosevelt Institute chief economist Joseph Stiglitz has promoted public options as "hallmarks of progressive capitalism."[55]

In their recent book *The Public Option: How to Expand Freedom, Increase Opportunity, and Promote Equality*, law professors Ganesh Sitaraman and Anne Alstott call for a dramatically expanded role for public options that guarantees access to important services and coexists—or could coexist—with private provision of the same service.[56] In addition to health care, Sitaraman and Alstott suggest that public options could help in a wide variety of sectors, including retirement, childcare, higher education, and banking. They note that "public options are evidence of our common civic faith; restoring our confidence in them, and expanding their reach, will ensure that the twenty-first century is a time of security and prosperity for all."[57] Like the Roosevelt Institute authors, Sitaraman and Alstott are careful to avoid "black-and-white assumptions about either government or the private sector." They argue against "assum[ing] that government always works well, or that government should muscle out private provision," but see a government option as critical to those areas where there is a need to "guarantee universal access to the basics of modern life."[58] Their vision is that "citizens can rely on the public option but also can turn to the marketplace for additional choices, combining public and private options in ways that work best for them."[59]

If we care deeply about the end goal of ensuring economic dignity, this larger approach of not allowing fixed views on government or markets to limit the tools at our disposal is both practical and most humane.

CHAPTER SEVEN

MARKETS OF THE PEOPLE, BY THE PEOPLE, FOR THE PEOPLE

Every presidential election brings charges that a Democratic president will usher in socialism. Still, even with the call for a government single payer on health care by some leading Democratic candidates, no one is seriously suggesting that our economy as a whole ban market competition, stop allowing prices of goods and services to be controlled by supply and demand, or prohibit start-ups, the stock market, or profit.

Market competition is here to stay in the United States. What we should be asking ourselves is whether such market competition is structured to raise the well-being of the many or of the few? Are our markets structured to provide financial rewards for those who compete in ways that promote or denigrate economic dignity?

In our current political dialogue, free-market proponents often approach any discussion of structuring or regulating markets as if it would constitute interference and disruption of markets that somehow originate in the state of nature. A call for a new regulation is often portrayed politically as akin to a child throwing a rock into a completely calm pond, creating ripples in an otherwise pure free market. Laws that seek to structure or regulate markets are often presumptively assumed to represent anti-market interference. Those advocating such policies are often asked to prove why the law or regulation in question is solving enough of "a market failure" to justify its acceptance. Republican presidential candidates often rail on Democratic predecessors for the pure number of regulations—as if the purpose, impact, and benefits are irrelevant. This can be seen in the Trump administration's simplistic notion that any new regulation—no matter what its virtue—can be justified only if it is paired with the repeal of two others.

This is not to say that some regulations are not oppressive, poorly constructed, out of date, and worthy of review or repeal. But that review should not start from the presumption that any new rule on market structure interferes with pure markets. Indeed, even Adam Smith, the father of market competition, based his famous argument—that the "invisible hand" of individual pursuit of self-interest in free competitive markets will benefit the common good—on the idea that competition would be structured by government policymakers to prevent government or private sector monopoly power.

Three guideposts should instruct our analysis of market structure and economic dignity.

1. **Market Structure Is Always Impacted by Government Policy:** As Robert Reich has written so persuasively for many years, every existing market is already deeply impacted by government policy, from laws that allow corporations to have limited liability to the structure of intellectual property law to the subsidies and public investments paid for with public revenues for everything from skills to infrastructure to basic science. That reality is made stark in the discussion below on for-profit higher education. It is inescapable that, one way or another, government policy already shapes markets. The real question we must ask is whether such policies incentivize market competition that promotes or that denigrates economic dignity.

2. **The Goal Is Better, High-Road Competition—Not Less Competition:** Nearly every critique of a regulation or government action—even on issues like for-profit higher education, payday lending, or predatory mortgages—is that it is an unwarranted restraint on market competition. But these critiques miss that, done right, consumer standards can

promote better, not less, competition. Structuring markets to reward competition principally on quality, price, and performance, and not race-to-the-bottom behavior, can lead competitive actors to focus on the elements that deliver better products and services to consumers and other stakeholders, without the concern that treating workers, consumers, and the environment with a level of basic decency might jeopardize their competitive advantage. Of course, rules that encourage high-road competition might impede profit margins compared to existing practices, where there is an open lane toward race-to-the-bottom competition. To the extent a textile manufacturer's profit margins require forcing workers to labor in extremely dangerous factories or rely on suppliers using ten-year-olds in Vietnam, regulations that limit these practices will reduce the company's profit margins. But that should be seen as a failure of past regulation and market structure to ensure competition was not structured to reward inexcusable exploitation—not as a disruptive, anti-market measure. In a democracy, markets should be structured by the people, for the people. If a given product's viability is based *only* on lower costs due to exploitation and predatory behavior, then it shouldn't be a viable market product or service. When everyone has to play by high-road rules, competition will not die but will shift, and those who excel at providing needed goods and services without resorting to the low road will emerge, profit, and thrive in a fundamentally better and robust competitive market.

3. **Never Structure Markets to Mean No Good Deed Going Unpunished:** Anyone—progressive or conservative—who promotes the values of dignity and ethical behavior toward their fellow Americans should be deeply troubled if market competition consistently punishes those who behave virtuously. It is important to realize that when we structure markets to allow companies to win through exploitation and predatory behavior, we can also create obstacles to individual companies and individual workers who want to take a higher road—who want to dissent on predatory practices and align their work with the values of

economic dignity. Some market purists who object to such consumer standards to limit race-to-the-bottom competition like to argue that it is unnecessary: the market will self-correct, with new entrants pushing out the unscrupulous. Yet that theory fails in reality, both for new entrants and individual employees. If competitors have the capacity to show dramatic profit margins or lower prices through exploitation, that can block the economic viability of entrants or existing companies seeking to compete on a high road. It can also make virtuous dissent by individual workers near impossible. When our nation had its breakdown of all common sense on housing finance, there was likely little room for a virtuous midlevel employee in 2006 to refuse to engage in such reckless subprime lending, because the market was structured to reward his competitors and peers at his own company for race-to-the-bottom competition. Virtuous employees may have indeed lost promotions, bonuses, and even their jobs. Structuring markets to prevent race-to-the-bottom competition ensures that we do not create business environments where no good deed and virtue go unpunished.

PUNCHING STEPHEN CURRY

As a thought experiment, imagine a slightly altered set of rules and regulations for the National Basketball Association (NBA). Consider for a second if the NBA *had always allowed* each team to throw a limited number of punches per game at the opposing team. If this punching rule existed, finding ways to most effectively punch out or protect opposing superstars like Stephen Curry or LeBron James would be a major feature of robust competition—and would help structure everyone's incentives. Innovative efforts might include bringing on "designated punchers." Books might be written on coaching strategies for whether you seek to use your punches early or late based on estimates of how quickly punched players could recover and whether you seek to deck James three times or use one of your punches on his supporting cast. Taunting players to waste one of the permitted punches would be refined to an art form. While perhaps this rule would have brought more Ultimate Fighting Championship (UFC) fans to basketball, most true basketball lovers would consider this a vicious race to the bottom. Those most effective in knocking out Curry or James—those who raced to the bottom—would have a serious leg up in pursuit of NBA championships.

In this scenario, there would be little room for virtue going unpunished. Members of any given NBA team might find this barbaric and prefer to refrain. Yet such Gandhi-like responses to the punching rule would likely not be well received. With the rules of competition structured to allow such violence, fans and owners would consider this unilateral disarmament. Coaches would pull aside conscientious objector players and tell them that they admire their values, but also that as long as other teams were doing it, they had no choice. Either punch or be let go.

Simply put, this rule would structure competition so that teams had little choice but to race to the bottom in terms of viciously punching opponents. Simultaneously, the rule would leave no room for individual players or teams to exhibit higher virtue and go unpunished.

A new, stricter regulation outlawing punching with a staggered set of penalties might be seen by market purists as a restrictive regulation that would limit freedom and competition. A no-punching rule might have been hotly contested by an NBA cost-benefit process. Yet we know that if rules in this hypothetical NBA were added that apply in the real NBA now—where flagrant fouls, technical fouls, and ejections for uncalled-for or extreme violence exist—no fan today would think competition had been reduced. We could see that the NBA had simply structured intense competition based on three-point shooting, rebounding, defense, and passing—as opposed to structuring competition on who can best deck Steph Curry.

We can see parallels in market after market. Where lower costs and higher market share can be achieved through predatory or abusive behavior that reduces social well-being and economic dignity, companies that race fastest and furthest to the bottom can win—and those who might wish to have competed on a higher ground are undercut and risk having any basic virtue punished in the market.

Consider a few real-life market examples that do not involve sports metaphors:

STRUCTURING COMPETITION FOR HIGH-QUALITY EDUCATION OR LOW-ROAD EXPLOITATION?

Few markets have been so dependent on and intertwined with government as the for-profit higher education market. This is indeed a textbook case of the rule that the structure of all markets is shaped substantially by government policy. Half of all for-profit colleges derive more than 70 percent of their revenues from Pell Grants or government-backed loans.[1] Without reliance on taxpayer dollars, there would likely not be a real for-profit education industry.

The only logical rationale for a for-profit higher education industry supported in any way by taxpayers is that it promotes competition tightly tied to clear, positive educational results that increase purpose and potential in people's lives. Yet nothing could be further from describing how the market rewards success in for-profit higher education. Simply put, this market has been structured to reward not educational results but enrollment, regardless of results or performance. Entities are usually guaranteed payment from the federal government upon a student's enrollment regardless of any issues of quality or even competence or value. The average student pays $14,600 per year at a for-profit college—much more than the cost of in-state public colleges.[2] If students qualify for Pell Grants, they will receive on average $4,000 each year in grant money.[3] Ninety-four percent of students at for-profit colleges take out federal loans,[4] and some also take out private student loans.

So when a student is lured into enrolling in a for-profit program, the school gets paid. It wins. If the for-profit fails to deliver any education of value, the loss is borne only by the student and us, the taxpayers. For example, if a two-year certificate is of poor quality, is not recognized by employers, or does not meet the standards necessary for the professional license promised, who loses out? The government loses $8,000—and more if loans are not repaid. The student is thousands of dollars in debt—on average $14,000—with higher forgone opportunity costs.[5] But once the for-profit college gets an enrollment, it receives its $14,000 a year—no risk, no skin in the game. Enrollment equals payment and profit, usually paid for with your taxpayer dollars.

Sound familiar? It should. It is precisely the formula that contributed to the subprime housing crisis. Once the secondary markets were willing to buy even the shadiest of mortgages and stamp them with AAA ratings, those actors who originated mortgages were going to get fully paid even if these mortgages were reckless or illegitimate. The government might lose because it was guaranteeing investors; the borrower might have massive debt and could even lose their home, down payment, and credit. But once the loan was originated, the bank got paid—no risk, no skin in the game. Origination equaled payment and profit.

We know the story in the housing market. Once market competition was structured to reward profits and payments to anyone who could originate a mortgage—regardless of quality or the odds of being paid back—the race to the bottom became fierce. Those who sought more responsible lending might look heroic in retrospect, but in the moment they were effectively punished for not more aggressively pursuing profits.

The for-profit higher education industry was no different. Yes, there are many products and services we buy where the business or even educational institutions get paid first—regardless of quality. Yet in cases like for-profit higher education, financial incentives lead companies to use marketing and pressure sales tactics that can easily swamp any clear consumer information on quality and risks. And the outcomes are particularly harmful because the institutions often target more vulnerable, less informed students. With enrollments—not educational quality or gainful employment of graduates—as the chief driver of revenue and profits, the ferocity of the race to the bottom can get especially intense.

At the height of the for-profit boom, spending on marketing and tactics to raise enrollment dwarfed investment in quality of the education for-profits provided. In 2009, for example, for-profit colleges spent $4.2 billion, or nearly 25 percent of all revenue, on marketing, advertising, recruiting, and admissions staffing. For comparison, nonprofit colleges spent less than 1 percent of revenue on marketing.[6] A Senate report found that for-profit colleges engaged in unscrupulous tactics to keep enrollments growing, such as creating a false sense of urgency in potential students to enroll, misleading potential students about the costs of the program, and giving out deceptive information about the reputation or accreditation of the school.[7] And the results? Only 20 percent of college students at four-year for-profits graduated from the institution they started at within six years, compared with 60 percent of those who attended nonprofit colleges and universities.[8] A Senate study of sixteen for-profit colleges and universities in 2008 to 2009 found that 57 percent of students withdrew in the first year of the program.[9] For-profit college students default on their student loans at nearly four times the rate of those who attend public programs.[10] The combination of lost years and crushing debt from fraudulent education can be deeply life altering. Yes, some students have benefited, and some for-profits care more about delivering for their students. But rather than being a good orchard with a few bad apples, the for-profit sector is more like a rotten orchard with a few good apples.

As usual, when the government sought to regulate for-profit colleges—through gainful employment regulations under the Obama administration—the reaction was an outpouring of lobbying dollars and outrage by the industry and its conservative congressional supporters. The notion that this is a case of Big Government contaminating a pure private market and squashing healthy competition is particularly ludicrous in the for-profit higher education sphere, where its very existence is due to taxpayer dollars. Such regulations were hardly a case of government interference versus no government interference. They were about trying to restructure market competition that involved government payments so those who triumphed did so based on the strength of educational and job results as opposed to how well they raced to the bottom with predatory, misleading tactics and poor—and in some cases even fraudulent—services.

Despite the for-profit industry fighting tooth and nail in the courts and the regulatory process, the Obama administration eventually finalized gainful employment regulations that required for-profit colleges to show that the typical student's loan payments did not exceed a certain level of earnings to avoid federal scrutiny or loss of federal funds.[11] These regulations were an important first step, though they never went nearly as far as needed. As evidence of how much the profit margins in the higher education industry were based on pure enrollment and predatory practices, even the announcement of the first modest regulations decimated market values. Between 2010 and 2016, for-profit college stocks sank up to 80 percent, which the *Wall Street Journal* attributed to increased federal and state government scrutiny as well as the strengthening labor market.[12] Several major for-profits went bankrupt, including ITT Technical Institute and Corinthian Colleges.

The election of Donald Trump raised the for-profit colleges' hopes that less scrutiny was on the horizon, and their stocks rose in response.[13] Betsy DeVos, President Trump's secretary of education, did not disappoint. Initially, Secretary DeVos delayed implementation of the gainful employment regulations. In 2019, DeVos successfully repealed them altogether.[14]

This is inexcusable. The condition for allowing government support for those attending such for-profits must be a market that rewards competitors solely on how effectively such institutions help educate Americans. At a minimum, that has to mean zero tolerance for predatory practices, and strong quality standards and protections related to student debt. Government must ensure such high-road competition in for-profit higher education or get out of subsidizing it altogether.

STRUCTURING ANTITRUST TO PROMOTE ECONOMIC DIGNITY

Antitrust is one area where it is no secret that government plays a critical role in structuring market competition. Yet for decades, there has been too little openness to considering whether antitrust law and competition policy should also incorporate values of economic dignity. The Chicago School revolutionized antitrust by establishing the premise that antitrust should be solely focused on judging whether economic concentration will lead to higher consumer prices. Since adherents held an idealized assumption that the threat of new entrants would hold down prices, only in the rarest cases—like cartels—did the Chicago School believe even massive economic concentration and monopolies would fail this test of higher consumer prices. This perspective became conventional wisdom and has dominated the courts for decades.

Even under a more price-based focus, antitrust economists like Fiona

Scott Morton and Carl Shapiro have called for more aggressive enforcement based on analyses of the many ways in which mergers and corporate behavior can result in higher prices, lower quality, reduced variety, and stunted innovation. The Obama Council of Economic Advisers, while led by Jason Furman as well as other economists like Thomas Philippon, documented how increased monopolization in everything from beer to airlines has raised prices for consumers, reduced economic growth, and increased inequality.

A new set of advocates and experts, from Barry Lynn to Lina Khan to Tim Wu, have advanced an even more fundamental critique that takes on the consumer welfare premise itself. They have argued that our antitrust laws were also supposed to serve other values—which they label "neo-Brandeisian," after the views of progressive advocate and former Supreme Court justice Louis Brandeis—such as limiting the broader abuses that excessive economic concentration can lead to in our economy and politics.[15] This rethink should draw our attention to a more focused type of abuse that should also be central to antitrust policy: those situations where concentration allows monopolists to wield the arbitrary use of brute market power to dominate and humiliate smaller competitors in ways that defy our values of economic dignity.

To be clear, there is nothing wrong with a company or entrepreneurs feeling dominated by a competitor through fair competition. If you get driven out of business by a competitor making a better hamburger or providing better food service, in terms of quality, lower costs to consumers, or better marketing, then that is no different than a baseball team being humiliated due to better pitching, fielding, and hitting. It's part of the game. Many Americans have seen real and substantial price and convenience gains from the rise of certain large operations like retail companies—particularly in rural areas where buying goods has long been difficult and costly. Fear from competition is part of what drives markets and innovation. But as Open Market Institute founder Barry Lynn has written, that should not apply to a different type of fear: "a fear of . . . the arbitrary edict, of the brute exercise of power."[16] This fear flies in the face of how FDR described the economic rights of the entrepreneur in the Second Bill of Rights: "the right of every businessman, large and small, to trade in an atmosphere of freedom from unfair competition and *domination* by monopolies at home or abroad"[17] (emphasis added).

BRIDGE, RAILROAD, AND TECH PLATFORMS

The harm from monopoly power that I highlighted in my discussion about the humiliation and devastation inflicted by Rockefeller on Ida Tarbell's father and his friends was precisely the type of brute force bordering on violence at odds with FDR's vision of "freedom from unfair competition and domination by monopolies."

Rockefeller's tactics resembled more the tactics of war than of fierce market competition. In war there is often a single bridge or single road, control of which ensures that one side can crush their enemy. That makes sense in war, which is fundamentally about domination and brute force.

What the Rockefellers and the Vanderbilts figured out in the late nineteenth century was that the creation of the railroad could be the economic equivalent of the essential bridge or supply road in war. Someone who controlled it could dominate or humiliate any competitor based on brute force—not on quality or price competition. According to Tim Wu, "Rockefeller liked to offer his smaller rivals the choice first popularized by Genghis Khan: Join the Empire or face complete destruction."[18] Whether attributed to Genghis Khan or Pablo Escobar, this type of "silver or lead" domination is what forced the smaller oil refiners in the Cleveland area (including Pennsylvania) to sell Rockefeller their operations at cut rates, and led to Tarbell's father's economic demise and his best friend's suicide. This episode is still referred to as the "Cleveland Massacre."[19]

While the Interstate Commerce Act of 1887 and antitrust lawsuits against railroads—beginning with Teddy Roosevelt's breakup of the Northern Securities Company in 1904—eventually put constraints on the type of railroad abuse that Rockefeller deployed in the Cleveland Massacre, the example remains relevant to the types of market structures we should avoid today to prevent new forms of such brute domination.

Once a platform—whether transportation, digital, or otherwise—becomes so dominant that anyone selling products and services must use that platform for economic survival, it can become the equivalent of controlling the essential bridge or railroad. While in Rockefeller's case it was telling small producers, "Face sky-high, discriminatory transportation costs or sell out," it would have been no better had he said, "Give me access to all of your data or intellectual property or I will deliver everything so late and damage your market share."

Today, we see the threat in the dominance of Amazon, Facebook, Google Play, and the Apple App Store, as well as in the battle over net neutrality. All of these can be seen as modern-day railroads—essential platforms, or to use Wu's term, the "key economic network of [its] time"—that can allow such giants to make "silver or lead" offers for economic survival.[20] For example, we see this brute economic force, similar to controlling the bridge or railroad, when Amazon forces retailers on its marketplace to pay for its costly warehousing and shipping service or else see their products buried in search results.[21] We see it when Google forces competing shopping comparison services to bid against one another for advertising slots in its dominant Google search results, giving spots to whoever will pay the most, regardless of how good the service is.[22] We see it when Facebook secretly spies on rival social media start-ups and tells the most promising ones either to sell out or face having their product copied.[23] And we see it when Apple forces app developers to pay a 30 percent commission for sales on its App Store and still demotes competing apps to ensure that its own products always appear first.[24] None of these examples represent the fear of fierce competition based on who designs better products. Instead, they are about the power to force concessions due to the brute force that comes from control over a modern-day "key economic network" of our time.

Solutions to this abuse could range from breaking up such companies to requiring those that have major platforms to not also be buyers and sellers to ensuring interoperability to regulations that forbid discriminatory treatment or information gathering of competing products on a platform—or some combination of those ideas. What is clear is that a modern-day antitrust law enforcement that promotes economic dignity should be structured at each turn to see where the modern essential bridges and railroads are being created, and to ensure market structures do not tolerate economic domination based on who controls the bridge or railroad, as opposed to who has the better product or service.

I will briefly note that this risk of economic concentration facilitating brute force is not just a problem with Big Tech. We see this kind of domination in the exploitation of the small farmers and ranchers in the agricultural sector who supply everything from the beans that go into canned goods to hogs sold to massive processing firms. Predictably, as industry concentration has increased, big companies have increasingly exploited their market power to dominate suppliers and squeeze their margins. For instance, in the chicken industry, farmer pay rose only 2.5 cents per pound from 1988 to 2016, while the wholesale price of chicken rose 17.4 cents in the same period.[25] ProPublica describes how, at a Department of Justice antitrust hearing in Alabama, many black farmers "detailed how chicken companies dictated contract terms and how they were powerless to resist, even if the terms were financially ruinous."[26] A farmer named John Ingrum, who later went out of business, noted that under his contract, he would be paid less if the chickens were "sick or underfed," even though the buyer—Koch Foods— actually supplied both the chicks and the feed he had to use.[27] As another farmer said of the contract he was presented with, "Either I sign it or I ain't got no chickens." Predictably, the Trump administration has reversed an Obama administration rule that would have given farmers access to legal remedies for such unfair practices.

STRUCTURING CORPORATE PURPOSE FOR SHAREHOLDER MAXIMIZATION OR OVERALL ECONOMIC WELL-BEING?

The question of whether the ultimate end goal of corporations should be the maximization of shareholder value is another textbook example of the rule that all market structure is shaped by government policy.

The idea that corporations must ultimately serve only the interests of shareholders has often been taught and presented as if it arises out of an intrinsic and long-standing market logic. The call for a broader corporate purpose is often seen as disruptive meddling with a long-standing market understanding and status quo. Yet the very capacity to organize as a corporation—with the special legal benefit of being able to raise funds without any investor liability—is an explicit privilege that exists solely due to laws passed by democratic legislatures. It is not even a principle that is deeply rooted in our history or even legal traditions. As scholars like Lenore Palladino and the late Lynn Stout, journalist Binyamin Appelbaum, and others have written, the idea of shareholder primacy became dominant only during the 1970s, as part of the rise of free-market economic ideologies pushed by economist Milton Friedman and others in the Chicago School.[28]

Today, there is a renewed willingness to ask, if corporations are creations of laws made by the people, should their end goal be something larger than shareholder maximization? There is increasingly a movement to go beyond shareholder primacy to a "stakeholder test"—one that allows corporations to consider the interests of employees, communities, suppliers, customers, and the environment on equal footing with shareholders. Recently, in 2019, even the high priests of the corporate community at the Business Roundtable endorsed the stakeholder view. The Roundtable explicitly stated that they were moving away from their previous statements going back to 1997, including the idea "that corporations exist principally to serve shareholders." In contrast, they defined "a more modern standard for corporate responsibility" that reflected "a fundamental commitment to all of our stakeholders."[29]

The endorsement of this stakeholder view by the Business Roundtable should not be dismissed as having no significance. Corporate culture can matter. Rich Wartzman writes in his book *The End of Loyalty* that when it comes to the deterioration of "good jobs," the "single" factor he saw in the history of General Electric, General Motors, Kodak, and Coca-Cola was "a reconstituting of corporate culture that has explicitly elevated shareholders above employees." He continues, "American workers won't be able to overcome these other challenges unless this perversion ceases."[30]

That said, there is also reason to question how impactful such a simple policy statement will be without more tangible legal changes. Leo Strine is the former chief justice of the Delaware Supreme Court, the state where most major corporations register and where considerable stockholder litigation takes place. He has written that despite the wide discretion courts provide corporate managers through the "business judgment rule," under

Delaware law, if a corporate executive or board "is treating an interest other than stockholder wealth as an end in itself, rather than an instrument to stockholder wealth, he is committing a breach of fiduciary duty."[31]

For example, when Craigslist founder Craig Newmark explicitly admitted that his main concern was for the services provided to the consumer, rather than monetizing the website, he was successfully sued for not being solely focused on shareholder wealth.[32] Think about how out of touch that is with widespread values. If a CEO made the candid admission in the middle of a recession that she was going to keep all her workers employed *solely because she was putting her workers first regardless of shareholder value*, she would be a folk hero, perhaps the subject of a Netflix movie. Yet the precise reason for such adoration—that she explicitly did it for the welfare of the workers and surrounding community alone—would be damning evidence in a lawsuit. This is a classic case of markets being structured in a way that virtue will not go unpunished.

If members of the Business Roundtable want to show their seriousness about a stakeholder value standard, they should start by pushing for legislative changes to ensure those who seek to promote the economic dignity of their employees will not risk legal action for a failure to fulfill their fiduciary duty. They could also change their corporate structures to become "benefit corporations." At least thirty-two states and Washington, DC, have created the "benefit" or "B Corporation" category, which gives corporate directors the leeway to legally declare their purposes as being beyond the sole aim of enriching stockholders as advocated for by groups like B Lab.[33] Benefit corporation legislation is the kind of government structuring of markets that adheres to the rule of not punishing corporate actors that are driven to put economic dignity at the pinnacle of their corporate aspirations.

The case for expanding corporate purpose to focus on a broader set of stakeholders like workers is often disparaged through unconvincing "slippery slope" arguments. Advocates for shareholder maximization remind us that the idea was meant to fix a conflict of interest called the "agency problem"—corporate managers choosing to pursue their own perks, preferences, power, and glory instead of being agents of shareholders. Some suggest that any movement away from a shareholder maximization goal will lead to a Wild West of corporate directors freed to pursue any personal pet cause or extravagant glorification without restraint. Really? With executive and board compensation still heavily stock-based, and given the needs for future financing and the threat of disinvestment, is there any serious basis for concern that if we moved to a stakeholder test, CEO after CEO would go hog wild in promoting workers and local communities at the expense of shareholder value?[34] Or that courts could not develop case law that distinguishes an effort to be a good employer from a reckless transaction that makes zero business sense?

Indeed, the entire notion that shareholders should be seen as the "owner" of the firm—the stakeholder who is the largest risk-taker in corporations—defies real-world experience. While shareholders may have their stock value at risk, most shareholders are passive and diversified precisely so that they have little risk in the success of any individual company in their portfolio. Workers, on the other hand, invest both their acquired skill set and their stake in the labor market, and usually rely on their paycheck as their biggest source of income. The paycheck may be a fixed payment, but workers' stake in the firm's success not only far exceeds the risk taken on by almost all shareholders, but is also their sole means of caring for family financially and usually a major reason for their family living in a particular location.[35] The workers' stake in the firm's success is thus critical to their economic dignity. The fact that some investors do take a more active interest in oversight does not mean that they should be the only class of stakeholders whose interests should be served by corporations.

The same arguments as to the high stake of workers in the future of a company also speak to the imperative that worker representation be required on corporate boards. While there are many design issues to be worked out about how such a requirement should be imposed in the United States, as Lenore Palladino discusses, such issues are manageable.[36] Furthermore, studies have shown that countries with greater use of such "codetermination" models in the European Union and OECD have less pay inequality,[37] and that such policies are associated with positive or neutral effects on productivity and innovation.[38] These results are not surprising: codetermination is a recipe against short-termism, with firms that have worker representation on boards more likely to focus on long-term investments—the types of investments that, while perhaps good for long-term shareholder value, might also be best for the end goal of serving larger societal interests.

All of us should be clear-eyed, however, about the limits of relying only on broadening the permissible goals for corporate purpose. Without actual laws requiring, or at least promoting, broader economic and environmental goals, corporate concern for stakeholders will be uneven and subject to the excuse that good corporate behavior will be punished because their competitors can still take a lower road. Yes, there is the occasional company like Costco that, out of some combination of corporate culture and a sense of how worker loyalty contributes to long-term market value, paid higher wages and benefits than its main competitor, Walmart. Nonetheless, only a significant increase in the minimum wage will help the workers in the much bigger pool of companies who would otherwise claim that an individual company alone raising its minimum wage would lead to competitive disadvantage. In addition, with the combination of short-termism and the advantageous tax treatment for stock buybacks, a company that chose long-term investment over joining the recent record-setting splurge of stock buybacks can end up being punished by short-term-focused investors. Again, to change the market rules related to corporate purpose and corporate behavior is not unprecedented government interference in markets; it is purely about how we the people want to structure our creation, the corporate entity, to better serve the economic dignity of the American people.

PREVENTING THE RACE TO THE BOTTOM IN TRADE AND TAX POLICY

When we think of how we structure competition for high roads or races to the bottom, tax and trade policies must also be prominent.

I was first involved with the fight to ensure environmental standards and International Labour Organization core labor standards in trade agreements in the 1990s. Although these efforts were often met with resistance from more conservative market purists, they presented a classic case not of limiting competition but of structuring competition to promote economic dignity, rather than denigrating it through race-to-the-bottom tactics. Without such standards and enforcement, trading partners could easily choose to increase their competitive edge and grab new markets by actually worsening already weak workers' rights and environmental standards. This was a point often and rightly made by labor advocates like the AFL-CIO's Thea Lee and Congressman Dick Gephardt's general counsel, Michael Wessell. In other words, without affirmative labor and environmental standards with strong enforcement, a simple agreement could not only fail to lift up workers, it could facilitate a race to the bottom where trading partners race for lower costs at the expense of economic dignity. While there are major trade and globalization issues at stake even when trading partners uphold fair standards, progressive lawmakers for some time have united to insist on core labor standards to prevent the use of exploitation and labor abuse as a source of competitive price advantage. Indeed, even in the 1990s, the AFL-CIO and progressive congressmen like Sander Levin found consensus with the Clinton administration on the free-trade agreements with Jordan and Oman, which imposed such labor conditions. The hard lessons have been on enforcement. With too many cases of nations not keeping their promises to enforce standards in trade agreements and laws on their books, progressive trade experts and lawmakers have rightly made vigilance through robust enforcement a make-or-break issue for any trade agreement.

As Emmanuel Saez and Gabriel Zucman write in their book, *The Triumph of Injustice: How the Rich Dodge Taxes and How to Make Them Pay*, there is no market structured more to be a race to the bottom than current global tax competition. Throughout the developed world, nation after nation is facing the challenges of a shrinking middle class and needed revenues and more progressive taxation to put the brakes on escalating inequality. Yet countries like Ireland, the Netherlands, Bermuda, the Cayman Islands, and numerous others participate in the world's greatest race-to-the-bottom competition with extremely low or nonexistent corporate taxation to attract corporate profits. These tax havens effectively put intense pressure on every other nation to cycle down their corporate tax rates or risk firms artificially shifting their profits to avoid paying taxes by using convoluted techniques with names like the "Double Irish with a Dutch Sandwich." In 2015, 45 percent of the profits of multinational corporations based in the United States and other advanced economies were put on the books in tax havens. To be clear, the underlying economic activity generating those profits did not take place in the tax havens—it took place in the United States and other countries, using those countries' advanced infrastructure, educated workforces, and legal systems that were paid for by those domestic taxpayers. Much of it is high-value intellectual property, like patents, that was developed in the United States but "located" overseas for tax purposes. This shifts the profits out of the country to tax havens to avoid contributing taxes that could be reinvested in future public investment. The United States loses tens of billions of dollars annually in corporate revenue due to the artificial shifting of profits to tax havens.[39]

Global corporate taxation is a true prisoner's dilemma. Every nation would be better off if no nation was able to compete principally by being a tax haven, but once some nations do, others are forced to race down. Their tax revenues shrink, either because of the reduced tax rates or their tax base leaving the country. And multinational companies will each claim that once their competitors engage in such tax games, not doing so would put them at a competitive disadvantage.

We should never downplay the prominent role American policy and U.S.-based corporations play in facilitating this race to the bottom—even with advancements on transparency under President Obama. Even if we cannot quickly gain global cooperation on a minimum tax as Saez and Zucman propose, the United States could attack this issue by applying a minimum tax to U.S. multinational firms' profits in each country, which would effectively create a tax "floor" and limit corporate incentives to shift profits to tax havens. President Obama proposed such a per-country minimum tax on the foreign profits of all U.S. multinational companies.[40] Because an American company was going to pay that minimum each year—even if a tax haven promised an extremely low rate—there would be less incentive for other nations, including tax havens, to race faster to the bottom. That might also make it easier for other major industrial powers to impose their own minimum tax, which could at least slow down the race to the bottom.

Sadly, while the Trump administration and the Republican Congress claimed that their tax bill would prevent profit shifting and offshoring, their "reform" actually encourages American companies both to move jobs overseas and move funds to tax havens. Instead of applying a minimum tax to each and every individual nation, they required only a 10.5 percent minimum tax, and required that this low rate simply be the "average" of their taxes on all their foreign profits. As I wrote in the *Atlantic* prior to the law's passage, this design incentivizes strategies to *combine* moving profits to tax havens and jobs abroad. How? If a company wants to move profits to a tax haven that has a zero tax rate, all it has to do to nullify the minimum tax is move production and jobs that generate the same amount of profits to a European nation that taxes at 20 to 25 percent, so that the *average* international tax rate is about 10.5 percent. The United States loses jobs, profits, and tax revenue.[41] Members of Congress including Representative Peter DeFazio and Senators Chris Van Hollen, Amy Klobuchar, and Tammy Duckworth have proposed legislation to fix this negative incentive. Yet, currently, this new provision of the Trump tax legislation not only fails to halt a global race to the bottom, it actually provides a reason to move jobs and profits out of the United States.[42]

Tax policy can also structure markets toward the high road or the low road not just abroad but here in the United States. Consider the common spectacle— seen recently with Amazon's announcement of a second headquarters—of states and localities competing to offer tax breaks to companies to locate in their state or city. When several states are fighting for the location of a single factory or headquarters, who wins will have zero impact on national jobs or growth. Yet once any state or city is allowed to give away their tax base to attract the jobs, they can trigger a race-to-the-bottom auction. In the case of Amazon's second headquarters, that meant proposing everything from billions of dollars in incentives to special regulatory shortcuts to even redirecting most of the state and local income taxes paid by employees back to the company.[43] Virtue in this case would be with the government officials who refuse to use their taxpayer dollars to give a handout to one of the world's wealthiest corporations—as some indeed did with Amazon—or who at least focus their promises on universal improvements to infrastructure or housing. But if the other states and cities also in need of job creation compete in a race-to-the-bottom sell-off of their taxpayer dollars, that means the city that refuses to do so is actually punished by losing any serious chance at "winning" the headquarters or factory.

Imagine for a moment if states and cities could still compete for company location, but not on the basis of tax or regulatory giveaways. They would instead have to compete solely on factors like improving infrastructure, affordable housing, K–12 education, and community colleges helping students gain skills for future jobs. And imagine if companies chose new locations based on which city was going to best expand investments in their people, in their quality of life and environment—and the company in question planned to contribute their part. A national race to the bottom would be transformed into a national race to the top.

CHAPTER EIGHT

STRUCTURING CHANGE TO PROTECT ECONOMIC DIGNITY

In Lin-Manuel Miranda's *Hamilton*, one lyric states: "You have no control, who lives, who dies, who tells your story."[1] This is too often true when it comes to the economic history of technology and dislocation. For example, consider the transition to the automobile in the early twentieth century. The history is often told—perhaps tongue in cheek—that many horses lost their jobs to the automobile in the early twentieth century. True. But make no mistake about it: a lot of humans did, too. In 1890, more than 90,000 Americans had jobs related to producing horse-drawn carriages or wagons. Another 368,000 people were employed as teamsters, the people who drove teams of animals pulling wagons.[2] Thousands more jobs were needed to deal with the five to ten tons of manure dropped per square mile in urban areas. Other common horse-related jobs at the turn of the last century included horseshoe and other horse clothing manufacturers, stable keepers, horse breeders, and coachmen.[3] But in the beginning of the twentieth century, the automobile industry rapidly replaced horse-powered transportation: between 1890 and 1920, the number of American companies building horse-drawn carriages dropped from nearly 14,000 to just 90.[4] While many displaced workers may have found new jobs and new industries, one can also be sure that many workers were hurt badly by this major technological and industrial innovation.

Economic historians often write that it is clear that the long-run verdict of the British Industrial Era was strong gains in standards of living for generations of Brits. But as economist Carl Benedikt Frey notes, the story would be quite different if told from the perspective of the millions of workers—including children—who were treated only as means to a long-term end from which they would never benefit. Millions worked under such harsh conditions that the poet William Blake called them "dark Satanic Mills."[5] Frey notes that for the Luddite generation, they and their children and grandchildren were worse off for three generations.[6] As Frey writes, "most economists will acknowledge that technological progress will cause some adjustment problems in the short run. What is rarely noted is that the short run can be a lifetime."[7] Or three.

Today, there are new looming threats that could cause even bigger upheavals than the automobile in the twentieth century—and they are occurring during an era of globalization that puts more pressure on jobs in the United States. Artificial intelligence (AI), robots, and autonomous vehicle technology are among the new technological advances that threaten major economic disruption. A quarter of American adults say the possibility that robots and computers could do many of the jobs done by humans makes them feel "very worried."[8] A widely cited study by Frey put the number of U.S. jobs at high risk of being automated in the next decade or two due to advances in AI and robots at 47 percent.[9] According to a Brookings Institution study, thirty-six million jobs "will face high exposure to automation in the coming decades."[10] Some experts project up to three million jobs could be at risk due to self-driving trucks and cars.[11] Martin Ford, author of *Rise of the Robots*, believes that artificial intelligence "could very well end up in a future with significant unemployment . . . maybe even declining wages . . . [and] soaring levels of inequality."[12]

Other experts believe that these concerns are overblown. Leading economists like Jason Furman have discussed how often previous projections of massive net job loss due to technological change did not come to pass.[13] Some point out that even the highly respected former Federal Reserve vice chair Alan Blinder admitted to being proven wrong after he estimated in 2007 that a quarter of white-collar jobs were vulnerable to offshoring.[14]

Economist David Autor has called such dramatic job loss estimates from AI "arrogant" predictions from "self-proclaimed oracles." Autor finds it a "bet against human ingenuity" for people to in effect say, "If I can't think of what people will do for work in the future, then you, me and our kids aren't going to think of it either."[15] Others have much lower—but still significant—estimates of job loss. The OECD estimates that only 9 percent of U.S. jobs are at risk from automation.[16] Similarly, analysis by McKinsey & Company found that fewer than 5 percent of jobs could be completely automated.[17]

My goal is not to litigate which side is right in this ongoing debate. My best guess is that we are less likely to see an unprecedented reduction in overall demand for labor in the coming decades. We're more likely to see the continuation of current trends in our economy that have led to widening income and wealth inequality with consequential job disruptions from globalization and technological trends.

Regardless of whose predictions are right, we as a nation must put policies in place that help shape change to promote and protect economic dignity. That means we need both affirmative policies to encourage the path of job creation to maximize dignified work and a true dignity net that ensures people can care for family and find new chances to pursue purpose and potential when economic disruption strikes. The United States has the weakest set of protections for economic security in the industrial world, which allows job losses to turn into a devastating spiral that destroys lives and communities. While some job churn is inevitable—even healthy—in a dynamic economy, in our current system a job loss is too often a direct threat to people's economic dignity. Fixing this requires far more than minimal adjustment assistance or retraining policies offered to grease a trade deal. It means real efforts to shape how technological and global trends can lift up, not tear down, the jobs and economic lives of millions of Americans. It means making the capacity to shape and cope with change in ways that protect economic dignity a proactive and central goal of our economic policies. As the Nobel Prize–winning economists Esther Duflo and Abhijit Banerjee put it, "The goal of social policy, in these times of change and anxiety," should be "to help people absorb the shocks that affect them without allowing those shocks to affect their sense of themselves."[18]

Neither a static model nor status quo policies can meet that test. So we will need a new model.

ECONOMIC DIGNITY CAN'T BE BASED ON STATIC ECONOMIES

We cannot achieve universal economic dignity based on a static view of the economy. The solution will never be to protect at all costs the workers in the obsolete horse industry from the coming of the automobile. As the MIT Task Force on the Work of the Future explains, "Transformative innovations such as the internal combustion engine, electricity, and telecommunications— among many others—improved quality of life, raised productivity and earnings; made work less dirty, dangerous, physically punishing, and dull; and increased the value of thinking, creativity, and expertise."[19] The Industrial Revolution brought on economic benefits at a scale that humanity had never before seen. As Frey writes in *The Technology Trap*, "Before 1750, per capita income in the world doubled every 6,000 years; since then, it has doubled every 50 years."[20] The auto was a major advance. It didn't just create a lot of good jobs that bolstered the American middle class—it also improved life for millions more. Consider just the number of people who have been able to see the wonder of our national parks thanks to the mass-produced automobile. In 1916, only about 14,000 people visited Yellowstone by car, with a similar amount visiting by train; two decades later, nearly half a million people visited Yellowstone by car.[21] Similarly, while many people lost their livelihoods of washing other people's clothes because of the availability of affordable electric-powered washing machines, the exploding share of dwellings with such appliances contributed to the shift in societal norms around women working outside the home[22] and progress toward gender equality. Indeed, if tomorrow our prayers were answered with an instant cure for Alzheimer's, it would undoubtedly disrupt many investments and jobs (home care workers, physicians, and nurses who provide the care for millions who live with the disease), but it would still be a net good. In short, the road to universal economic dignity for one generation cannot be based on blocking major life-enhancing progress for the next one.

When it comes to predicting the impacts of innovation and technology on jobs, it pays to be humble. Few economists in the past have had 20/20 vision about how technological change will create or destroy jobs even twenty years later. In the late nineteenth century, 98 percent of the labor needed to produce cloth became automated, but this led to an increase in weaving jobs. Cloth became much cheaper, leading to increased demand for clothes and job growth among weavers.[23] A century later, when ATMs became a staple in bank branches, many feared this would mean a major reduction in bank jobs. Instead, as the ATM made it cheaper to operate a bank office, more branches opened, leading to a net gain in such jobs.[24] Sometimes entirely new jobs that operate alongside the disrupted sector are created following the introduction of new technologies. No one predicted that after the automobile replaced the horse, the motel and fast-food industries would create new jobs, as the middle class was newly able to partake in the luxury of travel.[25] Certainly, when I left the White House in January 2000, I don't remember anyone predicting that if we returned only eight years later, every agency and department—including the White House and the State Department— would have multiple new jobs in "social media."

ECONOMIC DIGNITY CAN'T BE ACHIEVED THROUGH STATUS QUO POLICIES

While hoping for a static economy to prevent harmful disruption will never be the answer, neither will relying on our miserable status quo policies for protecting economic dignity in the face of economic change.

Despite all the attention paid to the issue of jobs being dislocated—or at risk of dislocation—due to robots, artificial intelligence, and trade, virtually no policy tools have been added to our barren policy toolbox to protect the economic dignity of workers in the face of disruptive change. There is no other industrialized nation where simply losing a job can cause more hardship. Former prime minister of Australia Julia Gillard has commented that while job loss certainly hurts in her country, in the United States, the weak protections for economic security create a sense of economic desperation. The reasons are manifold. In Belgium and Denmark, unemployed workers actively looking for work receive the great majority of their previous wages for up to one and two years, respectively.[26] In the United States, unemployment insurance provides benefits to fewer than a third of all unemployed workers.[27] Most states don't allow those looking for only part-time work to access unemployment insurance (UI) benefits.[28] For the few who are covered, UI benefits replace up to 47 percent of wages on average.[29] From 2008 to 2010, nearly three in four people who lost their health insurance when they lost their job said they skipped out on needed health care or prescriptions due to the cost. A similar ratio struggled with medical debt.[30] No doubt things have improved with the Affordable Care Act, but because it is under constant political and legal attack, and with some holes still needing to be plugged, too many still fear they could be one job loss and one illness away from financial ruin. Unlike Sweden and other nations, we have absolutely no system to help workers who know they will be laid off adjust and prepare for the road to new jobs *before* they fall into unemployment.

The United States also has no plan to help workers defer mortgage or rent payments in times of unemployment, raising the risk of foreclosure and eviction. In the Obama administration, I was proud to help orchestrate—at the urging of major housing and civil rights advocacy groups—a policy of one-year mortgage forbearance so that recovery housing programs could help people out of work stay in their homes while they looked for new jobs.[31] Yet there is no current national policy that does that. And for all the talk of retraining workers to help them land new jobs, there is no universal program that provides both income support and tuition to make it economically viable for workers who want to retrain to do so and still support their families. Indeed, the United States spends the least (other than Slovakia) in the OECD on measures to actively help unemployed and at-risk workers get back to work.[32]

At its core, much of the reason the United States provides such a pathetic policy response to economic disruption can be traced to two myths. The first is that providing support to the unemployed breeds dependency. The second is that any serious jobs-centric national economic strategy represents ill-conceived "industrial policy." Perhaps nowhere is the combination of these two myths so toxic as in the context of communities facing major factory closings or massive job loss.

As I have argued for over two decades, we have no policies to prevent or even slow the speed of devastating downward spirals communities face due to a major factory closing or concentrated job losses, despite the severe harm to economic dignity. Job loss is always painful, but there is an economic pathology that develops when a community dependent on a single form of production suddenly suffers a massive contraction. As anthropologist Katherine Newman explains:

> When steel mills close their gates, oil fields fall silent, and farm areas experience epidemics of foreclosures, downward mobility engulfs entire communities. The blight spreads from the shuttered factory to the town beyond its gates, undermining the firms that supplied the factory; the restaurants, supermarkets, and clothing stores where workers used to spend their money; and the public sector, which must struggle to support schools, police, and fire departments on a reduced tax base.[33]

The cycle is even worse than Newman describes. The increase in negative social and health outcomes amplifies the need for social, economic, and health assistance from governments just as their revenue is falling. This can leave local governments facing the impossible choice of either not addressing local suffering or raising taxes and making it even less attractive for businesses and individuals to move there in the future. As the downward cycle accelerates, the need for new economic activity grows, but the economic attractiveness of the location deteriorates.

The workers who suffer job losses in areas going through such vicious downward economic cycles end up getting hit particularly hard. A study of men with at least three years of job tenure who lost their jobs through mass layoffs or plant closings found they had a mortality rate of 50 to 100 percent greater the year after losing their jobs, and this increased risk of death persisted for the next twenty years at 10 to 15 percent.[34] Another study found that workers who lost their jobs through a mass layoff or plant closing and had no major health problem before losing their jobs had an 83 percent greater chance of developing a new stress-related health condition in the next eighteen months, whether or not they found a new job.[35] It is hard to read these statistics for downward cycles and not think that there is a causal connection between these downward economic cycles and the increase in the deaths of despair discussed earlier.

ECONOMIC CHANGE AND ALOOF WELFARE ECONOMICS

Our failure to address the challenges of economic change and economic dignity is impacted when our policy discussions display an aloof form of welfare economics. This is the field of economics that examines if policies, like a trade policy, are a good idea based on whether—when you add up all the economic wins and setbacks—the policy is a net win for the economy as a whole. If a new policy saves Americans $10 billion in spending but costs tens of thousands of workers jobs worth $5 billion in wages, then some will add up the costs and benefits and declare it a net win for the country. Academics often refer to the Kaldor-Hicks formula, which asks if the "winners" (those who saved $10 billion) have gained enough that they can pay off the "losers" and have everyone be ahead.

Make no mistake about it: in nearly every policy conversation I have been a part of, policymakers recognize that increased trade flows or new technologies create both "winners" and "losers" and that there is some moral obligation to help those who would be set back. Yet too often, there is little urgency around the policy table about making sure those who lost out were truly taken care of. Economist Dean Baker, a frequent critic of trade policies of both Democratic and Republican administrations, has noted that while the harsh dislocation of factory workers is often accepted as simply an unfortunate fact of economic dynamism, the same nonchalance is often not seen when professional jobs are at stake. As an example, he points to the resistance that would no doubt exist if there was wide-open immigration for doctors, even if it lowered overall medical costs for Americans.[36] James Carville once asked what debates on trade agreements would be like in Washington, DC, if the economic analysis determined that an agreement would lead to lower prices, more competition, and innovation but also to no one being able to get their child into their top two choices for private schools. In Binyamin Appelbaum's book *The Economist's Hour,* he echoes Nobel Prize winner Amartya Sen's reminder that somehow Kaldor-Hicks asks only whether the winners gain enough so that they *could* compensate all the losers—not that they actually do![37]

This aloof form of welfare economics or cost-benefit analysis is at stark odds with an economic dignity perspective. Determining that a certain policy was a net job creator fails to account for how deep the economic pain was for those who did lose jobs. A family that loses everything to a new policy will understandably draw little comfort from the fact that the same policy helped create a job for a young worker or two in another state. Cass Sunstein—one of the nation's top cost-benefit gurus and former regulatory chief under President Obama—stresses that even cost-benefit done right should be seen not as a cold, dollars-and-cents calculation, but as an effort to weigh ultimate impacts on well-being. Sunstein's discussion makes clear why even from a cost-benefit perspective, one could choose a policy with higher monetary cost (spread a non-consequential few dollars per person across millions) over a policy with a smaller monetary cost that would cause devastating harm to a small number of people. The latter may have a lower price tag, but it would inflict a far greater cost to human well-being.[38] This view is consistent with President Obama's Executive Order 13563, which, under Sunstein's supervision, specifically allowed agencies to consider nonmonetary "dignity" impacts in regulatory reviews.[39]

This is not to say that consumer costs—or consumer welfare—should be dismissed in an economic dignity analysis. Those of us who support a minimum wage increase do so because of how meaningful it can be for hard-pressed workers to have their paychecks go thousands of dollars further each year in caring for themselves and their families. We can't recognize the upside of that reality and then refuse to weigh the negative impacts of, for example, restrictive trade policies or tariffs that make that paycheck cover far less. And it makes little sense to ignore the fact that when trade barriers raise the costs of key inputs for American manufacturers, it could cost jobs by hurting their competitive edge in exporting their product. Our goal should not be to completely dismiss cost issues, but instead to ensure such benefits are weighed and balanced against other considerations of economic dignity. And at times we must be willing to recognize when harms resulting from our policies have such a negative impact on the capacity to care for family and pursue potential that they should be prevented regardless of any cost-benefit calculation due to the need to protect what should be an impenetrable sphere of economic dignity.

Even when business leaders or commentators note the importance of "compensating losers" or limiting the severity of such concentrated geographic harm, it is often based on a political economy argument for "saving capitalism" or preventing populist counterreactions or intense opposition to pro-market policies. But this type of reasoning misses the key point. We should avoid such devastating harms to concentrated groups of workers not as a tactic or means to achieve other goals. We should do so out of a national commitment to Kant's canonical definition of dignity—to never treat workers as only the means to larger national economic ends and not ends in themselves. The impact of policies and technology on workers and communities should not be an afterthought for "compensating losers" or a mere political strategy for passing legislation. Rather, it is an issue we should deal with preemptively and proactively, because how our policies impact economic dignity should be our lodestar.

ECONOMIC CHANGE AND ECONOMIC DIGNITY: IT'S POLICY, STUPID

We must commit to structure economic change so that it does not trample on economic dignity. Anton Korinek and Joseph Stiglitz write that "the proliferation of AI and other worker-replacing technological change can be unambiguously positive in a first-best economy in which individuals are fully insured against any adverse impacts of innovation, or if it is coupled with the right form of redistribution."[40] Technological innovation need not damage economic dignity if we shape such change to enhance dignified work and put in place policies that cushion disruptive change and offer adequate avenues to pursue potential and purpose. Indeed, we should be proactively and continually strategizing on how we can leverage technological innovation as part of a national strategy to create new jobs and tackle our greatest challenges—such as addressing climate change. If we recognize the inevitability and desirability of economic and technological progress but care about protecting and promoting economic dignity, policies that allow these priorities to coexist should be at the top of our economic policy agenda.

Taking economic change and economic dignity seriously means making significant progress in five areas.

FIRST, A BROAD ECONOMIC DIGNITY COMPACT

As I will discuss in Chapters Eleven and Twelve, the starting point should be a new compact that ensures more than a living wage (a true economic dignity wage) and a stronger safety net (a dignity net) for all those who work hard to support their families. That dignity net has to be part of our ongoing economic compact and broad enough to offer meaningful support when job loss represents a major dislocation. Beyond the most basic needs, like universal health care and stronger unemployment relief, this should include mortgage forbearance, renters' relief, and wage insurance for those who are facing serious dislocation, and special policies to offer dignified bridges to retirement for older workers.

SECOND, PREEMPTIVE POLICY TOOLS TO PROTECT COMMUNITIES FROM VICIOUS ECONOMIC DOWNTURNS AFTER MAJOR LAYOFFS

Today, unless a particular community or industry can make a case for temporary trade relief, assistance is typically available—if at all—only after the vicious downward cycle has left the community and families in desperate straits. We need a range of policies that are preemptive: that allow workers, businesses, and local governments to come together to design strategies to bolster or diversify or save jobs before the devastation hits—and to at least have serious resources to cushion the blow immediately when concentrated layoffs hit.[41] As the highest-ranking Michigander on the Obama Auto Task Force in 2009, I remember then governor of Michigan Jennifer Granholm calling to say she was trying to meet with General Electric to interest the company in a recently abandoned factory in an attractive location. Was there any incentive for such retooling before the community was so devastated? The answer was no. This poverty of policy options cannot persist.

There are a variety of policy options we should be proposing. We should finance a fifty-state manufacturing strategy fund to allow each state—or states working together as a region—to fund ongoing modernizations and low-carbon technology usages and to anticipate both threats and opportunities and prepare in advance. We should have a manufacturing community tax credit[42] so that a governor in the situation Granholm faced has the means to incentivize retooling of existing facilities. Major companies that received enormous public support and tax incentives in the United States should pay into a fund to help communities adjust when they close major U.S. factories. And the federal government should organize itself better to make it easier for hard-hit areas to facilitate needed federal relief. This has been done at times with federal "SWAT teams" after a military base closing. This was a model we deployed when President Obama asked me to coordinate help to Detroit as the city sought to claw its way back from bankruptcy in 2013—an effort Vice President Biden then led and ran from 2014 onward.

We also have to be willing to add targeted job creation to our policy toolbox to prevent such deep downward spirals from a major economic hit. In the Obama administration, we designed manufacturing innovation hubs that led entire regions to coordinate regional strategies for advanced manufacturing. Simon Johnson and Jonathan Gruber have taken the idea to an even broader level, calling for allocating funding for research and development based on regional economic strategies.[43] These are long-term strategic plans for regional economic development that make sense. But where we can see a major economic dislocation coming that can devastate a community or region, why should we not have a strategy for green renovations of buildings, school infrastructure modernization, and addressing deferred maintenance in order to spark economic activity and jobs that meet both immediate and long-term economic needs? An independent process could be set up to ensure such job creation decisions were made based on nonpolitical considerations. This effort could also include significant subsidies for and encouragement of apprenticeship programs in varied industries that are structured with unions and community colleges to meet employer needs. And we need real help and assistance for small as well as large suppliers when a major downturn hits or a factory closes.

THIRD, AFFIRMATIVELY SHAPING TECHNOLOGY AND GLOBALIZATION TO CREATE DIGNIFIED JOBS

Developing a stronger compact to protect economic dignity against devastating economic disruption must be a top national priority. We also have to reshape our trade and international economic strategies to do far more than put workers and job location front and center at every turn. Our response to the threats of AI, globalization, and economic inequality must also include national strategies to shape the future of dignified job creation and location—especially as we face the rising dangers of global warming and the competitive threat of a China often not playing by a fair set of rules.

We should, of course, be cautious of ill-informed industrial policies in which a set of government officials seeks to pick precise winners and losers by predicting the unpredictable when it comes to future economic trends. But we should also be careful not to allow simplistic, broad-brush caricatures of "industrial policy" to stymie our ambition or common sense in pursuing policies that would lead to stronger jobs and an economy that emits less carbon.

We can see the new economic case for such national strategies when we look at our manufacturing past and future. The efforts our government has and has not taken to ensure we have a competitive future in manufacturing on our shores have proven to be consequential for our current and future capacity to compete on the cutting edge.[44] Consider our history in consumer electronics and cutting-edge automobile technology. As a nation, we were indifferent to the movement of the production of consumer electronics out of the United States, as it seemed to offer little future for high-value production. When mobile phones swept the global economy, we lacked the production and supplier capacity to compete for these new products and lost huge potential economic value and jobs to China. In contrast, the Obama administration decided to save the U.S. automobile industry, even though doing so violated pure laissez-faire market principles. The result was not just saving at least one million jobs immediately; it was also ensuring that the United States has the domestic industrial capacity to compete for electric car production, next-generation batteries, and the high-value technologies of the future.[45]

National manufacturing requires looking beyond the isolated decisions of individual private companies. The power of a nation to make itself a magnet for the manufacturing jobs of the future can depend on the strength of what Harvard University professors Gary Pisano and Willy Shih have called the "industrial commons."[46] Simply put, the strength of university research and development, skilled workers, modern infrastructure, engineering capacity, and a vibrant supplier network help all manufacturers increase their chance of success. When firms and suppliers leave, it can create a negative cascading effect on the entire manufacturing base. This was never more evident than during the auto rescue. From everything we were taught in school, you would have thought that Ford CEO Alan Mulally would have opposed government assistance for his main rivals, GM and Chrysler. Yet it was a teaching moment when he testified to Congress that GM's and Chrysler's collapse "would have taken the supply base down and taken the industry down."[47] He recognized that the loss of the supply base triggered by the failure of GM and Chrysler could destroy the network for any American automaker having a claim on the economic future. This is why I argued, as cohead of the Obama administration's Manufacturing Task Force, that we needed to shift our thinking on manufacturing to an "innovation spillover" model, where we are focused on the degree to which manufacturing location in the United States leads to positive economic and innovation spillover benefits both for the specific communities impacted as well as for the broader economy."[48] This lesson can be seen today in the battle with China for leadership on 5G wireless technology, AI, and other industries of the future. To take on China for these jobs of the future, we have to understand and invest in the larger research and infrastructure networks needed for us to have industrial leadership in a world where we take China's behavior—and not idealized free markets—into account.

Nowhere is there greater urgency or opportunity to shape the future of jobs than in the range of technologies we need to accelerate the transition to a carbon-neutral economy. Across our economy, from zero-carbon energy production and energy storage to electric vehicles and net-zero buildings to advanced agricultural and land use practices to store more carbon in our soil, we need to build a new industrial commons in carbon-efficient technology. This will require a vast and sustained commitment to basic research on green technology that is supported by government, driven by university-industry partners, and accessible to large companies and smaller suppliers alike. We should be creative in using incentives and procurement commitments to pull forward private investment in these technologies and design them to ensure that those investments enhance our domestic industrial capacity and competitiveness. Such a commitment does not call for government to pick which companies or precise products or technologies will prevail. But it does call for shaping our public policies to structure and reward robust innovation, competition, and public strategies that will lead to a carbon-neutral future, bolster our domestic industrial base, and generate millions of high-wage jobs in the United States.

It is heartening that those strategizing on climate change—from different versions of a Green New Deal to implementation of the Obama administration's Clean Power Plan—have been focused on simultaneously achieving broad national goals and calling for policies to prevent devastating economic dislocation and downward economic cycles for workers and communities. This is the right approach for a nation committed to protecting economic dignity amid transformative change. But we should be clear-eyed about the magnitude of the task. Helping workers and communities vested in particular industries prosper through such difficult transitions will be challenging, involve significant resources, and require true partnership with labor. This will take bold action and creativity. But what better challenge is there than the biggest environmental and, in many ways, humanitarian issue of our time to demonstrate that we can pursue a national jobs-centric strategy that harnesses the benefits of economic change without a portion of our communities and workers feeling as though they were being treated as only a means to that end goal.

FOURTH, AMBITIOUS SECOND-CHANCE STRATEGIES

America lacks serious second-chance policies. Too many people either disparage policies to help dislocated workers find new job paths as ineffective or make simplistic assumptions about how easily steelworkers or miners can transition to coding or care work. Some go so far as to denigrate such policies as "burial insurance."[49] But if we want an economy that structures change to protect economic dignity, this is not an area where either failure or throwing in the towel is an option. This is, as FDR might say, an area where there is no choice but to engage in "bold, persistent experimentation" and try something.[50] We should start with innovating along the lines of policies like Sweden's job-security councils, which are funded by contributions from employers with collective bargaining agreements with their workers. The job security councils do have a preemptive element: they often work with employees well before the workers are laid off to figure out their next steps.[51] This is surely part of the reason why displaced Swedish workers are more likely to find a job within a year and experience smaller declines in earnings than U.S. workers.[52]

UBI to Rise: Our nation should have a simple-to-locate, easy-to-access second-chance program that gives all Americans who face a serious career dislocation an economically viable opportunity to seek new skills or quality credentials, and to secure whatever other support is needed to pursue a different career. Of course, in an economy where nearly six million people quit, are fired, or are laid off each month, most job losses and transitions, however uncomfortable, do not cause devastating harm or require in-depth policy responses.[53] For many people, guidance and skilled job search assistance may be enough—and those investments have high returns. But for those who have suffered a severe career or job dislocation and want something more, we offer far too little. For working parents who have lost their job and are under enormous financial and emotional stress, even free tuition can be an empty promise. They need direct financial support in order to participate in a time-intensive program to get back on their feet.

"UBI to Rise," a universal basic income (UBI) for a period of time where dislocated workers are trying to rise, makes sense. This simply recognizes that if we want workers—especially those in midlife and in the middle of raising families—to be able to take the gamble of exploring a new career or attaining a valuable credential or degree, we can't ignore that they need to be able to provide for their families at the same time. Right now, our nation has only one program that offers such income support, Trade Adjustment Assistance (TAA). The good news is research finds that TAA increases cumulative earnings for participants relative to nonparticipants.[54] However, it serves—by design—only a small fraction of those who might need it. From 2015 to 2017, only about 281,000 of 6.8 million—or 4 percent of—displaced workers received benefits through TAA.[55] Indeed, TAA is designed to help only a group of workers who, through an extensive process, can establish they lost their job due to trade. Yet why should it matter if someone lost their job due to trade, automation, AI, some combination of those factors, or simply changing consumer trends? Our goal should be to help people find a new career, not investigate why they lost their old one. A UBI to Rise should be for anyone who qualifies regardless of how their career was disrupted.

I have worked on versions of a UBI to Rise for years—in 1994,[56] in my 2005 book,[57] and in 2012 when President Obama proposed a version.[58] It is long past time to get it done. As part of that effort, we should provide workers with childcare, transportation subsidies, and other supports critical to completing a training program and finding a new career. A randomized controlled trial of sector-based employment programs in the United States found that "help with childcare or transportation or a referral for housing or legal services can be critical to staying in training or keeping a job."[59] UBI to Rise could also be structured to give workers a shot at starting their own business, a feature that would also be more effective if it was available before job loss hit. While regional strategies are critical when there is concentrated geographic job loss, jobs dislocated by automation—such as autonomous cars and trucks—could often be dispersed. A broad UBI to Rise can be helpful to such workers even if their regions or communities are not taking a hard hit. While, as I will discuss in coming chapters, we should not see such training as a magic bullet or a substitute for expanding worker power, we should also be giving people the power to shape their own destinies, whether they want to pivot to being a registered nurse, a high school sports coach, a store manager, or an information technology (IT) manager.

Programs that have features similar to UBI to Rise have shown great promise. A recent *New York Times* article tells the story of Amanda Lucas, who took advantage of a Kentucky program for miners' families that provided income support while covering the costs of tuition as she trained to become a respiratory therapist; her husband was out of work due to the collapse of the coal industry. The result was not only a needed paycheck but also a new sense of purpose. "I've always heard," she said, "if you love what you do, it don't seem like a job, and that's how I feel right now."[60]

A Rethink: Our failure as a nation to institute policies that protect against massive dislocation and devastating economic downward cycles for individuals and communities in the face of disruptive change has major implications for an economic dignity agenda. We must look at the degree of harm a concentrated group of working families will suffer and ask if the cost to their economic dignity is too great, even if the broader population of consumers will enjoy modest benefits. An economic dignity agenda must include shielding a sphere of economic dignity from any form of consumer welfare or cost-benefit analysis. For example, we simply forbid abusive child labor or the coercing of subordinates to provide sexual favors in exchange for promotions as per se violations of economic dignity. If we as a nation cannot develop comprehensive policies to cushion and provide new opportunities for individuals and communities severly harmed by our policies, we have to ask ourselves if we should go forward with such policies that can lead to this violation of economic dignity even if they can be seen as a positive for foreign policy or widespread economic gains.

This understanding offers a perspective for learning important lessons from the policies of previous decades—including the economic and job impacts from the North American Free Trade Agreement (NAFTA) and the efforts to bring China into the World Trade Organization (WTO) in the 1990s. It would be foolish for anyone to deny that these agreements had some serious failings and disappointments related to protections for workers and communities, a lack of enforcement against import surges in the immediate years following China's entry, and China's continuing unfair competitive policies and rejection of true political reform. The problem was not, however, that in the 1990s President Clinton wasn't focused on a broad economic security framework and enforcement to go hand in hand with the acceleration of globalization. He fought tooth and nail for universal health security and was far along with a universal worker adjustment strategy that his secretary of labor, Robert Reich, and many of us at the National Economic Council were developing. President Clinton also worked to triple dislocated worker funding during even extremely low unemployment and to create several economic development policies for hard-hit areas. An all-Republican Congress for his last six years in office, however, made major reform a legislative impossibility.

The core motivation for bringing China into the WTO was far less related to economics and far more part of a broader post–Cold War strategy aimed at bolstering the global rule of law and binding China to the liberal world order. Nonetheless, Clinton effectively held up the agreement for many months in part to secure an "anti-surge" provision to block or slow down imports if they were having severe impacts on jobs without having to prove any unfair trade practices. Had Al Gore followed Clinton as president, there is little question that the anti-surge provision would have been a powerful tool used again and again to both protect manufacturing communities and send a strong message to China. Instead, the Bush administration refused to ever use the anti-surge provision, even with a dramatic rise in Chinese imports, and even when their own U.S. International Trade Commission recommended such relief on multiple occasions. The extreme unwillingness to use this anti-surge provision effectively sent a green light for China to flood U.S. markets even faster. True enforcement of our anti-surge provisions, legislative progress on universal health care, stronger regional economic strategies, and a universal program of income support during new job training after any dislocation would not have been enough to deal with all the challenges of globalization and the economic rise and unfair economic practices of China. It could, however, have significantly helped prevent much of the devastation many American manufacturing communities faced.

In the first decade of the 2000s, the acceleration of globalization, as well as other factors, led to a period of capital taking a record share of income at the expense of labor. This coincided with more attacks on unionization, little progress on the minimum wage, and no important advancements in economic security policies.[61] The lessons from this history cannot be ignored. As more and more Democratic presidential candidates have proposed, there needs to be a new paradigm on trade where worker interests, not industry priorities, drive agreements. This is not a rejection of globalization or engagement. The economic benefits to our nation from trade that is open and fair are substantial, as are the foreign policy benefits that I believe have and can continue to come from more nations using trade within a global rule of law to promote peaceful relations. But things do need to change.

We need an overall economic strategy that puts workers first, reduces corporate influence, and does not violate our commitment to economic dignity for all of our people. Even if trade agreements are in pursuit of admirable foreign policy objectives or can be shown to have broad-based economic benefits, it is a violation of treating all people as ends in themselves to go forward *if we do not advocate for different terms at trade and have the comprehensive economic policies in place to prevent such devastating impacts for a concentrated group of families and communities who feel they were cast aside as means to those ends.* If we put economic dignity front and center in our economic policies, then, from trade provisions to our larger strategies, we will shape change to create jobs and lift up workers and communities proactively, preemptively, and continuously.

FIFTH, TECHNOLOGY IS NOT DESTINY

Much of the debate on the potential impact of automation and AI reflects a passive perspective. What will we do if technology renders millions of jobs obsolete? It is as if our only role were to watch—as if we were economic voyeurs. If we broaden and strengthen an economic dignity net and pass something like a UBI to Rise, we will be closer to what Korinek and Stiglitz described as a "first-best economy in which individuals are fully insured against any adverse impacts of innovation."[62] But beyond such policy measures to deal with the negative effects of technological change, we should ask what we can do to structure change. As Erik Brynjolfsson and Andrew McAfee conclude in *The Second Machine Age*, "Technology is not destiny. We shape our destiny."[63]

Economists Daron Acemoglu and Pascual Restrepo argue that automation and AI will take some tasks from workers and lower demand for some jobs— what they call "displacement" effects. However, they also believe that the creation of new tasks—"shaped by the decisions of firms, workers, and other actors in society"—in which labor has an edge over automation can provide a countervailing influence to the displacement effects.[64] Notably, the process of creating those new tasks is Acemoglu and Restrepo's framework thus underscores the fact that the decisions we make as a nation can have a powerful influence over what technological innovation means for our country.

We should be reimagining what is possible for the nation. Brynjolfsson and McAfee highlight several types of tasks in which humans have a clear advantage over machines: manual tasks like those that repairmen and home health aides do, creative tasks, and interpersonal tasks like those that teachers, nurses, and managers do.[65] By investing in leveraging what humans do well, we can help shape the possibility that technological advances serve our ends. We cannot be passive observers of artificial intelligence and job displacement. We should not only be looking for every option to help people in the workplace but also be imagining how we can use AI and automation to both create new jobs and better address national challenges. Consider a few ideas.

Brynjolfsson often cites Iora Health, winner of MIT's Inclusive Innovation Challenge—a contest for companies that create economic opportunity for moderate and low-income earners—as an example of how a company can use technology while also creating meaningful jobs, as opposed to just cutting them.[66] Instead of trying to constantly drive down its cost of labor, Iora chose to actually expand job opportunities for an outcome-based healthcare model. At Iora, an algorithm draws from patient data to create a "worry score" that informs staff of potential future problems the patient could face.[67] Iora pairs this ingenious use of technology with a more holistic version of health care that includes "health coaches." These health coaches come from the communities that Iora serves and help patients stay healthy by teaching them about exercise and eating well, texting them about their health, and visiting patients at home.[68] When a patient's worry score is high, indicating the level of care a patient needs, the care team, which includes health coaches, reaches out to the patient every day.[69] This creation of new meaningful jobs that strengthen health results for patients would not work if Iora followed an old-school model of getting paid by the number of services they provide as opposed to health outcomes. There would be little reason to create new health coach jobs in a fee-for-service model. It is only when health care is paid by virtue of value and results that there are more avenues for humans to add value beyond automation. Iora shows that smarter health policy could lead to more health jobs that leverage technology to create better care for patients.

Erik Brynjolfsson and Andrew McAfee also highlight 99Degrees Custom, an apparel maker in Lawrence, Massachusetts, as an example of how technology can generate jobs. "99Degrees Custom embraces a highly engineered, partially automated production line to make highly customized textile products."[70] That approach has allowed 99Degrees Custom to create new jobs that are "more varied, more highly skilled, and better paid" than "the old [textile] factory jobs."[71] The Massachusetts Executive Office of Housing and Economic Development gave the company a $2.8 million tax credit provided that the company hire 350 additional workers by 2023.[72] Why shouldn't all states provide tax credits for such companies that marry dignified labor and new technology?

While most of the focus on autonomous vehicles and job loss has been on truck drivers and taxicab drivers, about six hundred thousand bus driver jobs—more than twice the number of taxi driver jobs—are at risk.[73] Bus drivers typically work for the government and are disproportionately people of color and women.[74] Instead of simply pocketing a reduction in labor costs due to autonomous vehicles, local governments could use extra tax dollars to reimagine how public transportation works for its citizens. Bus drivers are already "highly skilled customer-service" workers who manage conflicts and help people with directions, among other things.[75] If we come to a day when fewer bus drivers are needed full-time, rather than just eliminate jobs, cities could train them and future "bus managers" to monitor and address bullying among schoolchildren, help older citizens explore their city, and better accommodate those with disabilities. This could lead to more people using public transportation, improve the quality of life for those in their cities, and protect and upgrade jobs and careers that minorities and women disproportionately occupy.

One of the areas in which Acemoglu and Restrepo see great potential for technology to improve jobs is education.[76] At first blush, one might think that AI and automation could be a threat to teachers' jobs. However, if you believe in the power of individualized education in public schools, AI may actually make teaching better and enhance the jobs of teachers. Acemoglu and Restrepo recognize the challenges to providing individualized education, specifically that "nobody has the information (and cannot easily acquire and process the information) to determine a student's optimal learning style in a specific subject or topic."[77] They suggest AI "can be designed to collect and process in real time data about the specific reactions, difficulties and successes students have in different subject areas, especially when taught in different styles, and then make recommendations for improved individualized teaching."[78] AI wouldn't replace the need for high-quality teachers but instead make teachers' efforts to provide individualized education easier. This type of individualized education can have important equity and dignity impacts. It takes away the rationale for tracking children and preventing them from sitting together by putting them in "gifted and talented" classes that can exacerbate racial and economic segregation within schools.[79] It is an offensive form of government-imposed negative dignity to compel children to go to school and then tell them that there are limits to their gifts, talents, and ambitions. Individualized educational methods can help children learn together, grow together, and see that everyone has talents.

Acemoglu and Restrepo's example struck a personal chord with me. My mother pioneered individualized education in Ann Arbor, Michigan, public schools four decades ago. She helped found the first public school in Ann Arbor focused on individualized education and taught there herself. While my mother rigorously made sure that all areas of achievement were met, she never forced her students to learn the exact same way or the exact same material, nor did she force them to switch classes each hour. She would let students enthralled in a science project or fascinated by the life of Harriet Tubman throw themselves into their newfound passion for hours or even days at a time. I saw firsthand the enormous benefits my mother's students received as she maintained high standards while allowing each of them to learn in different ways, recognizing and celebrating diverse learning styles and passions. Yet I also saw my mom grading and planning all the different learning paths of her students until ten o'clock each night. My family and I knew she was giving her students an education none of us had had as kids, but we also knew that it was likely too much to ask of most teachers. The use of AI might allow for there to be more Doris Sperlings but working fewer long hours.

If school districts come to realize the benefits of individualized education, AI may in fact raise demand for teachers. We have the ability to work with educators and innovators to shape the use of AI in individualized education in ways that enhance, not replace, the roles and impact of teachers in helping more young people pursue their passions, purpose, and potential.

If we prioritize meaningful work, it is also worth considering whether our tax code is actually favoring automation over jobs. Perhaps Bill Gates had not thought through all the policy angles when he floated his much-criticized idea of a "robot tax" in 2017.[80] Yet he was right to raise the larger issue. Legal scholars Ryan Abbott and Bret Bogenschneider argue that our current tax system "incentivizes automation even in cases where it is not otherwise efficient."[81] The 2019 MIT Task Force on the Work of the Future report calls for "rebalancing the tax code" to "create a (closer to) level playing field" for capital investment and human capital investments like training for workers.[82] The tax code should not be off-limits as we shape the future of AI and jobs.

Finally, to ensure we are taking every step to shape the path of technological change to promote economic dignity and jobs, federal procurement policies could be deployed to invest in research to develop how AI and other technology could improve—not cost—jobs. Our nation has benefited enormously from the Defense Advanced Research Projects Agency (DARPA), which "make[s] pivotal investments in breakthrough technologies for national security," and that has played a role in the development of everything from the internet to GPS technology.[83]

We could create an "ARPA AI Jobs" initiative. It would be a major fund promoting research only in usages of AI that enhance instead of replace jobs. Obviously, we should not be so naive as to think that it could stop a potential tidal wave of job-replacing AI if that turns out to be the overwhelming trend. But still, our nation has made extraordinary investments in science and technology in the past to achieve national goals—just think about the creation of NASA. Imagine providing major research rewards to the brightest, most idealistic minds across our technology and research communities to inspire more thinking on how AI can help spark the simultaneous creation of new jobs and innovative approaches to national challenges.

Of course, none of the above suggestions will ensure we get it right. But if we believe that we—not technology—should shape our destiny and our goals for economic dignity, we should at least be caught trying.

WORK AND DIGNITY

CHAPTER NINE

WORK AND ECONOMIC DIGNITY

When I was a junior economic staffer for the Dukakis for President campaign in Boston in 1988, those of us who burned the late-night oil in the policy shop often took turns answering the after-hours calls. These were usually voters and constituents, but every once in a while, it was a political celebrity like Senator Ted Kennedy. One night, I picked up the phone to hear a very disheartened owner of a small pizza shop in Chicago. He told me that out of his sense of civic duty, he tried to hire and mentor a number of disadvantaged minority youth to work in his pizza shop. He said he took pride that sometimes he closed his shop and took them to experiences they might not normally have. So that afternoon he had taken them to see Michael Dukakis so that they could witness a presidential campaign speech. He said it had been going great—until Dukakis repeated one of his standard stump speech lines: "We don't want to become a nation of pizza and hamburger flippers!" Of course, Dukakis, a son of an immigrant family doctor who often took vegetables for payment of his services, was only trying to make the case for America competing for the high-wage jobs of the future. But the call pierced my heart. "Why would he say that?" the owner asked. "Every day I am trying to convince these young men that there is worth in a hard day's work. Why would he mock the jobs they had?"

I promised myself then and there, if I could help it, I would never say or help write anything that put down any type of work or job. In our personal as well as professional lives, all of us should respect the dignity of all who work and contribute. Regardless of the prestige or skill level of any job, it is repulsive to a vision of economic dignity to not respect and appreciate the effort to care for family, the pride in a task well done, and the contribution of all we see and come in contact with—including those who choose to focus on raising their children or caring for loved ones. As Martin Luther King famously said: "All labor has dignity."

MARTIN LUTHER KING JR. AND THE DIGNITY COMPACT OF CONTRIBUTION

Martin Luther King Jr.'s statement about the universality of dignity for all labor is morally and spiritually correct. Too few of us treat all workers we meet with that degree of respect and appreciation for their work and dignity. We must do better.

But we must also not confuse that moral commitment to treat all with the respect they deserve with the issue of whether our policies enable workers to experience actual dignity in their economic lives.

As we should not assume that growth lifts all boats, we should not assume that because all who work deserve to be treated with respect, they automatically experience economic dignity in their lives. The ultimate test for that determination must be whether their work and contribution allows them to have the guarantees that they can in fact enjoy the three-part test of economic dignity. Does work allow one to care for family and loved ones without denying one the capacity to experience life's most precious experiences? Does it promote purpose, meaning, and potential? Does it lead to a sense of voice and respect at work as opposed to domination and humiliation?

As discussed in the next chapter, some conservatives who deploy the language of "dignity of work" seem to assume it is purely a psychological issue that can be resolved by the attitudes of workers and citizens. They feel no obligation to ask whether we have policies that ensure all workers can in fact work, care for family, and pursue their aspirations with dignity. They miss that economic dignity must operate as a compact of contribution. Honoring a commitment to the notion of dignity in all work must compel an obligation to ensure policies that make such economic dignity real.

No one made the case for both aspects of this economic dignity compact more powerfully than Martin Luther King Jr. King did not speak to the dignity of all work as simply a spiritual objective. He specifically spoke to it as creating an imperative to compel public policies that would remedy the economic dignity deficit that existed for so many Americans—especially African Americans who experienced disadvantage from discrimination and economic deprivation.

Indeed, King's famous "All Labor Has Dignity" speech came in the context of his support for a strike by public sanitation workers in Memphis in March 1968. After two sanitation workers, Echol Cole and Robert Walker, had been crushed to death by a garbage truck that the city neglected to update, leaving the families without any compensation,[1] thirteen hundred black men from the public sanitation department organized a strike seeking union rights, a fair wage, and better safety standards. The City Council, pressured by a sit in, voted in February of that year to recognize the union and grant a wage increase, but the mayor nullified the council's vote.[2] After police used mace and tear gas against nonviolent demonstrators, support for the sanitation workers' plight expanded, with daily marches occurring by the beginning of March, and over one hundred people were arrested.[3]

Speaking before the workers and their supporters in a crowded church of about twenty-five thousand, the largest indoor gathering of the civil rights movement up to that point, on what would be one of the last days of his life, King made the point that the strike was about "demanding that this city will respect the dignity of labor" for all the contributions such workers add. He famously said, "Whenever you are engaged in work that serves humanity and is for the building of humanity, it has dignity, and it has worth. One day our society will come to respect the sanitation worker if it is to survive, for the person who picks up our garbage, in the final analysis, is as significant as the physician, for if he doesn't do his job, diseases are rampant. All labor has dignity."[4]

Building on the recognition that "all labor has dignity," King called out two essential elements of the economic dignity compact: (1) that it is wrong for people who contribute not to be able to provide a basic standard of living for themselves and their families, and (2) that a true commitment to the equal dignity in all labor requires a commitment to creating conditions that ensure all who do their part are not denied the vital elements of economic dignity. In other words, there must be a vision of positive dignity. King asked,

> Do you know that most of the poor people in our country are working every day? And they are making wages so low that they cannot begin to function in the mainstream of the economic life of our nation . . . it is criminal to have people working on a full-time basis and a full-time job getting part-time income. You are here tonight to demand that Memphis will do something about the conditions that our brothers face as they work day in and day out for the well-being of the total community.

True dignity for all workers could not be realized, King stated, without the affirmative conditions to provide care for family and self, along with other essential elements of economic dignity.

> Now our struggle is for genuine equality, which means economic equality. . . . What does it profit one to have access to the hotels of our city and the motels of our highway when we don't earn enough money to take our family on a vacation? What does it profit one to be able to attend an integrated school when he doesn't earn enough money to buy his children school clothes?[5]

This strike called not only for a recognition of the dignity of all work, but also for actual policies at the city level that would make that recognition a reality for all who contributed to the economic life of the country. King said, "Now is the time to make real the promises of democracy. . . . Now is the time for city hall to take a position for that which is just and honest."[6]

FDR AND THE COMPACT OF CONTRIBUTION

As discussed earlier, economic dignity should involve a compact of contribution. We should be, of course, too humane a nation to let anyone starve or go without basic care regardless of their effort or circumstances. A moral nation should not allow children to live in poverty for any reason. So we should devise policy to support that basic humanity under all circumstances. But it is a mistake not to see the deep connection and unifying power in a compact of contribution: that each of us is expected to contribute to the best of our capacity, to pull our share of the load. A compassionate and smart compact of contribution organizes policy to encourage and enable all who can contribute in any way to do so, and provides the support to make it happen. Such policies should not be constructed as an arbitrary test to punish and deny benefits or to fuel resentment. Rather, they should be based on a commitment to affirmative government efforts to support and give every opportunity to every American to experience the sense of dignity that comes from adding value and pursuing purpose.

This compact of contribution requires a broadening and strengthening of what those who do their part can rightly expect in terms of economic security, opportunity, and dignity. Indeed, much of the economic dissatisfaction that exists today is not that people are expected to work or in some way contribute and do their part. The disillusionment emanates far more from a sense that people played by the rules and did everything that was expected of them but were nevertheless denied a basic degree of economic dignity—in terms of caring for family, having the capacity to pursue potential, and having second chances—that they thought they had earned. This indeed may be the great disappointment in the modern economy or modern capitalism today. An economic dignity compact must expand both what we offer to all people to help them do their part, and what those who do can rightly expect in terms of economic security, opportunity, and dignity. Two points underscore the importance of this idea.

First, the sense of social compact of contribution has deep roots in our national character. Like MLK's vision, FDR's New Deal vision was deeply rooted in the expansion of the two-way compact of contribution that asked individuals who could to carry their weight in exchange for a broader government guarantee of economic dignity in being able to care for family. FDR stated, "The Federal Government has no intention or desire to force either upon the country or the unemployed themselves a system of relief which is repugnant to American ideals of individual self-reliance."[7] In his book on FDR, Cass Sunstein points out that New Deal policymakers were willing to opt for "employment relief" even if it was more expensive than pure cash relief, as it honored the sense of a social compact "and was preferred by both the administration and recipients alike."[8] Frances Perkins wrote in *The Roosevelt I Knew* about the discussion within the Roosevelt White House of the resistance to just a handout strategy "when Americans wanted, above everything, to work and contribute."[9] She wrote of a favorite story that was "not lost on Roosevelt" of an elderly man getting $15 a week in relief who "went out regularly, without being asked, to sweep the streets of his village. 'I want to do something in return for what I get,' he said."[10]

When FDR first accepted the Democratic nomination, he spoke to the notion that the capacity to both work and care for family was core to his entire reconstruction policy:

> What do the people of America want more than anything else? To my mind they want two things: work, with all the moral and spiritual values that go with it; and, with work, a reasonable measure of security— security for themselves and for those who depend upon them. Work and security—these are the spiritual values, the true goal toward which our efforts for reconstruction should lead.[11]

Second, this social compact of contribution has the capacity to be a unifying force. There is no question that the concept of having to work to earn support has often been used as a mean-spirited way to exclude people who face health or economic barriers as an "undeserving" other. There has certainly been a failure to recognize the legitimate obstacles that limit the capacity of individuals to do their part, and to give them a helping hand up rather than callously deny them support. Yet the concept of a widely adhered to compact of contribution can also be unifying and humanizing. It can be a frame through which all people of our nation see the common values and humanity among people of different races, ethnicities, geographies, and political ideologies in a diverse nation like ours. This is especially the case when significant general revenues for the expansion of positive dignity are required. The more it is seen as furthering widely shared values of a compact of contribution, the more it can strengthen public support and diminish the degree it can be painted in ways designed to fuel resentment.

Consider Social Security. It was by no means a commitment to simply give old people money. It was instead rooted in a desire to prevent the devastating loss of economic dignity for older people precisely because such older Americans had done their part. The notion that so many Americans could work hard, sacrifice for their family and nation, and carry their load for their whole lives and yet still die on the streets defied an intrinsic sense of economic dignity. In addressing the Teamsters on September 11, 1940, FDR argued for "our old-age pension system . . . to be increased" but that "above all, these pensions must be given in a manner that will respect the *dignity of the life of service and labor which our aged citizens have given to the nation*" (emphasis added).[12] FDR felt that an explicit compact—that workers were contributing to earn a dignified retirement—would strengthen the longevity of Social Security because the design relied on the power of an earned and shared compact of contribution. FDR would later say to a critic, "We put those payroll contributions there so as to give the contributors a legal, moral, and political right to collect their pensions and their unemployment benefits. With those taxes in there, no damn politician can ever scrap my social security program."[13]

The values of this two-way compact of contribution were later relied upon by the first Republican president to succeed FDR to justify from a conservative frame continuing and expanding this crown jewel of progressive government, rather than seeking to dismantle it. In defending expansions of Social Security under his administration, Eisenhower stated:

> Retirement systems, by which individuals contribute to their own security according to their own respective abilities, have become an essential part of our economic and social life. These systems are but a reflection of the American heritage of sturdy self-reliance which has made our country strong and kept it free; the self-reliance without which we would have had no Pilgrim Fathers, no hardship-defying pioneers, and no eagerness today to push to ever widening horizons in

every aspect of our national life. The Social Security program fur-
nishes, on a national scale, the opportunity for our citizens, through
that same self-reliance, to build the foundation for their security. We
are resolved to extend that opportunity to millions of our citizens who
heretofore have been unable to avail themselves of it.[14]

This sense of a unifying compact of contribution was at the heart of President Clinton's case for expanding the earned income tax credit (EITC) and
the expansion and endurance of refundable tax credits tied to work over the
last twenty-five years. While conservatives sought to frame and deride the
EITC and the concept of refundable tax credits as "welfare" for "lucky duckies," Clinton was able to frame the case for the EITC expansions by rooting it
deeply in the values of a two-way social compact of contribution.[15] He pledged
to "ensure that no one with a family who works full-time has to raise their
children in poverty."[16] In doing so, he was essentially asking middle-class voters to see a shared value in the struggles and aspirations of lower-income
families, disproportionately of color, that would motivate middle-class support for a big EITC increase even though it went by definition to lower-income
workers. Clinton's frame has also been used by progressives from Barack
Obama to Bernie Sanders, and had lasting benefits.[17] Beyond the EITC battles
of the 1990s, winning the definition of the EITC as tax relief connected to
work and caring for family has dramatically reduced the partisan attacks on
it, set the frame for expansion of refundable relief in child tax credits, and
even led to some Republican policymakers now embracing at least targeted
expansions.

BROADENING—NOT DISMISSING—
A COMPACT OF CONTRIBUTION

While I believe it would be a setback to reaching the end goal of economic
dignity to upend this sense of mutual responsibility, I also do not believe that
only full-time work or traditional jobs should be seen as the only means of
fulfilling that responsibility. The value inherent in this sense of a dignity
compact of contribution is less specifically about traditional work than it is

about "doing your part" or "carrying your share of the load." Even as FDR prepared his Second Bill of Rights, he and his advisers explicitly described individual responsibility in the social compact as going beyond just work. Instead, they spoke to "the right to . . . command the necessities and amenities of life in exchange for work, *ideas, thrift and other socially valuable service*" (emphasis added).[18]

Strengthening and modernizing an economic dignity compact should mean recognizing where unpaid forms of contribution, service, and "doing your part" deserve more financial support—and then figuring out the best policy levers to do so. For example, there was recently a bipartisan expansion of a program that provides nontaxable stipends to family caregivers of injured veterans,[19] as well as a bipartisan push at federal and state levels to offset the thousands of dollars in out-of-pocket expenses family caregivers frequently accrue.[20] A modernized social compact of contribution would go further, for example, in making sure those serving the role of unpaid family caregivers to those with serious conditions or challenges are supported with compensation, training, community resources, and breaks to prevent burnout. Family caregivers are increasingly eligible for pay from Medicaid and veteran health programs, especially when they prevent more expensive forms of care. There is an important discussion emerging at both the national and state levels to consider how our current tax credits—from the child tax credit, to the child and dependent care credit, to the EITC—should be extended or made more refundable to ensure financial support for certain forms of unpaid caregiving. The UBI to Rise proposal advocated here is an example of a call for income support for periods when Americans are trying to actively invest in their education, future jobs, and careers.

We also now see and should support efforts to provide credit toward Social Security benefits for lost wages due to caring for loved ones—whether a spouse, child, parent, sibling, or other close family member.[21] An estimated 61 percent of the forty million Americans providing unpaid caregiving for an adult relative made changes in their paid work lives—like cutting back hours or taking a leave of absence—to accommodate their unpaid caregiving role, or received a warning about their attendance.[22] The effect of lost earnings due to caregiving brings down wages paid toward Social Security, especially for women, as they often take on a greater share of caregiving responsibilities.[23] A 2011 study found that men and women who reduced work hours to care for parents received about $38,000 and $64,000 less, respectively, in Social Security benefits, with losses substantially higher if they left the workforce entirely.[24] The United States lags behind most industrialized countries in offering credits for caregiving when calculating retirement benefits. The United Kingdom and Germany offer credits for caregiving for children as well as for aging and sick relatives.[25] More steps need to be taken along these lines to broaden our understanding of contribution beyond paid employment as part of strengthening our social compact.

Is there dignity in all work? Words matter. Respect for all who work is an imperative. But without a true compact of contribution that allows people to care for their families, pursue their purpose and potential, and have protections against mistreatment, words alone will never be enough.

CHAPTER TEN

THE EMPTY PROMISE OF "DIGNITY OF WORK" CONSERVATIVES

If all that mattered for a true compact on economic dignity were words, there might be hope of a new bipartisan convergence on the dignity of work. There may be no more current textbook example of failing the test of a two-way compact on dignity and work, as Martin Luther King Jr. so powerfully defined it, than the rise of dignity rhetoric among a handful of conservative senators and commentators. In addition to progressives like Joe Biden, Sherrod Brown, and Cory Booker, conservative senators Ben Sasse and Marco Rubio, as well as the former president of the conservative American Enterprise Institute Arthur C. Brooks, have all been associated with promoting "the dignity of work."

Brooks writes that "to feel dignified, one must be needed by others,"[1] and, invoking MLK directly, claims "ordinary work is a key driver of dignity for most people."[2] Similarly, Senator Sasse often invokes the American commitment to "inexhaustible, inviolable dignity."[3] Senator Rubio has said "the key challenge of our time is to conserve the classic American institution of dignified work."[4] Glenn Hubbard—former chairman of the Council of Economic Advisers under President George W. Bush and my frequent debating partner—acknowledges the "concerns about dignity" for workers in areas that have experienced industrial decline.[5] Former Manhattan Institute scholar Oren Cass, while not focusing on dignity, has stepped forward in thoughtfully encouraging conservatives to relax market orthodoxy and put less emphasis on GDP.[6]

So do we see a coming convergence at least with these Dignity of Work Conservatives around the imperative to promote policies to ensure a degree of economic dignity? Unfortunately, at the moment the answer is no. Not even close.

With limited exceptions, the conservatives mentioned are a classic case of those talking the talk but not walking the walk. I draw this conclusion not because, as conservatives, they approach economic issues with a greater focus on self-reliance or a larger skepticism of government and faith in markets than I do. I draw this conclusion because of the degree to which they highlight the dignity of work and then actively oppose, cast aside, or seek to set back nearly all policies that would support people's economic dignity— from the minimum wage to health-care protections to affordable food to bargaining power in the workplace—if they conflict even slightly with a rigid and preset ideological framework.

There are no Teddy Roosevelts here. Not so far, anyway. No conservatives willing to see the actual policy gaps that diminish economic dignity, and charge forward to solve them, regardless of whether it conflicts with conservative ideology about the desire to minimize government. The single affirmative policy to reward work that some of the Dignity of Work Conservatives have toyed with supporting is wage subsidies or small increases in the EITC— but even that support has been modest, and clearly not a high priority, as no one heard conservative howls at its complete exclusion from the nearly $2 trillion tax cut Republicans enacted in 2017.[7]

FAILING TO CREATE A TRUE COMPACT OF CONTRIBUTION

For the Dignity of Work Conservatives, dignity might be first in rhetoric, but it quickly takes a back seat almost every time to the ideology of market fundamentalism and small government. When it comes to actual policies, dignity loses out every time.

For example, while both Brooks and Sasse speak of dignity as a "need to be needed," they then brush by the assault on economic dignity many working parents feel due to not being able to meet their families' needs. Consider that the Dignity of Work Conservatives uniformly oppose any increase in the minimum wage, and some suggest even the current $7.25 an hour is unnecessary.[8] It is bizarre to use the claims, as Senator Rubio does, that "having a job that pays $10 an hour is not the American dream" and that Americans "can't live on $11 an hour" as a rationale for opposing any increase in the minimum wage for those with the least power and resources.[9] Most making $7.25 an hour would likely agree that $11 is not enough, but my guess is that those working full time would argue the extra $7,500 a year would help enormously—not to mention what a $15 minimum wage would do. A higher minimum wage would seem like the very least a conservative promoting the dignity of work could support. After all, a higher minimum wage does not increase the size of government or spending. And a higher minimum wage does not offend any values of self-sufficiency, as the increase will benefit only those who work.

The opposition to any higher minimum wage is powerful evidence that these Dignity of Work Conservatives' devotion is to market orthodoxy and minimalist government—not to helping people who work hard have the dignity of caring for family. *These are workers whose fundamental dignity gap is not that they "need to be needed," but that they are needed by the people they love and treasure the most in life and cannot fulfill those needs.* Compare this to Teddy Roosevelt, who two decades before the Depression or the New Deal called for "a living wage" that is "high enough to make morality possible, to provide for education and recreation, to care for immature members of the family, to maintain the family during periods of sickness, and to permit of reasonable saving for old age."[10]

Senators Rubio and Sasse vote consistently in opposition to expanded Trade Adjustment Assistance (TAA).[11] This is striking in that TAA is the federal government's only (and already underfunded) program to support workers in the communities harmed by trade and globalization often described by conservatives as taking dignity hits from being forgotten. To his credit, Hubbard acknowledges that "a government role" is needed to support "people that got left behind" by trade and the long-term unemployed, because the private sector will not make those investments, and that such investments "would require . . . taxes to pay for them."[12] And Cass has supported affirmative pro-manufacturing investments.[13]

This unfortunately is evidence that such conservative calls for "dignity of work" are generally just a kinder packaging for the more traditional punitive work compact favored by the right. Consider that while neither Sasse nor Rubio has been willing to defy market purism enough to call for a minimum wage increase critical to vulnerable workers supporting their families, they have had no problem calling for additional regulation when it has involved denying food or disability relief to those not meeting arbitrary work requirements.[14] Rather than a compact of contribution that asks what we can do to ensure that all can overcome barriers to work and contribution, the value of work is used simply as a pretext for often arbitrary designations of many struggling Americans as unworthy and undeserving.

Consider where we started this book: on the enormous assault on economic dignity when working parents cannot provide health care for their loved ones facing serious illness without risk of economic devastation. These parents feel desperately needed by their children. Their economic dignity is denied when they cannot care for the serious illness or disability of a loved one without bankrupting their families. This threat to economic dignity is directly due to a lack of adequate coverage, lifetime and annual limits on how much insurers will pay for critical care, limits on families' out-of-pocket costs, or price discrimination against those with preexisting conditions.[15] Take just one example of what this means. In October 2018, I spoke at the kickoff of the Nuns on the Bus tour with Sister Simone Campbell, Nancy Pelosi, Joe Sanberg, and nine-year-old Myka Eiler and her mom, Angela. Myka was born with a congenital heart defect and had two open heart surgeries before she was one year old. The family's health insurance was put at risk when Angela's husband was laid off, but because of the ACA, he was able to start his own business and still get coverage through the individual insurance market without facing discrimination based on Myka's serious health condition and high expenses. Without the ACA, Angela said, Myka would already be more than halfway to her lifetime cap on health expenses, and the family would likely have lost their home and business. Could there be any deeper dignity, "need to be needed," than Angela and her husband's need as parents to ensure their daughter can receive the health care she needs?

A conservative dedicated to a sincere dignity-of-work agenda could have at least taken a strong, clear position on health issues like ironclad protections against denial of coverage or discrimination on health prices or access due to the health conditions of loved ones. From an economic dignity perspective this would have been the least one could do.

However, none of the Dignity of Work Conservatives have been champions of preventing health discrimination based on preexisting conditions or ending lifetime limits on coverage. Instead, they have been in lockstep with conservative attempts to repeal the Affordable Care Act and its protections against discrimination based on preexisting conditions, prohibition on lifetime and annual limits, and subsidies to keep health care affordable. While three Republican senators—Susan Collins, Lisa Murkowski, and most dramatically, John McCain—refused to simply vote to repeal the Affordable Care Act in 2017, Senators Sasse and Rubio supported the effort all the way through.[16] The final bill Sasse and Rubio voted for would have "driv[en] up premiums and endanger[ed] the protections for people with preexisting medical conditions over time," as the Center on Budget and Policy Priorities noted at the time.[17] Rubio even claimed credit for leading the charge to eliminate the ACA provision that was specifically designed to prevent health-care plans in the new ACA marketplace from facing too much downside risk, frequently due to taking on clients who were disproportionally older, sicker, or had preexisting conditions.[18] It is striking to elevate the dignity of work, and then work against working parents who only want to not have their health-care costs jacked up or coverage denied because they have a child or spouse with a serious health condition.

Childcare provides another example where the Dignity of Work Conservatives' policy fails to match their stated concerns. Many conservatives have sought to argue against robust benefits for hard-pressed Americans on the unproven view that it would discourage work as their higher earnings reduced benefits and led to what they called high marginal tax rates on work.[19] Yet childcare costs actually represent the highest marginal tax rate on work that many low-income families face, because the high costs of providing care for children while working can soak up a large share of the earnings from work. But when it comes to childcare subsidies, we too often hear crickets or pure opposition from the Dignity of Work Conservatives. Indeed, just as conservatives have failed to put forward a serious proposal to achieve universal health-care coverage, so, too, have they failed to propose a serious plan to achieve universally affordable childcare for all parents.

Several of Senator Rubio's dignity proposals have a particularly unsettling attribute of increasing Peter's economic dignity only by sacrificing Paul's or future Peter's economic security. Rubio, to his credit, has been better than most Republicans on making the child tax credit more refundable for lower-income families. However, Rubio's proposal to expand the EITC for workers without children recognized the need for higher take-home pay for low-wage workers but then proposed paying for it by *cutting* the EITC for working parents trying to support their children.[20] In addition, Rubio claims to want to address the dignity gap whereby only 4 percent of very low-wage private sector earners have paid family leave following the birth or adoption of a child,[21] yet his free-market fundamentalism leads him to oppose a mandate on employers to provide paid leave or a small national tax that would fund a government-provided leave program. Instead, Rubio proposes allowing workers to take from their future Social Security benefits after the birth or adoption of a child—effectively forcing a trade-off between their immediate dignity needs to care for family and their future need for a dignified retirement.[22] Much was made of the small concession the Trump/GOP tax bill made to temporarily provide a tax credit for some employers who provide paid family leave, but that policy's design still leaves workers entirely at their employer's mercy for whether they provide paid leave or not and mainly subsidizes companies that already provide benefits. The insistence on promoting gains in economic dignity only by diminishing dignity from others can hardly be explained by an ironclad commitment to fiscal discipline. All the Dignity of Work Conservatives supported increasing the debt by nearly $2 trillion in the 2017 tax law, even when a large amount of the benefits went to the largest corporations and the most well-off Americans.[23]

Or consider Rubio's and Cass's policies on unions and collective bargaining. Rubio correctly acknowledges "the essential role of labor unions"[24] and says that "unions have historically served as an integrating force for the dignity of work."[25] But in the same breath, Rubio endorses policies designed to reduce if not decimate even the existing power of unions to bond together and protect the dignity of their members. Rubio supports Oren Cass's proposal for entirely voluntary "labor co-ops" that, as proposed, would make "negotiable" a raft of labor laws that are set up to protect spheres of dignity.[26] Even against the backdrop of the rise of inequality, the fall of unions, and the decline in labor's share of economic output the past several decades, Rubio supports Cass's policy, which is to "improve the [bargaining] position of the employer by design"—as if the central policy problem in the labor market is too much power in the hands of workers.[27] "Most employment regulation"— such as the minimum wage, mandated sick and family leave, break time, and overtime and workplace safety protections—"should be negotiable" between these co-ops and employers, according to the proposal.[28] Despite widespread retirement insecurity, the solution is that "defined-benefit pensions should be set explicitly outside the protection of federal insurance" so that workers must "bet" on their employers' solvency if they want such plans.[29] There may be alternative ideas of labor co-ops that might be worth exploring. Yet, as currently designed, these reforms turn back the clock from the protections for negative dignity in the private sector that grew out of the Progressive Era and were designed to ensure that the most vulnerable workers were not overwhelmed by the market power of employers.

A NARROW VISION OF PEOPLE SUFFERING

Some Dignity of Work Conservatives focus on the real policy neglect that many—particularly working-class white males—have felt in especially hardhit manufacturing and coal communities, or could feel through technological disruptions like autonomous vehicles. They are certainly correct to draw attention to such neglect. But too often, their deployment of the need for "dignity" seems reserved for this limited segment of the population. And, having raised the sense of neglect, they call for precious few tangible policies that could remedy such dignity gaps.

Much of the conservative rhetorical focus on dignity emerged in the shadow of Trump's victory. Brooks's writings on dignity were motivated by his observation that "Trump won . . . because he was the first major-party nominee in decades who even appeared to care about the dignity of these working-class voters whose lives are falling apart"—these being the "communities where [dignity] is most absent."[30] Hubbard emphasizes the need to address "concerns about dignity that neither party had addressed" for those in the "heartland who played by the rules" and have been left behind, like factory workers in towns experiencing economic decline.[31] Sasse emphasizes the threat of "cultural disruption" to those like truck drivers from automation, likening it to the decline of the coal industry in Appalachia.[32]

It is of course right and important to recognize any group of Americans who might have been invisible to policymakers and the media—including those white, working-class Americans hurt by trade and downward cycles in major factory towns and communities.

Both politicians and journalists need to be careful, however, not to elevate a universal theme like dignity and then seem to focus on only one segment of the population while offering few broad-based solutions. It runs the danger of feeding, even unintentionally, a more divisive dignity—to be discussed in the Conclusion. When we speak of the need for dignity of work, we should recognize at every turn that its denial is felt by varied groups across our nation. Yes, this should include the families in small, rural towns and manufacturing communities and the harder hit sections of Appalachia and the millions of mostly men whose jobs as truck drivers could be put at risk by automation and driverless cars.[33] But such discussions of dignity gaps must always include the diverse segments of our country that face denials of economic dignity. Certainly, this should include the millions struggling in lower-wage service jobs, such as pre-gig-economy workers—often minority women who care for households and the elderly—and poor children whose chances to pursue potential are deeply diminished by the accident of birth. Focusing on the dignity gaps of certain groups also misses the universal power of appeals to economic dignity: to help draw on unifying values and desire to care for family, pursue purpose and potential, and participate economically with respect.

Indeed, the danger of highlighting the dignity gaps of only specific demographics is enhanced when conservatives fail to match these calls with any serious policy responses to help those hard-hit workers or to take more universal steps to expand true first and second chances in the economy. The irony is deep. The small-government obsession of such conservatives has been one of the most stubborn obstacles to the type of targeted and broad-based economic and health policies that could have at least partially addressed the economic pain and loss of opportunity of so many who the conservatives now focus on in these discussions.

These criticisms of empty words by Dignity of Work Conservatives may seem harsh. But my words are designed to be more of a challenge than a condemnation. Arthur Brooks, for example, is a friend with a big heart whom I have seen repeatedly speak with passion in challenging other conservatives to acknowledge and address poverty. I have heard Senator Rubio speak with eloquence and emotion about the plight of minority children born into economic disadvantage and those like his own mother doing hard household work, even later in her life, to support her family. Senator Sasse speaks with nuance, intelligence, and concern about the likely economic and emotional plight of those who might be impacted by autonomous vehicle technology. Yet as impressive as each of these figures can be in their words, their policy actions never fail to disappoint. Simply put, they are unwilling to follow the logical policy consequences of their call for the dignity of work. They are unflaggingly unwilling to use their power to enact real policy solutions, because doing so would conflict with their preset ideology on small government and markets. I hope they someday realize that Teddy Roosevelt is chiseled into Mount Rushmore not because he let himself be boxed into his party's ideological purity, but because he was willing to see the real-world assaults on dignity faced by workers in a new economic era and put forward solutions focused on solving them—even if those solutions were ideologically out of the box. Are there modern Dignity of Work Conservatives? Not yet.

CHAPTER ELEVEN

AN ECONOMIC DIGNITY WAGE

Treating everyone who works or contributes in any way with dignity matters. But to paraphrase Martin Luther King Jr., even overcoming the indignity of being denied a seat at the lunch counter can be a cold victory if you cannot afford to buy your family a meal. We need more than words.

At long last, we need to commit to the ideal that those who do the best they can to work hard and pull their weight should be able to care and be there for family, and to live with a basic degree of economic dignity—and not just as an ideal but as a reality. We can't say there is dignity in all work but not a dignity wage for all work.

There are no doubt fiscal and labor market challenges to achieving such a goal. There will likely be no single silver bullet. There may be complexity in how we best combine wage and benefit policies and government subsidies and investment. We need to reward effort and contribution without cruel or punitive tests, while ensuring a stronger income floor for people with disabilities, and that no children are raised in devastating poverty. But no complexity or challenge can be an excuse any longer for allowing millions of Americans who do their part in a compact of contribution to live without a basic level of economic dignity. Failure cannot be an option. If we want the dignity of work to be a reality and not an empty promise, work must pay enough to allow all workers to care for their families without economic deprivation or extreme hours blocking them from being there and enjoying the precious moments of loving relationships.

This is hardly a new or radical concept. Even free-market champion Adam Smith said centuries ago, "They who feed, clothe, and lodge the whole body of the people, should have such a share of the produce of their own labor as to be themselves tolerably well fed, clothed, and lodged."[1] In *The Wealth of Nations,* he wrote that even for the lowest-skilled worker there must be a wage "consistent with common humanity" and that "a man must always live by his work, and his wages must at least be sufficient to maintain him . . . otherwise it would be impossible for him to bring up a family."[2] As noted earlier, in 1912, Teddy Roosevelt called for "a living wage" that was robust enough to ensure that workers have reasonable time off and enough resources to provide for young children, retirement, and periods of illness.[3]

Just over two decades later, FDR struck the same notes when he stated it is "plain that no business which depends for existence on paying less than living wages to its workers has any right to continue in this country." FDR was clear that "by workers I mean all workers, the white collar class as well as the men in overalls; and *by living wages I mean more than a bare subsistence level—I mean the wages of decent living*" (emphasis added).[4] It is long past time to turn these principles into reality for all workers.

I. ECONOMIC DIGNITY PURCHASING POWER

The first place to start in reaching this goal is to understand that what constitutes an economic dignity wage cannot be determined by simply looking at the size of one's paycheck. Whether we can say there is a true economic dignity wage requires looking at whether the entire set of resources together—taking into account wages, employer- or government-provided benefits, taxes, government subsidies, and public investments—allows a household to afford the foundations of economic dignity. Does a person have the capacity to ensure those aspects of life most critical to caring for family—stable housing, decent food, health care, childcare, retirement security—can be affordably achieved? Think of it as "economic dignity purchasing power" (EDPP).

While it is easy to look at wages or tax burdens or income grants in isolation, EDPP reflects the core notion that we must aim to achieve the end state of economic dignity for people through the culmination of all our policies.

This is most obvious for people who get a higher wage at a new job, but find they get no health and retirement benefits. Their paychecks are higher, but their capacity to ensure the most important foundations of caring for themselves and their families may have fallen. Or consider a working parent whose taxes go up by $1,000 to pay for a public childcare program that lowers their bills by $2,000. Their disposable income has gone down, but their EDPP has increased. Similarly, Social Security takes money out of each paycheck, but because of its progressive benefit structure, for most people it buys more retirement security and disability insurance down the road than the dollars set aside up front. The very good deal it provides in expanding dignified retirements makes Social Security a net plus for EDPP. While there are no doubt political consequences and calculations that are understandably considered by policymakers in whether certain costs are labeled a "tax" or "fee" or "premium" or "mandatory contribution," EDPP cuts to the chase: Does the policy at stake help or hurt workers' capacity to care for family with dignity? What matters most for an end goal of economic dignity is the degree that the combination of all our policies—income, taxes, incentives, subsidies, and public investments—affect Americans' EDPP.

An EDPP approach can also help give us insight into why, even when many working families see their real wages (adjusted for inflation) technically rising, they can feel like they are falling behind or running in place. If all of us were the typical family or the typical worker buying the typical basket of goods and services for our families, then a 1 percent increase in real wages would mean our EDPP had risen. But what if there is something vital to our capacity to care for our families—childcare, food, prescription drugs, rent, college tuition—where the costs are both rising unusually fast and are an outsized percentage of our family budget?

This is the case for millions of families. Consider those who may live in areas with a serious lack of affordable housing, which leads to their rent taking a higher than typical percentage of their budget, with higher than typical rent increases? Or those with young children in so-called childcare deserts? Or families with two children in college who find tuition rising at extremely high rates due to state budget shortfalls? In each of those cases and many more, despite the fact that their real wages may be rising, they rightly feel their

EDPP has decreased and they are falling behind. And as Matthew Desmond writes, expenses can be even higher in poorer communities—for example, groceries in inner cities can cost as much as 40 percent more—which further reduces EDPP for those families.[5] Xavier Jaravel, an economist at the London School of Economics, analyzed the rate of inflation of retail products and found that the goods purchased by low-income families had annual inflation rates about a half percentage point higher than goods purchased by higher-income families.[6] Annie Lowrey described in the *Atlantic* this growing focus on "inflation inequality."[7] If this analysis holds up, it could mean poverty has actually gotten worse than the picture shown by conventional inflation metrics.

All of this can be exacerbated further if you are aware that your parents and previous generations were able to afford the building blocks of economic dignity with similar or lower wages. The sense of falling behind or failing to rise in the way Americans have long expected is especially painful.

These challenges suggest that when families complain that they are worse off—perhaps even despite having a small increase in their income—they are not necessarily "economic hypochondriacs," as George Will put it.[8] Instead, it may reflect their high level of expertise at assessing their own EDPP.

II. AN ECONOMIC DIGNITY WAGE

When I was the economic policy director for the Clinton presidential campaign in 1992 in Little Rock, Arkansas, James Carville famously put up a sign in the "war room" with our three rules: CHANGE VS. MORE OF THE SAME. THE ECONOMY, STUPID. DON'T FORGET HEALTH CARE.[9]

To achieve a true economic dignity wage for all Americans, we need an analogous three-pronged approach: the dynamic duo of a robust minimum wage and an expanded earned income tax credit (EITC)—but don't forget about childcare. The minimum wage and EITC are complementary tools that both put cash directly in the pockets of workers to help them care for family. While it is critical to understand there are many economic costs that can serve as barriers to work—like transportation costs—childcare costs operate as the largest regressive tax on work and must be part of the equation.

STEP 1: A BOLD MINIMUM WAGE INCREASE

A robust minimum wage is the unique policy that is essential for the promotion of both negative and positive dignity. As former Supreme Court justice Felix Frankfurter observed, a minimum wage is a protection against pure domination and dehumanization in cases where workers' limited job options and desperation to care for family could allow an employer to force them to work for starvation wages.[10] It is also integral to positive dignity—the actions government must take to ensure that a person has the capability to affirmatively care for self and family and still enjoy the most meaningful moments of family life. Since the federal minimum wage was first established in the Fair Labor Standards Act (FLSA) of 1938, it has been linked to achieving a higher standard of living and increasing workers' purchasing power. As FDR explained, "Without question [FLSA] starts us toward a better standard of living and increases purchasing power to buy the products of farm and factory."[11]

While the call for an economic dignity wage requires the combination of a bolder minimum wage plus a wage supplement like an expanded EITC, there is little question that a higher minimum wage is the Batman in this dynamic duo for several reasons. Cash wages are still a worker's biggest-ticket item, accounting for about two-thirds of total resources the average household has full choice of how to spend.[12] The sense of a living wage for a hard day's work runs deep in the American value set and character. The minimum wage raises incomes without competing for the dollars from our nation's general revenue that are also needed to fund other vital investments in economic dignity. It is "pre-distribution," in the words of Yale political scientist Jacob Hacker.[13] The minimum wage is in essence a market structure rule: it structures competition to ensure a sphere of economic dignity—a wage that creates the capacity to care for family and, as Smith said, is "consistent with common humanity."

Unfortunately, the current federal minimum wage is disgraceful even by historic standards. If we were doing nothing more aspirational than restoring the minimum wage's value to its 1968 level, it would be over $10 as opposed to today's $7.25 level.[14]

Much of the opposition to a higher minimum wage comes on purely

ideological grounds—as we have seen, even from those conservatives who es-
pouse the "dignity of work" vision and from those seeking to protect business
profit margins. But it has also long been couched in the politically potent
name of "protecting jobs." From the time I started in the White House in
January 1993, even proponents of raising the minimum wage seemed to accept that if opponents could win the analytic and public debate, a higher
minimum wage would lead to fewer jobs in the economy, it was game, set,
and match. This is yet another example of how economic policymaking has
been held hostage by untested market fundamentalist assumptions and the
privileging of a specific economic metric without a deeper inquiry into what
policy would be best from a broader economic dignity perspective.

This case for the minimum wage increases got a strong boost in the 1990s
when economists started to test whether the purist market assumption—that
under traditional supply-and-demand economics, if the "price" of low-wage
labor increased, demand for labor would fall—was actually true. In 1993, two
Princeton economists, David Card and Alan Krueger, published a famous
study that shook the economic policy world. The Card-Krueger study analyzed what happened when New Jersey raised its minimum wage from $4.25
to $5.05 in 1992, while neighboring Pennsylvania maintained a $4.25 floor.[15]
To test the traditional theory that the minimum wage trades higher earnings
for fewer overall jobs, they examined low-wage fast-food chains along both
sides of the state line before and after New Jersey's minimum wage hike. They
found that, contrary to the conventional wisdom, the New Jersey restaurants
increased employment 13 percent, more than in comparable restaurants in
Pennsylvania. Why? Higher wages led to a more stable, better-motivated
workforce—delivering enough benefits and reduced recruitment costs to justify increasing employment.

Study after study has only bolstered this conclusion. As the Economic
Policy Institute (EPI) has summarized, the "overwhelming conclusion of [the
extensive] literature has been that past increases in minimum wages have had
little to no effect on employment."[16] In an important 2019 analysis, economists Doruk Cengiz, Arindrajit Dube, Attila Lindner, and Ben Zipperer
evaluated 138 state minimum wage changes over nearly four decades and

found "the overall number of low-wage jobs remained essentially unchanged over five years following the increase."[17] In another 2019 study, University of California, Berkeley, economists Anna Godoey and Michael Reich concluded that "the U.S. can raise the minimum wage to $15 without significant job loss, even in low-wage states."[18] These studies are reinforced by the fact that Fight for $15's inspiring wins in cities and states across the country have not seemed to cause major job loss or other harm to their economies.[19]

While those of us supporting a higher minimum wage have rigorous research on our side on the job loss question, that should not mean we buy into the assumption that if increasing the minimum wage was shown to cause some marginal reduction in demand for job hours, that should automatically rule out such policies. Yes, it should be part of the analysis. And of course, a hike in the minimum wage so bold that it was projected to cause a massive reduction in the demand for labor would very likely go too far. But the idea that any impact on the demand for labor should shut down consideration of a specific minimum wage hike should cease. First of all, as EPI has suggested, even in some situations where there might be marginal reduction in demand for labor, the "more likely scenario" is that those "lost hours are spread among the affected workers, who work a little less but earn more per year."[20] If that is the case, then it is a win for economic dignity to work less, make more, and have more time with loved ones.

More fundamentally, a small reduction in demand for job hours must be balanced against the enormous benefit to the moral fabric of our nation and to tens of millions of workers from at last having a true economic dignity wage. This would be the realization of the vision expressed from the start of the labor movement through the Fight for $15 that a hard day's work deserves a living wage and the ability to care for family with economic dignity.

Our policy choice should never be seen as either ensuring a living wage or protecting jobs. There are several policies in our toolbox that enable us to do both. If at some point in the future the evidence showed that a very robust minimum wage was creating too much risk of job loss, we could lean more on wage supplements like the EITC that add nothing to employer costs. A bold minimum wage increase could be packaged together with initiatives to create hundreds of thousands, or even millions, of new jobs through a dramatic expansion of national service, green jobs, or the "double-dignity jobs" I discuss in Chapter Thirteen. A strict assumption of job versus minimum wage trade-offs defies the rigorous research and suggests a lack of imagination about policy design and the multiple tools at our disposal.

STEP 2: A MAJOR EITC EXPANSION

While the minimum wage might be the Batman of the dynamic duo needed for an economic dignity wage, the EITC is a very consequential Robin. The EITC is a tax credit that bumps up the income of the most hard-pressed workers in our nation. Its main innovation is that it is refundable—meaning if your tax credit is supposed to be $2,000, then you would receive the full $2,000 even if you owed less than that in federal income taxes. While for decades many conservatives decried this "refundability" as a giveaway, many now see its value as offsetting payroll and state and local taxes and the cost of going to work.

I am proud to have been the main champion for expanding the EITC on the Clinton economic team and one of the main champions for further increases in the Obama White House. During the Clinton administration, we expanded the EITC for millions by doubling the credit for those with two or more children in 1993 and structured the new child tax credit (CTC) in 1997 so that it would also vastly expand EITC benefits for millions. Winning the public debate on refundable tax credits in the 1990s helped pave the way for President Obama and House leaders like Nancy Pelosi and Rosa DeLauro to successfully push—and continue to push—for making at least part of the CTC refundable, a position even some Republicans now support.

The cumulative impact of the piece-by-piece increases is no small step. In 1993, if anyone had suggested that it was possible to provide a worker making $17,000 with two children an income boost of $7,000 through policies like the EITC, it would have been considered an impossible dream. Yet that is exactly the case today, due to the culmination of all the steps forward.[21] Refundable tax credits now lift about nine million people out of poverty each year, including five million children, and help another twenty million people living in poverty do more to make ends meet.[22]

Furthermore, the EITC's reward for work has been linked directly to a feeling of dignity by recipients: the EITC "confers dignity by confirming claimants' identities as workers," "enhance[s] one's feelings of efficacy as a parent, and bring[s] pride in the status of 'worker' and a sense of social inclusion," according to an ethnographic study of EITC recipients by Sarah Halpern-Meekin, Kathryn Edin, Laura Tach, and Jennifer Sykes.[23] The authors also stressed its impact on pursuing potential. The EITC provides recipients "an opportunity to invest in a better future—to set aside money for a rainy day, buy a used car to get to a better job in the suburbs, or pay a semester's tuition at a community college. Maybe they could even manage to save for a down payment on a home, or perhaps treat the kids to something special. In this way, the once-a-year windfall allows poor, hardworking families to dream."[24]

It has not hurt that rigorous studies have shown such widespread benefits to the EITC. Based on significant economic research, the EITC "may ultimately be judged one of the most successful labor market innovations in U.S. history," according to leading anti-poverty scholar Hilary Hoynes.[25] Infants born to mothers with the largest EITC increases had stronger improvements across various health measures, including fewer low-weight births and premature births. Mothers receiving the biggest EITC increases had significant improvements across health indicators such as reduced mental stress, compared with otherwise similarly situated women who were not eligible for the increases. Additionally, EITC increases are linked to better academic outcomes for elementary and middle-school students as well as higher college enrollment for children from working poor families. The overwhelming weight of the evidence, even if not unanimous, has found the EITC has positive labor market effects, including being the biggest factor in the major increase in employment for single mothers in the 1990s.[26]

Yet to lead to a true economic dignity wage, the EITC needs to take a bold step forward with what I call an "EITC for All" proposal.[27] The EITC, together with the minimum wage, needs to create a guaranteed living wage that not only raises every working American above the poverty line but ensures the capacity to care for and enjoy family and to be a greater buffer for economic security for those in the middle class.

The first fix? The EITC does far, far too little for workers who do not have children they are claiming as dependents on their taxes. Since President Clinton created the EITC for so-called childless workers in 1993, it has not been expanded one single time. It tops out at only a bit more than $500 and provides no support to any workers with incomes over $16,000. Consider who this leaves out. A working mom making $16,000 might get up to $6,500 from the EITC when her children are young. When they get to be adults and she is still working, that benefit would shrink to only $50. It means workers who provide support for those they consider their children, like godchildren and grandchildren, but cannot list them as dependents on their tax returns get little or no support. It means it provides zero support to workers without kids if they are younger than twenty-five—and only a few hundred dollars if they are older—so it is virtually meaningless for young workers, particularly those from difficult economic circumstances struggling to find jobs and careers. And though often overlooked, an EITC for All could be a significant economic buffer for older working parents, like a fifty-five-year-old father with adult children who had worked in factories until recently and now takes a lower-paying job.[28]

A robust EITC for all workers could also put an end to taxing people into poverty. Today, more than five million workers are taxed into poverty, mainly because the Social Security and Medicare payroll taxes taken out of their paychecks still exceed any EITC they receive. For working parents with children at home, the generosity of tax credits prevents that from happening. But for those workers claiming no children as dependents, it happens far too often. An EITC for All proposal would fix that.[29]

The second element of an EITC for All is that it must go far higher up the income scale for all families, so it is providing real support well into what are seen as middle-class incomes—in at least the $50,000 to $80,000 range, depending on family size and what is needed to provide adequate EDPP. If we don't enact this type of expansion, a bold minimum wage increase could have the unintended consequence of largely wiping out the EITC for those working full-time. But even more, while there is power in ensuring that those who work full-time do not live in poverty, we must aim higher. An economic dignity wage means more middle-class workers who need support to have a level of security and comfort should receive it—including during the harder times when they take a fall in income. And as discussed in Chapter Nine, the EITC should be one of the policies considered for ensuring we as a country are recognizing the contribution of and providing adequate support to unpaid caregivers.

A CHILD ALLOWANCE FOR TRUE FIRST CHANCES

The contribution-based elements of an economic dignity wage defined here risk leaving a troubling hole. What if, for any reason, a child's parents or guardians have no wages? The EITC, CTC, and child and dependent care tax credit are currently structured so that children in the poorest families— those with little or no earnings—receive very little or no support. This design no doubt contributes to the unacceptably high levels of child poverty and one in twenty children living in *deep* poverty—meaning below half of the poverty line.[30] This reality is not only morally offensive, but a world of evidence confirms extreme childhood poverty makes a mockery of our commitment to the value of first chances.

While some may claim that disconnecting benefits intended to support children from the work effort of parents could have a negative impact on work incentives, as Hilary Hoynes has pointed out, when combined with the type of minimum wage and EITC increases proposed here, such proposals on net would still provide strong incentives for work.[31] Yet regardless of such incentive impacts, our commitment to dignity for all and first chances requires this to be an integral element of an economic dignity agenda. Whether it is through a new child allowance for low-income families or through full refundability for existing tax credits for children and childcare, our values require it.

STEP 3: DON'T FORGET ABOUT CHILDCARE— THE MOST REGRESSIVE TAX ON WORK

But don't forget about childcare.

Even the person most cynical about government could not imagine a room where policymakers conspired to create a special burdensome tax with the following features: the tax would apply solely to parents with younger children and no one else, the tax rate would be higher the less you made, and the whole tax would be triggered only by the decision to enter the workforce.

And yet those three conditions are a precise description of how childcare functions as a highly regressive tax on work for millions of families. This is why in crafting an economic dignity wage we can't forget childcare. For low-income parents, childcare costs can easily represent the highest tax they face on work. Consider the situation Theresa Carmouche faces as a mother of young twins in Marksville, Louisiana. As described by Joseph Williams in the Economic Hardship Reporting Project, Ms. Carmouche works as the director of a day care center, earning $11.75 an hour.[32] The bottom line is that "she can barely afford to send her own children to the center she supervises" because her monthly earnings are almost exactly the cost of sending her two children to the center.[33] Imagine this: she faces a 100 percent tax on her work if she sends her own children to the day care where she works.

For families living in poverty with childcare expenses, those costs average 30 percent of their income—well above the roughly 10 percent guideline recommended as part of a reasonable budget.[34] When 2.9 million families with children have housing costs exceeding half their income, it doesn't take a statistician to understand why any realistic vision of caring for family is out of reach.[35] One-third of low-income families with young children who pay for childcare are pushed into poverty by those expenses.[36] Supply constraints magnify the problems. Roughly half the U.S. population lives in a "childcare desert," including nearly three out of five Hispanic/Latinx families.[37] And waiting lists for childcare slots can often be years long.[38] Such a regressive tax on work hampers parents' ability to pursue potential and purpose. And each year taken off work because the cost of childcare was too high can reduce a worker's lifetime income by the equivalent of three to four years' salary.[39]

Unfortunately, only one out of every six children who qualify for federal childcare assistance receives any.[40] And the tax credit that exists for childcare expenses is not even refundable—meaning the families who need relief the most get nothing. Not a penny.[41] As Jason Furman wrote when he was chair of President Obama's Council of Economic Advisers, "While the gross cost of U.S. childcare is about average for the OECD, subsidies for childcare in the United States are considerably below the OECD average, making the net cost of childcare among the most expensive of any advanced economy."[42] As discussed in the previous chapter, there is great hypocrisy in conservatives who claim to prize the "dignity of work" and "self-sufficiency" yet continually oppose major resources for childcare programs that would enable working parents to provide for their families through employment.

This system must be fixed. Making childcare affordable is essential to ensuring that parents can fulfill their part of the compact of contribution and one of the most effective means to increase EDPP. Hillary Clinton, Elizabeth Warren, Kamala Harris, and Amy Klobuchar have each proposed plans in their presidential campaigns that would significantly cap childcare expenses as a percent of income.[43] Dayna M. Kurtz, director of the Anna Keefe Women's Center at the Training Institute for Mental Health, has proposed federally funded childcare centers modeled on the highly successful centers for working parents during World War II under the Lanham Act.[44] On the tax side, the child and dependent care tax credit must be made refundable for low-income families. Expanding affordable childcare is a win-win for economic dignity, as access to quality childcare subsidies is linked to better employment outcomes for parents[45] and improved health and development for children.[46]

III. UNIVERSAL BASIC ECONOMIC DIGNITY

In designing an economic dignity wage and economic dignity net, the goal should be to have a *universal* guarantee that all who work and contribute can afford the core components of economic dignity—what can be called universal basic economic dignity (UBED).

Critically, this is a different definition of "universal" than is used by those calling for programs like a universal basic income (UBI). Under that definition, the focus is on whether a particular policy is "universal" in the sense that everyone receives an identical basic income grant regardless of income or need. By contrast, under the UBED approach, "universal" is about the ultimate impact on people. Are our most critical protections for caring for family and pursuing purpose universally available to everyone when their economic dignity is at stake? This end goal does not require that everyone have an identical benefit every year, regardless of economic circumstances, but instead holds that a set of critical programs and benefits are universally *available* to all, not just those in poverty, but also middle-class families when they experience difficult circumstances or falls in income and benefits that threaten the capacity to care for family.

While UBED should be our end goal, the issue of whether more policies should adhere to universal benefits to all regardless of income or need is one that should require a case-by-case analysis. Such analyses should include an open recognition of the potential trade-offs between political benefits that come from including the largest possible pool of people versus the downside of not seeking a more progressive targeting of more resources to those most in need. It should also recognize the potential for greater political resilience that comes with broader participation versus the risk that the costs of providing for those who are already economically secure crowds out or causes a backlash against the government policies most essential to battling poverty and the continuing impacts of historic racial discrimination.

One idea that exemplifies where I think pure universal benefits go too far, and could end up being counterproductive to a full economic dignity agenda, is UBI. Most UBI plans offer around $12,000 a year for every adult—and sometimes $4,000 for every child—regardless of work, income, or need. While bold, sweeping proposals for expanding the EITC, college affordability, and universal childcare affordability can cost between $1 trillion and $2 trillion over ten years, major UBI proposals can be $3 trillion *annually*—or more than *$30 trillion over ten years*. Three trillion dollars is nearly double what the federal government currently collects in income taxes. It even approaches the total amount of revenues our nation raises from all existing federal taxes together, including income, corporate, and payroll.[47]

Advocates of UBI often stress the dignity and freedom component of no-strings-attached cash benefits and point to some success in developing nations.[48] Yet such a policy is not the best path forward in the United States for several critical reasons.

First, we are best off with an overall economic frame based on a compact of contribution. Such a compact must be compassionate by recognizing the real barriers to work people face when they have health issues, pain, or live in poverty. It must, as discussed above, include some form of a child allowance to prevent any child from being raised in deep poverty no matter what, and ensure that all have health care and basic housing. It should offer continual second chances, support, and incentives that allow all people to contribute the best they can—which can include a UBI to Rise to provide income support for people who are actively seeking to get back on their feet, improve their skills, work the best they can in light of disability, or overcome addiction or depression. I believe we are best off operating from the premise of a compassionate compact of contribution—not only because it will ensure stronger public support for an expanded economic dignity compact, but also because it is right to put our focus on helping the overwhelming number of people who want to contribute, to do their part, and to find purpose be able to do so.

Second, those who set a governing agenda have a responsibility to consider seriously the impact UBI could have on other critical investments for economic dignity and broader support for the concept of government responsibility. The fear I raise here is not a traditional fiscal discipline issue—a worry that higher deficits will raise interest rates and "crowd out" private investment—especially with recent economic experience showing little evidence of such effects, and the constant conservative hypocrisy on deficits when regressive tax cuts are at stake. What I am worried about is that the enormous costs associated with this pure universal grant that goes to so many people who do not need it will crowd out crucial existing programs, as well as future initiatives that are needed for a complete economic dignity agenda. Can we ignore the possibility that if we create a $3-trillion-a-year UBI plan, it might crowd out the potential for more intensive government efforts to provide deep assistance for people with disabilities or new investments in housing, universal health care, comprehensive support for low-income young people from pre-K into their careers, jobs, and schools in neighborhoods that have been victimized by past and present racial discrimination and barriers?

It is telling that UBI draws approval from strange bedfellows, including staunch conservatives like Charles Murray who support it only in exchange for *terminating* all other major government programs, including Social Security, Medicare, Medicaid, the EITC, and SNAP.[49] It is disappointing that even Andrew Yang—the one 2020 Democratic presidential candidate touting UBI—says his UBI will not be as expensive as $3 trillion a year because "we're spending $1.5 trillion-plus every year on an assortment of welfare and income support programs" and "if you're already getting $1,000 we're not going to stack this on top, then the headline cost comes down very, very quickly."[50] Translation: his proposal would reduce headline costs by giving less to those struggling Americans already getting help from existing programs—with full shares of this extremely large benefit going to those who are better off.

Some progressive UBI supporters even play into anti-government rhetoric and stereotypes as a means of supporting their plans—even though this works against the trust in government that is needed for major expansions of health care, higher education, and housing support. Even some people I deeply admire, like former Service Employees International Union head Andy Stern, have been willing to advocate for UBI by playing into the worst caricatures of government programs as by nature prone to stigmatizing and denigrating recipients. Stern invokes his own past experiences to promote out-of-date stereotypes about government bureaucracy, writing that "the state welfare bureaucracy had huge overhead costs, too much red tape, treated people as applicants, and enabled too much waste and fraud. It created perverse incentives for people to avoid work and to remain poor, and it allowed too many people to fall through the cracks."[51]

This is an unfair and unhelpful description that overlooks the dramatic improvements in efficiency and reducing stigma in our economic security programs. The EITC and CTC are provided to tens of millions as they file their taxes like everyone else—far from stigmatizing. Eligibility for healthcare subsidies on the individual market is determined through applications on the same website as unsubsidized coverage. In nearly all states, Medicaid applications can be submitted online and by telephone, and most states allow recipients to create an online portal for renewing their benefits.[52] SNAP benefits are now provided through an Electronic Benefits Transfer card that functions like a debit card for groceries. Most states automatically enroll people who are eligible for Supplemental Security Income in Medicaid, and many have joint applications for several benefit programs.[53] As longtime Social Security advocate Nancy Altman has testified, the "extremely low administrative expense is unachievable by employer-sponsored retirement plans or private insurance."[54] There is certainly further to go on preventing stigma, but a full economic dignity agenda is not advanced by such rhetoric.

Finally, UBI raises the issue of whether making programs universal always makes them more politically resilient and bulletproof during budget battles. The textbook case made for the political staying power of universal programs is the relative political strength of universal programs like Social Security and Medicare, as compared with means-tested programs like Medicaid or SNAP. Having lived through many of these budget battles, I can attest to the clear fact that there is more political cover in defending Social Security and Medicare—yet it is also the case that some of their political power comes from the fact they are both *earned* and largely universal. And while the evidence on the differential political power and resilience of targeted versus more universal programs is real, it is not airtight. For example, even though Medicaid and the EITC have been attacked repeatedly by Republican majorities in Congress, both have survived and have actually been *significantly expanded* over the last twenty-five years.[55]

In weighing the pros and cons of a universal program like UBI, it is also important to at least consider the potential for backlash risk. If, for example, the United States enacted a UBI and at some point faced a period of public backlash against high deficits or government spending, the fact that a UBI benefits upper-middle-class constituents might make it politically bulletproof. Yet this could lead to the risk that in protecting a generous UBI for those at higher income levels, the budget knives cut even deeper for those programs most targeted and essential for the poor and vulnerable. Indeed, we have recently seen that very dynamic playing out in Alaska, where its Permanent Fund Dividend (PFD)—an annual payment to each Alaskan drawn from the state's natural resources royalties—has become so politically popular that it is threatening the viability of other programs. After the PFD was reduced in 2016 to plug budget holes, Republican state senator Mike Dunleavy ran for governor on a platform of dramatically increasing the dividend—and won in a landslide. But the budget battle to increase the PFD led to defunding public broadcasting and cutting "31 percent [from Alaska's] its critical ferry system, $130 million from Medicaid, and $70 million from the University of Alaska system."[56] This recent budget move is not alone an argument against the potential of ideas like the PFD, but it does signify the need to weigh both the rewards and the risks of such programs.

An expansive UBED agenda could reach the best of both worlds. Yes, we should recognize the power of a program like Social Security where virtually everyone is included. But many broader programs draw much of their political power from the fact that they serve both poor and middle-income Americans, not because they provide the same benefits to every single person regardless of income or need like UBI does. Increased economic volatility means that programs targeted to hard-pressed working families will benefit a higher percentage of families at some point in their lives.[57] Studies have shown that, prior to the Affordable Care Act, close to half of non-elderly Americans went without health-care coverage at some point over a ten-year period,[58] and about half of taxpayers with children received the EITC at some point over an eighteen-year stretch, even prior to the EITC's most recent expansions.[59] If we expanded benefits and income eligibility up the income ladder to more middle-class levels—as I am proposing with the EITC, for example—in light of increased economic insecurity, it would benefit large shares of families at some point in their lives and gain political support without the excessive costs of some pure universal benefit programs. And given the growing concerns parents have that their children will be worse off than they are, more and more will believe that someone in their family might need the support of such public benefits at some point, even if they themselves are in the upper middle class or above.[60]

For all these reasons, an economic dignity wage and provisions that guarantee UBED—not UBI—are our best path forward.

CHAPTER TWELVE

A DIGNITY NET FOR ALL

"The right to adequate protection from the economic fears of old age, sickness, accident, and unemployment."[1] These were Franklin Roosevelt's words as he called for a Second Bill of Rights in his 1944 State of the Union. He knew, even with the creation of Social Security in the New Deal, more was needed for "a new basis of security and prosperity . . . for all."[2]

These protections are often referred to as our "safety net." Over time, we have taken strides toward FDR's vision by enacting programs like Medicare and Medicaid for health coverage in Lyndon Johnson's Great Society, expansions of unemployment insurance, the Food Stamp Program (now SNAP), the EITC, the Children's Health Insurance Program, and the Affordable Care Act. Yet the remaining holes in the net have become only more apparent in an age of increasing inequality and insecurity. Many I have already discussed, including the lack of universal health-care security and protections against housing foreclosures, evictions, and homelessness; and the imperative to preempt devastating downward cycles for people facing severe economic dislocation with broader unemployment insurance, job creation programs, and robust policies for second chances. I will not seek here to explore in detail all those crucial missing elements.

I will instead use this chapter to highlight a few critical areas that are too often overlooked as we reimagine a true economic dignity net.

1. A MODERN DIGNITY COMPACT THAT COVERS ALL WORK, ALL WORKERS, AND ALL FORMS OF WORK

Let's start from a simple, unifying principle: your employment status should not determine the strength of your economic dignity net. Whether workers have access to collective bargaining, health insurance, unemployment insurance, retirement savings programs, paid leave, and workplace protections like the minimum wage, workers' compensation, and antidiscrimination laws should not depend on how their job is classified or who their employer is.

Unfortunately, we are far away from that ideal. About thirty-two million Americans are contract workers who too often lack basic workplace protections, benefits, and the right to organize.[3] Your degree of economic security today is often largely determined by a binary decision: whether your employer gives you a W-2 as an employee or a 1099 as an independent contractor. W-2 employees for major companies are normally entitled to a slew of benefits and protections. Contractors and employees for subcontractors face—when it comes to handling precarious economic circumstances—what my former colleague Jared Bernstein calls YOYO: "you're on your own."[4] A classic example is FedEx workers. They wear FedEx uniforms to deliver FedEx packages in FedEx trucks—but FedEx does not call them employees, so they are not covered by government- or employer-provided benefits or protections.[5]

The difference can be night and day. Many of those who have gone from being a W-2 employee to a 1099 contractor know what it is like to receive comparable income but feel they are worse off because of the loss of health care, retirement, and other benefits; unemployment insurance; and workplace protections. During the Great Recession, Ken White, a worker in Providence, Rhode Island, lost a job he had held for two decades as a credit card processor. White now does similar work as an independent contractor for a technology services company that places him at a bank, "yet everything feels different. . . . He is paid less, and the bonuses and stock awards he once earned as a full-fledged employee are long gone."[6]

Some contractors perform work so similar to employees that they "might realize it only when they lose their job or are injured at work and learn that they aren't protected by the employment rules and safety protections that traditional workers are," says David Weil, dean of the Heller School of Social Policy and Management at Brandeis University.[7] Ariel Wilson Cetrone is one such worker. She did not realize she was an independent contractor, and not a traditional employee, until she was eight months pregnant and asked for maternity leave. Not only was she denied maternity leave, but the next day she was fired, and because she was not an employee, she did not have access to unemployment insurance.[8]

With so much riding on whether you receive a W-2 or a 1099, unions and worker advocates are correct to make the fight over misclassification a top-tier economic battle and insist that millions of gig workers—including most Uber and Lyft drivers—should be classified as employees, as they successfully did in a hard-fought 2019 legislative battle in California.[9] This is the right fight under our current structure. Too many workers today get the worst of all worlds. They have neither the true autonomy and flexibility of being their own boss nor the economic benefits and security of being a W-2 employee where at a minimum their employer pays its half of Social Security and Medicare payroll taxes and ensures they are part of the unemployment insurance system.

Yet we should also have clarity that getting more people classified as W-2 employees is a *means* to the end goal of economic dignity in our current legal framework—not an *end* in itself. True structural change would aim to build a new system where an economic dignity net is available to all and not based on one's form of work or whether they worked for someone else, were their own boss, or something in between. Our ultimate end goal is neither more W-2s nor fewer people working independently. Our end goal should be to create a robust economic dignity net that is the same regardless of how your work is classified.[10] If more people want to be their own boss, have more autonomy, and have greater day-to-day control over their work schedules, an economic dignity agenda should aim to empower them. We are a long way from that goal—which is why, for now, the battle against misclassification is essential.

At a time when more progressive policymakers are looking at major structural change in health care and other areas, we should be asking how we can best build an economic dignity net that maximizes choices for people to work as they see fit. Strong public options or universal provisions would be an important step in that direction. Another idea that should be in the mix is to expand on the innovative Shared Security System first proposed by Nick Hanauer and David Rolf.[11] Their proposal would create Shared Security Accounts "encompassing *all* of the employment benefits traditionally provided by a full-time salaried job," collected "via automatic payroll deductions, regardless of the employment relationship, and, like Social Security, these benefits would be fully prorated, portable, and universal."[12]

We should consider how to take their proposal to an even more sweeping level. Imagine, for example, a future system where a fraction of *any* dollar paid for *any* work—including that done by full-time workers, contractors, household employees, care workers, and gig economy workers—was added to individualized federal government accounts that would support a larger economic dignity net. With a singular and stable federal account, many problems of portability would vanish. These accounts could serve as a form of universal withholding and employer or customer contribution to ensure Social Security and Medicare benefits, unemployment assistance, paid leave, a new universal pension, and any other benefits for which there has not been a public provision de-linked from work. Advancements in payment technologies like those used by Venmo and Zelle make it easier to imagine how, with additional technological advances in the coming years and decades, a small portion of any payment to any worker could be added and electronically directed to a benefits account, automatically or with a single push or swipe.

My futuristic pondering is not meant to land on the best design or mix of direct public provisions for economic security, public options, or Super-Shared Security Accounts. It is instead to say that as we design the building blocks of a new economic dignity net, let's this time give all Americans maximum choice in being a full-time employee or their own boss, or multiple options in between, without holding their economic security in the balance. There may be better ways to arrive at this larger goal, but we should make our long-term ambition to develop ideas like this that would weave an economic dignity net for all workers, regardless of their type of employment, and to secure adequate resources for those benefits.

2. REPAIRING THE FAILED ECONOMIC DIGNITY NET FOR PEOPLE WITH DISABILITIES AND THEIR FAMILIES

"Included. Supported. Empowered." These words define not only the campaign to tell the stories of the 4.6 million Americans with intellectual or developmental disabilities (I/DDs) like autism and Down syndrome, but also the values inherent in a compact of contribution to promote economic dignity. The "Included. Supported. Empowered." campaign reflects the courage, resilience, and accomplishment of those with I/DDs and the depth of commitment of the families and caregivers who go to the greatest lengths to ensure those with I/DDs pursue their sense of purpose and meaning and capacity to contribute. As the Tierra del Sol Foundation, a nonprofit working to support individuals with I/DDs in education and employment, states, "Regardless of the notion of disability, each person has the potential and the right to lead a full, productive, and personally meaningful life."[13] Yet from a public policy perspective, our existing social compact continually fails these individuals and their families.

Last chapter, I talked about economic dignity purchasing power, which looks at all resources, income, and support and measures the degree to which people can afford the main components of economic dignity. Every time a parent has less economic dignity purchasing power due to a child having a disability, it is a policy failure. It is evidence of failure to provide the public support for any additional medical costs, educational services, and direct and technological support that are needed simply to fulfill what should be a national commitment to true first chances and an opportunity for every child to thrive. Our current social compact fails miserably and unnecessarily to meet that test. For example, while those working as direct support professionals are often a critical lifeline for those with I/DDs, as I will discuss in the next chapter, they are grossly underpaid, leading to a shortage of experienced workers and disruptive turnover. Consider home- and community-based services, which honor the overwhelming preference of people with disabilities to live with dignity in their communities and provide higher-quality care at a lower cost than institutional care.[14] Because of underfunding, two-thirds of the over 700,000 people on the waiting list for this care are people with I/DDs such as autism. How long is the wait list for people with I/DDs to get home- and community-based care? Days? Weeks? Even months? Try *five and a half years*.[15] The fact that families must often bear the responsibility of paying the thousands of extra dollars those with disabilities need to simply maintain the same standard of living as everyone else is rightly described by advocates as nothing short of a tax on disability.[16] Certainly it means families can have less economic dignity purchasing power simply due to a family member having an I/DD or other disability.

As journalist Ron Fournier says in *Love That Boy*, his book about getting care for his autistic son Tyler, Hillary Clinton's mantra that "it takes a village" is even more true for parents who "can't afford private services."[17] Many of these should be publicly provided, even for middle-class families. As parents will go to any length for their child, our failure to provide full public support ends up also diminishing the economic dignity of family members who are forced to limit their own pursuit of work and potential to fill the holes in our current safety net. As Brian Field writes for the Autism Spectrum Disorder Foundation, "It is not uncommon in this cycle for families to dig themselves into debt, sell their assets, and in some cases be forced into foreclosure or bankruptcy over the medical costs incurred in seeking to better their autistic child's circumstances."[18] Too often, parents and family members struggle with basics in their own lives due to waiting lists and denied or meagerly supported services. My first cousin Dara and her husband, Rob, are fierce advocates for their son with autism and extremely dedicated parents to both their children. Yet, the need for constant care for their son and lack of public support in providing highly qualified respite care has made it near impossible for them to attend normal life events like weddings. While Dara found a way to travel to my father's funeral in August 2018, she confessed to me that the difficulty in arranging specialized care had meant she and her husband had not gone on a true vacation in sixteen years—since their son with autism had been born.

A caring society committed to economic dignity would go to every length to ensure that parents of children with disabilities have all the support possible at every stage of life to provide the children they so desperately love with every opportunity to thrive, contribute, find purpose, and live independently. Instead, we too often tell those individuals and families they are on their own. If we want to turn our porous safety net into a dignity net worthy of our hearts and values, we can start here.

BREAKING DOWN BARRIERS TO PURPOSE, POTENTIAL, AND CONTRIBUTION

As Judy Heumann, one of the nation's leading disability rights advocates, has noted, when our economic policy provides those with disabilities the right support and opportunity, it is "reducing the unemployment rate, it's increasing the education level, it's facilitating the ability of disabled people through their sense of pride and dignity to be able to be integrated members of the community, holding meaningful and valuable jobs."[19]

Our current model fails a compassionate and smart compact of contribution for people with disabilities with "appropriate opportunities and supports."[20] Current policies too often force people with disabilities into arbitrary boxes that provide minimal support if you are deemed unable to work; no support if your disability is deemed not debilitating enough; and rarely adequate support to ensure you have every opportunity to contribute to the best of your capacities. It is hard to imagine a more impoverished vision for economic dignity.

Similarly, Julia Bascom, director of programs at the Autistic Self Advocacy Network, notes, "as with the broader disability community, [autistic people] see high rates of unemployment and underemployment—the result of a complex combination of factors, including low expectations, misconceptions about autism, and insufficient funding for supported employment programs." Bascom notes that these challenges "have very little to do with the actual job skills and talents of autistic people. . . . We face many of the same challenges as the rest of the disability community in that we have many people who want to work but are actually being prevented from doing so."[21] While conservatives continually call for smaller government in the cause of increasing self-sufficiency, as discussed in Chapter Six, this is an area where *more* government help would mean *more* people working and being more self-sufficient.

Our national policy to affirmatively help people with disabilities gain entry into the workforce is abysmal. We begin to fail by starting too late. As Rebecca Cokley, the director of the Disability Justice Initiative at the Center for American Progress, describes, the tendency to not even ask those with disabilities what they aspire to do with their lives until they reach the age of sixteen leads to poor transition planning and the false "expectation that we can't achieve, we can't succeed, and that we're unable to contribute."[22] For adults, a lack of investment in boosting accessible transportation, affordable and accessible housing, high-quality job training, and universal health care and paid family and medical leave remain widespread barriers.[23] Accessible technology is a "powerful ally" toward helping autistic people work, Bascom notes, but is "another area where we see a real lack of resources."[24] The federal government provides less than $30 million in funding a year, distributed to state programs, to help people with disabilities gain assistive technologies, even though there have been dramatic developments.[25] Technological advances from one-handed keyboards to a hands-free computer mouse to app-based technology for the visually impaired can provide quality-of-life improvements and make it easier for people with disabilities to work. Unfortunately, lack of funding leaves them inaccessible for too many.[26]

Job intermediaries are key for matching people with disabilities with job opportunities, but we do little at the national level, leaving too much of the work to nonprofits and state and local governments that decide to help. The support system for people with disabilities that we do have can put up perverse barriers to work and pursuit of potential. Anna Landre is a Georgetown University student and high school valedictorian who has spinal muscular atrophy type 2. She has written about the difficulties she has had maintaining Medicaid coverage that funds a home care aide who supports her and enables her to attend college. When she secured a summer internship that paid $14 an hour, she found out those earnings would cause her to lose Medicaid coverage for sixteen hours a day of support from her home care aide. That means she would receive less than six hours a day of government-funded support, leaving her to make up the ten-hour-a-day difference, a cost she couldn't afford on her own. The system gives her a brutal choice between pursuing her potential and accessing the care she needs. As her mother said, "My daughter wants to work and contribute to society. . . . She doesn't want to sit home without a job and ride the system." As Ms. Landre notes, by limiting her ability to take the internship, she "can't even get to that point" where she might "have a career and maybe one day not need the state."[27] Later, Medicaid nearly rescinded her personal care support—a decision that "would have ended [her] pursuit of a college education and prohibited [her] from ever living independently" had it not been reversed.[28] Such arbitrary and inflexible barriers are exactly the opposite approach of what our nation needs to do to support people with disabilities and ensure economic dignity for all.

We must also end the indignity of some employers being allowed to pay workers with disabilities less than the minimum wage, and do more to promote inclusive workplaces. These practices make it harder for workers with disabilities to provide for themselves and loved ones. As Azza Altiraifi writes for the Center for American Progress, "95 percent of employees being paid subminimum wages are also employed in sheltered workshops, or segregated workplaces designed solely to employ people with disabilities."[29]

The lack of a comprehensive and universal approach to supporting people with disabilities is unacceptable and means that too many who need help getting to work aren't able to.

And a key place where we must improve our compact of contribution is Social Security Disability Insurance (SSDI). Unfortunately, many policymakers—especially conservatives but unfortunately some progressives, too—focus on exaggerated claims of abuse.[30] They treat SSDI reform as a budget-cutting issue, impugning the overwhelming number of people who have worked their whole lives, often through painful and challenging disabilities, before going on SSDI. They ignore that the United States has the most restrictive and least generous disability benefit system of all OECD member countries.[31] They seem to forget that the average SSDI recipient has worked for twenty-two years before receiving benefits; that it has a stringent application process; and that evidence reveals that the vast majority of those just barely denied SSDI appeals do not get jobs. As the Center on Budget and Policy Priorities notes, "Evidence suggests that few beneficiaries could earn more than very small amounts if they did not receive SSDI."[32]

Yet for those who have some hope of working again, it can be our policies that make it extremely hard for them to even explore work options. Most have struggled to work with a disability for years. Their disability gets worse or the employer that had been able to accommodate them lays them off, and they can find no other jobs they can do with their disability. They have to find a lawyer and battle—often through an extensive appeal—to get benefits that are far below any notion of a living wage. Some may want to experiment with getting back in the workforce, but because of their disability they are unsure if they will be able to maintain their hours. What if the disability flares up again and they need to go back on SSDI, and must go through the entire legal process over again? For the minority of workers on SSDI who might be able to reenter the workforce in some fashion, perhaps with part-time work, we have created a system that tells them that if they experiment with this difficult leap and fail, we may permanently pull the rug out from under them. They will have given up critical benefits they may never get back to try to pursue an uncertain path back to some form of work.

Consider the case of Paul Khouri. After he started receiving SSDI benefits, he wanted to get back to work—both because it was challenging to live only on his monthly benefit and because he wanted to contribute by working at a disability rights organization.[33] But he quickly found that starting to work put his benefits at risk. He said he "had to basically cut down [his] hours and say 'I'll volunteer the rest of my time, but I can only get paid for fifteen hours a week'" to avoid jeopardizing his benefits.[34] That's because workers receiving SSDI can receive only up to $1,220 a month over the long term before they lose their benefits—creating a major risk if they try to work.[35] While SSDI recipients can maintain eligibility while earning for a few years, the limits create uncertainty and fear among recipients. As the advocacy group The Arc notes, "unrealistically low limits on assets and earnings make people fear losing vital public benefits if they work too many hours or earn too much."[36] For very poor people with disabilities who also receive Supplemental Security Income, asset limits before workers become ineligible are only $2,000 for an individual and $3,000 for a household—putting recipients in an impossible bind of either forgoing immediate assistance or being trapped in permanent poverty.[37] And SSDI and SSI provide access to Medicare and Medicaid, so people with disabilities who work more than a certain amount may be putting their access to affordable health insurance at risk as well.[38] The Affordable Care Act provides new avenues for people with disabilities to sustain health care. Still, broader approaches to universal health care—from a public option to single payer—would help more.

Rather than focus entirely on the very few who might cheat, or blaming those who have no choice but to stay on SSDI for long periods, or seeing reform as just a budget-balancing exercise, we should be clear as a society: we are going to do everything in our power to support you and your dignity. Rather than promote punitive policies or those that disincentivize work, we should create a more compassionate compact of contribution that asks what we can do to support people with disabilities coming in and out of the workforce to the extent they can.[39]

3. BUILDING DIGNITY IN RETIREMENT AND SPREADING WEALTH CREATION

We face huge wealth inequality and growing retirement insecurity beyond anything we have seen since the 1920s. In the late 1990s, as President Clinton's national economic adviser, I thought we had a way to tackle both. With large projected budget surpluses, we could keep Social Security solvent without benefit cuts and still use some of the surplus to help seed a universal pension or savings vehicle we would call universal savings accounts (USAs). The idea was also a way of neutralizing the Republicans' call to cut Social Security benefits and privatize a portion of Social Security through individual market-based accounts.

Time, experience, and economic developments have somewhat changed what I would prioritize and have my guard up for. I now believe that the first order of business must be to expand Social Security benefits not just for the poor but for a broader swath of the middle class. For those who saw their pensions and housing values collapse in the Great Recession, it only reconfirmed FDR's vision that Social Security would be the one rock-solid foundation for retirement security guaranteed under any economic circumstance.[40] Today, about one in four seniors relies entirely on Social Security for their retirement income, and most elderly Americans rely on Social Security for most of their retirement income.[41] Fewer than one in five private-sector workers has access to a defined benefit plan.[42] Three out of five working-age Americans—over 100 million people—do not have *any* retirement savings beyond Social Security.[43] About one-third of *retirees* have less than $50,000 in savings.[44] Too many Americans go from living paycheck to paycheck to relying on a modest Social Security check each month that averages just $1,356 a month, or $16,272 a year.[45]

We need to give serious attention to proposals to increase benefits for the broad numbers of retirees who rely on them.[46] By contrast, the growing disparity in longevity by education and income should hopefully take all proposals to raise the retirement age completely off the table.[47] Beyond Social Security, we can and should be bolder, particularly when it comes to our mounting long-term care needs. The ability to grow old with dignity often depends on the ability to receive quality individualized care at home or a quality senior living facility.[48] But many seniors and their families can't afford the expenses associated with such care, with the cost of a full-time home health aide running more than $4,000 a month—and often much more.[49] A dignity net must meet this challenge. Potential solutions include exploring proposals like those from Caring Across Generations for a universal social insurance program for home- and community-based care, expanded access to long-term care insurance, and increasing coverage for critical care through existing or future government health programs. Washington State recently enacted an ambitious long-term care benefit of $100 per day for up to one year, which will be paid for by a small payroll tax.[50]

To support the expansive policies needed to achieve an economic dignity compact, our first goal should be to raise revenues from the most well-off 1 percent—and especially the top one-tenth of 1 percent—in our society and prevent the exploitation of offshore tax havens by major companies and well-off individuals. In particular, we need to do far better at taxing the immense, often never-taxed, super-wealth in our society. While there are several positive ways to do this, from ending tax-free transfers of wealth to heirs to raising the top tax rate on capital gains, I strongly advocate imposing a small annual wealth tax on those who are worth over $50 million.[51] Such measures can go an enormous way toward funding the types of broad economic dignity policies espoused in this book.

Yet if we are to be successful at making our tax system far more progressive, we should not shut down the consideration of asking all Americans and employers to pay a little more to ensure a stronger economic dignity net for one's older years—in terms of long-term care, paid family leave, and Social Security benefits—if it can be shown to directly increase overall economic dignity purchasing power (EDPP). All of us would tell a relative to withhold an extra percent or two of their wages at work if it meant a more solid annuity they could count on, disability benefits, and long-term care insurance. Once we have made our tax system more progressive and fair, we should not allow fear of political attacks to prevent us from considering a modest contribution that would increase Social Security benefits, paid leave, and long-term care, and that represents a major step forward to our end goal of universal economic dignity.

DON'T GIVE UP ON WEALTH BUILDING

A wealth tax and other policies to reduce the obscene concentration of wealth in our society should be a critical economic priority. But a plan to both decrease wealth inequality and promote economic dignity must also focus on how to build wealth for tens of millions of Americans who have little or no savings or wealth. With so many Americans living paycheck to paycheck, and some estimating that 40 percent of American households don't have $400 to meet an emergency expense, policymakers can be hesitant to put forward more aspirational wealth-building policies that go beyond helping families make ends meet. Yet even with the need to prioritize expansions in guaranteed economic security, it is a mistake to give up on helping average working Americans have a better shot at building wealth as a form of security or a modest nest egg. An economic dignity net extends to the capacity to save and provide for family and loved ones over the long term.

This is also critical for repairing the enormous, persistent wealth divide by race. Due in large part to our history of discrimination, particularly in employment, housing, and neighborhood segregation, the average black household today has only roughly one-tenth of the average wealth among white households.[52] As discussed in Chapter Four, wealth disparities driven by generations of discrimination end up reducing first chances and economic mobility for children today.

Helping to close the racial wealth gap is one key motivation for not giving up on the wealth creation benefits of homeownership. While we certainly must provide more support to affordable housing for renters and take the steps needed to eradicate homelessness, we should also do more to support hard-pressed working families having a shot at homeownership. Improving access to credit and providing support for down payments to groups with subpar homeownership rates is a start. This could put homeownership in reach for more families and could be particularly targeted to redress the legacy of redlining and disparities in black and Latinx homeownership— and include first-time homebuyer assistance for a broad swath of working families. Currently, we are moving in the wrong direction. The homeownership rate among black Americans has actually gotten worse since the financial crisis. Shockingly, it is now virtually unchanged from when the Fair Housing Act was enacted in 1968.[53] At 44 percent, it remains far behind that of white households, nearly three-quarters of whom own their homes.[54]

Furthermore, as I have long highlighted, we have an upside-down tax policy on wealth: We have actually created a tax code that by design gives the most public support for savings to those with the highest incomes and the least need for savings incentives, and the very least wealth-building support to the least fortunate. How? Tax incentives for homeownership and retirement in individual retirement accounts and 401(k) plans are provided through tax deductions. For every dollar Americans pay into retirement savings or for mortgage interest, they can deduct a dollar from their income for tax purposes. This turns our progressive structure of marginal tax rates for taxing income into a regressive one for savings. While earners in the highest income bracket get a nearly 40 percent federal tax deduction for savings, the hardest-pressed workers get only a 10 percent deduction or less for every dollar they manage to put away, because that's the rate at which they're taxed. The result? In the midst of the highest levels of wealth inequality we have seen since the Roaring Twenties, the top 5 percent of taxpayers currently get more tax benefits for savings than the bottom 80 percent combined.[55]

We must reverse this upside-down policy by providing generous support for wealth building and saving for retirement beyond Social Security. Whether we call them USAs or universal 401(k)s, we should turn our upside-down system right-side up by offering matching savings for workers trying to save, and even double-matching or automatic yearly deposits for low- and modest-income Americans.[56] This is a great place for a public option. A government-provided savings vehicle—based on the highly efficient thrift savings plan (TSP) available to government employees—could be available to all workers. Such a federal public option could help eliminate all of our current challenges with pension portability. As I discuss above, this would fit the test of building a new economic dignity net where benefits would be universally available to all regardless of their job classification, how many sources of income they have, or how often they change jobs. To stem the decline in Americans getting the security of defined benefits, we should explore how to extend incentives to encourage defined benefit plans to unions and other sectoral arrangements, and to offer government-backed annuity options that could provide the same type of certain, guaranteed payout retirees can count on.

Policies that address these disparities and help affirmatively build wealth and homeownership should be core components of a modern dignity net for all.

CHAPTER THIRTEEN

DOUBLE-DIGNITY JOBS

What if the robot apocalypse prophecies are right? What if this time is different? What if some combination of AI, robots, and autonomous vehicles actually means not just job disruption, but less demand for human workers in the private economy? What would our economic model be in an economy where there is no need for millions to work at all?

Some, from presidential candidate Andrew Yang to Silicon Valley icons like Mark Zuckerberg and Elon Musk to former head of the SEIU Andy Stern, think this is a primary virtue of a universal basic income (UBI). If unprecedented technological advances make us wealthier, more productive, and less in need of workers, we need a different model of income support.

But hold it. Even if it did come to pass that the private sector demands less labor, does that lead to "end of work" scenarios with massive job shortages?

I have a very different view. I don't buy that if someday our private sector demanded less labor, it would mean that there would not be enough jobs that need workers. From an economic dignity perspective, we have massive numbers of unfilled jobs in need of workers right now that will never be filled by automation or AI. They won't be outsourced to other countries either.

I am referring to the massive jobs deficit we face in helping millions in our nation close devastating dignity gaps. These include jobs to help autistic people pursue their potential, to experts to help those leaving prison or with serious disabilities connect with the workforce, to tutors and coaches and counselors to help children from economic disadvantage travel the pipeline to college opportunity, to more and higher-paid teachers, to therapists to help young children struggling with trauma or middle-aged folks struggling with opioid addiction. We have a deep need for higher-skilled, higher-valued care workers to help our children's brains advance and provide comfort to our parents when their memories fade.

So I have a different idea. If there are more people in need of dignified work, and we can tap wealth from gains in robots and AI (or just our current excessive wealth in the top one-tenth of 1 percent), why not fund dignified jobs that provide economic dignity to Americans who could use a helping hand? Why, oh why, would we call for the largest spending project in our history—a whopping $3 trillion *a year*, which is what UBI could cost—and have zero of it specifically directed toward funding jobs to fill the pervasive dignity gaps in our nation?[1]

The double-dignity jobs promoted here would *not* be low-wage jobs with no career paths or chance to develop skills or a sense of autonomy. To qualify as double-dignity jobs, they must both serve the dignity of others *and* offer the compensation and paths for skills and career advancement that can enhance meaning, purpose, and the pursuit of potential for those holding those jobs.

The beauty of a double-dignity jobs strategy is that it does not require us to wait to find out who is right about the future of robots and jobs. This is a jobs strategy that makes sense today and tomorrow. This strategy would promote jobs, growth, and economic dignity whether a robot apocalypse comes to fruition or we see a continuation of accelerating labor market polarization and economic inequality.[2] Double-dignity jobs would also be—if you can handle another "double"—double wins. In scores of areas, the investment in jobs with higher pay and higher value would be repaid to the economy through higher returns in promoting our goals of economic dignity for all.

Some of these will be direct government jobs. Others will be nonprofit jobs and even private sector jobs, sparked by making such services affordable to millions more families.

The following list is not intended to be exhaustive; it is intended instead to show that the profound need for dignified work that can raise the well-being, fulfillment, happiness, and dignity of our fellow Americans is vast.

EXAMPLE ONE: CHILDCARE WORKERS AND EARLY EDUCATION TEACHERS

Let's start with a case study involving childcare in the military. In the 1980s, experts found that service members with children were commonly losing time on duty due to a lack of quality childcare.[3] Like other employed parents, service members need to know their kids are in good hands. As M. A. Lucas, the founding director of the army's Child Development Services System, described it, "It became clear that childcare, or lack of childcare, could impact the nation's security, the military's ability to be ready to defend the country."[4] So what did the Department of Defense do? It didn't just expand childcare slots; it built a network of quality, affordable (service members pay based on their income) childcare providers with skilled, valued professional caregivers. The military transformed what was once a shabby system with low standards and high turnover into one that is regarded as among the best in the country. The military ensures that all childcare workers receive training, specialist support, and professional development. To attract and keep such workers from leaving with their newfound skills, the military increases their pay and ties obtaining more training to systematic raises, much like the rest of the military.[5]

This is a textbook case of crafting and expanding double-dignity jobs. Top-notch childcare meant more of those defending our nation could better care for and enjoy their families while also pursuing careers in the military. The upskilling of the jobs meant that childcare positions that are often poorly paid or undervalued were instead truly dignified jobs with fair pay, purpose, and potential. Harvard economist David Ellwood rightly stressed the multiple wins to this investment: parents were comforted, children reaped long-term returns from improved early education, workers found dignified jobs, and the military better retained its soldiers in a volunteer army.[6]

The potential for expansions of double-dignity jobs for childcare and early education is huge. There is overwhelming evidence that quality preschool provides the highest returns for true first chances, but the funding in the United States is shockingly low.[7] It is tragic and shortsighted that the jobs held by the early care and education (ECE) workforce—the caregivers we trust with looking after and enriching the minds of our youngest—have been among the worst in the economy. Childcare workers make below 97 percent of the average wages of all occupations,[8] and one in seven childcare workers live in households below the federal poverty line.[9] In twenty-one states and Washington, DC, childcare workers would have to spend over half their earnings to pay for center-based infant care.[10] Preschool teachers make only slightly more but earn only about 50 to 80 percent of what kindergarten teachers earn, even when such teachers have similar credentials and work with children only slightly older.[11] It's not enough to say, "We should have more skilled early learning teachers." We also have to pay them in ways that value their work.[12]

Making early care and education positions double-dignity jobs means ensuring that compensation supports economic dignity for a skilled, valued workforce and that there is ongoing training and opportunities for meaningful advancement—all of which serve the dual purpose of providing dignity to the workforce and retaining the best teachers in the field.

EXAMPLE TWO: COLLEGE ADVISORY JOBS

The deficit in jobs is also acute in the area where we see some of the most accelerating inequality in our nation: college preparation and college advisory support. The inequalities in this area supercharge broader economic inequality. Many children in higher-income families have at their disposal parents with personal knowledge of the path to college success. Well-off parents—even if they restrain themselves from cheating on SATs or Photoshopping pictures to make it look like their child is a top swimmer to gain admission—have considerable avenues to give their child a leg up, all of which are legal. Some are able to pay thousands to high-priced consultants and tutors to help with everything from preparing personal statements to standardized test prep.[13] Once in college, low-income students are still at a disadvantage relative to their wealthier peers, struggling to stay enrolled and graduate without many of the same financial and nonfinancial supports.[14] While it may be human nature for parents with resources to take reasonable measures to support their children, that only makes it more imperative for public policy to play a role in equalizing opportunity. What if we had enough career professionals to advise and coach low- and middle-income children to get every advantage to level the playing field?

Currently, in the poorest school districts, the median student-to-school counselor ratio is 435 to 1. In Arizona and California, the median ratio is more than 750 students to 1 school counselor.[15] With such overwhelming numbers of students needing guidance from one counselor, it is impossible that many students are getting attentive guidance when it is needed.[16] Many of those overwhelmed school counselors not only lack training in helping their students transition to college and careers, but they also have zero specialized training around the complexities of financial aid, meaning more students are left underserved in terms of preparing and applying for college.[17] Meanwhile, wealthy parents can pay for private admissions counselors to give their kids a boost in the college admissions process, with packages that cost up to $10,000 and hourly fees of $200.[18] The immense disparity in guidance for high schoolers in the transition to college is totally legal. Yet research suggests that for each additional counselor a high school has, there could be as much as a 10 percent increase in rates of students enrolling in four-year colleges.[19]

With more pay, training, and reasonable caseloads that can lower burnout, the college adviser position could be a double-dignity job with a big impact. Advisers can ensure that low-income children get individualized, comprehensive help on everything from student aid applications, to high school course selection, to advice on financing, to identifying the most suitable schools, to obtaining application and standardized test fee waivers. They can engage with and inform parents about the process, giving the entire family the knowledge required to navigate the college-going process. We can look to the College Advising Corps (CAC) for a promising model of creating such double-dignity jobs. CAC offers meaningful, full-time jobs for recent college graduates, many of them first-generation college students themselves, to create a college-going culture in 670 high schools across 16 states. These jobs give advisers the chance to use their personal experience and growing professional knowledge to give more high schoolers a chance to pursue potential while offering a stepping-stone to other careers in education for the advisers. The kids that CAC advises in person and virtually are 30 percent more likely to apply to a college, 24 percent more likely to be accepted, and 25 percent more likely to submit a Free Application for Federal Student Aid (FAFSA).[20] Advisers can address a host of issues that are associated with dropping out of postsecondary programs before students even enroll in a program.

We should also be increasing the number of dedicated advisers to address the myriad needs of students in both four-year and community colleges. As I will discuss in greater depth in a later chapter, there is promising evidence that having such dedicated advisers supporting students in college can have high returns. One example: in the City University of New York (CUNY) Accelerated Study in Associate Programs (ASAP), advisers work with smaller cohorts of students to provide intensive tutoring and support. The advisers are a key reason ASAP students graduate in three years at nearly double the rate of comparable students.[21]

EXAMPLE THREE: JOBS TO EMPOWER THOSE WITH INTELLECTUAL OR DEVELOPMENTAL DISABILITIES

There are few jobs that so directly uplift the economic dignity of millions of American families than those that provide direct support services (direct support professionals, or DSP) to people with intellectual or developmental disabilities (I/DD), including autism and Down syndrome. As one grandmother of an autistic young man described these jobs, "These are the people who bring a child with autism to the hospital in the middle of the night . . . reinforce what is being taught in the classroom . . . collaborate with other staff . . . be familiar with laws protecting those with disabilities . . . communicate regularly with families . . . work overtime (no matter how exhausted they are) or give up holidays."[22] A health-service executive described the work as "a job unlike many others," in which workers "perform complex job duties that include administering medications, teaching hygiene, overseeing behavioral health plans, communicating effectively with both verbal and nonverbal individuals, and supporting community participation."[23]

Yet even these statements do not encapsulate the full value of these jobs. Listen to families discuss how DSP workers form close relationships of trust, support, and affection with those with I/DD, and how they can be a person's key to contributing economically and living with independence and autonomy. You would think jobs that are essential to ensuring economic dignity would indeed be economically valued in terms of compensation. You would be wrong. Nicole Jorwic, a high-level staffer at The Arc—one of the top policy shops in the nation advocating for those with I/DD—estimates that the average wage for such vital work is $11.76 an hour, and even in relatively high-cost-of-living states like Illinois, it can be less than $10 an hour.[24] The failure to provide a true economic dignity wage to these vital DSPs ends up diminishing the economic dignity of those they seek to serve. While long-term relationships are especially crucial in both trust and expertise, the low wages lead to such high turnover rates that 38 percent of DSPs leave this invaluable work within six months.[25] For Jorwic, the issue is professional as well as personal. She has an adult brother with autism. She recounted in congressional testimony how the departure of her brother's trusted DSP due to low wages was not only devastating for her brother but now also threatens her mother's peace of mind and ability to work. "The word 'crisis' doesn't really do it justice—having a skilled, properly trained, and fairly paid workforce is the linchpin for success for so many people with disabilities to live the independent life they choose."[26]

In state after state, there is now increasing demand to significantly raise the wages and benefits of DSP workers. Advocacy organizations like The Arc support all measures to ensure that we honor the "professional" in these direct service professional jobs. That means, as Arc calls for, combining far stronger compensation with "development and implementation of a national credentialing system for DSPs to professionalize the industry and programs that direct qualified people into the industry via pipeline programs."[27]

For those who choose forms of behavioral therapy for their children with I/DD, many families cannot afford the available specialists. For a behavioral therapy available for autistic people, many specialists do not take Medicaid,[28] and health insurance has varying degrees of coverage for specialists.[29] One special-needs parent from Greenville, South Carolina, who volunteers with other parents struggling to access treatment, states, "These families have no-where to turn for help. . . . It just breaks my heart to talk with so many moth-ers who are so desperate, who do not know what to do."[30] Rural communities tend to be the hardest hit by the shortage of trained specialists to support and empower people with I/DD. In South Dakota, for example, there is roughly one child psychiatrist for every one hundred thousand children un-der age eighteen;[31] one estimate places the share of developmental pediatri-cians that practice in rural areas at just 7 percent.[32] There is a further silent crisis for many of these families: the fear that their kids will not have ade-quate housing and assistance as adults to live as independently as possible. Thinking more broadly about the millions of special-needs kids, we also have a chronic need for more special-education teachers. Forty-eight states in the 2015–2016 academic year reported a shortage of special education teachers.[33]

These jobs—whether DSPs, educators trained in helping young people with I/DDs, those who help young people with verbal communication, or those who assist with housing and independent living—are careers that could offer so many Americans the dignified work of providing care, op-portunity, and dignity for individuals and families.

EXAMPLE FOUR: THE NEED FOR AN ARMY OF JOB NAVIGATORS

Millions of Americans face difficulty in securing employment. Sixty percent of people ages twenty-five to fifty-four with disabilities are unemployed or out of the workforce.[34] Each year 650,000 people return from prison in need of a home and work.[35] One million workers were still not reemployed in early 2018 after being displaced from a job between 2015 and 2017.[36]

These Americans exemplify a far too common struggle: one's path to pur-suing potential and economically caring for family hinges on navigating a labor market that is extremely hard for people already facing employability challenges to successfully surmount alone. The Obama administration rec-ognized the importance of health-care navigators to advise and guide people on selecting and signing up for the right health insurance plan for their families from a panoply of options. The need for such navigators and coaches[37] can be critical for helping those struggling to enter or reenter the workforce, identify opportunities, find the right training, and practice for interviews. At the same time, the intermediary role that job navigators play can allow them to build critical relationships of trust with employers, increasing the willingness of the employer to fill the job with candidates who would otherwise be struggling on their own to get a foot in the door.

When I led President Obama's initial effort to address the discriminatory hiring practices used against those who were long-term unemployed, we searched for programs that successfully connect these people in these situations with new jobs. Skills for Chicagoland's Future, led by its CEO Marie Trzupek Lynch, and Platform to Employment (P2E), led by Joe Carbone, were two places that stood out. With so many people still struggling with long-term unemployment in the aftermath of the Great Recession, Skills functioned as an intermediary that matched overlooked job seekers with open positions at businesses at no cost to either job seekers or businesses. The staff at Skills had big hearts but hard heads and no illusions about the difficulty of their task. They would approach, say, United Airlines when it had fifty job openings, and ask them to save ten for Skills to try to fill. Lynch and her team would survey their pool of those who were long-term unemployed, find qualified candidates, and then get them ready to interview for their return to the labor force.

Lynch was appreciative of my enthusiasm for their work but did not want me to have an overly romantic view of this endeavor. The companies, she said, are willing to help give people second chances, but they expect her organization to deliver strong candidates. And, she cautioned me, many are struggling with depression, have forgotten basic grooming measures, and need significant counseling and coaching to show up ready to succeed in their interview. Yet their results are impressive. In 2018 alone, Skills's business partnership staff and recruiters placed over thirteen hundred people in sought-after positions in the Chicago area, the vast majority of whom had only a high school education. Hundreds of these matches involved people from high-poverty neighborhoods.[38] Matches earn on average $6,120 more per year than comparison job seekers.[39] Platform to Employment has also shown success with the job navigator model. Operating in eleven states, with 90 percent of their placements keeping the jobs, P2E offers an intensive course to help the long-term unemployed navigate the job search process as well as to connect them to jobs.[40] The job seekers often have extensive work histories and college degrees but are extremely discouraged and deeply affected by a long period of trying unsuccessfully to rejoin the workforce.

These job navigator and career coaching positions require intensive understanding of the challenges of the population served, plus the expertise, trust, and performance generated in relationships with employers. Nonprofits like Skills and Platform to Employment can offer a more efficient and effective way to help struggling job seekers than having each company attempt to replicate the expertise involved in connecting qualified but overlooked candidates to jobs with specific challenges. When I told several CEOs about a competitive grant program we were designing to fund citywide programs for the long-term unemployed using intermediary models, one told me he only wished his firm had taken that approach when they had agreed to Michelle Obama and Jill Biden's effort to commit to hiring veterans, as it was inefficient to have each company trying to gain expertise on veterans' issues on its own.

For those with disabilities, job navigators and coaches could help companies know what is needed to accommodate workers of different disabilities, how to proceed, and which state and federal programs can provide support. The fact that roughly only two out of five of those with disabilities are in the workforce but the vast majority want to work speaks to the need for more employment intermediaries and coaches who specialize in overcoming the challenges faced by people with disabilities in the labor market. Some nonprofits and state agencies are leading the way but need additional funding to reach more people with disabilities who want to work. For example, Triumph Services in Birmingham, Alabama, working with a very small staff, provides individuals with developmental disabilities with interview and job skills and connects them to jobs at over 180 employers, mostly funded by state and federal grants.[41]

Consider the need for job coaches to support and connect the approximately ten thousand former offenders who return to communities from prison each week. The Center for Employment Opportunities, led by Sam Schaeffer, provides former prisoners with both job coaches, who offer support for participants to get unsubsidized private sector jobs, and job developers, who work with employers and participants to move people into permanent employment. The staff also teaches formerly incarcerated people financial education and, more important, help to "build their vision of their future—any future they want other than incarceration—and light a fire under that vision."[42] The program, which also includes transitional employment, has a successful track record of reducing recidivism and helping connect former offenders to jobs.[43] The regional director of the Center for Employment Opportunities' Los Angeles office, Sarah Glenn-Leistikow, said that the staff members "show up day in and day out because the work has meaning to people's lives. . . . There's a mutual love of the work we do, both from staff and participants. They're doing hard work every day, improving the community, the city, the county. They come here because that's meaningful to them."[44]

EXAMPLE FIVE: JOBS THAT FOCUS ON THE WHOLE CHILD

Perhaps the clearest example of a double-dignity job that improves children's lives is that of a public school teacher. By ensuring that teacher pay reflects their expertise and contribution to society, we can create better jobs for Americans while improving the educational outcomes for our children. In addition to an effort to ensure teachers receive the pay and respect they deserve, there is a need for broad investment in a diverse number of double-dignity jobs that address all of a child's needs—the "whole child" approach. While there is no one definition of a "whole child" approach, it certainly means addressing physical and mental health, the personal development that comes from meaningful after-school activities, and individualized attention. Low-income students facing economic disadvantage often also face a host of challenges in schools, such as dealing with more stressors on average than their wealthier peers.[45] Too many fall behind quickly in math and reading[46] and have dramatically less individualized tutoring and fewer summer and after-school activities.

Currently, there is a deep deficit of psychologists in schools to address behavioral and trauma-related issues among kids. The current ratio of school psychologists is a pathetic 1 for every 1,400 students.[47] In a master's or specialized degree program, school psychologists receive extensive training to perform a range of services, from assessing a student's cognitive abilities to providing crisis intervention services after a child experiences a traumatic event.[48] Public schools recognize the critical role that school psychologists should play. The Chicago Teachers Union went on strike in October 2019 demanding "support staff focused on students' well-being," including psychologists.[49] In Los Angeles, school psychologist Alejandra Gurrola works in several schools each week, serving more than two thousand students, and worries about what that means for her students: "It interferes with our quality of work because we don't have enough time to serve as many students as we could. . . . What if a student is having an emotional crisis on a Tuesday and I'm not there because I'm assigned to another school? Then the resource for that student is not there for that day."[50] We should invest in training school psychologists and paying them a strong enough wage to support their families and allow them to pay off graduate school debt. By doing so, we would create meaningful jobs that would fill a desperate need in our public schools.

The deficit in double-dignity jobs is broad and deep. Across this nation, perhaps the most common attributes of even the most high-performing nonprofits are underfunding, understaffing, economic uncertainty, and burnout. This is a hidden jobs deficit. You would think that when talented people choose to pursue professions of relatively low pay to serve others, we as a society would at least help ensure they have the secure pay and benefits and support to encourage long-term service and careers. We don't. My mother, Doris Sperling, founded a successful, inspiring tutoring nonprofit, the Family Learning Institute (FLI) in Ann Arbor, Michigan, which primarily serves students from lower-income neighborhoods throughout Washtenaw County. This model helps nearly 90 percent of students gain one to two reading levels in a single year of one-on-one tutoring.[51] But even a program with such impressive returns as the FLI, which relies on volunteer tutors, can function effectively only with skilled professionals who are specialists in assessment, reading, and nonprofit management.

Even the highest-performing nonprofits in youth development struggle to get the strong, steady funding needed to hire dedicated young professionals and then convince them to build careers with the nonprofit. This is even more true when those same funding challenges also translate to excessive hours due to understaffing. I saw that struggle even with the Mosaic Youth Theatre of Detroit, which was founded by my brother, Rick Sperling, in 1992, and has been continually recognized as one of the nation's top youth theater programs and by the Carnegie Foundation and others for its stellar performance on youth development.[52] "It's really heartbreaking," describes Rick. "We get on board such amazing, dedicated young people who want nothing more than to stay and transform lives through the arts. But we lose them because funding limitations make it very hard for them to see a path to real career growth." This story can be told time and time again about successful after-school programs across the nation. As one director of an effective after-school program in Kansas noted, she "lost some good support staff over the years, including a future Kansas teacher of the year, because she couldn't offer the stability employees needed. 'If we didn't have to worry all the time about funding, how could we expend that energy?' she wondered. 'We could have this great plan going forward.'"[53] The deep deficit in double-dignity jobs makes all the difference in whether young people born into economic disadvantage get true first and second chances.

EXAMPLE SIX: JOBS CARING FOR OUR PARENTS

One of the most common evocations of "dignity" in our current economic dialogue is the call for everyone to have a "dignified retirement." For too long this has been seen as only a matter of retirement income and savings. Increasingly, however, the dominant issue of a dignified retirement is the capacity to ensure quality care for parents and loved ones experiencing chronic conditions and Alzheimer's or other dementias. As the population ages, more and more people experience how economic dignity is impoverished without the capacity to ensure quality care for parents. This issue goes to the heart of our ability to care for family and experience its most meaningful moments. It also represents a profound opportunity for double-dignity jobs.

The number of people aged sixty-five and older who will require assistance with daily living is expected to double in the next twenty-five years, but we have not seriously addressed the need for more caregivers.[54] The typical situation today is that when a loved one needs long-term care services—and 70 percent of those aged sixty-five and older will need such services at some point[55]—a family member or friend steps in to provide that care. This describes the situation for nearly 40 million people who provide some form of unpaid care for a close family member or friend.[56] While this is often felt to be a part of our cycle of life—a sense of repaying our parents for the years they cared for us—it can also come with serious sacrifices to the capacity to be there for one's own children and to pursue one's potential, not to mention immense financial strain.

The direct care workforce, which includes personal care aides, home health aides, and nursing assistants, doubled in size over roughly the past decade, and is projected to add more jobs than any single occupational category by 2026.[57] Whether those positions can be double-dignity jobs will depend on policy. As Ai-jen Poo has written, "At the same time that millions of people in the United States are struggling to survive long-term unemployment, there are far too few workers who are positioned and prepared to provide care for the growing number of elders and people with disabilities. The demographic shift creates a moment when we can set in place a system to affirm the dignity of people at every stage of life and in every walk of life and create millions of good jobs in the process."[58]

But much like jobs in childcare, elder-care jobs currently do not support economic dignity very frequently. Despite most working full-time, more than half of direct care workers live in households below 200 percent of the poverty line.[59] On top of doing physically and emotionally draining work for poverty-level wages, direct care workers have few opportunities for advancement. Even when there are opportunities, the compensation gains are often inadequate to incentivize anyone to invest the necessary time toward upskilling. Most states don't require personal care aides to receive any training,[60] and the wage differential for home health aides, who are able to perform certain clinical tasks in addition to helping with basic daily living after undergoing training, is far too low to be a real opportunity for mobility.

Many older adults, like me, who have a parent with dementia often feel like they are struggling to provide the best care possible for their parent in a system that is ill equipped. Despite the fact that one in three clients of home care agencies lives with Alzheimer's and related dementias,[61] there is no requirement of actual training or knowledge in dementia care at a federal level, and only thirteen states have dementia-specific training requirements.[62] The astronomical turnover of home care workers—estimated to be between 40 and 82 percent annually[63]—means that any valuable on-the-job experience gained is quickly lost. This is happening precisely because the jobs are so undervalued and underpaid. Enhancing the role of the home care worker to be a trained and valued member of the health-care delivery team—as SEIU president Mary Kay Henry and others have long called for—means providing robust initial and ongoing training, higher compensation, peer mentoring, and meaningful opportunities for advancement in the profession.

Done right, the costs of such investment in double-dignity jobs will pay high returns. When home care workers were integrated into the health-care delivery team for patients, the results were impressive: one cohort saw a 41 percent decline in the average rate of repeat ER visits and a 43 percent decline in the average rate of rehospitalizations by the second year after the training.[64] According to the authors of the study, the savings from reduced repeat ER visits and rehospitalizations could be as high as $12,000 per patient.[65] In New York City, a pilot demonstration created an opportunity for home care workers to obtain an advanced role in their profession, termed a Care Connections Senior Aide (CCSA), creating precisely the kind of professional, valued job that could be scaled. With an advanced title in the field, CCSAs received two hundred hours of training and coaching, were integrated into the health-care delivery team, and earned a salary 60 percent higher than the average for entry-level home care workers.[66] The result: improved job satisfaction, improved relations with clients and communication with clinical managers, plus a decline in emergency department visits.[67] I distinctly remember an on-the-ball caregiver who stayed overnight for my father, who was dealing with congestive heart failure. This person, still in college, had the training to spot a pattern in my father's breathing that led her to wake him up and alert a nurse. It saved a several-day visit to the University of Michigan hospital that likely would have cost more than the full-year's salary for most caregivers.

This reflects the multiple wins in double-dignity jobs. Higher skills and higher pay reduce wasteful turnover, protect a sense of value and respect that is deserved by workers, and deliver economic security and dignity to their families, all while reducing unnecessary health expenditures.

CHOOSING JOBS PROGRAMS WISELY

I have focused on double-dignity jobs that involve the direct services from one American to another, services that provide dignified work and lift up the dignity of those being helped. Yet these jobs should be seen as part of a larger principle: we should ask how much we can align jobs for those in need of dignified work with our most compelling national priorities. An expansion of AmeriCorps or national service jobs programs may not always lead to career paths but could address pressing social needs, instill a greater national ethic of civic participation, and lead to a tighter job market. Building on the Civilian Conservation Corps concept to undertake a generational upgrade of our public lands and national parks is an example of a worthy and deeply needed national project that could create jobs and experience connected to the natural environment. More ambitiously, there are potentially millions of jobs that can be created or enhanced by making good on the vision of a Green New Deal—from energy-efficient installations, to lead removal, to installation and maintenance of new infrastructure like electric vehicle charging stations. These jobs may not involve direct assistance to promote the dignity of specific individuals, but they can represent dignified work that furthers an environmental future that will have a profound impact on health, happiness, and overall well-being. As Lawrence Summers has argued, with economic trends pointing toward weakened demand and lower interest rates in the future,[68] the economic argument for even borrowing to create jobs through public capital investment with high national economic returns has rarely been stronger. Jobs created through addressing deferred maintenance, modernizing schools, and creating a carbon-free national infrastructure would be another win-win mechanism to create dignified work in the face of temporary or structural declines in private sector demand for workers.

Another option that has been proposed in various forms is a guaranteed jobs program to ensure all people can work at all times. From a values perspective, such a guaranteed jobs program incorporates the compact of contribution and the value of dignity. It is an idea that deserves to be considered and piloted in particularly hard-hit communities and economically disadvantaged areas, for the long-term unemployed, and especially during serious economic downturns.[69] There is strong evidence from an Obama administration emergency jobs program in 2009 that subsidizing private employers to hire unemployed workers during the downturn is quite effective. Studies have shown that 63 percent of the employers created jobs that would not have otherwise existed, helping the unemployed reenter the job market and boost earnings—and even helping those facing the barriers of long-term unemployment and a prior criminal record.[70] Certainly, initiatives like this should be expanded.

But we will change more lives by focusing our investment on double-dignity jobs. Why?

There is enormous temporary job loss and job change in our economy. As many as six million a month—yes, *a month!*—change jobs willingly or unwillingly. Guaranteeing that each person is employed at all times could be a herculean managerial challenge that fails to target our greatest job and social needs. And the imperative to move quickly can lead to temporary employment that may lack the serious training, skills, wraparound services, and career building that can be most game-changing in the lives we are trying to lift up. As mentioned earlier, a study compiled lessons from forty years of subsidized jobs programs and identified two of the most promising elements of effective subsidized employment programs as ensuring opportunities for skills and career development and providing critical, but often forgotten, wraparound services.[71] Bottom line: guaranteed jobs programs are worth exploring, but may be best in situations of more targeted economic circumstances.

A focus on double-dignity jobs sets a higher bar with more lasting value to both workers and society. It embraces the end goal of economic dignity for all and creates thousands of well-paid jobs that repair the dignity gaps felt by far too many of our people.

CHAPTER FOURTEEN

CAN ALL WORK HAVE MEANING?

[Work] is about a search, too, for daily meaning as well as daily bread, for recognition as well as cash, for astonishment rather than torpor; in short, for a life rather than a Monday through Friday sort of dying.[1]

STUDS TERKEL, *Working*

Can all work have meaning?

In an economy where we ensure an economic dignity wage, respect the value of all who contribute regardless of income or job prestige, and protect against abuse and mistreatment at work, we will have gone a long way toward ensuring a basic level of dignity at work. We go even further when all of us as individuals—and collectively as a society—is deeply committed to never stigmatizing, shaming, or looking down on any job or means of contributing to society. We make progress toward promoting dignity for all when we recognize and appreciate the commitment, pride, and high standards so many Americans bring to working at a job, helping their community, or devoting themselves to the hard and meaningful work of raising their children or caring for other loved ones.

Ending the conversation there would, however, skip over a profound question for this journey: Is it actually realistic to aspire to an economy where every person would be able to find a sense of meaning and pursue some form of purpose in their work and their economic lives beyond a paycheck?

It goes without saying that providing the opportunity for children to have a better life is a major driver of purpose for millions of Americans. This was expressed poignantly in former president Barack Obama's eulogy at the funeral of Congressman Elijah Cummings. Obama described Cummings's parents as sharecroppers who transitioned to factory and housecleaning work. His father would take his son to the airport to watch planes, saying, "I have not flied. I may not fly. But you will fly one day. We can't afford it right now, but you will fly."[2]

But as important as the sense of purpose in caring and providing opportunity for family or contributing to one's community is, to achieve a test of universal economic dignity, I still believe we should aim higher. We should shape our economy and workplaces to achieve a world where work offers the possibility to find meaning and purpose and pride beyond simply a paycheck, even in the service of caring for family.

It is perhaps of little surprise that the top libertarians and progressive philosophers disagree on whether such a goal is achievable. Philosopher Robert Nozick rejects the idea that all work can be meaningful—which he defines as allowing the capacity to "exercise one's talents and capacities" in an activity "of worth" that one understands as part of a larger goal.[3] Nozick implies that "some jobs . . . may not seem at all meaningful . . . [but] are nevertheless necessary."[4] He suggests that some people might actively choose to have a less meaningful job in order to get higher compensation—though we know that is far from always the case.[5]

John Rawls, on the other hand, believed meaningful work for all was possible, even for jobs some today think of as being mundane or requiring specialized skill. The philosopher wrote in A Theory of Justice that such work can be crafted in ways that allow all workers a sense of respect and meaning. "The worst aspects of division [of labor]," Rawls stated, "can be surmounted: no one need be servilely dependent on others and made to choose between monotonous and routine occupations which are deadening to human thought and sensibility. Each can be offered a variety of tasks so that the different elements of his nature find a suitable expression."[6]

Philosopher Norman Bowie seeks to imagine how Immanuel Kant's vision of never being treated as a pure means to an end should shape our conception of meaningful work and identifies "six Kantian characteristics of meaningful work." These are perhaps helped by higher skills but not dependent on them.

The characteristics include work that "is freely entered into," "allows the worker to exercise . . . autonomy and independence," "enables the worker to develop . . . rational capacities," "provides a wage sufficient for physical welfare," "supports the moral development of employees," and "is not paternalistic in the sense of interfering with the worker's conception of how she wishes to obtain happiness."[7]

I tend to side with Rawls. Yes, not everyone will inevitably find the same levels of challenge or fulfillment at work. But we have the power—through how we treat one another and construct public policy—to ensure the compensation, respect, and chance to contribute needed for a basic level of dignity and meaning for all who work. Is that too idealistic? Perhaps. But what is clear is that we will never know until we do everything in our power to test that proposition. What I can say with confidence is we are not there, or even close to making that effort. There is far, far more we can do if we are committed to economic dignity as our end goal.

WHAT DO WE KNOW?

It is perhaps convenient to quote philosophers because the empirical evidence on which job characteristics are linked to meaning at work is not perfectly clear. Despite the mixed literature on this subject, one common theme shines through: meaning at work depends on far more than compensation and benefits.

Americans place a high value on finding meaning at work, but their relationships with their jobs vary widely. In 2006, when Americans were asked to rank five work characteristics including "high income" and "working hours are short [with] lots of free time," work that is "important and gives a feeling of accomplishment" was the most preferred job characteristic overall.[8] However, in 2017, only 34 percent of people said that their job gave them "a great deal" of meaning and fulfillment, 36 percent said they got "some" meaning and fulfillment from their job, and 29 percent got "not much" or "none at all" from their job.[9] Answers did not vary with income level. Perhaps not surprisingly, a different economic study found that men with at most a high school degree had experienced a decline in finding meaning in their work since 1970.[10] The statistics on meaning at work align with those about engagement at work—about a third of people are "engaged" at work, meaning enthusiastic about and committed to their work and workplace. Discouragingly, 13 percent of workers essentially said they are miserable at work, or "actively disengaged."[11] The remaining folks fall in between.

When it comes to whether Americans get a sense of identity from their jobs, people are almost evenly split. "About half (51 percent) of employed Americans say they get a sense of identity from their job, while the other half (47 percent) say their job is just what they do for a living."[12] Education mattered in this study: 77 percent of workers with a postgraduate degree and 60 percent of those with a college degree say their job gives them a sense of identity, while only 38 percent of those who have a high school diploma or less say the same.[13] The type of employment also matters. Over 60 percent of those in government jobs, self-employment, or nonprofit work report deriving identity from work, compared with 42 percent in the private sector.[14] The RAND Corporation found somewhat more positive outcomes than other studies. It asked Americans ages twenty-one to seventy-five if their work provides them with the "satisfaction of work well done," a "feeling of doing useful work," a "sense of personal accomplishment," the ability to "make positive impact on community/society," "opportunities to fully use talents," and "goals to aspire to." About 80 percent of Americans say their job provides at least one of these qualities always or most of the time. Only one in three, however, say their job provides all six sources of meaning.[15]

While these varied measures are difficult to put into a neat narrative about the meaning all Americans find in their work, the research does suggest that there is much we can do as members of our society, employers, and policymakers to move in the right direction.

Researchers in organizational behavior have long studied what job characteristics produce meaning and satisfaction at work. Two leaders of the field, Richard Hackman and Greg Oldham, developed a model of what makes a job meaningful, identifying important attributes such as being able to complete tasks from start to finish, using a variety of skills, having autonomy, receiving feedback, and performing work that positively affects others.[16] Practices found to destroy meaning have less to do with the status of one's job than about creating a disconnect between employees' values and employers' values, giving people pointless tasks, treating people unfairly, and disconnecting people from supportive relationships.[17]

One of the most thoughtful approaches to the issue is the concept of "job crafting" that Yale School of Management professor Amy Wrzesniewski has put forward. Wrzesniewski finds that by job crafting—by which she means "the physical and cognitive changes individuals make in the task or relational boundaries of their work"—employees can change the amount of meaning they derive from work.[18] Take an example Wrzesniewski found in the food-service industry. Professional cooks and kitchen staff changed "the number of their tasks" and "the way they saw their tasks" to utilize their creative talents. "Rather than simply prepare food that served customers' needs, the cooks tried to make the food as 'nice' as possible, thus changing the task boundary of the work. Instead of thinking about the preparation of meal elements as separate tasks, the cooks . . . [saw] their work as being about the gestalt of the entire meal. The cooks used their own artistic standards in trying to create a product worthy of pride."[19] The cooks reframed their work, changing it from a rote task that required following management's policies to one that allowed them to use their creativity.

Perhaps Wrzesniewski's most illuminating study of job crafting was of cleaning workers at a hospital. She and her coauthors interviewed twenty-eight janitorial staff at a hospital and found striking differences in how they defined the tasks and overall mission of their work. Some described their work as pure cleaning, involving few skills, and thus found their job unsatisfying. Yet others defined the range of their tasks and goals in ways that went far beyond the technical description and added higher meaning, skills, and job satisfaction. This latter group performed tasks outside their job description that created more meaning in their work. One janitor changed the paintings in the rooms of comatose patients, hoping that the change in visual stimulation might help the patients' healing. Another worker took care to clean anything on the ceiling, where many patients lying in bed would look but the average healthy person would not.[20] These workers saw themselves as part of the broader service mission of the organization itself, saying, "I'm an ambassador for the hospital," and "I'm a healer. I create sterile spaces in the hospital. My role here is to do everything I can to promote the healing of the patients."[21] Both the janitors at the hospital and the food-service workers exercised their autonomy to enhance their own meaning at work, aligning themselves with the broader mission of their organization—helping the sick or creating amazing meals for people—and altering "the meaning of the work and their work identity" in the process."[22]

Wrzesniewski's research and the organizational behavior literature supports Rawls's view that the "worst aspects of division [of labor] can be surmounted." Neither the nature of capitalism nor the fact that there is some division of labor by skills and pay nor the path and pace of technology has to make misery at work inevitable. What we do as policymakers, employers, and consumers can make a major difference.

A FRAMEWORK FOR DEFINING MEANINGFUL WORK

Based on this discussion and my research and life experience, I would summarize meaningful work—beyond compensation and benefits—through five elements.

First, feeling connected to a larger purpose or mission that a worker can take pride in. This does not mean that every worker has a double-dignity job or is working toward curing cancer or helping refugees. Nor does it mean that every worker has to be a CEO or the star engineer or the plant manager or the owner of the restaurant. Instead, this tenet gets at the idea that all employees should feel pride and connection to the ultimate goal of their organization, whether they are equipment managers of a pro sports team, waitresses who take enormous pride in providing topflight service, steelworkers who know they supply quality inputs for our bridges and cars, or janitors at a hospital who see themselves as integral in caring for the sick.

Second, respect for the basic common humanity of all workers. Dignity at work must include the sense that even as a subordinate, even with the goals of efficiency and profit, your basic common humanity is recognized and respected. In Kant's terms, you are an end in yourself. That means we must design work and jobs so that they do not require nonstop, mind-numbing, high-pressure, repetitive tasks. Workers need breaks, new tasks, and basic respect because they are ends in themselves. It also means going beyond providing the legally mandated protections for workers and structuring work with the recognition that all of us have basic human needs that manifest in the need to check in on sick children, take time off for the birth of a child or loss of a loved one, or cope with depression.

Third, a sense of voice. As I discussed earlier in the book, having dignity at work is also about being valued and having one's input considered. As a spot welder at a Ford plant in the 1970s stated when asked about pride in his job: "Proud of my work? How can I feel pride in a job where I call a foreman's attention to a mistake, to a bad piece of equipment, and he'll ignore it."[23]

Fourth, all workers—regardless of pay and status—should be treated as first-class citizens and full members of the team. What defines first-class citizenship is not pure equality of status, pay, or prestige. It is that there is a common baseline of respect, rights, and responsibilities that applies to the highest- and lowest-ranked person in the organization or society. It is better to be the starting quarterback on a high school football team than the third-string guard, but each is considered a part of the team and has to be on time, do the same workouts, and live by the same rules.

Fifth, workers should feel they always can pursue their potential to contribute, be better, and even move up and be recognized for their work. Of course, not every job at every stage of a worker's tenure provides clear opportunities for promotion. Not every person will have the opportunity or luck to literally pursue their full potential. This does not mean, however, that workplaces cannot offer opportunity for workers to continually feel proud of their work, be recognized individually or as part of a group, take on new tasks, or have opportunities to expand their sense of making a difference. The best managers will realize that deploying these strategies will both expand the individual dignity of their workers and result in stronger company performance and productivity.

WHAT CAN WE DO? THE ROLE OF POLICY

But can policy matter in what are fundamentally matters of basic respect in employer-employee relationships? We are obligated to try. As we discussed in Chapter Seven, when markets or workplaces are structured to reward race-to-the-bottom practices that denigrate economic dignity or meaning at work, we should feel compelled to fix them.

Consider the critical issue of segmentation at work. As previously discussed in Chapter Twelve, a major policy challenge is correcting misclassifications of workers like FedEx or Uber drivers whose classification as "contractors" denies them basic economic security benefits. Beyond this, however, is a deeper segmentation or "fissure," as David Weil calls it, in our workforce that has only picked up steam in recent decades. Segmentation involves the wholesale shifting of jobs that were once part of our largest, well-known American companies to subcontracting companies. This practice is infiltrating every major business sector. In 2012, Apple, for example, had only 63,000 full-time employees out of more than 750,000 workers globally responsible for its products.[24] In 2019, Google's global temporary and contracted workforce, at 121,000 people, is larger than its full-time employee workforce of 102,000.[25] Despite working alongside full-time employees, Google's temps and contractors wear different-colored badges, reinforcing separation, and earn lower wages and fewer benefits for the same or similar jobs.[26] If, as Weil notes, the twentieth century marked the concentration of an economic system dominated by large corporations, now we have shifted to a model where that dominance is deployed through employment that has been split off to various secondary actors. This arrangement lets companies have their cake and eat it, too—at the expense of the workers on the wrong side of the fissure. The larger company retains significant control over subcontracted workers' actions and hours, but it has less accountability. The worker is still serving the goals of the larger company, but is now often denied both the economic benefits and psychological status of being a first-class member of the larger company's team.[27]

To be clear, this is not subcontracting as we think of it in construction, where the person you hire to build a house subcontracts out the pouring of concrete to another company. This type of segmentation gets at the subcontracting out of jobs that could easily be in-house. It's subcontracting out data entry, food service, and janitorial workers at major tech and manufacturing companies or housekeeping at major hotel chains. It was once common for such workers to be actual employees of that company, whether it be GM or Kodak or most of the Fortune 500. Being officially part of the team was consequential. It mattered. When such workers were part of the larger company, it was harder for executives to have a lower-rung employee denied the basic benefits of paid time off and health care offered to the rest of a company's employees (and in some cases, like retirement benefits, discouraged in the tax code). As Weil writes, when "lead companies directly employed many workers, workers received a significant share of the profitability in terms of both wages and benefits. . . . By shifting work out, lead firms no longer face a wage determination problem for that work, but rather a pricing problem in selecting between companies vying for it."[28]

Now more and more companies seek to limit full-time jobs within their companies to those they believe are directly focused on the company's "core competencies." These are the elements of work that companies claim truly add value to their competitiveness. Ancillary tasks are subcontracted out to the lowest bidder. The behavior of some companies suggests a preference to subcontract out anything that can lower costs, even if it is related to their core competencies: "Hershey outsources elements of production of its chocolate liquor—the chocolate core of products like Kisses—to other companies, leaving only final reassembly steps to its own facilities and workforce."[29]

This explosion of segmentation in the workforce creates a negative cycle, as subcontractors can offer more and more competitive bids the more they slash and deny the pay, paid leave, and health and retirement benefits employees would have received if still working for the major corporation being serviced. So, while these workers may be doing the very same task for the company that was done previously by the same or similar workers, they now have a fundamentally different relationship to their employer and their place of work than in prior years.

The impact on inequality is staggering. Economist Larry Katz estimates "the sorting of workers into high- and low-end employers accounts for a quarter to a third of the increase of wage inequality in the United States since 1980."[30]

This segmentation trend hinders workers' ability to pursue purpose, potential, and meaning at work. I will focus on two critical ways in which segmentation violates our tenets for meaningful work: the ability to pursue potential and the right to be treated as a first-class member of the team.

A SHOT AT MOVING UP?

Even if it was largely in the movies, the notion of the person in the mailroom moving up to the C-suite by working hard and showing initiative represents a classic American value and aspiration. This upward mobility success story goes from improbable to nearly impossible in the segmentation or fissure era. By subcontracting out jobs to other companies, large organizations essentially cap the ability of the employees of the subcontractor to rise up in the ranks.

Few tales make this more vivid than Neil Irwin's piece in the *New York Times* on two janitors at leading technology companies—Gail Evans, a janitor working as an employee for Kodak in the 1980s, and Marta Ramos, a janitor contracted out to Apple today. The janitors at Kodak had robust employee benefits, including paid vacation, reimbursement of tuition costs for part-time college, and bonuses. Moreover, when Kodak recognized talent in its low-wage workers like janitors, it promoted them. Gail Evans was a janitor at the Kodak campus in Rochester, New York, in the early 1980s. After a manager found out Evans knew how to use spreadsheets, the manager asked her to teach other employees the skill. "When she eventually finished her college degree in 1987, she was promoted to a professional-track job in information technology. Less than a decade later, Ms. Evans was chief technology officer of the whole company, and she has had a long career since as a senior executive at other top companies."[31] Evans told the *New York Times*, "One thing about Eastman Kodak is they believed in their people. It was like a family. You always had someone willing to help open a door if you demonstrated that you were willing to commit to growing your skills and become an asset that was valuable for the company."[32] Evans's story is the canonical "mailroom to boardroom" journey that represents our ideal for upward mobility and opportunity in the American workplace.

Contrast Evans's experience with the situation Marta Ramos faces in the era of segmentation. An employee of a contractor Apple uses to clean its buildings, Ramos has almost no opportunities for advancement. The most she can hope for is a 50 cent raise for "becoming a team leader keeping tabs on a few other janitors."[33] The segmentation model essentially puts a ceiling on the skills Ramos can develop and utilize.

As Ramos's story illustrates, the downsides of contracting do not end at benefits and wages. Wharton School of Management professor Matthew Bidwell has noted that contracting can permanently damage someone's career, as contractors fall behind on developing their skills and potential. As Bidwell stated, "As an employee, your employer may pay to train you and keep you up to date on new technologies. They will also give you a chance to try new kinds of work and learn that way. As a contractor, nobody is paying for you to learn. [Businesses] only want to hire you to do things that you have already demonstrated you can do elsewhere. That means you have to pay for your own training."[34]

BEING A FIRST-CLASS CITIZEN AND PART OF A TEAM

Segmentation not only hurts opportunities to advance but also leads to dignity harms at work, as people can be treated like second-class citizens when they aren't officially part of the company "team." First, there are the big-ticket differentiators between employees of the main company and workers from the subcontracting company, including pay and benefit discrepancies. Employees of subcontractors often do not have the same access to bereavement leave or family leave that employees of the main company do. Ramos, the janitor working at Apple, doesn't get a paid vacation or a bonus, whereas most Apple employees get generous benefits.[35] Then there are the smaller, quieter dignity harms. In Silicon Valley, many technology companies employ armies of contractors and use things like badge color to distinguish between employees and contractors, marking out who truly belongs and who doesn't.[36] At some companies, the process of creating exclusion and boundaries is reinforced by keeping contractors out of work events, meetings, and work parties. One Apple contractor told the *New York Times* that though he had worked extensively on a new version of Apple's operating system, he wasn't invited to the fancy release party in San Francisco that the Apple employees attended when the operating system debuted, so he and other contractors headed for beers at a neighborhood pub.[37]

Some of the practices that arise from segmentation offend dignity in multiple ways. Facebook reportedly refused to let its cafeteria workers, who are employed by a food-service contractor, participate in its annual Take Your Child to Work Day.[38] Indeed, the *Wall Street Journal* reports that contractors at many companies cannot "attend important meetings, go to the company gym, or bring their kids to Take Your Child to Work Day."[39] This special day serves as a way to bring employees together over the shared experiences of parenting. Everyone from the executives to the administrative staff can bond over the travails of getting a child to do their homework or experiences with bullying in school. Because such events promote bonding and a sense of being part of a team among workers across positions, they also function as networking events. As political scientist Robert Putnam notes in his 2007 essay, "*E Pluribus Unum:* Diversity and Community in the Twenty-first Century," "Networks have value, first, to people who are in the networks. For example, economic sociologists have shown repeatedly that labor markets are thoroughly permeated by networks so that most of us are as likely to get our jobs through whom we know as through what we know. Indeed, it has been shown that our lifetime income is powerfully affected by the quality of our networks."[40] If cafeteria workers can't interact with Facebook employees in a company-wide social function, they face diminished networks. At a more basic level, one of the main points of Take Your Kids to Work Day is to expose your children to different types of careers they could aspire to and show them what a day at your company looks like. Why should a cafeteria worker who serves "core competency" employees every day be denied that opportunity?

WHAT CAN BE DONE THROUGH POLICY?

There is no evidence that this trend—or the corporate culture that helps drive it—is reversing or even slowing. While a few companies are becoming more conscious of ensuring contractors get higher minimum wages, there seems to be no interest in bringing such employees back in-house. Only changes in legislation and regulation are likely to restructure the market to better serve our economic dignity ideals. Currently, the market is set up for a classic race to the bottom: major companies see their top competitors choosing to reduce costs by taking bids to find the lowest cost subcontractor, making it more unthinkable that any of them would consider restoring these outsourced jobs back into company jobs with first-class citizenship. It may be very difficult for the human resources manager at a large company to advocate for keeping janitors on as employees when all of their competitors are cutting costs through segmentation.

There may be no easy off-the-shelf answers, but it is important to start reimagining our labor market policy approaches to reverse the downsides of the segmentation or fissure era.

One idea is to expand how we look at "nondiscrimination" rules in the provisions of benefits. Under current Employee Retirement Income Security Act law, employers do not get the tax benefits associated with contributions to employees' retirement plans if the plans "discriminate in favor of highly compensated employees."[41] That rule was designed to prevent companies from offering senior management much better retirement plans than lower-level staff. In the segmentation era, we need to consider expanding this principle to whether major companies also provide or ensure that subcontractors essentially working full-time for them also receive the same benefits.

Congress could also explore rethinking who is defined as "the employer" for a host of legal responsibilities beyond collective bargaining, as discussed earlier. Weil argues for broadening multiemployer liability in subcontracted industries. Multiemployer liability essentially says that "more than one employer may be responsible for a workplace hazard and therefore citable for a violation of health and safety standards."[42] This policy has traditionally been used in the Occupational Safety and Health Administration regulatory context and specifically in the area of construction. However, we should be thinking about how we might use a similar principle to expand liability and responsibility for subcontractors and franchisees in every area of work.

Expanding our legal view of who the responsible employer is and then expanding transparency could create momentum for such subcontractors to bond together to press for higher benefits, better pay, and more flexible work rules, especially if there are more avenues for such workers to unionize. What if we said that any company that is competing for a government contract must list publicly a side-by-side comparison of the benefits it pays its core workers and those paid to its segmented workers? This could create opportunities to put public pressure on companies to equalize benefits and, with a broader employer definition, create energy and possibility for new versions of collective bargaining and bonding together.

Finally, as suggested in my discussion on a new economic dignity net in Chapter Twelve, we should be aspiring toward more universal access for all workers to major health, employment, and retirement benefits. As we work toward this goal, we should be asking what structures would minimize the incentive for dignity-denigrating treatment of so many workers. Policies for universal health coverage would surely help. The more we reform our economic security benefits so that any employer is going to have to pay the same costs whether the worker is in-house or subcontracted out, the less incentive there will be to cut costs through a race to the bottom that treats some workers as second-class citizens.

WHAT CAN CONSUMERS AND MANAGERS DO?

The focus of this book has been on policy, but it is important to remember that we as consumers have the power to vote our values with our purchases. If we place economic dignity for all people and all work at the top of our economic agenda, we can, in our role as consumers, vote against products and services that are the result of degrading or dehumanizing practices toward workers.

Consider the effect of the "electronic whip," which I explained in Chapter Five. Emily Guendelsberger, a journalist who worked in low-wage jobs at Amazon, McDonald's, and Convergys, vividly recounts these experiences in her book *On the Clock*. She writes that technology "constantly corralled [her] and [her] coworkers . . . like a sheepdog snapping at a herd's heels."[43] The McDonald's "phone-book-size operations and training manual" lists every work activity down to the second ("target sandwich assembly time: 22 seconds"), with accompanying constant electronic alarms sounding when targets are not met. At Amazon, Guendelsberger walked sixteen miles a day fulfilling orders with a GPS monitor tracking her movements and counting down the seconds for her to finish every task.[44] In highlighting the conditions that millions of Americans are subjected to on a daily basis, she asks her readers a series of key questions: "When was the last time you asked to go to the bathroom? Would you panic over running two minutes late? Is it normal to be constantly monitored at work, to have everything you do timed by the second?"[45]

Using technology to regulate employee behavior every minute prioritizes microefficiencies over human treatment of workers. As I noted in Chapter Five, Amazon "pickers," the workers who locate an item in the warehouse and put it on a conveyor belt to be shipped, have to pick up four hundred items per hour, or one every seven seconds.[46] While it is reasonable for employers to encourage higher productivity and to not tolerate slacking, that is far different than seeing workers only as instruments of efficiency—with the type of microefficiency developed during slavery.[47] At base, such practices treat people as means and not ends. GM worker Gary Bryner told Studs Terkel in 1976 how the auto giant had determined that for every second the company can make workers more efficient it can save $1 million:

> You know, [managers] use the stopwatches, and they say, look: we know from experience that it takes so many seconds to walk from here to there. . . . And our argument has always been, you know, that's mechanical. That's not human. Look: we tire. We sweat. We have hangovers. We have upset stomachs. We have feelings, emotions, and we're not about to be placed in a category of a machine. . . . I just think they want to be able to be treated with dignity and some respect. And you know, that's not asking a hell of a lot.[48]

Treating people as you would a machine has always been an affront to dignity. Even Henry Ford's automobile assembly, with its famed $5 wage for an eight-hour day, was romanticized. He paid twice what any other auto company did because he had a turnover rate of 370 percent a year. To put that in context, Walmart's turnover rate today is a very high 100 percent. Historian Stephen Meyer notes of the workers, "They wouldn't stay. . . . They hated the work and they would just walk off the job or not show up."[49]

In the face of disturbing employer practices, we, as consumers, have to decide that we are willing to say no when work policies offend our values of economic dignity. The Delano grape workers strike of 1965–70 to protest miserable pay and work conditions—no toilets in the fields, no cold drinking water, no rest periods, and poverty-level wages (70 cents per hour, or $6 per hour updated for inflation)—was more effective when 17 million Americans answered the call of the United Farm Workers to boycott grapes.[50]

On *Last Week Tonight with John Oliver*, the host highlighted the impossible conditions that many warehouse workers face in the quest to get consumers two-day delivery of packages.[51] Oliver poked fun at consumer complicity in this system with a tongue-in-cheek ad for Amazon titled "Amazon: Try Not to Think About It."[52] As Oliver pointed out, there is an onus on the consumer to be part of the shift away from dehumanizing work. But are consumers willing to pay a little more to ensure that they're not supporting companies that work their employees or contractors to the bone for meager pay? Is it worth it to consumers to wait an extra day or two for a package to arrive if it means the person who packaged the item got to use the bathroom without fear of losing their job? As writer Anne Helen Petersen put it, "Are you willing to be slightly less comfortable so that a whole lot of other people can have a slightly higher quality of life?"[53] We all know that warehouse workers and janitors will be paid less than CEOs, but we don't have to accept a world in which lower-wage workers face degrading conditions.

For example, one measure that consumers could take would be to boycott goods and services produced or delivered in ways that violate economic dignity. When you see the "fair trade" symbol on a bar of chocolate or a pound of coffee, you know that the item was produced according to internationally agreed-upon social, environmental, and economic standards.[54] A modern-day economic dignity or "fair work" code could include basic protections for workers against oppressive microefficiency or electronic whip treatment.

The issue of seeking universal meaning and purpose of work is also a challenge to anyone who plays a role in managing or structuring organizations. There is evidence from the workplace democracy literature that respecting and actively engaging the input of workers both promotes meaning at work and leads to better business results. Political theorist Robert Dahl argued in 2001 that workers have a "moral right to democratic voice at work."[55] Studies of Toyota's assembly line approach demonstrated that workers were happier and more efficient when they were able to autonomously "own" their portion of the production process, could contribute suggestions for continual improvement of the system, and felt part of the greater whole, through the core production model philosophy of "respect for humanity."[56] One stellar example I lived through was in the famed "war room" that served as the central command for the 1992 presidential campaign for then-governor Bill Clinton. James Carville and George Stephanopoulos made a startling decision: the major morning and evening strategy meetings would be attended by *all* campaign employees in Little Rock, Arkansas. Not only could you come, but you were supposed to be there! Even in the days before the internet and social media, it seemed like a huge leak risk. But their instincts were spot-on. The pride that every person on that campaign felt at being able to hear the top strategic thinking on the campaign every day and to have a chance to weigh in was immense and made the idea of anyone leaking to the press unthinkable. And as everyone knew the goals for each day, there were repeated examples of very junior staffers spotting and correcting potential errors.

Let us carry with us the lessons of Amy Wrzesniewski's research with hospital janitors. The janitors in her study creatively enhanced their own meaning and value in their jobs, but as Wrzesniewski noted in an interview, they had to be almost subversive to add this extra value.[57] Why shouldn't every worker in a hospital get some skills and training on how to deal with patients, family members, and grief? Why shouldn't every adult in a school be trained to recognize bullying and depression? The list can go on and on. There are no doubt endless ways that we could craft work to both add value to the larger mission of organization and bring more dignity, meaning, and opportunity to every job if we accept economic dignity as our end goal.

Can all work have meaning? We won't truly know till we truly try.

WORKER POWER AND WORKER POTENTIAL

CHAPTER FIFTEEN

WORKER POWER

In October 1977, country music singer and Grand Ole Opry member Johnny Paycheck released a song about the bitterness of working for meager rewards:

I been workin' in this factory
For nigh on fifteen years
All this time I watched my woman
Drownin' in a pool of tears
And I've seen a lot of good folks die
That had a lot of bills to pay
I'd give the shirt right offa' my back
If I had the guts to say

Take this job and shove it
I ain't working here no more
My woman done left and took all the reasons
I was workin' for
You better not try to stand in my way
'Cause I'm walkin' out the door
Take this job and shove it
I ain't workin' here no more

"Take This Job and Shove It" appeared on Paycheck's album of the same name, which went platinum and spent eighteen weeks on the country charts, including two weeks at number one.[1] The success of the song was in no small part due to the striking emotions it evokes: the craving for the dignity that comes with the power to exit a bad job.

It is also a reminder that when we aspire to structure labor markets to enable worker power, it is not just about negotiation for better wages and benefits—it is also about the power to say no to forces of domination and humiliation.

Vast numbers of workers lack the power to contest assaults on economic dignity by their employers. Philosopher Elizabeth Anderson estimates that as many as 80 percent of American workers have so little power that they are "subject to dictatorship at work."[2] First Amendment rights don't extend to the workplace: workers can be fired for remarks they make outside work or for their political beliefs. Many companies surveil the activities of their employees. A 2007 survey from the American Management Association found that 66 percent of companies monitor the internet use of their employees, 45 percent track keystrokes, and 43 percent monitor email.[3] Since then, those numbers have likely increased as monitoring technology has become more sophisticated and widespread. Apple has required its employees to undergo searches of their belongings for stolen merchandise; several workers have complained these mandatory searches caused them to lose a half hour of unpaid time each workday.[4] Anderson argues that such rules would be "unconstitutional for democratic states to impose on citizens who are not convicts or in the military."[5] However, this phenomenon is not new. As Anderson reports, "Workers were eligible for Ford's famous $5 daily wage only if they kept their homes clean, ate diets deemed healthy, abstained from drinking, used the bathtub appropriately, did not take in boarders, avoided spending too much on foreign relatives, and were assimilated to American cultural norms."[6]

LAWS ON WORKPLACE TREATMENT: NECESSARY BUT NOT SUFFICIENT

Our nation's major civil rights laws—from the Civil Rights Act of 1964 to the Americans with Disabilities Act of 1990—are milestones in protecting against abuses of negative economic dignity in the job market and beyond.

They are a critical and essential part of securing dignity for all Americans. Yet we also know progress comes through a dynamic of how changes in laws, cultural norms, political mobilization, and enforcement interact to make progress real. Laws do not make it on the books without powerful mobilization and battles for hearts, minds, and political power, and they often require that same commitment to ensure they are implemented and enforced. *Brown v. Board of Education* was a result of the interactive power of brilliant and brave political mobilization and legal strategy. The disturbing gap between the high constitutional values of equal protection articulated by the Warren Court and the remaining on-the-ground discrimination faced by millions has been the source of both intense political mobilization to close the gap and deep pain at the distance still to go.[7] Obviously racial discrimination in housing and employment is still too commonplace, as are barriers for those with disabilities. Racial and gender wage gaps still persist. Women and men in the same roles earn different pay.[8] For every dollar a white male makes, black women earn 61 cents and Latinas earn only 54 cents, leading to losses of about $1 million over a forty-year career.[9] Enforcement, political commitment, and widespread public pressure are always critical for civil rights and labor rights laws to have a positive impact on those they are intended to protect.

Take workplace sexual harassment. In 1986, in *Meritor Savings Bank v. Vinson*, the U.S. Supreme Court finally recognized sexual harassment at work as a violation of federal civil rights law.[10] Prior to this ruling, the U.S. Equal Employment Opportunity Commission (EEOC) saw fewer than ten cases per year. However, in the year after the ruling, the EEOC received 624 complaints, and its caseload eventually grew to 4,626 by 1995.[11] Yet a 2017 poll showed that 40 percent of American women still report having experienced sexual harassment at work.[12] Recognizing how crucial such larger political mobilization and cultural changes are, some see special power in the #MeToo movement. As Catharine MacKinnon, feminist legal scholar and co-counsel for Mechelle Vinson in *Meritor*, observed, "The #MeToo movement is accomplishing what sexual harassment law to date has not."[13]

The gap between legal rights and outcomes should always be a call for greater mobilization and enforcement, not a diminishment of the importance of such laws in expressing our national values. As Frederick Douglass wrote after an earlier civil rights act was struck down by the Supreme Court in 1883, there is a dignity value in a clear national statement against discrimination:

> It is said that this decision will make no difference in the treatment of colored people; that the Civil Rights Bill was a dead letter, and could not be enforced. There is some truth in all this, but it is not the whole truth. That bill, like all advanced legislation, was a banner on the outer wall of American liberty, a noble moral standard, uplifted for the education of the American people. There are tongues in trees, sermons in stones, and books in the running brooks. This law, though dead, did speak. It expressed the sentiment of justice and fair play, common to every honest heart. Its voice was against popular prejudice and meanness. . . . It told the American people that they were all equal before the law; that they belonged to a common country and were equal citizens. The Supreme Court has hauled down this broad and glorious flag of liberty in open day. . . . It is a concession to race pride, selfishness and meanness, and will be received with joy by every upholder of caste in the land, and for this I deplore and denounce that decision.[14]

There are still major areas where we lack even laws on the books that express such a "noble moral standard." Only twenty-one states and Washington, DC, offer protection from employment discrimination based on sexual orientation and gender identity for all workers—and as of this writing it's far from hopeful that the Supreme Court will be a force for progress.[15] Domestic workers, including live-in housekeepers, nannies, and caregivers, have long been deprived of the protections of federal labor laws. They can often be fired without notice and may not be entitled to overtime. Moreover, because the Civil Rights Act of 1964 applies solely to employers who have fifteen or more employees,[16] it's technically legal under federal law for domestic workers to be subject to sexual harassment and discrimination on the basis of race, religion, gender, or national origin.

One thing should be clear: in the ongoing political, legal, and social battle for workers to be treated with economic dignity—regardless of their race, ethnicity, gender, sexual identity, or status in the workforce—workers must be able to exert power in the workplace and labor market.

STRUCTURING LABOR MARKETS FOR WORKER POWER

For too long, much of the economics profession—like the U.S. Supreme Court of the pre–New Deal era—operated under the formalistic assumption of equality between workers and employers in labor markets. In 1908, while striking down a federal law that prohibited railroad companies from firing or discriminating against workers who were part of a union, the Supreme Court endorsed the fanciful idea that "the right of a person to sell his labor upon such terms as he deems proper is . . . the same as the right of the purchaser of labor to prescribe [working] conditions."[17] Fortunately, more and more policymakers and economists realize that worker inequality in labor markets is the correct starting point—the default position—for policy analysis. Globalization and the spread of information technology have exacerbated this power imbalance in labor markets, with the threat of global sourcing often used to depress wages. Sections of the business community have attacked unions by funneling millions of dollars into the campaigns of politicians who support so-called right-to-work laws, which allow employees who benefit from union contracts to free ride and not contribute to the union's costs of representation.[18] Economists including Joseph Stiglitz, Jason Furman, and Peter Orszag are also increasingly highlighting the degree that growing economic concentration is exacerbating income inequality through monopoly's close cousin, monopsony—when firms exploit their market power as buyers of goods and services to gain advantage over suppliers or their own workers.[19] Furman has focused on monopsony in labor markets, in particular, and how employers in concentrated industries can also push down wages by implicitly or explicitly colluding, which can affect workers ranging from nurses in cities with few hospitals to software engineers in Silicon Valley.[20] As Stiglitz notes, "Even if a firm with monopsony power passes on some of the gains to consumers, there's extortion in the economy and societal welfare is lowered."[21]

While laws that prevent discrimination and abuse—and set basic rules and minimums for pay, safety, and benefits—are vital for economic dignity, they will never be detailed enough or forward-looking enough to foresee all constantly evolving issues of dignity, domination, and humiliation. Nor will they on their own end the power imbalance between workers and employers.

An economic dignity agenda must structure labor markets to enhance worker power and thereby overcome the imbalance between firms and workers. This means focusing on three goals: (1) expansion in workers' capacity to bond together, (2) zero tolerance for involuntary servitude, and (3) "Take this job and shove it" power.

EXPANSION IN WORKERS' CAPACITY TO BOND TOGETHER

As Justice Ruth Bader Ginsburg wrote in her dissent to the recent *Epic Systems Corp. v. Lewis* decision, "Forced to face their employers without company, employees ordinarily are no match for the enterprise that hires them. Employees gain strength, however, if they can deal with their employers in numbers. That is the very reason why the NLRA [National Labor Relations Act] secures against employer interference [in] employees' right to act in concert for their 'mutual aid or protection.'"[22]

Employees who threaten to quit or strike risk their ability to care for themselves and their family, while employers who lose employees can simply replace them. In a few cases—a handful of superstars in the NBA or engineering whiz kids in Silicon Valley—employees may have sufficient market power and wealth that they can walk away, but these examples are the exceptions to the normal asymmetry of the importance of a job to an employee versus an employer. In most cases, even the bravest worker standing alone can be like Tank Man, the unidentified protester in Tiananmen Square.

This fundamental reality underscores the importance of all workers having the capacity to bond together regardless of job categories, changes in corporate structure, or the evolution of technology. Our labor laws must evolve as our economy evolves in order to ensure that the principle of workers being able to bond together expands rather than diminishes. And when legal reform is blocked, creative mobilization strategies must seek to plug the holes. Advancing this goal will require us both to (1) *repair* the damage done to traditional unions and (2) strengthen labor laws and *broaden* the set of options for collective action.

REPAIR THE DAMAGE DONE TO TRADITIONAL UNIONS

Unions have long been the most successful way for workers to come together to demand better treatment. The Bureau of Labor Statistics reports that non-union members in the United States make only 82 percent of what union members make.[23] Moreover, the OECD has found that unions are linked to better job quality, particularly in more training and career advancement.[24] Unions can also increase workers' ability to resist humiliation. Oxfam found that unionized workers in the poultry industry reported feeling more comfortable leaving their workstation to use the restroom when their requests were denied compared to their nonunionized peers.[25]

However, union membership has declined precipitously, with negative consequences for workers. In 1954, 34.8 percent of wage and salary workers belonged to a union.[26] In 2018, only 10.5 percent of such workers were union members.[27] One-third of the rise in income inequality among men over the past forty years can be attributed to declines in union membership.[28]

Unions have struggled in part due to employers' aggressive and illegal anti-union tactics during union elections. While it is illegal under federal law for employers to threaten to close plants, discharge or punish employees for engaging in union activity, threaten employees with loss of jobs or benefits, or question employees about union sympathies in a way that interferes with their rights,[29] these activities are widespread. One study found that in 57 percent of union elections, management threatened to close plants; in 34 percent, management discharged workers; in 47 percent, management threatened to cut wages and benefits; and in 63 percent, management forced workers to attend anti-union one-on-one sessions with a supervisor that included interrogations about their position in the election at least weekly.[30] The Department of Labor has estimated that three-quarters of employers hire outside firms to run misinformation and intimidation campaigns.[31] In 2017, Boeing ran 485 anti-union television ads in a week, targeting three thousand workers during a unionization drive in South Carolina, and additional ads from the South Carolina Manufacturers Institute aired 350 times, including one local ad during the Super Bowl.[32] Currently, employers have little incentive to follow the law when engaging in anti-union tactics. Although employees can receive back pay or reinstatement for being discriminated against or fired illegally, these remedies do not account for the often irreparable harm to the broader union campaign.

Another benefit of unionization is that it makes it easier to facilitate the types of works councils prevalent in Germany. Unionization is critical to ensuring that such worker councils promote the voice and influence of workers and are not co-opted by employers to block or replace collective bargaining. Done right, such worker councils are made up of employer and employee representatives who have rights over a number of issues, including work schedules, temporary work reductions, overtime, vacation policies, bonuses and targets, safety rules, and salary structure.[33] Importing this system could give workers a real voice at the table in deciding the critical conditions of their employment—a sense of voice and dignity in the conditions of their daily work.[34] When I was in the Obama White House in 2014, we expressed our enthusiasm for the prospect of United Auto Workers (UAW) and Volkswagen collaborating to bring such works councils to a plant in Tennessee.[35] As Justin King, a worker at the plant, wrote in the *Chattanooga Times Free Press*, "We all want to have a voice. We all want to be able to discuss decisions with management, and find solutions that everyone agrees on. We all want to be a part of Volkswagen's success in Chattanooga."[36] However, national anti-union groups and Republican leaders campaigned against the unions, leading to a narrow loss,[37] and more recent efforts have been squashed by all-out efforts to defeat the unionizing movement.[38]

While the decline in unionization rates is real and harmful, there are also signs of resurgence. AFL-CIO president Richard Trumka frequently reminds audiences that public support for unions is near its highest level in fifty years, at 64 percent.[39] A Pew poll shows that 75 percent of millennials have a favorable view of unions.[40] Trumka also points to polls that show nearly 60 million more nonunionized American workers would join a union if given the opportunity.[41] In February 2018, teachers in West Virginia—responding to low salaries and inadequate benefits in the face of rising health-care costs—

organized a walkout and a protest at the state capitol attended by thousands,[42] which Randi Weingarten, head of the American Federation of Teachers, called a "fight for dignity and respect."[43] These strikes have inspired teachers' unions to organize actions demanding more education funding and higher salaries in a diverse group of other states, including Kentucky, Oklahoma, Colorado, Arizona, and North Carolina with exceptionally strong public support.[44] In 2018, UNITE HERE locals representing Marriott hotel workers in major cities across the nation won not only raises and improved benefits but also a landmark agreement to be consulted on the use of new technology and automation.[45]

In 2019, legislation was introduced that would rewrite labor laws by imposing stricter remedies on employers for illegal activities, strengthen the power of strikers, and facilitate collective bargaining—the Protecting the Right to Organize (PRO) Act—which Trumka called "our strongest bill yet."[46] It has enough cosponsors to pass the House[47] and is endorsed by most of the 2020 Democratic presidential candidates. The PRO Act would go further, banning the type of intimidating action that Kumho Tire took against the United Steelworkers (USW). Former USW president Leo Gerard described these tactics, including firing the leader of the organizing drive, as "daily, mandatory captive audience meetings, designed to coerce workers into voting against union representation," and a series of additional actions that "violate the intent of the NLRA, which was to encourage collective bargaining, not hinder it."[48]

We must repair the damage done to traditional collective bargaining. At the same time, we should seek out new options for workers to bond together—including those who have been excluded from the benefits of unionization for too long.

INDEPENDENT CONTRACTORS

In 1914, the Lehigh Valley Coal Company claimed that it was "not in the business of coal mining at all" but merely gave miners access to its mines and then bought coal from those miners. Lehigh argued that these miners were not employees and accordingly were not covered by the workers' compensation statute at issue. Judge Learned Hand rejected this argument as "absurd," since these miners "carr[y] on the company's only business" of owning mines and selling coal.[49]

Lyft, Uber, and FedEx drivers likely would use Hand's "absurd" language to describe the denial of their status as "employees." In our modern economy, gig workers and independent contractors are a large and growing group. However, many have not been able to achieve economic security. In response, workers have organized strikes and protests overcoming challenges inherent in organizing these groups. As organizer and driver Rebecca Stack-Martinez notes, "There is no directory out there of who's driving, how many drivers, how we can reach them. And so we have to be really creative about how we get to drivers and get them involved in the movement."[50] However, they also face a significant legal obstacle. Under the NLRA, only workers considered employees and not independent contractors are guaranteed the right to organize. Being classified as a contractor, as gig workers like Uber workers are, impacts not only your benefits but your federal right to unionize or collectively bargain as well.

Reforms to federal law to reduce misclassification, such as the PRO Act, and to expressly give independent contractors the right to unionize are required to address this issue nationwide. While California's new law—Assembly Bill 5 (AB5), or the "gig worker bill"—instituted a stricter test for classifying a worker as an independent contractor for the purposes of California state law, it does not itself create a right to unionize for workers considered independent contractors under federal law.[51] Governor Gavin Newsom and worker advocates are now seeking to use the passage of the law as leverage to craft a deal that would give workers the right to organize under California state law.[52] However, these kinds of legislative changes will not be enough to address the plight of all workers excluded from unions. As our economy continues to evolve, we will need new models of organizing and bolstering worker power.

WORKERS FOR FRANCHISES

The McDonald family opened their first restaurant in 1937 and after multiple iterations opened the original McDonald's, selling a limited number of items (including hamburgers), in San Bernardino, California, in 1948.[53] By

1954, the restaurant had gained the attention of Ray Kroc, who sold milk-shake machines being used in the McDonald brothers' restaurant. Kroc went on to lead a nationwide franchise model that became an industry practice for fast food.

The practice of franchising has made it nearly impossible for fast-food workers to take advantage of traditional collective bargaining. Under the NLRA, if a majority of workers within a unit designate a union to bargain on their behalf, that union represents all employees within that unit. However, in the fast-food case, because an individual franchise or small number of locations are typically established as separate corporate organizations, workers are considered employees of the individual franchise (rather than the corporation itself) and therefore would have to organize at the franchise level to gain collective bargaining rights.[54] This kind of dispersion of workers makes it nearly impossible to organize through traditional routes, especially when employees turn over frequently, as they do in the fast-food industry.

Can fast-food workers combine organizing efforts across employers? Yes, but it is very challenging. Employers must voluntarily agree to be part of multiunit bargaining[55]—and it can be considered illegal for a union to pressure employers to engage in multiunit bargaining by threatening a boycott or strike.[56] And even if all McDonald's workers could be organized and strike under a "joint employer" test, their power to bond together could be limited. Management—and even some of the workers—may fear that Burger King and other competitors without unions would undercut their prices by keeping their wages lower. This could create a race to the bottom where both unionized employers and employees lose.

Unions have historically addressed this problem through sectoral "pattern bargaining," where the first agreement between a union and a major player in the industry becomes a "take-it-or-leave-it" template for all future negotiations.[57] At its height, comprehensive sectoral pattern bargaining was the norm in many industries including manufacturing, mining, and transportation. However, due to declining union membership and power, national pattern bargaining threatens to become a conduit for management to demand industry-wide concessions.[58] There are some areas where pattern bargaining survives to some extent. For example, the recent UAW strikes against GM may lead to negotiations over similar terms with Ford and Fiat Chrysler.[59] USW spearheads significant efforts to coordinate pattern contracts in industries such as steel, paper, and tires. There are also some sectors where workers retain significant leverage, such as in groceries, where union membership is higher than in other retail environments, the product is perishable, and margins are low—making strikes a powerful tool.[60] The United Food and Commercial Workers International Union has recently used strikes to demand better wages and working conditions across the grocery industry and across the country.[61] Nevertheless, many workers today do not have the same power to negotiate across sectors.

Sector-wide agreements in an industry like fast food can ensure that employers who agree to better compensation and working conditions will not be undercut by race-to-the-bottom competitors. This type of bargaining at the regional or sectoral level is common in many European and Latin American countries. In these systems, such as in Sweden, negotiations occur at multiple levels: (1) at the national level for all industries between unions and an industry association representing all employers, (2) at the national level for each industry between relevant unions and employers, and (3) at the company level.[62] However, because collective bargaining in the United States occurs at the individual employer level and workers cannot exert pressure to engage in multiunit bargaining through boycotts or strikes, sectoral bargaining may be too hard to force without legislative changes.

The Fight for $15, perhaps the most inspiring and successful national grassroots economic movement in recent decades, had its origins in efforts for sectoral collective bargaining. The movement's primary demand was not just for a living wage but also for a union for fast-food workers.[63] The Service Employees International Union (SEIU), led by its first female head, Mary Kay Henry, helped organize and fund the campaign.[64] Their goal was not just to persuade one employer to raise wages but for the entire fast-food industry to change. As Henry has said, "The ultimate dream is to get McDonald's, Wendy's, and Burger King to a national fast food bargaining table."[65] The first action took place in New York City on November 29, 2012, when hundreds of workers at McDonald's, Burger King, Domino's, KFC, Taco Bell, Wendy's, and Papa John's walked out on their jobs[66] and chanted slogans like "Hey, hey, what do you say? We demand fair pay," and "How can we survive on seven twenty-five" (at the time, $7.25 an hour was the federal and New York State minimum wage). Pamela Waldron, who worked at the KFC in Penn Station for eight years earning $7.75 an hour with often limited hours, explained her reason for protesting: "I have two kids under six, and I don't earn enough to buy food for them."[67]

The current legal barriers to organizing a union across franchises and companies and the decline in pattern bargaining forced fast-food workers to pursue a different path to setting a sectoral wage standard. They took to the streets to pass state and local laws that would raise the minimum wage not only for the entire fast-food industry but also for all lower-wage labor. The original action led to strikes across the nation, including strikes in sixty cities in August 2013.[68] Over time, the campaign expanded to represent a broader set of low-wage workers, many of whom were not involved in existing union campaigns—such as home care aides, childcare workers, airport workers, gas station attendants, and convenience store employees.[69] As Abera Siyoum, an electric cart driver at Minneapolis–St. Paul airport, noted, "When I look at the fight of fast-food workers, I see my fight. We live in the same community and suffer the same problems."[70]

This public pressure has led to an incredibly impressive and consequential number of legislative victories across the country. As of May 2019, seven states—California, Connecticut, Illinois, Maryland, Massachusetts, New Jersey, and New York—as well as Washington, DC, have passed $15 minimum wage floors; together, these states account for a little more than 30 percent of the U.S. workforce.[71]

FARMWORKERS

The need to both expand protections for traditional organizing and evolve new organizing tactics to bolster worker power is seen most clearly in sectors with the most highly vulnerable workers. Consider the plight of farmworkers. As discussed earlier, a massive organizing effort and boycott led by Dolores Huerta, Cesar Chavez, and Larry Itliong resulted in the first collective bargaining agreements between farmworkers and growers in California in 1970.[72] These agreements increased wages, required growers to contribute to workers' health care and economic development, and included safety protections from pesticides.[73] This activism importantly led to the state's Agricultural Labor Relations Act (ALRA), which established and protected the right of farmworkers to form unions in California.[74] After decades of pressure from activists, New York recently passed a state law to expand protections to collective bargaining to farmworkers.

Today, however, farmworker unions represent a very small share of workers,[75] in part because of their historic exclusion from labor laws at the federal level and in many states, but also due to the fierce fear tactics that growers can wage over workers even when the right to unionize is protected.[76] A high proportion of farmworkers fear deportation if they speak out, and many are dependent on growers for basic needs—whether housing or opportunities to make a day's wage, with little economic security to fall back on.

While we must push forward with ensuring traditional organizing rights, we can see success in alternative organizing tactics. For example, the Coalition of Immokalee Workers (CIW), founded in 1993 by workers and activists—including Greg Asbed, Laura Germino, and Lucas Benitez—has for a quarter century pressured major buyers of Florida tomatoes to agree to buy exclusively from growers who meet certain humane standards for farmworkers, a groundbreaking model termed "worker-driven social responsibility."[77] This effort, called the Fair Food Program, has seen the wages and working conditions of thirty-five thousand farmworkers improve. As Steven Greenhouse has documented, because neither federal nor Florida law provides farmworkers with a right to unionize, the coalition instead became a standards-setting organization that has successfully persuaded companies and growers to embrace worker rights as well as safety from human trafficking and gender-based violence at work and mechanisms to enforce those standards.[78]

DOMESTIC WORKERS: LEGISLATE TO NEGOTIATE

Even if domestic workers had all the basic protections of the NLRA and Fair Labor Standards Act (FLSA) that other workers do, the nature of household employee work can make traditional strategies for bonding together extremely difficult—even with inspiring exceptions such as Dorothy Bolden's efforts to organize African American household employees in the South in the 1960s. For household employees who work for a single household, the notion of strikes and collective bargaining with thousands of household employers just doesn't fit. Yet Bolden's National Domestic Workers Union and Poo's National Domestic Workers Alliance are dedicated to ensuring that legal and practical obstacles to traditional organizing cannot mean a failure to devise legal and political strategies to ensure such household workers can have the power of bonding together.

The strategy employed by domestic workers has been one of bonding together to both legislate to secure basic labor rights and create new forums for negotiations. Like fast-food workers, domestic workers who cannot unionize and negotiate across many employers have experimented with new ways of setting standards across the sector. As a result of the advocacy of the NDWA and others, in 2010, New York became the first state to pass a law that included domestic workers in all major labor laws protecting other workers.[79] These protections include overtime pay, a minimum of one day of rest per week, and protection from discrimination and harassment. Oregon, California, Connecticut, Illinois, Massachusetts, Hawaii, and Nevada have followed suit.[80]

Seattle followed suit with an important innovation. In addition to providing employment protections for domestic workers (regardless of whether they are considered independent contractors or employees) such as a minimum wage, overtime pay, and rest breaks, Seattle's 2018 law created a thirteen-member wage board that includes domestic workers and will make sector-wide recommendations on compensation, benefits, and employment conditions.[81] By creating this industry-wide board, the Seattle law secures long-term power for domestic workers that will allow them to continue to bond together and demand better employment conditions in the future. As Sage Wilson of Working Washington noted, "There's no practical way for domestic workers to engage in collective bargaining or any form of collective power when they're individual employees in households, so establishing a place where people can build community, organize in a way that matters, and raise industry standards on things like wages and benefits, but also harassment, is really a huge deal."[82] The Seattle law has since inspired the 2019 passage of a similar law in Philadelphia that sets new standards for domestic workers and creates an enforcement and implementation board that will make ongoing recommendations.[83]

This model has been used in the Fight for $15. In Seattle, then mayor Ed Murray, who campaigned on a $15 minimum wage, appointed a task force to produce a plan that both workers and businesses could accept. After months of intense negotiations led by David Rolf on the labor side, the group produced a recommendation that twenty-one of the twenty-four task force members endorsed. In 2014, the Seattle City Council unanimously approved a path to a $15 minimum wage.[84]

STRUCTURING SECTORAL BARGAINING

Law professor Kate Andrias of the University of Michigan has noted that the future of employment law is one where the law is not just "a collection of individual rights bestowed by the state" but instead "it is a collective project to be jointly determined and enforced by workers, in conjunction with employers and the public."[85] Movements like the Fight for $15 and organizing by domestic workers have set a precedent for future negotiations. However, broad sectoral bargaining that sets base national wages for entire industries (with cost-of-living increases as necessary) will require us to rethink the way we've structured the relationships between unions and companies. For example, as Andrias and Temple University law professor Brishen Rogers have proposed, Congress could empower the Department of Labor to create a process to set sector-wide wages and other minimum terms through consultation with workers and employers. Congress could also expand unions' rights to organize, negotiate, and strike at the sectoral level—rather than the individual company level.[86] In rare cases, employers have found it in their interest to voluntarily engage in sectoral bargaining. In the television and film industry, for example, hundreds of production companies have formed a trade association: the Alliance of Motion Picture and Television Producers, which engages in collective bargaining with trade unions such as the Writers Guild of America.[87] As a result, television writers in the union have negotiated quality health coverage and a singular defined benefit plan, which writers keep even as they change jobs and employers repeatedly. There is no reason why this model could not work in other industry sectors as well—only if workers had the right to such industry-wide bargaining, instead of having to hope the major employers in their industry found it to their advantage.

Such innovations would update the relationship between workers and employers, harmonizing our labor laws with how the modern economy is structured and ensuring more workers receive the benefits of collective bargaining.

BARRED AT THE COURTHOUSE DOOR

Another way that workers can bond together and demand better working conditions is through collective litigation. Our judicial system provides a mechanism for bonding together through class-action lawsuits.[88] This can strengthen workers' access to justice and the opportunity to change their employers' practices. This is the approach that Loretta Lee, an engineer who was fired from Google, took when she brought a class-action lawsuit on behalf of all female harassment victims at Google.[89]

Over the past few decades, however, employers have increasingly blocked this path for workers. They have further consolidated their power over their workers through insisting on forms of mandatory arbitration that cut off the option for collective litigation. Typically, arbitration is private and confidential, meaning that records are sealed and not available to the public. Even if there is a pattern of sexual harassment or other abuse at a company or by particular members of management, other workers might not be aware. The lack of such information can lead new employees to unknowingly sign on to work with predatory managers. In arbitration, employers define the procedures and providers, which means that workers are less likely to win, and when they do actually win, their awards are likely to be smaller.[90]

Lee, for example, initially brought an individual case alleging that her male coworkers spiked her drinks with alcohol, shot Nerf darts at her, and made sexual comments to her. Google's attorneys then attempted to have her individual lawsuit dismissed and forced into arbitration.[91]

Employers typically make such arbitration agreements a condition of employment. If workers truly had equal bargaining power, of course they could just say no. In reality, almost all workers have no choice but to sign the agreement if they want to have a job. And because more and more companies are using arbitration, workers cannot simply change employers to avoid it. Research by the Economic Policy Institute has found that since 1991, mandatory arbitration has skyrocketed and is now being used by 65.1 percent of companies with one thousand or more employees.[92]

The prevalence of mandatory arbitration has been enabled by several anti-consumer and anti-worker Supreme Court decisions. In 1925, Congress enacted the Federal Arbitration Act to ensure the validity and enforceability of agreements to settle disputes through arbitration.[93] The 1991 Supreme Court decision *Gilmer v. Interstate/Johnson Lane Corp.* upheld the enforceability of agreements that required employees to go through arbitration to enforce federal civil rights law, in this case the Age Discrimination in Employment Act.[94] Other decisions have upheld waivers of class-action rights by consumers and businesses.[95]

The most recent legal interpretations by a conservative Supreme Court majority have further eroded the ability of workers to join together to enforce their rights. In the 2018 decision in *Epic Systems Corp. v. Lewis*, the Supreme Court held that the Arbitration Act required courts to enforce such agreements and that Section 7 of the NLRA does not apply to class- or collective-action legal procedures.[96]

In dissent, Justice Ginsburg argued that a proper interpretation of the NLRA would allow these collective actions, regardless of mandatory arbitration clauses in employment contracts: "Employees' rights to bond together to meet their employers' strength would be worth precious little if employers could condition employment on workers signing away those rights."[97] Since this view has lost in the courts (for now), Congress could affirm these protections by passing new legislation to shield workers from mandatory arbitration clauses by employers.

ZERO TOLERANCE FOR INVOLUNTARY SERVITUDE

The Thirteenth Amendment of the U.S. Constitution—which abolished slavery and involuntary servitude—was ratified in 1865 in the aftermath of the Civil War. As the Supreme Court stated in the 1944 case *Pollock v. Williams*,

"The undoubted aim of the Thirteenth Amendment as implemented by the Anti-Peonage Act was not merely to end slavery but to maintain a system of completely free and voluntary labor throughout the United States. . . . In general, the defense against oppressive hours, pay, working conditions, or treatment is the right to change employers. When the master can compel and the laborer cannot escape the obligation to go on, there is no power below to redress and no incentive above to relieve a harsh overlordship or unwholesome conditions of work."[98] However, a number of labor practices in our modern economy seem to violate the spirit of that amendment—especially by restricting the ability of workers to exit or protest harsh conditions.

INDENTURED SERVITUDE AND OUR VISA SYSTEM

Workers are at high risk for abuse when a single employer petitions for a visa, is the only person the immigrants can work for, and can control their destiny without any real accountability. This situation can create a structure for domination and elements of involuntary servitude. To be clear, this is not an argument against legal immigration but instead recognition of the importance of structuring our system to avoid any semblance of indentured servitude.

The H-2A visa allows agricultural employers to import foreign workers on an employment contract, typically on a temporary or seasonal basis.[99] Workers who come on an H-2A visa may work only for the employer who petitioned for them.[100] When Juan Antonio Lara came from El Salvador to Washington to pick apples and found his room infested with bedbugs, local farmworkers said of him and his fellow migrant workers, "You are like prisoners. You can't make much money and you are stuck there."[101] The U.S. Government Accountability Office reported that this feature of the H-2A program creates a disincentive for reporting abuse because workers may fear retaliation if they complain, such as threats of deportation, violence, and exclusion from future employment.[102] Unlike U.S. workers who can leave abusive working conditions and seek other work, these immigrant workers are relatively powerless to combat mistreatment.

A prime example is sheepherders—one of the oldest professions in the world. Sheepherders remain active in the United States and are among the worst-treated workers. They are frequently bound to employers by H-2A immigration contracts. As a result of their tenuous immigration status, sheepherders often face exploitative conditions. For example, Colorado Legal Services found that "80 percent of sheepherders were not permitted to leave their ranch," about "70 percent reported never having access to a functioning toilet," and "50 percent reported not having the opportunity or ability to read their employment contracts."[103] Many sheepherders never report their health issues, such as injuries or chronic pain from the repetitive nature of the work, because they are afraid they'll lose their jobs. Colorado representative Daniel Kagan visited herders in August 2009 and found deplorable conditions: "Sheepherders are completely at the mercy of their employers, depending on them utterly for food, shelter, medical care, clothing, and, even, for human contact. That state of total dependency is wrong, and almost invites abuse of the employee. A day off is something a sheepherder can only dream about."[104]

Our existing legal immigration system can also lead to higher-skilled workers being trapped by employers. For example, the H-1B visa allows U.S. employers to temporarily employ foreign workers in specialty occupations as long as they are connected to a specific employer who applies for the H-1B opening. Most workers therefore feel they have few options to exit or find employment elsewhere and could face the prospect of deportation. As a result, H-1B workers are reluctant to protest poor employment conditions, even if they are paid less than the prevailing wage or experience wage theft. This lowers the power of their coworkers as well: it is harder to protest working conditions or ask for higher wages if your fellow workers have no power to stand up with you against an abusive employer.

H-1B workers also often pay large fees to recruiters, meaning they arrive in debt to their employers, leading to human trafficking and financial bondage in severe cases.[105] The *Boston Globe* found that a recruiting firm brought more than 350 Filipino teachers to Louisiana and demanded that the workers cover the costs of school administrators' travel to the Philippines (nearly $20,000), and pay $12,550 each in fees (the equivalent of multiple years' salary in the Philippines), in addition to a percentage of their second year's salary.[106] Ingrid Cruz, one of the teachers, recalled being told, "If you don't sign it, you are going back home."[107] A California-based IT company, Cloud-wick Technologies, lured workers from India with the promise of up to $8,300 per month in pay while actually providing as little as $800 net per month.[108] Although a relatively small company, Cloudwick provided data solution services to major corporations including American Express, Apple, Bank of America, Cisco, Comcast, Verizon, and Visa.

A zero-tolerance policy for involuntary servitude means that when U.S. companies truly cannot find U.S. workers and must hire H-1B visa holders, those foreign workers have real options to quit or find new employment. This change would increase worker bargaining power and make them more equivalent to others in the workforce, thereby reducing the risk of involuntary servitude.[109]

NONCOMPETE CLAUSES

There is a threat of involuntary labor whenever employers can prevent an employee from being able to work for anyone else but them. Our "involuntary servitude" antennae should go up when we hear about the growing prevalence of "noncompete clauses." Not all noncompete clauses should raise danger signs. If you sign as a top executive for Pepsi, it might seem highly reasonable that you agree not to work for Coca-Cola for a couple of years—in order to protect Pepsi's trade secrets, encourage you to invest in your personal growth within the company, and strengthen Pepsi's incentive to train you. Whether such noncompete clauses verge into problematic territory depends on issues like how highly skilled and compensated the job is, whether the employer provided you with significant training that they want to ensure you do not instantly take to a competitor, and how long the noncompete requirement is.

But there is never a justification for agreements that are used to ensure that companies do not have to compete for low-wage workers by offering higher pay or matching a competitor's better benefits. These are just a form of domination designed to compound inequality in labor markets. MIT professor Matt Marx has found that employers typically present these agreements when workers lack negotiating leverage, such as on their first day of work and after they have turned down other offers.[110]

Jimmy John's famously required employees to sign agreements that prohibited them from working at any business that made more than 10 percent of its revenue from sandwiches within three miles of a Jimmy John's store for two years after leaving the company.[111] In 2016, after an investigation by the New York attorney general and a lawsuit by the Illinois attorney general, Jimmy John's agreed to stop including noncompete agreements in its hiring processes.[112] However, the practice remains commonplace, with growing negative consequences for workers as employers seek to intimidate them by increasingly taking them to court to enforce such questionable agreements.[113] When the company is not investing in significant training, these noncompete clauses for low-income workers are a new form of economic domination that should simply be outlawed.[114]

Some states, such as California, North Dakota, and Oklahoma, do prohibit noncompete agreements, and Illinois bans noncompetes for low-wage workers. Yet even these laws have proved inadequate because the typical remedy for violations is nonenforcement. Employers too often have nothing to lose by inserting noncompete language into contracts, which can still serve to intimidate workers and prevent them from demanding better conditions or quitting.

WAGE THEFT

Too many employers have found mechanisms to avoid paying workers what they are owed. Some of the most obvious ways include refusing to pay workers for all their hours, paying them less than the minimum wage, denying overtime pay, or asking them to work unpaid—such as when employers require workers earning an hourly wage to clock out before closing up.

Sometimes employers will deduct costs, like uniforms, from an employee's paycheck, causing their income to—illegally—drop below the minimum wage. Taking 20 percent of a worker's pay is like forcing them to work 20 percent of their hours for free—a blatant form of involuntary servitude.

Stealing tips is another clear form of wage theft. When consumers tip workers, we believe we are rewarding them for good service and the tips legally belong to the employees, as was solidified under an Obama-era rule.[115] This has not, however, kept all tips out of unscrupulous employers' pockets. The restaurant industry is particularly vulnerable. "We have the highest rates of wage theft because we have the most complicated system of any industry," Saru Jayaraman, cofounder of the Restaurant Opportunities Center United, told *Eater*. "Now you layer on top of that all these rules around a two-tiered wage system and all the regulations around paying people a sub-minimum wage and making sure tips make up the difference, and you've got the Wild West."[116] This type of theft frequently occurs when employers "pool" workers' tips (ostensibly to ensure tips are shared equitably) but take a cut for themselves. Some employers divert money from the tip pool away from servers in a bar or restaurant and use it to pay the salaries of workers who ordinarily do not receive tips, such as cooks and dishwashers. In this way, employers are using the tips their employees receive to cover business costs.

A survey by the National Employment Law Project of 4,387 workers in low-wage industries found that 68 percent experienced at least one pay-related violation in the previous workweek.[117] This translates to a loss of about 15 percent of earnings. Women, foreign-born, black, and Latinx workers were significantly more likely to be targeted. These widespread violations are the result of several factors, including a decline in the enforcement of worker protections. As Heidi Shierholz of the Economic Policy Institute has noted, in 1978 there were 69,000 workers for every wage-and-hour investigator, but today that ratio is 175,000 to 1. Given the limited resources devoted to enforcement and relatively weak penalties for violations, unscrupulous employers have a low likelihood of getting caught and little incentive to follow the law.[118] In addition to federal efforts to take on wage theft through higher penalties and more resources for enforcement, state attorneys general could do more to fight wage theft as well.

"TAKE THIS JOB AND SHOVE IT" POWER

Simply put, the power of workers to demand respect and more dignified treatment is largely a function of having options—the power to say "take this job and shove it." Such power is strongly enhanced by what are called "full-employment policies." This refers to the deployment of both monetary and fiscal policy to foster full-employment, or "tight," labor markets. When everyone who wants to work has a job, the power balance can alter. Employers have to do more to court employees as opposed to the other way around. Workers have more leverage in negotiations not only for better wages and benefits but also for more dignified treatment at work, because they have more confidence that they can land on their feet and find another job if they exit.

Unfortunately, the ability to tell an abusive employer to "take this job and shove it"—and the full employment that makes it possible—has not been central to the dictates of monetary policy. The twin goals of monetary policy have historically been to pursue a balance between full employment and inflation. The theory is that as unemployment goes down, employers need to offer higher wages to attract workers. Because these higher wages translate to higher costs for businesses, this theory predicts that businesses will raise their prices, leading to inflation. This relationship between unemployment and inflation is known among economists as the Phillips curve. The Federal Reserve has traditionally operated on the assumption that some version of this relationship holds in the short run. As a result, when unemployment starts to fall, the Fed will respond by raising interest rates to avoid inflation rather than keeping rates low in order to take every possible step to reach full employment.

In recent years, there has been renewed advocacy—including by the Fed Up campaign spearheaded by Ady Barkan—for monetary policy tilted far more toward an aggressive full-employment focus. Some of this has been based on recent evidence that the Phillips curve is broken: that unemployment can be driven lower and lower than previously thought without sparking an uptick in inflation. A more basic critique, however, is that conventional monetary economics have overweighted the fears of inflation compared with the vast benefits of tight labor markets with the economy at full employment, including the power of workers to demand more respectful treatment at work.[119]

In much the same way, expansionary fiscal policy—think government spending and stimulus—is often the most powerful tool to promote full employment by boosting the economic demand. This is especially and obviously true in economic downturns. The stimulus enacted early in the Obama administration saved or created about nine million jobs from 2009 to 2012 and helped prevent a second Great Depression.[120] The decreasing evidence over the last two decades that deficits lead to inflation has bolstered the already strong case for the use of government investment on an ongoing basis to expand economic demand and reap the economic dignity benefits of full employment.

From a perspective of ensuring that work leads to economic dignity for all workers, the case for tighter labor markets and full-employment monetary and fiscal policy is very strong. As economists Dean Baker and Jared Bernstein summarized in their book *Getting Back to Full Employment,* "Unemployment is not just a problem that affects those unable to find jobs; it hurts the entire labor force. Unemployment reduces the bargaining power of all job holders."[121] Recent empirical work by Bernstein and Keith Bentele has further reinforced that the largest beneficiaries of such full-employment policies are low-income workers, particularly those non-white or single moms.[122] Simply put: beyond wage growth, tight labor markets give higher capacity to make demands or exit to the very same workers who normally have the least power to say no to mandatory arbitration, no to noncompete clauses, no to erratic work schedules, and no to abuse at work.

A tighter labor market where employers are forced to court workers can be one of the most potent remedies to prevent such domination by giving employees the power to exit without fearing they will be unable to care for their families. Instead of job applicants feeling so desperate that they subject themselves to inferior wages and working conditions, employers desperate for workers start being willing to do what is necessary to give workers on the edge of the workforce a chance.[123] When I was in the White House in the late 1990s, I remember how major employers would start calling me as unemployment kept falling, suddenly expressing interest in corporate citizenship efforts to hire people out of prison or the long-term unemployed. And as former Federal Reserve chair Janet Yellen notes, those gains may be lasting and make workers more resilient; it's possible "the skills and experiences [disadvantaged workers] are acquiring in today's tight labor market will yield long-run benefits—enabling them to do better even if the economy experiences another downturn."[124] In short: "Low-wage workers' best friend is a very tight job market," as Bernstein says.[125]

To end this chapter where we started: laws that outlaw abuse are essential but not enough without a labor market structured for worker power. We must also realize there are limits to what market structure can achieve. Even in the tightest of labor markets, some workers will be devoid of opportunities for exit due to their location, their language abilities, or the fear that they cannot fully replace a well-paying job they desperately need to hold on to. As a result, many workers will always feel trapped and devoid of "take this job and shove it" power. This is why we will always need laws that ensure fundamental economic dignity that can never be trampled on. It is why standards like requiring a 50 percent bump in wages for overtime is critical not only for a living wage but also to put some guardrails on the demands of employers. There will always be a need for both specific legal protections of basic spheres of economic dignity and a labor market structured to ensure true worker power.

CHAPTER SIXTEEN

WORKER POTENTIAL: YES, EDUCATION AND SKILLS STILL MATTER

There is no single policy or path to economic dignity. There are many roads to a sense of meaning and contribution. An economic dignity wage, expansions of labor power, and a culture of respect for all who do their part are each critical to ensuring the aspiration of economic dignity for all. The opportunity to achieve a quality higher education, of lifelong learning and skills, has long been seen as a critical component of the capacity to pursue potential and to rise economically regardless of the accident of your birth.

And yet over the past two decades, more and more progressive policy advocates have raised a notable concern: whether the focus on education and skills as an answer to economic inequality has distracted from a broader focus on issues of concentrated economic power at the top, declining unionization, and the erosion of the minimum wage. While progressive labor economists like Larry Mishel, former head of the Economic Policy Institute, supported the public investment agenda in the 1990s pushed by President Bill Clinton and advisers like Robert Reich and me, they felt the strong focus on human capital led to too little emphasis on the structural issues of concentrated economic power.

This is an important critique that must be taken seriously. It does not require, however, an "either–or"—worker potential or worker power—answer. On one hand, there is no doubt strong historical evidence that raising the skill level of the overall workforce can be integral to shared prosperity. Harvard labor economists Claudia Goldin and Larry Katz found that the universal high school movement helped large swaths of Americans gain the skills to benefit from the technological progress that came from electrification and other developments. Goldin, Katz, David Autor, Alan Krueger, and other top labor economists found that the "wage premium" associated with higher education and skills was, if anything, growing in the internet era and argued it was a key driver of the rise in economic inequality.

On the other hand, there is now widespread agreement that structural issues like economic concentration and the declines in unionization and the real value of the minimum wage have played major roles in widening economic inequality. While Goldin and Katz argue that returns to higher education still explain the majority of rising inequality in the 1980–2017 period, even they agree that structural issues may have been a more decisive factor in rising economic inequality in the 2000s.[1]

The critique by Mishel and others of an overfocus on skills was at its strongest in the recovery after the Great Recession, when many in the business community argued that stubbornly high unemployment was due to a "skills gap" or "skills mismatch"—that our primary labor market challenge was that workers didn't have the right skills for available jobs—as opposed to lack of demand in the economy. When I became national economic adviser for the second time in 2011, this was a dominant message we repeatedly heard from CEOs in the business community and read in newspaper articles across the country. The problem was, when we invited our top labor economists for a special NEC meeting, the reaction was unanimous: there was no evidence of a skills gap in the data. A skills gap should have led to wages going up for skills in need, but no one could find that to be the case. This suggested that companies either were not offering high enough wages or were unwilling to bear the extra costs of training workers for those jobs. Indeed, there was evidence that companies had often exaggerated the skills needed as a way of sorting out the flood of job applicants when the labor market had been weaker. If I tried to start a fancy law firm but offered only $10 an hour, I might find there was a "skilled lawyer shortage"—but that would be more about the wages offered than about the lack of available lawyers. As Paul

Krugman wrote at the time, "Show us the money: If employers are really crying out for certain skills, they should be willing to offer higher wages to attract workers with those skills. In reality, however, it's very hard to find groups of workers getting big wage increases, and the cases you can find don't fit the conventional wisdom at all."[2] Worse still: many of those who focused only on the skills-gap thesis were unwilling to follow the logic of their argument by supporting major new public investment—as opposed to seeing it as an act of individual responsibility or requiring the support of high-wealth donors.

PREVENTING AN OVERREACTION: SKILLS STILL MATTER

Regardless of the exact breakdown of the factors driving economic inequality, it does not take the wisdom of King Solomon to conclude that *both* quality education and structural issues matter in battling economic inequality and promoting economic dignity.

That recognition requires people like me to acknowledge the foresight of progressive economists like Mishel and union leaders in seeing the rising challenges of structural power issues, even in the 1990s at a time of rising income across the board. It also means that many of us who focused on progressive public investments at the time should have done more to focus on and foresee issues of economic power.

Yet it also requires recognition by those who stress economic power as the dominant issue to not make the same mistake from the other direction: we must not now let a proper focus on worker power lead to playing down the importance of skills and higher education to an economic dignity agenda. Two wrongs in underappreciating the full spectrum of needed policies for workers do not make the right economic policy.

Ensuring equal opportunity to access some form of quality higher education is still a core requirement of a nation seeking to live up to its ideals of upward mobility, caring for family, and having continual opportunity to pursue one's sense of purpose and potential. Policies expanding public investment in the full pipeline—from pre-K, to more individualized help in schools, to after-school opportunities and college guidance, to a focus on completing quality higher education programs—are far from all that is needed to battle deep economic disadvantage and patterns of neglect or discrimination, but they are not small potatoes either. And finally, any of us who are highly educated policymakers need to check ourselves anytime we are at risk of essentially telling other people's children something different than we are telling our own children.

In short, worker power and skills should not be seen as in tension with one another: they are but another dynamic duo on the path to universal basic economic dignity.

1. COMPLETING QUALITY HIGHER EDUCATION STILL MATTERS

We must structure economic policy to ensure that all who contribute—regardless of whether they attend college—can live with economic dignity. But we should not ignore the reality that completing a quality four-year college degree is currently still one of the best overall investments a person can make in themself—and that we should break down every barrier we can so that those who want to pursue their potential through a college education can do so.

Consider the following. College graduates have average annual incomes of roughly $62,000, compared with roughly $37,000 for high school graduates, a wage premium of more than 60 percent.[3] And wage premiums are even more substantial for those with advanced degrees. College graduates have consistently lower unemployment than other workers, especially among younger workers,[4] and about double the wealth of nongraduates.[5] Over 20 percent of Americans without a high school diploma live in poverty, compared with fewer than 5 percent with a college degree.[6] According to research by the Social Security Administration, men who graduated from college make $655,000 more—and women make $450,000 more—over their lifetimes than high school graduates, even controlling for key demographic variables.[7] While it is true that higher supplies of workers with quality higher education could dampen some of the wage benefits, that does not mean individual college graduates would not, on the whole, be far more likely to be better off economically than high school graduates. Moreover, a more educated labor supply over the longer run could attract more high-wage, high-value job creation in the United States.

The payoff is typically most significant for students from poor backgrounds and thus a boost for upward mobility. Tim Bartik and Brad Hershbein found that those from low-income backgrounds who complete college make 71 percent more in lifetime earnings than those who complete only high school. For African Americans from lower-income backgrounds, the return is 173 percent.[8]

And while a college degree is not a requirement for all good jobs with strong wages, in our current economy it is still a form of economic dignity insurance—providing a buffer against an economic downturn, erosion of an industry, or displacement from a career whether due to technology, globalization, or just normal competition. Consider the Great Recession. As Brookings Institution scholars explained, "Those with postsecondary degrees saw more steady employment through the Great Recession . . . and the vast majority of net jobs created during the economic recovery went to college-educated workers."[9] And "only those with a bachelor's degree or more had returned to prerecession [employment-to-population] levels by early 2017."[10]

And while there are tens of millions who find dignity and meaning in their work and contribution without a higher education, we also should not ignore evidence that for many people a college education can have broader positive effects on overall well-being and satisfaction in careers and in the pursuit of potential. Economists Philip Oreopoulos and Uros Petronijevic write that "recent evidence shows that even after controlling for different measures of family background and income, workers with more schooling hold jobs that offer a greater sense of accomplishment, more independence and opportunities for creativity, and more social interactions than jobs available to noncollege graduates."[11] They note that "several studies have also shown that college graduates tend to enjoy better health outcomes on average."[12] Goldin and Katz found that jobs requiring higher educations are part of an increasing trend of women working into their sixties and seventies due to personal fulfillment at work, rather than necessity.[13]

Completing college may not be the "guaranteed passport" to a secure middle-class life it once was, as Nick Hanauer puts it.[14] Yet based on existing evidence and the potential threats to some jobs requiring less education due to AI and other technological advances, completing a high-quality higher education degree is still nonetheless one of the best bets that one can make on furthering their economic future.[15] We should aspire to an economy where education or skill level is not a prerequisite to caring for family, finding purpose and meaning at work, or being treated with dignity. Yet we should also aspire to an economy where every person has every opportunity to pursue their potential and sense of purpose, including having access to quality higher education.

TAKING RISK OUT OF THE EQUATION

Even if the payoff for the typical college graduate is substantial, with student debt at $1.5 trillion and mounting, does it represent too much risk? A good bet is still a bet. Getting it wrong can be devastating. We have all heard about millennial college graduates saddled with high debt who cannot find jobs that pay enough to pay back those debts—no less the jobs they aspired to when they chose to attend college. About two-thirds of four-year college graduates have student loans averaging nearly $30,000.[16] Although the unemployment rate is very low for recent four-year college graduates, about two-fifths are underemployed, meaning they work in jobs that often don't require the degree they earned. All of this can make such college graduates question the investment, opportunity costs, and risk they took.[17] There is evidence that loan debt can also hold back opportunity after college in areas like homeownership and entrepreneurship.[18]

Yale political scientist Jacob Hacker describes this situation as an example of the "Great Risk Shift" from government and business to individuals. Hacker states that as costs and debt skyrocket and "people with the same number of years of schooling have much more disparate economic experiences than they used to . . . investing in education, wise as it may be, is also increasingly risky."[19]

How should we address that risk? Not by discouraging people from seeking a quality higher education when for most young people—including from low-income backgrounds—the decision to forgo it would be riskier economically, for all the reasons noted above. Graduates with a bachelor's degree—

even those who are underemployed—fare better in today's labor market than high school graduates and also frequently transition out of underemployment more quickly than people without college degrees.[20] Completing a two-year college degree is also associated with a 13 percent earnings boost for men and a 22 percent boost for women compared to completing high school only.[21] Instead, the answer should start with making the experience of getting a higher education accessible to all and less risky. As with universal health care, there may be more than one way to get there. Proposals for free public college tuition for all—or at least lower- and middle-income students—as well as larger Pell Grants for low-income students that can also help with living expenses would all sharply reduce the risk of pursuing a higher education. And even with such reforms, when students choose to take on debt for private colleges or for living expenses, such debt should never be crushing for those who are unemployed, work public service jobs, or earn low or moderate incomes. Despite progress in the Clinton and Obama administrations, there remains a need for a simpler, consolidated, and more generous income-contingent repayment program to ensure repayment of any education-related debt is capped at only a small percentage of income.[22] Regardless of the exact path chosen, each of these policies would remove the massive financial risk from the college equation by ensuring no one is inhibited from pursuing their potential by not going to college or leaving with crushing debt.

DON'T FORGET COMPLETION AND QUALITY

Two of the best ways to "de-risk" a college education are to ensure it is high quality and that students actually earn a valuable degree or credential. Overall, one-third of students who enroll in four-year colleges do not graduate within six years, and graduation rates are even lower for black and Hispanic students.[23] Fewer than half the students starting at public two-year schools graduated within six years.[24] And the graduation rates at for-profit schools are pathetic: only 20 percent. These schools fail even worse in serving black students, whose graduation rate is only 13 percent within six years.[25] The wage premium for workers with some college but no postsecondary degree is still about $5,000 a year,[26] but that is often outweighed by the debt a student has taken on. As Ellen Ruppel Shell has highlighted in her op-ed in the

New York Times, the combination of not graduating, taking on high debts, and the opportunity costs of not working hits low-income students the hardest.[27] It is clear we must prioritize not just getting students into a quality college but ensuring they have the support they need to complete their degree. What can we do to boost college completion?

Economist and current dean of the Woodrow Wilson School of Public Policy Cecilia Rouse—who spearheaded this focus on college completion for the Clinton National Economic Council in the late 1990s—has stressed that support must be individualized and include a "comprehensive approach including pre-freshman summer programs, support services and scholarships for students."[28]

As Rouse has recently explained, "One of the more successful models for encouraging post-secondary degree completion is the City University of New York's ASAP (Accelerated Study in Associate Programs)," which "has shown phenomenal success."[29] ASAP has three-year graduation rates of nearly three times the national average, and nearly double those of similar students in other CUNY community colleges. What is ASAP doing differently that makes such an impact? For one, they provide the type of extra support for tuition and living expenses that allow their students to enroll full time, so they can devote the majority of their time to the rigors of their coursework. As discussed earlier, the program's success is in part attributed to the skilled professionals who provide mentoring to students. The staff includes a dedicated ASAP adviser, a dedicated career and employment adviser, and tutoring services, among other benefits.[30] Students meet with advisers thirty-eight times a year, rather than seven for non-ASAP CUNY students. Typical CUNY advisers have a caseload of six hundred to fifteen hundred students, which is common at community colleges. In contrast, ASAP counselors serve just sixty to eighty students each.[31] The results are staggering, and are cost effective, as the gains from the program substantially improved graduation rates, resulting in lower costs per degree.[32] And they are scalable: three Ohio community colleges have successfully replicated the ASAP model and more than doubled graduation rates.[33]

Another proven intensive model to increase completion rates is the Posse Foundation model, which recruits talented disadvantaged students during their senior year of high school and groups them together into "posses" of ten students who attend the same college. The students are provided with workshops and mentoring, along with full scholarships, and the results are remarkable: 90 percent of Posse scholars graduate from college, even though their SAT scores are typically 300 points below the average for the selective colleges they attend.[34] These are the types of human capital investments that deserve more—not less—focus and expansion.

KEEP A CLOSE EYE ON QUALITY

Not all colleges are of equal quality—not even close. While some people might be focused on a small sliver of the most prestigious schools, the fact is that there are many high-performing four-year and two-year colleges across our country. There are just too few admissions slots. A focus on true first chances must keep our eye on the ball: increasing the number of high-quality higher education slots across our nation and making sure people of all backgrounds have fair access to them.

For all the focus on privileged parents maneuvering to get their children into selective colleges, it is actually those from lower-income households who benefit the most from attendance at these colleges. Graduates of elite colleges from low- and high-income backgrounds have very similar earnings outcomes, reaching the top 20 percent at about the same rate, which suggests that some colleges can level the playing field among students.[35] Attending an elite college increases the chances that a child from a family in the bottom 20 percent will rise to the top 20 percent by about *fourteen times*, while the difference for children from upper-income families is far less dramatic.[36]

Yet recent data show that these elite schools are terrible at taking in lower-income students. Children with parents in the top 1 percent are a mind-blowing seventy-seven times more likely to attend an "Ivy-plus" college than children with parents in the bottom 20 percent.[37]

The key is to expand and ensure fair access to these prestigious schools as well as high-performing schools of all types. Public colleges like California State University–Los Angeles, Stony Brook University, the City University of New York system, Glendale Community College, the University of

Texas at El Paso, and many others excel at enrolling low-income students and creating upward mobility by moving them into higher-income groups, according to research by Raj Chetty, John Friedman, and others.[38] These colleges are "engines of upward mobility," as Chetty and his coauthors put it.[39] We need to learn from, expand, and reward schools with strong mobility and opportunity outcomes.[40]

Consider the case of Carlos Escanilla. He is a psychotherapist at a Florida high school, but in high school he was an aspiring rock star with C+ grades and average test scores, according to David Leonhardt's profile in the *New York Times* titled "College for the Masses."[41] How he got from there to a comfortable and rewarding career all started when a friend persuaded him to apply to Florida International University. As it happened, Mr. Escanilla's credentials were just above the admission thresholds for the school, and he got in. While there, he "fell in love with learning," earned a liberal arts degree, and learned how to "fall, dust yourself off, and keep going."[42] Research by University of Chicago economist Seth Zimmerman found that students on the margin for acceptance to Florida International University, like Escanilla, receive a 22 percent earnings bump between eight and fourteen years after graduating from high school if they attended, relative to those who just miss the threshold.[43]

A major problem is that we as a nation do not invest nearly enough in expanding high-performing schools like Florida International and other high-performing schools. Economist Marshall Steinbaum points out that since the Higher Education Act of 1965, there has been a harmful deemphasis on directly funding quality and high-performing higher education institutions.[44] We should be directly increasing—not contracting—funding for high-performing institutions, particularly public universities, that encourage economic mobility so that they can enroll and graduate more students. As Larry Katz explains, we need "the equivalent of the high school movement—developing more University of California campuses or more Florida public universities, so we [aren't] rationing access to quality public colleges."[45] He adds, "In the past 40 years, California's population has almost doubled again, growing by 15 million, and we've gone from eight UC undergraduate campuses to just nine. . . . There's no reason there shouldn't be another five 30,000 or 40,000 student UC campuses given how much the population has grown."[46]

We have to focus just as strongly on expanding quality slots in public community colleges. These can serve as accessible entry points to higher education and can help promote upward mobility for low-income and non-traditional students, such as those raising children and those who are mid-career. Indeed, these institutions enroll nearly half of all college students.[47] More needs to be done to improve quality and pathways from community colleges to four-year colleges. While about four-fifths of entering community college students hope to earn a four-year degree, fewer than one-sixth actually do within six years.[48] Clearly, more resources are needed to strengthen community college quality, invest in effective advising like ASAP and other interventions that boost completion, and smooth the pathway to four-year colleges.

Investing more in quality, free, public community colleges would also be a powerful tool to diminish the lure of low-performing for-profit schools.[49] This would allow more students like Carlos Escanilla to find a quality slot and have a better shot at pursuing their dream potential.

LET'S CALL ALL HIGHER EDUCATION "COLLEGE"—AND SAY IT IS FOR ALL

When you have been engaged in economic policy for as long as I have, one of the things you get used to is being part of the same conversation and the same debates with different people in different decades. One recurring debate is the emphasis on "college" versus "technical education." The debate goes like this. Someone correctly states that encouraging everyone to go to "college" leads too many people to inadvisably seek a traditional four-year college education they will not complete and leads to high debt, and that a skill-related education is far better for many people. Others will also rightly caution that this message can sometimes be used to track or limit the opportunities of young people, especially minorities, who are steered away from the college education that often leads to income mobility. They also have a point.

But it may be time to change this dichotomy and the language we use to define it. Why not call all higher education "college"? Why not encourage college for all and mean that every young person should have a post-high-school plan for additional education? This can involve different paths and different types of programs for folks at different points of their lives. We should do more to inform people—young, midcareer, or reskilling later in life—which schools and types of education can offer the highest returns.

There is a stronger and stronger argument that we should be breaking down the typical vocational-versus-liberal-arts-college dichotomy anyway. If there are more opportunities to start vocational training in high school that continues into higher education, like the IBM-sponsored P-TECH (Pathways in Technology Early College High School) in Brooklyn, is that college or tech training?[50] Students who enter an exciting job-related vocational education program may have a transformative experience that convinces them to keep extending their higher education—especially as we improve the pipeline from community colleges to four-year colleges. Another promising model is degree apprenticeships, which help students get work-based learning opportunities while earning credits toward a bachelor's or associate's degree.[51]

Moreover, as I've said before, educating a child today is like training for the 2032 Olympics when you do not know what sport you will compete in. What would you do? You would have to develop a set of skills—speed, endurance, strength, and so on—that you hope would help you adapt and excel at whatever sport you were assigned. As someone who graduated from law school in 1985 with no clue that within a decade people would be using mobile phones, the internet, and laptop computers, I can certainly see the future workforce needing to adjust the same way.

Finally, if students are trained solely for a narrow, technical job, it can leave them unprepared for the first change in technology that comes their way—and prevent them from attaining aspects of a liberal arts education that are important for transferable, critical thinking and civic participation.[52] Indeed, even the bump in pay that some recent graduates with STEM majors receive immediately after graduation fades after a few years, and "by age 40, the earnings of people who majored in fields like social science or history have caught up," according to David Deming.[53] On the other hand, it may make more and more sense for those who receive a strong liberal arts education to learn some practical technical skills as well. Shakespeare experts who can code and software engineers who understand world religions may be the best positioned for the job market of the future.

2. WORKER POTENTIAL: SKILLS AND TRAINING STILL MATTER

A skills mismatch theory was a very bad argument for why unemployment was so high in 2010. That does not mean, however, we should pretend there are not workers who could benefit from a far more effective workforce training, skills, and credential system. We should push for more full-employment policies and a broader and longer-term stakeholder view of companies, which should lead to greater investment in training by private employers. But it would be unwise and naive to assume markets alone can answer the needs of all workers without better-designed and increased public investment. As discussed earlier, even in tight labor markets, individual companies will often underinvest in what workers need out of fear they will leave for a competitor after receiving training. And almost no company offers workers who are being laid off significant support for finding their next job—unless it is compelled by a union contract. This is why strengthening unionization and strong public investment in training and skills programs are essential to ensuring we as a nation do not underinvest in providing pathways to help workers pursue their potential in careers and increase their capacity to care for family.

When it comes to skills training, we still face serious trust gaps. Workers fear sacrificing to gain credentials and skills that will prove unsatisfactory for employers. Those hiring, on the other hand, too often do not trust that training programs were done with adequate employer consultation, and thus worry that they are not designed to meet their needs. Both support for on-the-job training and massive increases in apprenticeship funding where training is tied to a job no doubt are popular in part because they avoid such trust gaps. In these cases, all parties trust that the effort to gain skills is connected to filling a job.

Expansions of unionization can help reduce trust gaps in workforce training and help develop "highly skilled workers who earn family sustaining wages" through careers, as the AFL-CIO notes.[54] Because union-organized training is often more industry-wide, employers and workers in an entire industry can benefit, thereby reducing workers' fears that they are tying their fortunes to one employer and individual companies' fears that they will invest in training that a free-riding competitor will seize by hiring away their workers.

Unionization also expands opportunities for the best solution to closing trust gaps: on-the-job training where workers know their efforts will be connected to job attainment or promotion. The union apprenticeship programs work best when they are formed in partnership with management and registered with government agencies. For example, unions and the AFL-CIO Working for America Institute partner to support, design, and provide feedback for the Industrial Manufacturing Technicians (IMT) apprenticeship program, which trains workers for technical and highly specialized manufacturing jobs with 2,700 hours of on-the-job training and 260 hours with technical college instructors.[55] The Swedish job-security councils that provide serious guidance and training for workers even before they are laid off are co-run by unions and could provide a potential model for the United States, as discussed in previous chapters.[56]

Efforts by sectors to identify specific, clear credentials that will be accepted job- or industry-wide can help close trust gaps. Sectoral training programs provide skills for a specific industry or industries in a local economy, rather than for just one company, to enable mobility across companies. And they are often facilitated by intermediaries and developed with employers' input to ensure that the credentials and skills developed are valued by the companies that will be hiring program graduates. We are now seeing hard evidence from randomized controlled trials that these types of programs are producing strong results in giving Americans second chances and potential careers. For example, the nonprofit Year Up provides young adults in urban areas with six months of training in IT or financial services, followed by a six-month paid internship at a major firm in that sector. Participants had earnings boosts of 40 percent (more than $7,000) three years after completing the program.[57] WorkAdvance focuses on helping long-term unemployed workers with training and placement services in sectors where there are both strong local demand and career advancement opportunities. Participants had 14 percent higher earnings (about $1,930) after three years.[58]

One standout is Project QUEST (Quality Employment through Skills Training), based in San Antonio, Texas. The program provides participants, overwhelmingly women of color, with comprehensive support and resources to earn community college degrees in high-demand areas like health care and IT.[59] QUEST arose in response to a loss of good-quality low-skill manufacturing jobs in the San Antonio region. The nonprofit organization works with employers to determine fields and credentials that will be valuable, and provides tuition subsidies and a host of critical support services to low-income job seekers while they participate in two-year associate's degrees or one-year certificate programs at area community colleges to earn those credentials. As CEO David Zammiello explains, many participants have "fragile life circumstances, whether it's . . . home insecurities, food insecurities, so funding alone will not cure that particular issue."[60] Staff at QUEST provide intensive counseling, connections to assistance with childcare and transportation, and help in remedial education, fine-tuning a résumé, navigating the job search, and practicing for interviews. This strategy pays off: participants had average annual earnings 20 percent higher a full nine years after the end of the program.[61] As management scholar Paul Osterman noted about Project QUEST, "It is scalable, and there is no reason every city and town in America can't have something like it."[62]

We as a society should also ensure that employers recognize the skills people already have and focus squarely on whether people can do the job, rather than requiring unnecessary degrees. There can be a disconnect between tech employers and high-ability young people without traditional degrees who can do the needed work but lack the traditional education credentials that tech employers often assume are the only evidence of whether such young people have the skills to succeed in those jobs. My former National Economic Council colleague Byron Auguste has attacked this trust, or information, gap through the organization he conceived and cofounded,

Opportunity@Work. It understands the credentials and skills needed, makes sure young or midcareer people have or develop those skills, and then matches these workers with employers. Opportunity@Work closes these information and trust gaps and ensures that talented workers who might typically get screened out by a computer algorithm or recruiter early in the hiring process get a fair shot at quality careers.[63]

Take Wilkin Sánchez's experience. An immigrant from the Dominican Republic without a college degree, Sánchez worked at McDonald's when he arrived in the United States. Sánchez built up his IT skills through online programs and then got those skills verified through the TechHire initiative launched by the Obama administration and supported by Opportunity@Work, which enabled him to move into a good-quality job that he finds much more fulfilling as an IT support specialist.[64] Rhode Island governor Gina Raimondo built on this model to expand pathways into technology, manufacturing, health care, design, and other middle-class jobs through her flagship Real Jobs Rhode Island initiative.[65] Other similar models include Skillful, a nonprofit initiative of the Markle Foundation that works with employers to improve their skills-based hiring practices and supports career coaches for job seekers.[66]

3. BUILDING A PIPELINE TO PROMOTE EQUALITY AND FIGHT ENTRENCHED DISCRIMINATION

If we de-emphasize the importance of higher education to an economic dignity agenda, we are also downgrading a major tool for promoting mobility for people in deep poverty, especially those also impacted by historical racial discrimination. To be sure, education should never be seen as some form of silver bullet. The remnants of slavery, Jim Crow, and government-orchestrated residential segregation require a multitude of broad and targeted policies, such as truly combating housing discrimination, promoting equity and community input in economic development, providing a fair shot at jobs, and ensuring all have an opportunity to rise, regardless of parental income, age, or geography. Beyond a higher minimum wage or unionization or even free college, we need comprehensive investment throughout the pipeline from birth through college to attack the disadvantage of the accident of birth for those born into poverty. Indeed, "direct investments in the health and education of low-income children" all the way into their mid-twenties have the highest return on investment of government programs, with those programs often paying for themselves over time, according to a meta-analysis conducted by Harvard economists Nathaniel Hendren and Ben Sprung-Keyser.[67]

EQUAL OPPORTUNITIES MUST START EARLY

Equal opportunities start with universal quality early education. As Isabel Sawhill and Jens Ludwig summarize, "Findings from a number of rigorously conducted studies of early childhood and elementary school programs suggest that intervening early, often, and effectively in the lives of disadvantaged children from birth to age ten may substantially improve their life chances for higher educational attainment and greater success in the labor market, thereby helping impoverished children avoid poverty in adulthood."[68] Nobel Prize–winning economist James Heckman and his coauthors famously found that every $1 investment in quality early learning initiatives returns $8.60, with the greatest gains coming from the most intensive investments.[69]

Yet despite the strong evidence that early education provides major long-term benefits and that the achievement gap starts in early childhood, the United States spends less than half of the OECD average for the size of our economy on childcare and early childhood education—only 0.3 percent of GDP.[70] The result? About one-third of four-year-olds and three out of every five three-year-olds still lack early education, largely due to government underfunding.[71] This inadequate investment flies in the face of equality of opportunity and true first chances, and we as a nation need a real commitment to making universal pre-K a reality to address it.

INDIVIDUALIZED SUPPORT FOR K–12 STUDENTS

Through the third grade, as the saying goes, you learn to read so you can read to learn after that. Those who fall behind can begin to feel shame, act out, and lose confidence. Indeed, 88 percent of the students who do not earn a high school diploma struggled with reading in the third grade.[72] A large percentage of parents with means know well that individualized tutoring or coaching can be game-changing for children struggling to keep up or even excel enough to compete for selective colleges. Yet for many parents in even middle-class families—no less low-income families—an hourly tutor can be an unaffordable luxury.

A randomized controlled trial evaluated the impact of two-on-one math tutoring in twelve low-income Chicago public schools in the 2013–14 academic year. Participating students received fifty minutes of math tutoring every school day by specially trained tutors organized through Match Education, now called SAGA.[73] This innovation allowed Match to create a scalable model that public schools could adopt. The results of the intervention were staggering: participants learned an additional one to two years of math above what is typically learned in a year and had improved test scores, math grades, and even grades in other subjects. The improvement was so substantial that it narrowed the black-white test score gap by nearly a third.[74]

The Family Learning Institute (FLI) has shown similarly impressive results. At FLI, nearly nine out of ten low- or moderate-income students gain one to two reading levels in a single year of one-on-one tutoring.

Programs like Match and FLI show how individualized tutoring can help close the achievement gap and have a major impact on young people's confidence and self-esteem. Nick Hill received tutoring through FLI and testifies to its life-changing impact. As an African American fourth grader far behind in reading, he was embarrassed to read aloud in front of his classmates out of fear they would make fun of him. According to Hill, three years of one-on-one tutoring with FLI changed his direction, boosting his "confidence more than anything else," both in reading and in life.[75] Hill went on to graduate from Michigan State and is now a financial adviser at Morgan Stanley in Cleveland.

If we are committed to true first chances, low family income cannot mean a blocked door to individualized educational help.

CLOSING THE ACTIVITY, SUMMER, AND AFTER-SCHOOL GAPS
Access to high-quality extracurricular activities is increasingly limited to children from upper-income families, driving an "alarming" "activity gap."[76]

Scholars Kaisa Snellman, Jennifer Silva, and Robert Putnam find "many school districts have cut back on their funding for drama clubs and music programs and either reduced the number of after-school sports offered or put a hefty price tag on participation. The end result is that an increasing number of low-income students find themselves left on the sidelines."[77] The authors discovered that while more affluent kids became more involved in extracurricular activities, since the 1970s working-class students have become increasingly disengaged and disconnected, with their participation rates plummeting.[78]

Nearly 60 percent of after-school programs report that their program budget was "inadequate to meet the needs of their community."[79] Government support tends to be inconsistent and susceptible to budget cuts, leading to instability for staff in the programs and limited access for kids.[80] Sadly, while 56 percent of children in areas of concentrated poverty would be enrolled in an after-school program if one were available to them, only 24 percent actually are.[81]

Quality matters here as well. Close to home, I have watched the triumphs of the Mosaic Youth Theatre of Detroit—which, as previously mentioned, my brother, Rick, founded and ran for twenty-five years—and the struggles it faced to secure adequate funding. Mosaic is one of the acclaimed nonprofits to pioneer the field of creative youth development, which demonstrates how rigorous, high-quality arts programs can help develop confidence, critical thinking, and collaboration in youth from all backgrounds.[82] The University of Michigan studied Mosaic and found that its intensive arts training led to statistically significant leaps in students' professional development and educational aspirations. A striking 95 percent of these young people from Detroit schools have gone on to college—many on scholarships Mosaic helped arrange.[83] Programs like this can have transformative effects on the lives of countless young people from low- or moderate-income families, but they rarely have any meaningful government support. That has to change.

And it's clear that we must address activity and learning gaps even when school is not in session. The "summer slide" or summer "enrichment gap" or "Harry Potter divide"[84] shows that much of the gap between poor and wealthier students gets even worse in the summer, when students of more means are much more likely to participate in enriching activities including camps, learning programs, and even reading Harry Potter books. Trials by the Wallace Foundation and RAND Corporation found that low-income students who consistently attended free, voluntary five- or six-week summer programs received significant reading and math gains compared with students who applied for the programs but were not accepted.[85]

PAVING THE ROAD TO COLLEGE

Many, like me, realize only later in life the gift we inherited at birth of a high—almost assumed—expectation of going to college, and a tremendous support system that served as a magnet to keep us on track. Those of us blessed to be born into a family of college achievement, expectation, and support can do almost everything wrong, but with one right step we can be back on track. A low-income young person without such strong support systems, on the other hand, can do virtually everything right, but with one misstep is too often thrown off track.

The question is: Can we do enough early on to create such a magnet and support system for younger people with the odds stacked against them? I was inspired in my late twenties by the story of millionaire Eugene Lang, who, upon returning to his elementary school in Harlem for a commencement speech, tore up his prepared remarks and promised every sixth grader that if they graduated from high school he would pay for their college. Decades later, *60 Minutes* checked and found that an unusually high percentage had indeed graduated and gone to college, inspired by Lang's promise.[86] Lang's example offered a great hope: if you could instill in poor adolescents the promise of college, would it serve as that magnet of high expectations that so many kids of higher means take for granted?

The lesson of the Eugene Lang story is that, as with most things, it is never that simple. A promise like Lang's does help, but it does not alone remedy all that low-income teens—particularly very poor, minority teens—have to face, such as a lack of resources in schools, economic insecurity at home, and few after-school activities. For minority teens, this is often coupled with discriminatory treatment in terms of school discipline and the criminal justice system.[87]

We need earlier intervention and support—certainly by middle school—to ensure younger people from poor backgrounds are getting the support and taking the steps needed for a college track. As education theorist and University of Texas–San Antonio professor emerita Laura Rendón explains, "By the time students get to 12th grade, it is too late to improve college-eligibility. . . . It could be said that students begin to drop out of college in grade school."[88] Laurene Powell Jobs, who cofounded the successful non-profit College Track, reiterated to me when I was in the White House that to get students from situations of terrible economic disadvantage into and through college requires not just inspiration but early, intensive, continuous support through college completion.[89]

We could go so much further if, to start, it was considered part of the fundamental mission of colleges to do early outreach and have ongoing programs—not just a few visits or one-year programs—to encourage, inspire, and mentor disadvantaged children in the colleges' own backyards to aspire to and be prepared for college. This could include college mentors, summer programs on college campuses, intensive help on the college application process, and SAT/ACT preparation. This was one of the key motivations behind the founding of Gaining Early Awareness and Readiness for Undergraduate Programs (GEAR UP), which I played the lead White House role in creating in the late 1990s for President Clinton.[90] There are also successful evidence-based approaches that begin in high school and carry through college completion, like Career Academies, "I Have a Dream" Foundation, Project GRAD, and College Track.[91]

We also must close troubling gaps for ACT/SAT test and college application preparation. As Paul Tough highlights in *The Years That Matter Most*, there is a compelling case that test scores currently play a troubling role in exacerbating inequalities in the college admissions process.[92] If test scores continue to play such a central role in admissions, we need more advisers for public schools and for programs like CollegeSpring that provide test prep services to primarily low-income students, and have been shown to increase SAT scores substantially.[93] We should also encourage efforts—like those used by the Posse Foundation—to recognize the tremendous potential in those from economically disadvantaged backgrounds that do not rely on standardized test scores. And, as discussed earlier, students need adequate support from advisers both in navigating the college admission process and in succeeding while they are in college.

This is just the tip of the iceberg. As we wrote in the report for the first college opportunity summit I coordinated in early 2014 for President Obama, "Getting more students ready for college will require an all-hands-on-deck approach with multiple early interventions to tackle the myriad obstacles low-income students face in preparing for college."[94]

A focus on these important programs and paths to pursue potential need not be a trade-off with a focus on worker power. We can and *must* do both.

CONCLUSION

INCLUSIVE DIGNITY OR DIVISIVE DIGNITY?

This book has made the case that the three pillars of economic dignity should be our end goal for economic policy. It is a fundamentally inclusive vision. The premise is that these basic guarantees are universal goals that can be achievable for everyone—and not based on a zero-sum game where some people's economic dignity must come at the expense of others.

No doubt the elephant in the room—and in this book—is the rise and prominence of appeals by President Trump and far-right, anti-immigrant parties in Europe to Brazil and elsewhere to what could be called "divisive dignity." By divisive dignity, I mean the subtle or explicit appeal to the perceived reclaiming of superiority in status over a resented "other"—normally a racial or religious minority or immigrant group. Whereas this book calls for an inclusive economic dignity based on the universality of human dignity, divisive dignity derives its power by appealing to lifting up the status of members of an aggrieved majority—usually white—at the expense and subjugation of the dignity and status of scapegoated minorities. Sadly, in the last several years we have seen the capacity for Trump and other leaders with authoritarian tendencies to achieve electoral success with divisive dignity appeals that stoke resentment by emphasizing harsh, exclusionary rhetoric and punitive policies.

In the United States, some see the recurrent appeals to divisive dignity as evidence that the core instigation of the Trump presidency was currents of racism and sexism, and thus, issues that are less amenable to being addressed by inclusive economic policies. Sociologist Diana Mutz, who studied the shifts in opinions and vote choices of the same voters in 2012 and 2016, concluded that Trump's win could be explained by a tactic of helping "members of a dominant group" (whites) "regain a sense of dominance and wellbeing."[1] She argues that Trump voters were not motivated by being "left behind" economically, but rather by "a sense of a threat to their group's position, whether it is the status of Americans in the world at large or the status of whites in a multiethnic America."[2] Likewise, political scientists John Sides, Michael Tesler, and Lynn Vavreck use an extensive analysis of survey data of voters before the 2016 election to argue that economic factors paled in importance compared with identity-related prejudice in explaining his support.[3] Many others disagree. They remind that one out of eight Trump voters voted for Obama[4] and point to the significant gap in economic output of hard-hit rural and former manufacturing communities versus thriving metropolitan economies as an indication that the stronger rationale for Trump's support is economic.[5]

This seems like a false, oversimplified dichotomy. Economic disappointment and racial appeals are less separate explanations than they are interrelated. A more accurate analysis is likely that the loss of faith in the basic economic compact creates an opening for demagogues to connect with divisive racial appeals. Johns Hopkins sociologist Andrew Cherlin studied the perceptions of voters in two economically hurting communities in Maryland and found that "whites . . . tend to racialize their economic anxieties, but racial issues and the industrial decline are so bound together that it is virtually impossible to separate them into two independent components." He quotes a local journalist on the perceptions of people in a heavily white community: "If you're fearful, desperate, alienated, you start looking for ways to be suspicious of other people." Cherlin's research concludes that Trump simply seized on the economic unhappiness of such white voters to inflame and "encourage their tendency to racialize that desperation."[6]

There is a long, painful tradition in the United States of elites and politicians racializing economic disappointment and desperation as a divisive tactic to prevent cross-racial coalitions from bonding together to support inclusive economic policies. In writing about the period after the Civil War, for instance, W. E. B. Du Bois referred to this perverse offering of divisive dignity as a substitute for inclusive economic policies as the "psychological wage" in which "the white group of laborers, while they received a low wage, were compensated in part by a sort of public and psychological wage. They were given public deference and titles of courtesy because they were white." Writing in the 1930s, Du Bois stated that as a result of this division, "there probably are not today in the world two groups of workers with practically identical interests who hate and fear each other so deeply and persistently and who are kept so far apart that neither sees anything of common interest."[7]

Ta-Nehisi Coates also writes of how subordinating blacks to poor whites was done to foster a sense of common superiority between working-class whites and white oligarchs. Coates quotes Jefferson Davis, the eventual president of the Confederate States, who explicitly proclaimed that slavery functioned to "elevat[e] every white man in our community. . . . It is the presence of a lower caste . . . that gives this superiority to the white laborer."[8] This system served as a foundation for Jim Crow laws. As Michelle Alexander writes, "These discriminatory barriers were designed to encourage lower-class whites to retain a sense of superiority over blacks, making it far less likely that they would sustain interracial political alliances aimed at toppling the white elite. The laws were in effect another racial bribe."[9]

Dan Carter, a historian and biographer of George Wallace, the former Alabama segregationist governor and presidential candidate, sees this appeal to divisive dignity as a continuing plague on our politics. In 2016, before the election, he wrote that "both George Wallace and Donald Trump are part of a long national history of scapegoating minorities: from the Irish, Catholics, Asians, Eastern European immigrants and Jews to Muslims and Latino immigrants. During times of insecurity, a sizable minority of Americans has been drawn to forceful figures who confidently promise the destruction of all enemies, real and imagined, allowing Americans to return to a past that never existed."[10] This same tendency for economic grievance to be answered with racial and ethnic division is happening across the globe. As Fareed Zakaria argues, "Countries where mainstream politicians have failed to heed or address citizens' concerns have seen rising populism driven by political entrepreneurs fanning fear and latent prejudice."[11] Political scientist Jack Snyder argues that "nationalist political entrepreneurs have combined [economic and cultural] grievances into a narrative about perfidious elites who coddle undeserving outgroups—immigrants and minorities—while treating the nation's true people with contempt."[12]

Some may argue that the rise of harsh anti-immigrant, anti-multiculturalism politics in nations with very strong economic security policies like Sweden and Denmark rebuts the notion that it is a failure to develop inclusive economic security policies that creates the critical opening for such divisive dignity appeals. In Denmark, a country with a vast welfare state and much lower levels of inequality than the United States, the center-left prime minister Mette Frederiksen recently campaigned on a platform of tougher immigration restrictions, kept in place a ban on Muslim women wearing burqas, and permitted a policy that requires children living in areas with high shares of "non-Western immigrants" to undergo seminars in "Danish values."[13] On the other hand, her campaign promised to increase spending on social and welfare programs.[14] Sweden, long famous for its robust, universal safety net and efforts to protect multiculturalism, has seen a party with origins in the neo-Nazi movement, the Sweden Democrats, rise to gain the third-largest bloc of seats in parliament.[15]

While the experiences of Sweden and Denmark are no doubt a caution against seeing strong economic security policies as silver bullets to combat divisive dignity appeals, it is also critical not to overstate their significance. First, the parliamentary systems in Europe allow significant influence and representation of far-right groups without approaching their majority support.[16] The rise of Sweden's far-right party is disturbing but was still at 18 percent in a recent major election. From a longer-term perspective, Sweden should be seen, rather, as providing strong evidence of the power of an inclusive economic dignity compact. It has for a long time been extremely successful at incorporating significant numbers of immigrants and refugees with a compact that offers newcomers broad universal benefits but also focuses on moving them smoothly into the workforce in a clear two-way compact.[17]

The last decade has also seen a powerful confluence of factors that will take time to fully analyze and comprehend. The increasing pressure on middle-class manufacturing and service jobs due both to technological advances and to competition from countries like China and India, the rise of spreading hate through social media, and high levels of refugee flows, all in the context of a major global financial crisis, have no doubt put pressure on elements of even nations with strong economic security policies. Part of the story in Sweden's radical far-right rise is that as in numerous other Western democratic states, the rise of nativist sentiment has been fueled in part by an online disinformation campaign coming from Russian and American far-right entities.[18] Indeed, the deep economic pain caused by a severe global financial crisis—and the resentment of remedies that were seen as protecting either wealthy financial culprits or undeserving fellow citizens—may have lit on fire these brewing economic pressures. German economists Manuel Funke, Moritz Schularick, and Christoph Trebesch have established a strong relationship between financial crises and polarization, finding that after financial crises, but not after a typical recession, "voters seem to be particularly attracted to the political rhetoric of the extreme right." Studying the impact of nearly one hundred financial crises on hundreds of elections in twenty different countries, they found that the share of the vote going to far-right parties increases by 30 percent in the five years after a financial crisis.[19] They argue that "when social groups fear decline and a loss of wealth, they turn to right-wing parties that promise stability and law and order."[20] Left-wing parties do not benefit because "right-wing populists are much more willing to exploit cultural cleavages and blame economic problems on foreigners and those who supposedly put the interests of a global elite above those of their fellow citizens."[21]

It is always hard to test the counterfactual: How much worse could appeals to divisive dignity be in Nordic nations if they had weak policies to promote economic dignity? Perhaps much worse. Indeed, if we are to make country comparisons, the most compelling example may be found in the 1930s. In that decade, while FDR rallied a nation in economic despair and desperation through an appeal to an inclusive economic dignity compact based on universal responsibilities of the individual and its government, Germany and Italy saw the ugliest of appeals to division and dignity through horrid subordination and a brutality to a scapegoated "other."

I remain strongly convinced that while we should never believe that economics is the answer to all issues of racial hate and anti-immigration fears, a commitment to inclusive and universal economic dignity will leave less of an opening for appeals to what Du Bois called a "psychological wage" of superiority over a scapegoated other. Broad policies that prevent devastating falls, provide true first and second chances, and ensure that millions never feel that their economic despair is invisible or overlooked are still the best recipe we have to reduce the appeal of hateful rhetoric over tangible and affirmative economic policies. One of the great ironies in the United States is that right-wing policymakers who most exploit economic despair have often been on the front lines of blocking the broader economic and health security measures that could have been powerful tools to address existing economic pain and disappointments.

These three pillars of economic dignity provide a unifying vision for addressing our nation's economic challenges. Some commentators suggest that Democrats should talk less about issues impacting specific groups that suffer from distinct economic disadvantage and discrimination, and focus only on more generalized economic policies. They argue that this strategy is the best means to reduce the risk of turning off some alienated white, working-class voters, who represent Trump's base. Yet an economic dignity focus does not force policy or political strategy into that unfortunate dichotomy. It does not require us to accept such a false choice that could betray our values and blind us to pressing problems in our nation.

The beauty of an economic dignity agenda is that it speaks to universal end goals for all people—while not making invisible any of the distinctive challenges experienced by different groups in our nation. It allows us to see a rural jobs program for laid-off workers and an apprenticeship program for urban youths not as distinct policies for different political constituencies, but as common components of a shared strategy to achieve the universal goal of ensuring that everyone has true first and second chances in life.

And yet I must finish where I started. The fundamental motivation for making economic dignity our end goal is not as a means to any other goals. Economic dignity is our end goal in itself. It is motivated by the basic belief that the capacity to care for and experience the most meaningful moments with family, to pursue purpose and potential, and to contribute economically with respect, free from domination and humiliation, is a fundamental and universal aspiration, core to each of us as humans. Amid all the metrics, means, policies, labels, and debates over political strategies that bombard us daily, it is this vision of economic dignity that should be the North Star for economic policy that guides us every step of the way.

ACKNOWLEDGMENTS

I will start where many people end—thanking my spouse. My wife, Allison Abner, normally responds to my queries about what I should do professionally with the supportive assurance that I should do "whatever I think is best." Not this time. "This book," she said, "is a chance to speak from your heart. You have to do it." Our close friend, the journalist (and bridesmaid at our wedding) Linda Villarosa, piled on. After listening to my equivocations about writing a broader-vision book, she firmly told me I was being afraid to write bigger: I had to get over that. A united Team Allison is a persuasive and powerful force. I knew I had to take the plunge. Throughout the actual writing of the book, Allison—an accomplished TV writer—was always there to edit, advise me on the most sensitive issues, and provide support when I most needed it. I could not be more grateful.

I also have to mention up front my thanks to three editors. Jeff Goldberg, who was editor-in-chief when I wrote for the *Daily Pennsylvanian* thirty-two years ago and later as I wrote columns for the *Atlantic*, encouraged me to try a long article as a means to get my overall views down and out to the world. I knew *Democracy Journal* was the perfect place for such an essay, and their editor, Michael Tomasky, was just terrific in his advice, editing, and support for my "Economic Dignity" piece in their Spring 2019 issue.

Most of all, I cannot thank enough Scott Moyers, my editor at Penguin Press. Once Scott expressed to me his belief in this book and his enthusiasm for doing it together, I never thought for a second about doing it with anyone else. Over the last many months, I have been able to see firsthand why Scott is considered one of the top policy editors in the nation. He was wise, candid, supportive, and an outstanding editor and counselor. Scott also told me from the start that no one would be more valuable to the book-writing process than Mia Council, the assistant editor. There was simply no part of the process where she was not invaluable, from excellent editing to enormously helpful (and patient) guidance and advice. I am indeed so grateful to the entire team at Penguin Press, including our production editor, Megan Gerrity, the book's lead publicist, Juliana Kiyan, head publicist Sarah Hutson, production manager Hannah Dragone, managing editor Aly D'Amato, and Lauren Louzon.

I remain truly touched that Bob Barnett—with all his epic book deals—not only found time to advise me on my book, but gave me his 100 percent care, concern, and wise counsel as if I were actually one of those mega-deals. He certainly did not need my business: he helped me out of the same loyalty and friendship he has always shown me going back to our days doing debate prep for candidate Bill Clinton back in 1992.

Like many books, this was perhaps written both too slowly and too quickly. I first started outlining my initial ideas for a book on economic dignity in late 2014. Yet, with other work and family commitments (and no deadline), I would always start again and then put the idea to the side. But, once it officially landed with Penguin Press in May 2019, the heat was on and it meant researching and writing at an accelerated pace. This means my thank you to friends and researchers must include those who reviewed my earliest outlines in 2015–2016, the writing of the *Democracy Journal* essay, and the more fast-paced work to get this book out by May 2020.

On the earlier side, Danielle Lazarowitz was one of the first to help me explore current and past definitions of dignity, and Dan Sheehan was among the first to do research for me on the pace of technological change so I could consider its impact on economic dignity. Max Harris, a brilliant young Harvard PhD and economic historian, was extremely helpful in much of my historical research for this book—especially on debt prisons—and only had to back off this year to focus on writing his own book on post–World War I monetary policy. Mira Patel helped me explore the use of the word "dignity" by past prominent Americans and was of significant help on key chapters in the last few months of writing. Keshav Poddar offered significant and diverse research that found its way into this book on issues from Justice Brennan to antitrust policy. Ted Lee did extensive and strong research for me on worker power, job creation, and job training issues that significantly informed key chapters. Taylor Cranor was a lifesaver the last several months, doing excellent research on early labor laws, economic change, and the larger issue of meaning of work that also informed critical chapters in the book.

Two people deserve special mention. Brandon DeBot has been a star researcher and policy partner for the last three years, while also attending Yale Law School. He is one of the top young policymakers in the nation on fiscal policy and progressive taxation, and he played an essential and invaluable role in the research and drafting of a significant number of chapters in this book. No one helped more on the book over the final eight months than Maya Goodwin. Her exceptional research, sharp analytical insights, and willingness to push (and usually win) on her ideas have strengthened this book in numerous chapters. Her management in quarterbacking the final production was also essential. It would have been hard to do this book without so many people, but most especially Brandon and Maya.

I am so grateful to those who somehow found time to review specific chapters and offer their comments and share their expertise. These include Rebecca Cokley, Lenore Palladino, Julia Bascom, David Kamin, Ai-jen Poo, Janet Kim, Adam Grant, Chris Jennings, Mary Kay Henry, Vanita Gupta, Lisa Hall, Judy Heumann, Bharat Ramamurti, David Edelman, James Kvaal, Bob Shireman, Kathleen Romig, Heather Boushey, Cecilia Rouse, John Friedman, Dan O'Sullivan, Danielle Gray, Paige Shevlin, Andrew Imparato, and Byron Auguste. A very special shout-out to Jason Furman, who cut into his very deserved downtime near Thanksgiving to offer me helpful comments on several chapters. Another special mention goes to Damon Silvers, who gave me several consequential edits and suggestions after reading several chapters during his train rides in Japan while visiting his son.

Three very good friends somehow found time to read the entire manuscript and gave multiple helpful suggestions at different times in the writing— Michael Waldman, Michael Wessel, and Jacob Leibenluft. I am so grateful to each of them, especially Jacob, who was a key sounding board for both the essay in *Democracy Journal* and the book.

There were so many people who, while not reviewing drafts, gave me valuable thoughts and ideas through conversation or work together. These include, but are not limited to, Larry Mishel, Tom Kalil, LaPhonza Butler, Sasha Post, Neera Tanden, Thea Lee, Ron Klain, Bill Godfrey, Felicia Wong, Michael Calhoun, Bob Reich, Judy Lichtman, Andrew Kassoy, Wade Henderson, Jackie Woodson, Brian Highsmith, Joe Sanberg, John Podesta, Pauline Abernathy, Rick Samans, Meeghan Prunty, Bob Greenstein, Josh Steiner, Dan Porterfield, Barry Lynn, Sarah Bianchi, Sarah Miller, Samantha Power, Victoria Palomo, Leo Gerard, Tom Conway, Kelly Friendly, Rebecca Winthrop, Monique Dorsainvil, Liz Fine, Michael Shapiro, Jason Miller, Nick Merrill, Sheryl Sandberg, and Trelaine Ito. After all this time, I still often ask what Chris Georges would think on so many issues—and am grateful to have his parents, Jerry and Mary Georges, still in my life.

A special thanks to Cass Sunstein, the most prolific book author most of us know, for his passion for the concept of dignity and his advice and early encouragement of me writing this book. Thanks to another amazing author, Walter Isaacson, as well for his early encouragement. So much of this book was written at my favorite café. I am so grateful for the incredibly kind and supportive efforts of Kyle Jones, Selina Tapangco, Megan Fodran, and many others who went so out of their way to support my writing at every turn, month after month.

When I needed counsel and advice and editing on the actual writing of this book, no single person was more helpful throughout than Dan Schwerin. He is a special talent in the world of policy and writing and I was so lucky to have his guidance. While I was supposed to be in the consultant role to Jennifer Harris as she helped Larry Kramer and the Hewlett Foundation in their consequential work to develop a new progressive economic paradigm, my book certainly benefited from research I did with them on issues like corporate purpose and worker power.

In the first couple of years that I was contemplating this book, no single individual suffered through more nascent early outlines that Brian Deese, who, as always, offered the wisest of counsel and also swooped in at the very end to provide critical advice. Thanks as well to Jake Sullivan for very thoughtful advice on an early draft of what later became the *Democracy Journal* essay.

I cannot come close to thanking all of the people I have worked with in my policy jobs or advised. But I must mention the elected officials I have worked for—and their commitment and heart—starting with interning for Senator Carl Levin, campaigning for Mike Dukakis, and working for three years for the inspirational Governor Mario Cuomo, whom I am grateful to have had as an adviser and a mentor till the end of his life. I am also deeply and forever proud and appreciative to have advised Hillary Clinton in two presidential campaigns. Obviously, I will always be in debt to Bill Clinton and Barack Obama. Their brilliance and commitment made them a policy wonk's dream, and I will always be grateful that they gave me one of the highest opportunities to serve our nation.

I benefited from ideas, inspiration, and various forms of help from so many in my family. My daughter, Nina, helped with the design of the cover, researched flap jackets for me, proofread part of the galleys, and so often made my day by sitting with me on the couch as she did her homework and I wrote. My son, Miles, was a constant source of encouragement and support as I wrote the book, always checking in with me on how it was going and always impressing me with his ideas and fresh thinking. As always, I am so proud of and inspired by Samantha Chapman and Derick Chapman, who are in every way to me another daughter and son. I was so proud to be Derick's best man (a whole forty-eight hours after the book was due) and delighted that he has brought his wonderful new wife, Maddy, into our lives. My sister, Anne Sperling, and her husband, Ethan Israelsohn, have always been my science advisers on any policy I do. My sister-in-law, Marian Short, and my brother, Rick, bring the artistic element to my thinking as well as inspiring passages on the power of quality arts programs in the development and lives of young people. I was very moved by my discussions with my sister-in-law Peggy Kirkeeng on her personal commitment to treating everyone in every job with respect and dignity, while my brother Mike was, as always, one of my most trusted sounding boards on policy issues and everything I do. I benefit often from hearing the views and analysis of my brilliant nephew Erik Sperling. We may disagree at times on policy or strategy, but always with respect for each other's heart and motivation. Dara, Rob, Samantha, and Daniel

Sparling inspired me every day to think more about what more we can do to support loving families with a member with autism. I am deeply thankful for having JoAnn and Stephen Spencer and their three wonderful children in our lives, and am so inspired by the zest for life of my unstoppable aunt, Irene Sperling. I am so very grateful for the constant and tireless support and love of my wonderful mother-in-law, Olivia Abner. Nothing in our lives would go as well or be as good without the blessing of having her and my other brother, Tony Abner, living so close and so much a part of our lives. I only wish I had had met Allison early enough to have known her amazing father, Ewart Abner.

While I cannot thank all of the close friends I have been blessed with in life, I must thank Howard Shapiro and Shirley Brandman, the couple in my life who has never stopped being a second family to me since we lived together at law school thirty-seven years ago. And with everything I have done over the last forty years, Paul Dimond has been the most dedicated mentor and adviser and friend anyone could ever ask for—and on this book as well.

Even as she battles with dementia, I treasure every moment and "I love you" with my mother, and she remains a continuing source of inspiration to me. Throughout her career, she sought to close the achievement gap, push for individualized education in public schools, support collaborative assessment, and fight for equity for all children—decades before many of these issues were topical. It still amazes all of us that, while being a public-school teacher and reformer for forty years and a Supermom, she somehow managed to found three organizations—Family Learning Institute, Ann Arbor Young People's Theatre, and the first open school in Ann Arbor. All survive and thrive today.

Of course, with all the joy during the writing of this book, there was also loss. I miss my father every day—though my relationship with him lives on, including in my reflections as I wrote this book. His unconditional love, wisdom, judgment, and commitment to civil rights, social justice, and fighting for those with disabilities shaped my worldview and life's direction. I will never forget his compassion, expertise, and skill as I was there to watch him in action in his last year—at eighty-five years old—win a difficult case for a client with serious disabilities. In the first month of writing this book, our hearts were broken when we lost Josie Caintic, at only fifty-one years old, suddenly to breast cancer. She was a blessing in our and so many others' lives. We will be forever grateful for the extraordinary care, dedication, and support she provided our family for thirteen years, and the example of kindness and resilience she set for our daughter and all of us. I often thought of both Josie and my father during the writing of this book. They were from different nations and different backgrounds with different opportunities. But they both shared the exceptional admiration and affection of so many whose lives they touched, the pride in the professionalism and impact of their work, and the deep satisfaction of providing so much opportunity for so many family members they loved. In their own way, and in every way, they personified dignity.

NOTES

INTRODUCTION

1. Kathryn Schulz, "The Many Lives of Pauli Murray," *New Yorker*, April 10, 2017, https://www.newyorker.com/magazine/2017/04/17/the-many-lives-of-pauli-murray.
2. Pauli Murray, "An American Credo," *Common Ground* 5, no. 2 (December 1945): 22–24.

CHAPTER ONE: ECONOMIC METRICS AND INVISIBILITY

1. See Richard H. Thaler, "Mental Accounting Matters," *Journal of Behavioral Decision Making* 12, no. 3 (1999): 183–206, https://doi.org/10.1002/(sici)1099-0771(199909)12:3<183::aid-bdm318>3.0.co;2-f); and Richard H. Thaler, "Behavioral Economics: Past, Present and Future," *SSRN Electronic Journal*, May 27, 2016, https://doi.org/10.2139/ssrn.2790606.
2. "Robert F. Kennedy, Remarks at the University of Kansas, March 18, 1968," JFK Library, accessed November 4, 2019, https://www.jfklibrary.org/learn/about-jfk/the-kennedy-family/robert-f-kennedy/robert-f-kennedy-speeches/remarks-at-the-university of-kansas-march-18-1968.
3. "Robert F. Kennedy, Remarks at the University of Kansas, March 18, 1968."
4. For example, Norway from 1994 through 1997, and Saudi Arabia from 2003 through 2005 and 2010 through 2012. "GDP Growth (Annual %)," World Bank Group, accessed November 4, 2019, https://data.worldbank.org/indicator/NY.GDP.MKTP.KD.ZG.
5. See, for instance, Ruth Umoh, "This Royal Family's Wealth Could Be More than $1 Trillion," *CNBC*, August 18, 2018, https://www.cnbc.com/2018/08/18/this-royal-familys-wealth-could-be-more-than-1-trillion.html; and Heba Kanso, "Saudi Women 'Still Enslaved,' Says Activist as Driving Ban Ends," *Thomson Reuters Foundation*, June 22, 2018, https://www.reuters.com/article/us-saudi-women-driving/saudi-women-still-enslaved-says-activist-as-driving-ban-ends-idUSKBN1JI2XH.
6. See, e.g., *Nomination of Dr. John W. Snow: Hearing before the Committee on Finance*, 108th Cong. (2003), 52, https://www.finance.senate.gov/imo/media/doc/86516.pdf. Snow stated, "I think it was President Kennedy who talked about, 'a rising tide lifts all boats,' when asked to characterize his tax plan back in 1962, I think. There is a lot of merit in that idea."
7. Donald Lazere, "A Rising Tide Lifts All Boats: Has the Right Been Misusing JFK's Quote?" *History News Network*, accessed November 4, 2019, https://historynewsnetwork.org/article/73227.
8. Robert E. Lucas, "The Industrial Revolution: Past and Future," Federal Reserve Bank of Minneapolis, May 1, 2004, https://www.minneapolisfed.org/publications/the-region/the-industrial-revolution-past-and-future.
9. "GINI Index (World Bank Estimate)—United States," World Bank Group, accessed November 25, 2016, https://data.worldbank.org/indicator/SI.POV.GINI?end=2016&locations=US&start=1979&view=chart.
10. This measure is known as the Supplemental Poverty Measure. See Indivar Dutta-Gupta, "New Poverty Measure Shows Government's Anti-Poverty Impact," Center on Budget and Policy Priorities, November 9, 2011, https://www.cbpp.org/blog/new-poverty-measure-shows-governments-anti-poverty-impact.
11. Stiglitz, Fitoussi, and the OECD have continued with their book *Beyond GDP: Measuring What Counts for Economic and Social Performance*. Their recent report highlights steps taken by ten countries to better incorporate measures of well-being and sustainable development into the policymaking process, though there is little consistency in the type of indicators the countries use and how they are incorporated into policy. But what remains true is that indicators that are better snapshots of well-being have the power to inform the entire policy dialogue of how people's lives are truly faring and support a paradigm shift that prioritizes well-being over just growth. See Joseph E. Stiglitz, Jean-Paul Fitoussi, and Martine Durand, "Country-Experiences with Using Well-Being Indicators to Steer Policies," in *Beyond GDP: Measuring What Counts for Economic and Social Performance* (Paris: OECD Publishing, 2018), 103–14, https://www.oecd-ilibrary.org/economics/beyond-gdp/country-experiences-with-using-well-being-indicators-to-steer-policies_9789264307292-7-en.
12. There are efforts to design more comprehensive indexes like the United Nations' Human Development Index, the World Economic Forum's twelve-factor Inclusive Development Index, and the sixteen critical factors comprising the Institute for Innovation in Social Policy's Index of Social Health, including teenage suicide and food insecurity.

13. Stiglitz, Fitoussi, and Durand, *Beyond GDP*, 13.
14. Heidi Shierholz, "Low Wages and Scant Benefits Leave Many In-Home Workers Unable to Make Ends Meet," Economic Policy Institute, November 26, 2013, https://www.epi.org/publication/in-home-workers/.
15. Linda Burnham and Nik Theodore, "Home Economics: The Invisible and Unregulated World of Domestic Work," 2012, National Domestic Workers Alliance and Center for Urban Economic Development, University of Illinois at Chicago Data Center, https://idwfed.org/en/resources/home-economics-the-invisible-and-unregulated-world-of-domestic-work/@@display-file/attachment_1.
16. This is due to the fact that taxi drivers were generally classified as independent contractors.
17. Annette D. Bernhardt, Siobhan McGrath, and James DeFilippis, *Unregulated Work in the Global City: Employment and Labor Law Violations in New York City* (New York: Brennan Center for Justice at New York University School of Law, 2007), https://www.brennancenter.org/sites/default/files/legacy/d/download_file_49380.pdf.
18. Ariel Ramchandani, "There's a Sexual-Harassment Epidemic on America's Farms," *Atlantic*, January 29, 2018, https://www.theatlantic.com/business/archive/2018/01/agriculture-sexual-harassment/550109/.
19. Restaurant Opportunities Centers United, "New Report: 90% of Female Restaurant Workers Experience Sexual Harassment," October 14, 2014, http://rocunited.org/2014/10/new-report-90-female-restaurant-workers-experience-sexual-harassment/.
20. Ginger C. Hanson, Nancy A. Perrin, Helen Moss, Naima Laharnar, and Nancy Glass, "Workplace Violence against Homecare Workers and Its Relationship with Workers Health Outcomes: A Cross-Sectional Study," *BMC Public Health*, January 17, 2015, https://www.ncbi.nlm.nih.gov/pmc/articles/PMC4308913/.
21. Pew Charitable Trusts, "How Income Volatility Interacts with American Families' Financial Security," March 2017, http://www.pewtrusts.org/-/media/assets/2017/03/incomevolatility_and_financialsecurity.pdf.
22. Board of Governors of the Federal Reserve System, "Report on the Economic Well-Being of U.S. Households in 2017," May 2018, https://www.federalreserve.gov/publications/files/2017-report-economic-well-being-us-households-201805.pdf.
23. Kim Parker, Rich Morin, and Juliana Menasce Horowitz, "Public Sees America's Future in Decline on Many Fronts," Pew Research Center's Social & Demographic Trends Project, March 21, 2019, https://www.pewsocialtrends.org/2019/03/21/public-sees-an-america-in-decline-on-many-fronts/.
24. *Jacobellis v. State of Ohio*, 378 U.S. 184, 197 n. 2 (1964).
25. Will wrote three columns in the *Washington Post* that highlighted the term: George F. Will, "Prosperity amid the Gloom," *Washington Post*, October 19, 2006, http://www.washingtonpost.com/wp-dyn/content/article/2006/10/18/AR2006101801502.html; George F. Will, "Democrats' Prosperity Problem," *Washington Post*, June 10, 2007, http://www.washingtonpost.com/wp-dyn/content/article/2007/06/08/AR2007060802397.html; George F. Will, "Horrors of a 'Crisis,'" *Washington Post*, April 13, 2008, http://www.washingtonpost.com/wp-dyn/content/article/2008/04/11/AR2008041103250.html; AEI published approvingly of the use of the term on multiple occasions: Mark J. Perry, "Quote of the Day II: Economic Hypochondriacs," American Enterprise Institute, June 11, 2007, https://www.aei.org/carpe-diem/quote-of-the-day-ii-economic-hypochondriacs/; and John H. Makin, "Print Money and Cut the Payroll Tax," American Enterprise Institute, December 1, 2008, https://www.aei.org/research-products/report/print-money-and-cut-the-payroll-tax/.

CHAPTER TWO: DEFINING DIGNITY

1. Rudyard Kipling, "If—," Poetry Foundation, accessed November 4, 2019, https://www.poetryfoundation.org/poems/46473/if—.
2. Michael Rosen, *Dignity: Its History and Meaning* (Cambridge, MA: Harvard University Press, 2018), 11.
3. "Preamble to the Declaration of Independence," National Archives and Records Administration, accessed November 5, 2019, https://www.archives.gov/founding-docs/declaration.
4. Rosen, *Dignity*, 15.
5. Michael J. Sandel, *Justice: What's the Right Thing to Do?* (New York: Farrar, Strauss and Giroux, 2009), 122.
6. Rosen, *Dignity*.
7. Immanuel Kant, *Kant: Groundwork of the Metaphysics of Morals* (Provo, UT: Renaissance Classics, 2012).
8. See Martin Luther King Jr., foreword to "A Freedom Budget for All Americans: A Summary," by A. Philip Randolph and Bayard Rustin, A. Philip Randolph Institute, January 1967, https://www.prrac.org/pdf/FreedomBudget.pdf.
9. Cesar Chavez, address at the Commonwealth Club of California (San Francisco, November 9, 1984), United Farm Workers, accessed November 5, 2019, https://ufw.org/research/history/cesar-chavez-laid-vision-farm-workers-latinos-1984-commonwealth-club-address/; and Samuel Gompers, October 4, 1904, Samuel Gompers Papers, accessed November 4, 2019, http://www.gompers.umd.edu/quotes.htm. "We don't love to work only. The mule works, too. Work alone is not the ideal and hope for the attainment of the human kind. I have said that we want to work and ought to work, but the work we perform for our fellow man should yield to us a better life. It won't do to tell us that our forefathers lived on coarser food than we do now. It is not satisfactory or convincing. The fact of the matter is that we live in the United States of America, the richest country on the face of the globe—and the millions of honest toilers of America are willing to work to produce the great wealth and place it at the feet of the people of our country, but in return the toiling masses, the great

producers of wealth . . . insist that there should be a better life and better home and better surroundings for the great producers of wealth."

10. Chavez, address.

11. Elizabeth Cady Stanton, "Address Delivered at Seneca Falls," in *The Boisterous Sea of Liberty: A Documentary History of America from Discovery through the Civil War*, by David Brion Davis and Steven Mintz (Oxford University Press, 1998), 404.

12. Ai-jen Poo, *The Age of Dignity: Preparing for the Elder Boom in a Changing America* (New York: New Press, 2015).

13. "Strengthening and Growing the Middle Class," Biden Foundation, accessed November 4, 2019, https://archive.bidenfoundation.org/pillars/strengthening-middle-class/.

14. Benjamin Wallace-Wells, "Sherrod Brown Wants to Bring a Working-Class Ethos Back to the Democratic Party," *New Yorker*, December 13, 2018, https://www.newyorker.com/news/the-political-scene/sherrod-brown-wants-to-bring-a-working-class-ethos-back-to-the-democratic-party; and "The Dignity of Work," accessed November 5, 2019, https://dignityofwork.com/.

15. Mark Paul, William Darity Jr., and Darrick Hamilton, "The Federal Job Guarantee—A Policy to Achieve Permanent Full Employment," Center on Budget and Policy Priorities, March 9, 2018, https://www.cbpp.org/research/full-employment/the-federal-job-guarantee-a-policy-to-achieve-permanent-full-employment.

16. Alexander Hamilton, "Federalist No. 1," October 27, 1787, https://teachingamericanhistory.org/library/document/federalist-no-1/.

17. Gunnar Myrdal, *An American Dilemma: The Negro Problem and Modern Democracy* (New York: Harper & Brothers Publishers, 1944).

18. Isaiah Berlin, "Two Concepts of Liberty" (lecture, 1958), Isaiah Berlin Virtual Library, accessed November 10, 2019, http://berlin.wolf.ox.ac.uk/published_works/tcl/tcl-a.pdf.

19. Berlin, "Two Concepts of Liberty."

20. William J. Brennan, "Reason, Passion, and 'The Progress of the Law,'" *Cardozo Law Review* 10, no. 3 (1988): 15, https://heinonline.org/HOL/LandingPage?handle=hein.journals/cdozo10&div=12.

21. *Trop v. Dulles*, 356 U.S. 86, 100 (1958).

22. *Furman v. Georgia*, 408 U.S. 238, 273 (1972).

23. "Convention (III) Relative to the Treatment of Prisoners of War. Geneva, 12, August 1949," International Committee of the Red Cross, accessed November 10, 2019, https://ihl-databases.icrc.org/ihl/WebART/375-590006.

24. William J. Brennan Jr., "The Great Debate" (speech, Text and Teaching Symposium, Georgetown University, Washington, DC, October 12, 1985), Federalist Society, accessed November 10, 2019, https://fedsoc.org/commentary/publications/the-great-debate-justice-william-j-brennan-jr-october-12-1985.

25. Brennan, "Great Debate."

26. Brennan, "Great Debate."

27. *Goldberg v. Kelly*, 397 U.S. 254, 265 (1970).

28. *Goldberg v. Kelly*, 397 U.S. 254, 265 (1970).

29. *Planned Parenthood of Southeastern Pa. v. Casey*, 505 U.S. 833, 851 (1992).

30. *Obergefell v. Hodges*, 135 S. Ct. 2584 (2015), 2608, https://www.law.columbia.edu/sites/default/files/microsites/gender-sexuality/Gender_Justice/combined_-_what_obergefell_should_have_said.pdf.

31. 1912—Massachusetts. 1913—California, Colorado, Minnesota, Nebraska, Oregon, Utah, Washington, and Wisconsin. 1915—Arkansas and Kansas. Arthur F. Lucas, "The Legal Minimum Wage in Massachusetts," *Annals of the American Academy of Political and Social Science* 130 (March 1927): 1. http://www.jstor.org/stable/1016389.

32. Thomas Reed Powell, "The Oregon Minimum Wage Cases," *Political Science Quarterly* 32 (June 1917): 308, https://www.jstor.org/stable/pdf/2141734.pdf.

33. William F. Ogburn, *Progress and Uniformity in Child-Labor Legislation: A Study in Statistical Measurement.* (New York: Columbia University Press, 1912), 273–493; table XVII, 76.

34. Michael Schuman, "History of Child Labor in the United States—Part 2: The Reform Movement," Bureau of Labor Statistics, *Monthly Labor Review*, January 2017, 13, https://www.bls.gov/opub/mlr/2017/article/pdf/history-of-child-labor-in-the-united-states-part-2-the-reform-movement.pdf.

35. David Robertson, "The Bias of American Federalism: The Limits of Welfare-State Development in the Progressive Era," *Journal of Policy History* 1, no. 3 (July 1989): 279, doi:10.1017/S0898030600003523.

36. *West Coast Hotel Co. v. Parrish*, 300 U.S. 379, 398 (1937).

37. *Epic Systems Corp. v. Lewis*, 138 S. Ct. 1612, 1634 (2018).

38. Theodore Roosevelt, *Theodore Roosevelt: An Autobiography* (New York: Charles Scribner's Sons, 1913), 25.

39. Roosevelt, *Theodore Roosevelt*, 25.

40. George Ruiz, "The Ideological Convergence of Theodore Roosevelt and Woodrow Wilson," *Presidential Studies Quarterly* 19, no. 1 (1989): 164, https://www.jstor.org/stable/pdf/40574572.pdf; and Aida D. Donald, *Lion in the White House: A Life of Theodore Roosevelt* (New York: Basic Books, 2007), 43.

41. Doris Kearns Goodwin, *The Bully Pulpit* (New York: Simon & Schuster Paperbacks, 2013), 77.

42. Roosevelt, *Theodore Roosevelt*, 80.

43. Goodwin, *The Bully Pulpit*, 77.

44. Goodwin, *The Bully Pulpit*, 213–14.

45. Roosevelt, *Theodore Roosevelt*, 119–200.

46. "Sound Recordings of Theodore Roosevelt's Voice, Social and Industrial Justice," Library of Congress, accessed November 25, 2019, https://www.loc.gov/collections/theodore-roosevelt-films/articles-and-essays/sound-recordings-of-theodore-roosevelts-voice/#SIJ.

47. Roosevelt, *Theodore Roosevelt*, 200.

48. Roosevelt, *Theodore Roosevelt*, 201.

49. Ruiz, "Ideological Convergence," 164.

50. Roosevelt, *Theodore Roosevelt*, 160–61.

51. Franklin D. Roosevelt, "A Proof of Democracy: Ours Is a Great Heritage" (speech, International Teamsters Union, Washington, DC, September 11, 1940), accessed November 10, 2019, http://www.ibiblio.org/pha/policy/1940/1940-09-11a.html.

52. Daniel Nelson, "The Origins of Unemployment Insurance in Wisconsin," *Wisconsin Magazine of History* 51, no. 2 (1967–68): 111, 120, www.jstor.org/stable/4634308.

53. Edwin Amenta, Elisabeth S. Clemens, Jefren Olsen, Sunita Parikh, and Theda Skocpol, "The Political Origins of Unemployment Insurance in Five American States," *Studies in American Political Development* 2 (1987): 145, doi:10.1017/S0898588X00000444.

54. Eleanor Roosevelt, "The Great Question" remarks (United Nations, New York, March 27, 1958), available at https://harpers.org/blog/2007/12/roosevelt-on-human-rights-in-the-small-places/.

55. Franklin D. Roosevelt, "State of the Union Message to Congress," January 11, 1944, Franklin D. Roosevelt Presidential Library and Museum, accessed November 13, 2019, http://www.fdrlibrary.marist.edu/archives/address_text.html.

56. Franklin D. Roosevelt, "State of the Union Message to Congress."

57. Franklin D. Roosevelt, "State of the Union Message to Congress."

58. Martin Luther King Jr., *Why We Can't Wait* (New York: New American Library, 1964), 10.

59. Bayard Rustin, "Reflections on the Death of Martin Luther King, Jr. (1968)," in *Time on Two Crosses: The Collected Writings of Bayard Rustin*, ed. Devon W. Carbado and Donald Weise (San Francisco: Cleis Press, 2003), 191.

60. Bayard Rustin, "The Total Vision of A. Philip Randolph 1969," in *Time on Two Crosses: The Collected Writings of Bayard Rustin*, 197.

61. Lyndon B. Johnson, "Special Message to the Congress: The American Promise" (speech, Washington, DC, March 15, 1965), LBJ Presidential Library, accessed November 13, 2019, http://www.lbjlibrary.org/lyndon-baines-johnson/speeches-films/president-johnsons-special-message-to-the-congress-the-american-promise.

CHAPTER THREE: IT STARTS WITH FAMILY

1. Claire Cain Miller, "Americans Are Having Fewer Babies. They Told Us Why," *New York Times*, July 5, 2018, https://www.nytimes.com/2018/07/05/upshot/americans-are-having-fewer-babies-they-told-us-why.html.

2. OECD, "PF2.1. Parental Leave Systems," OECD Family Database, August 2019, 2, https://www.oecd.org/els/soc/PF2_1_Parental_leave_systems.pdf.

3. Kaiser Family Foundation, "Health Insurance Coverage of the Total Population: 2018," https://www.kff.org/other/state-indicator/total-population.

4. Bureau of Labor Statistics, "National Compensation Survey: Employee Benefits in the United States, March 2018," September 2018, 311, https://www.bls.gov/ncs/ebs/benefits/2018/employee-benefits-in-the-united-states-march-2018.pdf.

5. This is derived from the finding that only 7 percent of workers with wages in the bottom 25 percent of the wage distribution have any paid family leave. Most childcare workers (caring for children below preschool age) and personal care aides and home health aides fall within this wage category. Bureau of Labor Statistics, "National Compensation Survey," 311; Bureau of Labor Statistics, "Occupational Outlook Handbook: Childcare Workers, 2018," accessed November 13, 2019, https://www.bls.gov/ooh/personal-care-and-service/childcare-workers.htm; Bureau of Labor Statistics, "Occupational Outlook Handbook: Home Health Aides and Personal Care Aides, 2018," accessed November 13, 2019, https://www.bls.gov/ooh/healthcare/home-health-aides-and-personal-care-aides.htm; and Elise Gould, "State of Working America Wages 2018," Economic Policy Institute, February 20, 2019, https://www.epi.org/publication/state-of-american-wages-2018/.

6. Sharon Lerner, "The Real War on Families: Why the U.S. Needs Paid Leave Now," *In These Times*, August 18, 2015, http://inthesetimes.com/article/18151/the-real-war-on-families, citing data in Alyssa Pozniak, Katherine Wen, Krista Olson, Kelly Daley, and Jacob Klerman, "Family and Medical Leave in 2012," Abt Associates, September 6, 2012, https://www.dol.gov/sites/dolgov/files/OASP/legacy/files/FMLA-Detailed-Results-Appendix.pdf.

7. Alyssa Pozniak, Katherine Wen, Krista Olson, Kelly Daley, and Jacob Klerman, "Family and Medical Leave in 2012: Technical Report," Abt Associates, September 6, 2012, 141–42, https://www.dol.gov/sites/dolgov/files/OASP/legacy/files/FMLA-2012-Technical-Report.pdf.

8. Lerner, "The Real War on Families."

9. See U.S. Department of Labor, Wage and Hour Division, FMLA Surveys, accessed November 21, 2019, https://www.dol.gov/whd/fmla/survey/.

10. Bryce Covert, "Too Often, a New Baby Brings Big Debt," *Nation*, May 15, 2012, https://www.thenation.com/article/too-often-new-baby-brings-big-debt/.

11. Covert, "Too Often a New Baby Brings Debt."
12. Referring to private industry workers. Bureau of Labor Statistics, "National Compensation Survey," 311.
13. Pew Research Center, "Where Americans Find Meaning in Life," November 20, 2018, https://www.pewfo rum.org/2018/11/20/where-americans-find-meaning-in-life/.
14. Wendy Wang, "Parents' Time with Kids More Rewarding than Paid Work—and More Exhausting," Pew Research Center, October 8, 2013, https://www.pewsocialtrends.org/2013/10/08/parents-time-with-kids -more-rewarding-than-paid-work-and-more-exhausting/.
15. Martin Luther King Jr., "American Federation of State, County and Municipal Employees (AFSCME) Memphis, Tennessee, March 18, 1968," in *All Labor Has Dignity*, ed. Michael K. Honey (Boston: Beacon Press, 2011), 176.
16. Lerner, "The Real War on Families."
17. Lydia Saad, "The '40-Hour' Workweek Is Actually Longer—by Seven Hours," *Gallup News*, August 29, 2014, http://news.gallup.com/poll/175286/hour-workweek-actually-longer-seven-hours.aspx.
18. Daniel Schneider and Kristen Harknett, "It's About Time: How Work Schedule Instability Matters for Workers, Families, and Racial Inequality," October 2019, https://shift.berkeley.edu/its-about-time-how -work-schedule-instability-matters-for-workers-families-and-racial-inequality/.
19. Schneider and Harknett, "It's About Time."
20. Rachel Garfield, Kendal Orgera, and Anthony Damico, "The Coverage Gap: Uninsured Poor Adults in States That Do Not Expand Medicaid," Kaiser Family Foundation, January 14, 2020, https://www.kff.org/medicaid /issue-brief/the-coverage-gap-uninsured-poor-adults-in-states-that-do-not-expand-medicaid.
21. Sarah Kliff, "'Am I a Bad Mom?' Why One Mom Didn't Take Her Kid to the ER—Even After Poison Control Said To," *Vox*, May 10, 2019, https://www.vox.com/health-care/2019/5/10/18526696/health-care-costs-er -emergency-room.
22. Christine Herman, "To Get Mental Health Help for a Child, Desperate Parents Relinquish Custody," Shots Health News from NPR, January 2, 2019, https://www.npr.org/sections/health-shots/2019/01/02/673765794 /to-get-mental-health-help-for-a-child-desperate-parents-relinquish-custody.
23. The charge was later amended to "no-fault dependency," which means the child did not enter the state custody through fault of the parents. Herman, "To Get Mental Health Help for a Child, Desperate Parents Relinquish Custody."
24. U.S. General Accounting Office, "Child Welfare and Juvenile Justice: Federal Agencies Could Play a Stronger Role in Helping States Reduce the Number of Children Placed Solely to Obtain Mental Health Services," GAO-03-397, April 2003, https://books.google.com/books?id=v2K9ZbnWXI0C&printsec=frontcover.
25. Robert F. Kennedy, "Remarks at the Cleveland City Club, April 5, 1968," John F. Kennedy Presidential Library, accessed November 13, 2019, https://www.jfklibrary.org/learn/about-jfk/the-kennedy-family/robert -f-kennedy/robert-f-kennedy-speeches/remarks-to-the-cleveland-city-club-april-5-1968.
26. Emily A. Benfer, "Contaminated Childhood: The Chronic Lead Poisoning of Low-Income Children and Communities of Color in the United States," *Health Affairs*, August 8, 2017, https://www.healthaffairs.org /do/10.1377/hblog20170808.061398/full/.
27. See, for instance, Union of Concerned Scientists, "Inequitable Exposure to Air Pollution from Vehicles in California (2019)," January 28, 2019, https://www.ucsusa.org/resources/inequitable-exposure-air-pollution -vehicles-california-2019#ucs-report-downloads.
28. For discussion, see Vann R. Newkirk II, "Trump's EPA Concludes Environmental Racism Is Real," *Atlantic*, February 28, 2018, https://www.theatlantic.com/politics/archive/2018/02/the-trump-administration-finds-that-environmental-racism-is-real/554315/.
29. Newkirk, "Trump's EPA Concludes Environmental Racism Is Real."
30. Alan B. Krueger, "The Rise and Consequences of Inequality in the United States" (speech, Center for American Progress, Washington, DC, January 12, 2012), https://cdn.americanprogress.org/wp-content/uploads /events/2012/01/pdf/krueger.pdf.
31. Bill Chappell, "U.S. Kids Far Less Likely to Out-Earn Their Parents, as Inequality Grows," *The Two-Way* (blog), *NPR*, December 9, 2016, https://www.npr.org/sections/thetwo-way/2016/12/09/504989751/u-s-kids -far-less-likely-to-out-earn-their-parents-as-inequality-grows.
32. Hamilton Project, "Enrichment Expenditures on Children," July 18, 2013, https://www.hamiltonproject .org/charts/enrichment_expenditures_on_children.

CHAPTER FOUR: THE PURSUIT OF POTENTIAL AND PURPOSE

1. Martha C. Nussbaum, *Creating Capabilities: The Human Development Approach* (Cambridge, MA: Belknap Press of Harvard University Press, 2011), 31–32.
2. Robert F. Kennedy, "Remarks at the University of Kansas, March 18, 1968," John F. Kennedy Presidential Library, November 13, 1968, https://www.jfklibrary.org/learn/about-jfk/the-kennedy-family/robert-f -kennedy/robert-f-kennedy-speeches/remarks-at-the-university-of-kansas-march-18-1968.
3. Robert F. Kennedy, "Remarks to the Cleveland City Club, April 5, 1968," John F. Kennedy Presidential Library, November 13, 2019, https://www.jfklibrary.org/learn/about-jfk/the-kennedy-family/robert-f-kennedy/robert -f-kennedy-speeches/remarks-to-the-cleveland-city-club-april-5-1968.
4. James Truslow Adams, *The Epic of America* (New York: Blue Ribbon Books, 1931), 404–5, 411–12, 416, accessed November 13, 2019, http://gerdthiele.de/Talkolleg/epic.

5. Ganesh Sitaraman, *The Crisis of the Middle-Class Constitution* (New York: Alfred A. Knopf, 2017), 12–13.

6. Ryan Teague Beckwith, "Read Paul Ryan's Speech on the State of American Politics," *Time*, March 23, 2016, https://time.com/4269260/paul-ryan-speech-donald-trump-politics-transcript/.

7. "President Barack Obama's State of the Union Address," White House Office of the Press Secretary, January 28, 2014, https://obamawhitehouse.archives.gov/the-press-office/2014/01/28/president-barack-obamas-state-union-address.

8. The 3.2 percent figure specifically refers to children who are poor for at least half of their childhoods and graduated by age twenty-five. Caroline Ratcliffe, "Child Poverty and Adult Success," Urban Institute, September 2015, https://www.urban.org/sites/default/files/publication/65766/2000369-Child-Poverty-and-Adult-Success.pdf. The 60 percent figure refers to students whose socioeconomic status is high based on a composite score of parents' education, occupations, and family income when the child is a sophomore in high school. Graduation rate for the latter group is based on eight years after completing high school. National Center for Education Statistics, "Postsecondary Attainment: Differences by Socioeconomic Status," in Grace Kena et al., *The Condition of Education 2015*, NCES 2015-144, U.S. Department of Education, Washington, DC, https://nces.ed.gov/programs/coe/pdf/coe_tva.pdf.

9. Caroline Ratcliffe and Signe-Mary McKernan, "Childhood Poverty Persistence: Facts and Consequences," Urban Institute Brief 14, June 2010, https://www.urban.org/research/publication/childhood-poverty-persistence-facts-and-consequences.

10. National Academies of Sciences, Engineering, and Medicine, *A Roadmap to Reducing Childhood Poverty* (Washington, DC: National Academies Press, 2019), 4, https://www.nap.edu/read/25246/chapter/2.

11. Ratcliffe and McKernan, "Childhood Poverty Persistence."

12. Fifty-nine percent of sophomores with parents with lower educational attainment and income (for ease, these groups are referred to here by income) planned to earn at least a bachelor's (incorporates those planning to earn a bachelor's and an advanced degree), compared with 88 percent of children from households with higher income. What's more, there is a stark drop-off in students from low-income households who in sophomore year expect to earn at least a bachelor's and then by senior year no longer have that expectation (59 percent in sophomore year, compared with 47 percent by senior year). For wealthy and middle-income students, this decline is much smaller. National Center for Education Statistics, "Postsecondary Attainment."

13. Specifically referring to bachelor's completion by age twenty-five. National Center for Education Statistics, "Postsecondary Attainment."

14. Ratcliffe and McKernan, "Childhood Poverty Persistence."

15. Adam Looney, "5 Facts about Prisoners and Work, before and after Incarceration," Brookings Institution, March 14, 2018, https://www.brookings.edu/blog/up-front/2018/03/14/5-facts-about-prisoners-and-work-before-and-after-incarceration/.

16. It matters where a child grows up, too. If children grow up poor in an area with better-quality primary schools, less residential segregation, and less income inequality, they have a better shot at escaping poverty and rising to the upper class in adulthood. Also, poor children growing up in the Southeast have less chance of rising economically, compared with poor children on the West Coast: for example, a child born to a low-income family in San Jose, California, has three times the odds of rising to the top fifth as a child from a low-income family in Charlotte, North Carolina. For points in text: Raj Chetty, Nathaniel Hendren, Maggie R. Jones, and Sonya R. Porter, "Race and Economic Opportunity in the United States: An Intergenerational Perspective," Equality of Opportunity Project, March 2018, http://www.equality-of-opportunity.org/assets/documents/race_paper.pdf; And for endnote: Raj Chetty, Nathaniel Hendren, Patrick Kline, and Emmanuel Saez, "Where Is the Land of Opportunity? The Geography of Intergenerational Mobility in the United States," National Bureau of Economic Research, June 2014, https://www.nber.org/papers/w19843.

17. Chetty et al., "Race and Economic Opportunity."

18. Alexandra Killewald and Brielle Bryan, "Falling Behind: The Role of Inter- and Intragenerational Processes in Widening Racial and Ethnic Wealth Gaps through Early and Middle Adulthood," *Social Forces* 97, no. 2 (December 2018): 705–40, doi: 10.1093/sf/soy060.

19. Richard Rothstein, *The Color of Law: A Forgotten History of How Our Government Segregated America* (New York: Liveright, 2017); Trymaine Lee, "A Vast Wealth Gap, Driven by Segregation, Redlining, Evictions and Exclusion, Separates Black and White America," *New York Times*, August 14, 2019, https://www.nytimes.com/interactive/2019/08/14/magazine/racial-wealth-gap.html; Andre M. Perry, Jonathan Rothwell, and David Harshbarger, "The Devaluation of Assets in Black Neighborhoods: The Case of Residential Property," Brookings Institution, November 27, 2018, https://www.brookings.edu/research/devaluation-of-assets-in-black-neighborhoods/; and Paul R. Dimond, *Beyond Busing: Reflections on Urban Segregation, the Courts, and Equal Opportunity* (Ann Arbor: University of Michigan Press, 2005).

20. In terms of mobility of educational attainment (the likelihood that if one's parents are in the bottom half of the educational attainment spectrum the offspring will make it to the top quartile of educational attainment), the United States sits among the worst fifty countries around the world—almost entirely developing countries. Ambar Narayan, Roy Van der Weide, Alexandru Cojocaru, Christoph Lakner, Silvia Redaelli, Daniel Gerszon Mahler, Rakesh Gupta N. Ramasubbaiah et al., *Fair Progress?: Economic Mobility across Generations around the World* (Washington, DC: World Bank Group, 2018), 10–12.

21. Amartya Sen, *Inequality Reexamined* (New York: Oxford University Press, 1992), 40–41.

22. Franklin Delano Roosevelt, "Remarks on the 50th Anniversary of the Statue of Liberty, October 28, 1936," Re-imagining Migration, accessed November 13, 2019, https://reimaginingmigration.org/fdr-on-the-statue -of-libertys-50th-anniversary/.
23. "Text of President Bush's 2004 State of the Union Address," *Washington Post*, January 20, 2004, https:// www.washingtonpost.com/wp-srv/politics/transcripts/bushtext_012004.html.
24. Richard M. Johnson, *Speech of Col. Richard M. Johnson, of Kentucky, on a Proposition to Abolish Imprisonment for Debt, Submitted by Him to the Senate of the United States, January 14, 1823* (Boston: Society for the Relief of the Distressed, 1823), 5–10, accessed November 13, 2019, https://books.google.com/books? id=rPZCAQAAMAAJ.
25. Bradley Hansen, "Bankruptcy Law in the United States," EH.net, Economic History Association, accessed November 13, 2019, https://eh.net/encyclopedia/bankruptcy-law-in-the-united-states/.
26. Jill Lepore, "I.O.U.: How We Used to Treat Debtors," *New Yorker*, April 6, 2009, https://www.newyorker .com/magazine/2009/04/13/i-o-u.
27. Edward J. Balleisen, *Navigating Failure: Bankruptcy and Commercial Society in Antebellum America* (Chapel Hill: University of North Carolina Press, 2001), 13.
28. Alexis de Tocqueville, "Chapter XVIII: Of Honor in the United States and in Democratic Communities," in *Democracy in America*, vol. 2, bk. 3 (New York: The Colonial Press, 1899), https://web.archive.org/web /20110217015834/http:/etext.lib.virginia.edu/etcbin/toccer-new2?id=TocDem2.sgm&images=images/mod eng&data=/texts/english/modeng/parsed&tag=public&part=59&division=div2.
29. As a percentage of GDP. See OECD, "Public Expenditure on Activation Policies in 2015," accessed November 13, 2019, http://www.oecd.org/employment/activation.htm.
30. OECD, "Figure 4.8. Unemployment Benefit Schemes Are a Key Source of Income Support," in *OECD Employment Outlook 2018* (Paris: OECD Publishing, July 2018), 167, https://read.oecd-ilibrary.org/employment /oecd-employment-outlook-2018_empl_outlook-2018-en#page169.
31. OECD, *Back to Work: United States: Improving the Re-employment Prospects of Displaced Workers* (Paris: OECD Publishing, 2016), 16, https://www.oecd.org/unitedstates/back-to-work-united-states-97892642665 13-en.htm.
32. See Chris Stokel-Walker, "Why Getting Fired Is Worse Than Divorce," *Bloomberg*, April 26, 2017, https:// www.bloomberg.com/news/articles/2017-04-27/why-getting-fired-is-worse-than-divorce-or-the -death-of-a-spouse, citing the What Works Centre for Wellbeing, "Unemployment, Re-employment and Well-Being," March 2017, https://whatworkswellbeing.files.wordpress.com/2017/02/unemployment-reemployment -wellbeing-briefing-march-2017.pdf.
33. Rich Morin and Rakesh Kochhar, "Lost Income, Lost Friends—and Loss of Self-Respect," Pew Research Center, July 22, 2010, https://www.pewsocialtrends.org/2010/07/22/hard-times-have-hit-nearly-everyone -and-hammered-the-long-term-unemployed/.
34. Philip Oreopoulos, Marianne Page, and Ann Huff Stevens, "The Intergenerational Effect of Worker Displacement," *Journal of Labor Economics* 26, no. 3 (July 2008): 455–83, https://www.jstor.org/stable/10.1086 /588493.
35. Ann Huff Stevens and Jessamyn Schaller, "Short-Run Effects of Parental Job Loss on Children's Academic Achievement," *Economics of Education Review* 30 (2011): 289–99, https://poverty.ucdavis.edu/sites/main /files/file-attachments/stevens_2011eer.pdf.
36. Milena Nikolova and Boris N. Nikolaev, "Family Matters: Involuntary Parental Unemployment during Childhood and Subjective Well-Being Later in Life," GLO Discussion Paper Series 212, Global Labor Organization, 2018, https://ideas.repec.org/p/zbw/glodps/212.html.
37. Timothy J. Classen and Richard A. Dunn, "The Effect of Job Loss and Unemployment Duration on Suicide Risk in the United States: A New Look Using Mass-Layoffs and Unemployment Duration," *Health Economics* 2, no. 3 (March 2012): 338–50.
38. Rand Ghayad, "The Jobless Trap," MIT Institute for Career Transitions Job Market Paper (working paper, 2013), http://media.wix.com/ugd/576e9a_f6cf3b6661e44621ad26547112f66691.pdf.
39. Kory Kroft, Fabian Lange, and Matthew J. Notowidigdo, "Duration Dependence and Labor Market Conditions: Evidence from a Field Experiment," *Quarterly Journal of Economics* 128, no. 3 (August 2013): 1123–67, https://doi.org/10.1093/qje/qjt015.
40. Annie Lowrey, "Caught in a Revolving Door of Unemployment," *New York Times*, November 16, 2013, https://www.nytimes.com/2013/11/17/business/caught-in-unemployments-revolving-door.html.
41. Laid-off workers, once reemployed, have wages about 13 percent lower than continuously employed workers, one to twenty years after layoff. Justin Barnette and Amanda Michaud, "Wage Scars from Job Loss" (working paper, University of Akron, February 16, 2011), https://www.uakron.edu/dotAsset/2264615.pdf.
42. Daniel S. Hamermesh, "What Do We Know about Worker Displacement in the U.S.?" NBER Working Paper 2402, National Bureau of Economic Research, Cambridge, MA, 1987, http://www.nber.org/papers/w2402.
43. Ben S. Bernanke, "Recent Developments in the Labor Market," National Association for Business Economics Annual Conference, Arlington, VA, March 26, 2012, http://www.federalreserve.gov/newsevents/speech /bernanke20120326a.htm.
44. White House, "Best Practices for Recruiting and Hiring the Long-Term Unemployed," accessed November 13, 2019, https://obamawhitehouse.archives.gov/sites/default/files/docs/best_practices_recruiting_longterm _unemployed.pdf.

45. United States Sentencing Commission, "Demographic Differences in Sentencing," November 14, 2017, https://www.ussc.gov/research/research-reports/demographic-differences-sentencing.
46. Ashley Nellis, "Color of Justice: Racial and Ethnic Disparity in State Prisons," Sentencing Project, June 14, 2016, https://www.sentencingproject.org/publications/color-of-justice-racial-and-ethnic-disparity-in-state -prisons/.
47. Christy Visher, Sara Debus, and Jennifer Yahner, "Employment after Prison: A Longitudinal Study of Releasees in Three States," Urban Institute, October 2008, https://www.urban.org/sites/default/files/publica tion/32106/411778-Employment-after-Prison-A-Longitudinal-Study-of-Releasees-in-Three-States.PDF.
48. Cory Booker and Mignon Clyburn, "The Unnecessarily High Cost of Inmate Calling Charges Is an Injustice," *Huffington Post*, October 13, 2016, https://www.huffpost.com/entry/high-cost-of-inmate-calling -charges-injustice_b_8285802.
49. Bernadette Rabuy and Daniel Kopf, "Separation by Bars and Miles: Visitation in State Prisons," Prison Policy Initiative, October 20, 2015, https://www.prisonpolicy.org/reports/prisonvisits.html.
50. Patrick Oakford, Cara Brumfield, Casey Goldvale, Laura Tatum, Margaret diZerega, and Fred Patrick, "Investing in Futures: Economic and Fiscal Benefits of Postsecondary Education in Prison," Vera Institute of Justice, January 2019, https://storage.googleapis.com/vera-web-assets/downloads/Publications/investing -in-futures-education-in-prison/legacy_downloads/investing-in-futures.pdf.
51. Robert Bozick, Jennifer Steele, Lois Davis, and Susan Turner, "Does Providing Inmates with Education Improve Post-Release Outcomes? A Meta-Analysis of Correctional Education Programs in the United States," *Journal of Experimental Criminology* 14, no. 3 (2018): 389–428, https://perma.cc/NKE4-KDFK.
52. E. Ann Carson, "Prisoners in 2014," U.S. Department of Justice, September 2015, https://www.bjs.gov /content/pub/pdf/p14.pdf.
53. Mike McPhate, "California Today: Firefighters, at Less Than $2 an Hour," *New York Times*, September 1, 2017, https://www.nytimes.com/2017/09/01/us/california-today-firefighters-at-less-than-2-an-hour.html.
54. Katherine Katcher, Sonja Tonnesen, and Neeraj Kumar, "Prisoners Who Risk Their Lives during Calif. Wildfires Shouldn't Be Shut Out of Profession," *USA Today*, November 3, 2017, https://www.usatoday.com /story/opinion/policing/2017/11/03/prisoners-who-risk-their-lives-during-calif-wildfires-shouldnt-shut -out-profession/827215001/.
55. Lucius Couloute, "Nowhere to Go: Homelessness Among Formerly Incarcerated People," Prison Policy Initiative, August 2018, https://www.prisonpolicy.org/reports/housing.html.
56. J. J. Prescott and Sonja B. Starr, "The Case for Expunging Criminal Records," *New York Times*, March 20, 2019, https://www.nytimes.com/2019/03/20/opinion/expunge-criminal-records.html.
57. J. J. Prescott and Sonja B. Starr, "Expungement of Criminal Convictions: An Empirical Study," University of Michigan Law & Econ Research Paper, No. 19-001, University of Michigan Law School, Ann Arbor, MI, July 2019, https://papers.ssrn.com/sol3/papers.cfm?abstract_id=3353620.
58. New York awarded $7 million to various New York higher education institutions in 2017 to offer in-prison college-level courses to an estimated 2,500 inmates, all of whom must have only five years or less in their sentences. Jesse McKinley, "Cuomo to Give Colleges $7 Million for Courses in Prisons," *New York Times*, August 6, 2017, https://www.nytimes.com/2017/08/06/nyregion/cuomo-to-give-colleges-7-million -for-courses-in-prisons.html. California expanded access to in-person, in-prison college courses, and in 2017, nearly every prison offered at least some in-person college courses. Wayne D'Orio, "Propelling Prisoners to Bachelor's Degrees in California," *Hechinger Report*, July 12, 2019, https://hechingerreport.org /propelling-prisoners-to-bachelors-degrees-in-california/.
59. Beth Avery and Han Lu, "Nationwide Trend to Reform Unfair Occupational Licensing Laws," National Employment Law Project, July 17, 2019, https://www.nelp.org/publication/nationwide-trend-reform -unfair-occupational-licensing-laws/.
60. Eric Westervelt, "Scrubbing the Past to Give Those with a Criminal Record a Second Chance," *NPR*, February 19, 2019, https://www.npr.org/2019/02/19/692322738/scrubbing-the-past-to-give-those-with-a-criminal -record-a-second-chance.
61. Hannah Knowles, "Criminal Records Can Be a 'Life Sentence to Poverty.' This State Is Automatically Sealing Some," *Washington Post*, July 1, 2019, https://www.washingtonpost.com/nation/2019/07/01/criminal-records -can-be-life-sentence-poverty-this-state-is-automatically-sealing-some/.
62. Alicia Bannon, Mitali Nagrecha, and Rebekah Diller, "Criminal Justice Debt: A Barrier to Reentry," Brennan Center for Justice at New York University School of Law, October 4, 2010, https://www.brennancenter .org/our-work/research-reports/criminal-justice-debt-barrier-reentry.
63. Patrick Liu, Ryan Nunn, and Jay Shambaugh, "Nine Facts about Monetary Sanctions in the Criminal Justice System," Hamilton Project, March 2019, https://www.brookings.edu/research/nine-facts-about-monetary -sanctions-in-the-criminal-justice-system/.
64. Michael W. Sances and Hye Young You, "Who Pays for Government? Descriptive Representation and Exploitative Revenue Sources," *Journal of Politics* 79, no. 3 (July 2017): 1090–94, https://www.journals.uchica go.edu/doi/abs/10.1086/691354.
65. U.S. Department of Justice Civil Rights Division, "Investigation of the Ferguson Police Department," March 4, 2015, https://www.justice.gov/sites/default/files/opa/press-releases/attachments/2015/03/04/ferguson _police_department_report.pdf.

66. Liu, Nunn, and Shambaugh, "Nine Facts about Monetary Sanctions in the Criminal Justice System."
67. Joseph Shapiro, "As Court Fees Rise, the Poor Are Paying the Price," *NPR*, May 19, 2014, https://www.npr .org/2014/05/19/312158516/increasing-court-fees-punish-the-poor.
68. Shapiro, "As Court Fees Rise, the Poor Are Paying the Price."
69. Shapiro, "As Court Fees Rise, the Poor Are Paying the Price."
70. Council of Economic Advisers, "Fines, Fees, and Bail: Payments in the Criminal Justice System That Disproportionately Impact the Poor," December 2015, https://obamawhitehouse.archives.gov/sites/default/files /page/files/1215_cea_fine_fee_bail_issue_brief.pdf.
71. Shapiro, "As Court Fees Rise, the Poor Are Paying the Price."
72. Karin Martin, Sandra Susan Smith, and Wendy Still, "Shackled to Debt: Criminal Justice Financial Obligations and the Barriers to Re-entry They Create," National Institute of Justice, January 2017, no. 4, https:// www.ncjrs.gov/pdffiles1/nij/249976.pdf.
73. Liu, Nunn, and Shambaugh, "Nine Facts about Monetary Sanctions in the Criminal Justice System."
74. Shapiro, "As Court Fees Rise, the Poor Are Paying the Price."
75. *Bearden v. Georgia*, 461 U.S. 660 (1983), https://supreme.justia.com/cases/federal/us/461/660/.
76. Liu, Nunn, and Shambaugh, "Nine Facts about Monetary Sanctions in the Criminal Justice System."
77. Rhode Island Family Life Center, "Court Debt and Related Incarceration in Rhode Island from 2005 through 2007," April 2008, https://csgjusticecenter.org/wp-content/uploads/2008/04/2008-RI-CourtDebt .pdf.
78. U.S. Department of Justice Civil Rights Division, "Investigation of the Ferguson Police Department," 13–14; and Matt Apuzzo and John Eligon, "Ferguson Police Tainted by Bias, Justice Department Says," *New York Times*, March 4, 2015, https://www.nytimes.com/2015/03/05/us/us-calls-on-ferguson-to-overhaul -criminal-justice-system.html.
79. Liu, Nunn, and Shambaugh, "Nine Facts about Monetary Sanctions in the Criminal Justice System."
80. Council of Economic Advisers, "Fines, Fees, and Bail."
81. Shapiro, "As Court Fees Rise, the Poor Are Paying the Price."
82. Liu, Nunn, and Shambaugh, "Nine Facts about Monetary Sanctions in the Criminal Justice System."
83. Adam Looney and Nicholas Turner, "Work and Opportunity before and after Incarceration," Brookings Institution, March 14, 2018, https://www.brookings.edu/research/work-and-opportunity-before-and-after -incarceration/.
84. Mario Salas and Angela Ciolfi, "Driven by Dollars: A State-by-State Analysis of Driver's License Suspension Laws for Failure to Pay Court Debt," Legal Aid Justice Center, Fall 2017, https://www.justice4all.org/wp -content/uploads/2017/09/Driven-by-Dollars.pdf.
85. Bannon, Nagrecha, and Diller, "Criminal Justice Debt."
86. Joseph Serna, "A New Push in California to Automatically Clear Old Arrest and Conviction Records," *Los Angeles Times*, March 7, 2019, https://www.latimes.com/local/lanow/la-me-ln-ting-gascon-criminal-justice -bill-20190307-story.html.
87. Anne Case and Angus Deaton, "Rising Morbidity and Mortality in Midlife among White Non-Hispanic Americans in the 21st Century," *Proceedings of the National Academy of Sciences* 112, no. 49 (December 2015), https://doi.org/10.1073/pnas.1518393112.
88. Uptin Saiidi, "US Life Expectancy Has Been Declining. Here's Why," *CNBC*, July 9, 2019, https://www.cnbc .com/2019/07/09/us-life-expectancy-has-been-declining-heres-why.html.
89. To name a few other explanations contributing to the rise of deaths of despair: the overprescribing of highly addictive opioids, particularly to whites (Mark J. Pletcher, Stefan G. Kertesz, Michael A. Kohn, and Ralph Gonzales, "Trends in Opioid Prescribing by Race/Ethnicity for Patients Seeking Care in US Emergency Departments," *Journal of the American Medical Association* 299, no. 1 (2008): 70–78, doi:10.1001/jama.2007.64); followed by a surge in the availability of illicit drugs, namely, heroin and the more potent fentanyl; and the stigma around drug use and the subsequent grossly inadequate access to evidence-based drug treatment.
90. Carol Graham and Sergio Pinto, "Unequal Hopes and Lives in the USA: Optimism, Race, Place, and Premature Mortality," *Journal of Population Economics* (2018), https://www.brookings.edu/wp-content/uploads /2017/06/working-paper-104-web-v2.pdf.
91. Graham and Pinto, "Unequal Hopes and Lives in the USA"; and having a sense of purpose has been found to not only improve quality of life, but also results in decreased mortality. Aliya Alimujian, Ashley Wiensch, and Jonathan Boss, "Association Between Life Purpose and Mortality Among US Adults Older Than 50 Years," *Journal of the American Medical Association Network Open* 2, no. 5 (2019), https://doi.org/10.1001 /jamanetworkopen.2019.4270.
92. Eleanor Krause and Isabel Sawhill, "What We Know and Don't Know about Declining Labor Force Participation: A Review," Brookings Institution, May 2017, 21, https://www.brookings.edu/wp-content/uploads /2017/05/ccf_20170517_declining_labor_force_participation_sawhill1.pdf.
93. Alan B. Krueger, "Where Have All the Workers Gone? An Inquiry into the Decline of the U.S. Labor Force Participation Rate," Brookings Papers on Economic Activity, BPEA Conference Drafts, September 7–8, 2017, https://www.brookings.edu/wp-content/uploads/2017/09/1_krueger.pdf.
94. Sabrina Tavernise, "Black Americans See Gains in Life Expectancy," *New York Times*, May 8, 2016, https:// www.nytimes.com/2016/05/09/health/blacks-see-gains-in-life-expectancy.html.

95. Steven H. Woolf and Heidi Schoomaker, "Life Expectancy and Mortality Rates in the United States, 1959–2017," *Journal of the American Medical Association* 322, no. 20 (2019): 1996–2016, https://doi.org/10.1001/jama.2019.16932.

96. Sarah Holder, "Life Expectancy Is Associated with Segregation in U.S. Cities," *CityLab*, June 6, 2019, https://www.citylab.com/equity/2019/06/segregation-life-expectancy-study-research-racism-map/591028/.

97. Emily E. Peterson et al., "Vital Signs: Pregnancy-Related Deaths, United States, 2011–2015, and Strategies for Prevention, 13 States, 2013–2017," Centers for Disease Control and Prevention, *Morbidity and Mortality Weekly Report* 68, no. 18 (May 2019): 423–29, http://dx.doi.org/10.15585/mmwr.mm6818e1.

98. Quoted in Gene Demby, "Making the Case That Discrimination Is Bad for Your Health," *NPR*, January 14, 2018, https://www.npr.org/sections/codeswitch/2018/01/14/577664626/making-the-case-that-discrimination-is-bad-for-your-health.

99. Barry P. Bosworth, Gary Burtless, and Kan Zhang, "What Growing Life Expectancy Gaps Mean for the Promise of Social Security," Brookings Institution, February 12, 2016, https://www.brookings.edu/research/what-growing-life-expectancy-gaps-mean-for-the-promise-of-social-security/#recent/.

CHAPTER FIVE: ECONOMIC RESPECT

1. Richard White, *The Republic for Which It Stands: The United States during Reconstruction and the Gilded Age, 1865–1896* (New York: Oxford University Press, 2017), 344.

2. Stanley Lebergott, "The Pattern of Employment Since 1800," in *American Economic History*, ed. Seymour Harris (New York: McGraw-Hill, 1961).

3. Elizabeth Anderson, *Private Government: How Employers Rule Our Lives (and Why We Don't Talk about It)* (Princeton, NJ: Princeton University Press, 2019), 34.

4. Anderson, *Private Government*, 45–46.

5. Edgar T. Davies, "The Enforcement of Child Labor Legislation in Illinois," *Annals of the American Academy of Political and Social Science* 29 (January 1907): 93–103.

6. Viviana A. Zelizer, *Pricing the Priceless Child: The Changing Social Value of Children* (Princeton, NJ: Princeton University Press, 1994), 6.

7. Hugh D. Hindman, *Child Labor: An American History* (Armonk, NY: M.E. Sharpe, 2002), 31.

8. "Toiling for Their Bread: Children Who Are Employed in Workshop and in Factory," *New York Times*, December 26, 1882, https://timesmachine.nytimes.com/timesmachine/1882/12/26/103431768.pdf.

9. Michael Schuman, "History of Child Labor in the United States—Part 2: The Reform Movement," Bureau of Labor Statistics, *Monthly Labor Review*, January 2017, https://www.bls.gov/opub/mlr/2017/article/history-of-child-labor-in-the-united-states-part-2-the-reform-movement.htm.

10. Ruth Firestone Brin, *Contributions of Women: Social Reform* (Minneapolis: Dillon Press, 1977), 85.

11. Brett Clark and John Bellamy Foster, "Florence Kelley and the Struggle against the Degradation of Life: An Introduction to a Selection from 'Modern Industry,'" *Organization and Environment* 19, no. 2 (June 2006): 251–63.

12. Florence Kelley, "The Sweating System," excerpted from Florence Kelley, *The Sweating System in Chicago, in Bureau of Statistics of Labor of Illinois Seventh Biennial Report*, 1892. Appears in *American Journal of Public Health* 95, no. 1 (January 2005), https://ajph.aphapublications.org/doi/pdf/10.2105/AJPH.2004.052977.

13. Kelley, "The Sweating System."

14. Nancy Woloch, *A Class by Herself: Protective Laws for Women Workers, 1890s–1990s* (Princeton, NJ, and Oxford: Princeton University Press, 2015), 6.

15. Florence Kelley, "The Working Boy," *American Journal of Sociology* 2, no. 3 (November 1896): 358–68.

16. Florence Kelley, *Our Toiling Children* (Chicago: Women's Temperance Publication Association, 1889), cited in Clark and Foster, "Florence Kelley."

17. William F. Ogburn, *Progress and Uniformity in Child-Labor Legislation: A Study in Statistical Measurement* (New York: Columbia University, 1912), 350, table XVII, https://books.google.com/books?id=5_o8AAAAYAAJ.

18. Ogburn, *Progress and Uniformity*, 350.

19. Melvin I. Urofsky, "State Courts and Protective Legislation during the Progressive Era: A Reevaluation," *Journal of American History* 72 (June 1985): 69, https://www.jstor.org/stable/pdf/1903737.pdf.

20. Schuman, "History of Child Labor," 15.

21. Elliott J. Gorn, *Mother Jones: The Most Dangerous Woman in America* (New York: Hill and Wang, 2005).

22. Virginia Commonwealth University, "Company Towns: 1880s to 1935," accessed November 10, 2019, https://socialwelfare.library.vcu.edu/programs/housing/company-towns-1890s-to-1935/.

23. Gorn, *Mother Jones*.

24. Mother Jones, "Girl Slaves of the Milwaukee Breweries," *Western Federation of Miners, Miners Magazine* (April 4, 1910), 5–6, http://www.motherjonesmuseum.org/wp-content/uploads/2014/05/Mother-Jones-Girl-Slaves-of-the-Milwaukee-breweries.pdf.

25. Gorn, *Mother Jones*, 89; and David A. Corbin, *Life, Work, and Rebellion in the Coal Fields: The Southern West Virginia Miners, 1880–1922*, 2nd ed. (Morgantown: West Virginia University Press, 2015), accessed August 9, 2019, https://muse.jhu.edu/.

26. Mary Harris Jones, *Autobiography of Mother Jones* (Mineola, NY: Dover Publications, 2004), 34.
27. Leo Troy, "Trade Union Membership, 1897–1962," National Bureau of Economic Research (1965), 1, https://www.nber.org/chapters/c1707.pdf.
28. Howard Berkes and Robert Benincasa, "Mines Not Safe Despite $1 Billion in Fines, Federal Audit Says," *NPR*, August 22, 2019, https://www.npr.org/2019/08/22/752868484/no-link-between-fines-and-safety-in-mines-government-audit-says; and Department of Labor, Office of the Inspector General, "MSHA Did Not Evaluate Whether Civil Monetary Penalties Effectively Deterred Unsafe Mine Operations," August 16, 2019, https://www.oig.dol.gov/public/reports/oa/viewpdf.php?r=23-19-002-06-001&y=2019.
29. Berkes and Benincasa, "Mines Not Safe"; and Department of Labor, Office of the Inspector General, "MSHA Did Not Evaluate."
30. Kirstin Downey, *The Woman behind the New Deal* (New York: Doubleday, 2009).
31. David Brooks, "How the First Woman in the U.S. Cabinet Found Her Vocation," *Atlantic*, April 14, 2015, https://www.theatlantic.com/politics/archive/2015/04/frances-perkins/390003/.
32. Joseph Berger, "Triangle Fire: A Half-Hour of Horror," *New York Times*, March 21, 2011, https://cityroom.blogs.nytimes.com/2011/03/21/triangle-fire-a-half-hour-of-horror/.
33. Brooks, "How the First Woman in the U.S. Cabinet Found Her Vocation."
34. Hadassa Kosak, "Triangle Shirtwaist Fire," Jewish Women's Archive, accessed November 10, 2019, https://jwa.org/encyclopedia/article/triangle-shirtwaist-fire.
35. Tony Michels, "Uprising of 20,000 (1909)," Jewish Women's Archive, accessed November 10, 2019, https://jwa.org/encyclopedia/article/uprising-of-20000-1909.
36. Peter Dreier and Donald Cohen, "The Fire Last Time," *New Republic*, March 11, 2011, https://newrepublic.com/article/85134/wisconsin-unions-walker-triangle-shirtwaist-fire.
37. Thomas R. Layton and Einer R. Elhauge, "U.S., Fire Catastrophes of the 20th Century," *Journal of Burn Care & Research* 3, no. 1 (January–February 1982): 24, https://doi.org/10.1097/00004630-198201000-00003.
38. Richard A. Greenwald, *The Triangle Fire, the Protocols of Peace, and Industrial Democracy in Progressive Era New York* (Philadelphia: Temple University Press, 2005), 147.
39. Downey, *The Woman behind the New Deal*, location 904.
40. "Remembering the 1911 Triangle Factory Fire," Cornell University, 2018, accessed November 10, 2019, https://trianglefire.ilr.cornell.edu/legacy/legislativeReform.html.
41. Frances Perkins Center, "Her Life: The Woman behind the New Deal," accessed November 10, 2019, http://francesperkinscenter.org/life-new/.
42. Ida M. Tarbell, *All in the Day's Work: An Autobiography* (New York: Macmillan, 1939; Ravenio Books, 2015), location 315. Citations refer to the Ravenio edition.
43. Gilbert King, "The Woman Who Took on the Oil Tycoon," Smithsonian.com, July 5, 2012, https://www.smithsonianmag.com/history/the-woman-who-took-on-the-tycoon-651396/.
44. Ida M. Tarbell, *The History of the Standard Oil Company, vols. 1 & 2* (New York: McClure, Phillips, 1904), location 1296.
45. Ron Chernow, *Titan: The Life of John D. Rockefeller, Sr.* (New York: Vintage, 1998), 147.
46. Tarbell, *All in the Day's Work*, location 324.
47. Tarbell, *All in the Day's Work*, location 2726.
48. Tarbell, *All in the Day's Work*, location 1265.
49. Tim Wu, *The Curse of Bigness: Anti-Trust in the New Gilded Age* (New York: Columbia Global Reports, 2018), 70–77.
50. Linda Burnham and Nik Theodore, "Home Economics: The Invisible and Unregulated World of Domestic Work," National Domestic Workers Alliance, 2012, http://www.idwfed.org/en/resources/home-economics-the-invisible-and-unregulated-world-of-domestic-work/@@display-file/attachment_1.
51. Sean Farhang and Ira Katznelson, "The Southern Imposition: Congress and Labor in the New Deal and Fair Deal," *Studies in American Political Development* 19 (2005): 1–30; and Juan Perea, "The Echoes of Slavery: Recognizing the Racist Origin of the Agricultural and Domestic Worker Exclusion from the National Labor Relations Act," *Ohio State Law Journal* 72, no. 1 (2011): 95–138.
52. Quoted in Kamala Kelkar, "When Labor Laws Left Farm Workers Behind—and Vulnerable to Abuse," *PBS NewsHour*, September 18, 2016, https://www.pbs.org/newshour/nation/labor-laws-left-farm-workers-behind-vulnerable-abuse.
53. "Atlanta's Washerwomen Strike," AFL-CIO, accessed November 26, 2019, https://aflcio.org/about/history/labor-history-events/atlanta-washerwomen-strike.
54. Dorothy Bolden, interview by Christine Lutz, August 31, 1995, Voices of Labor Oral History Project, Southern Labor Archives, Special Collections and Archives, Georgia State University, https://digitalcollections.library.gsu.edu/digital/collection/voicelabor/id/4.
55. Premilla Nadasen, *Household Workers Unite: The Untold Story of African American Women Who Built a Movement* (Boston: Beacon Press, 2015), 42.
56. Nadasen, *Household Workers Unite*, 43.
57. Daniel E. Slotnik, "Overlooked No More: Dorothy Bolden, Who Started a Movement for Domestic Workers," *New York Times*, February 20, 2019, https://www.nytimes.com/2019/02/20/obituaries/dorothy-bolden-overlooked.html.

58. Burnham and Theodore, "Home Economics"; and Alexia Fernandez Campbell, "Housekeepers and Nannies Have No Protection from Sexual Harassment under Federal Law," *Vox*, April 26, 2018, https://www.vox.com /2018/4/26/17275708/housekeepers-nannies-sexual-harassment-laws.

59. Ivette Feliciano and Corinne Segal, "'You're Mostly Isolated and Alone.' Why Some Domestic Workers Are Vulnerable to Exploitation," *PBS NewsHour*, August 12, 2018, https://www.pbs.org/newshour/nation/ai-jen -poo-domestic-workers-exploitation.

60. Burnham and Theodore, "Home Economics."

61. Nadasen, *Household Workers Unite*, 40.

62. Slotnik, "Overlooked No More."

63. Alexia Fernandez Campbell, "Kamala Harris Just Introduced a Bill to Give Housekeepers Overtime Pay and Meal Breaks," *Vox*, July 15, 2019, https://www.vox.com/2019/7/15/20694610/kamala-harris-domestic -workers-bill-of-rights-act.

64. Steven V. Roberts, "26 Grape Growers Sign Union Accord; Boycott Nears End," *New York Times*, July 30, 1970, https://www.nytimes.com/1970/07/30/archives/26-grape-growers-sign-union-accord-boycott-nears-end -26-grape.html.

65. Gosia Wozniacka, "Less Than 1 Percent of US Farmworkers Belong to a Union. Here's Why," *Civil Eats*, May 7, 2019, https://civileats.com/2019/05/07/less-than-1-percent-of-us-farmworkers-belong-to-a-union -heres-why/.

66. Mary Kay Henry, "We Need Unions for All. It's a Bold Agenda for Helping Everyone Get Ahead in Our Economy," *USA Today*, August 30, 2019, https://www.usatoday.com/story/opinion/2019/08/30/2020-democrats -must-endorse-seiu-unions-for-all-mary-kay-henry-column/2122608001/.

67. National Academies of Sciences, Engineering, and Medicine, *Sexual Harassment of Women: Climate, Culture, and Consequences in Academic Sciences, Engineering, and Medicine* (Washington, DC: National Academies Press, 2018), https://doi.org/10.17226/24994.

68. Diana Falzone, "'You Will Lose Everything': Inside the Media's #MeToo Blacklist," *Vanity Fair*, April 16, 2019, https://www.vanityfair.com/news/2019/04/the-metoo-blacklist.

69. Elyse Shaw and Ariane Hegewisch, "Sexual Harassment and Assault at Work: Understanding the Costs," Institute for Women's Policy Research, October 15, 2018, https://iwpr.org/publications/sexual -harassment-work-cost/.

70. Shaw and Hegewisch, "Sexual Harassment and Assault at Work."

71. Helen Chen, Alejandra Domenzain, and Karen Andrews, "The Perfect Storm: How Supervisors Get Away with Sexually Harassing Workers Who Work Alone at Night," UC Berkeley, May 2016, http://lohp.org/wp -content/uploads/2016/05/The-Perfect-Storm.pdf.

72. Bernice Yeung, "Under Cover of Darkness, Female Janitors Face Rape and Assault," *Reveal* and *Frontline*, June 23, 2015, https://www.revealnews.org/article/under-cover-of-darkness-female-janitors-face-rape-and -assault/.

73. Yeung, "Under Cover of Darkness."

74. Good Jobs First, "Violation Tracker Parent Company Summary: ABM Industries," accessed November 10, 2019, https://violationtracker.goodjobsfirst.org/parent/abm-industries.

75. Bernice Yeung, "A Group of Janitors Started a Movement to Stop Sexual Abuse," *Frontline*, PBS, January 16, 2018, https://www.pbs.org/wgbh/frontline/article/a-group-of-janitors-started-a-movement-to-stop-sexual -abuse/.

76. Alex Press, "Women Are Filing More Harassment Claims in the #MeToo Era. They're Also Facing More Retaliation," *Vox*, May 9, 2019, https://www.vox.com/the-big-idea/2019/5/9/18541982/sexual-harassment-me-too -eeoc-complaints.

77. Debbie Berkowitz, "Big Poultry Workers Are Literally Peeing Their Pants So That Americans Can Have Cheap Chicken," *Quartz*, May 11, 2016, https://qz.com/681025/big-poultry-workers-are-literally-peeing -their-pants-so-that-americans-can-have-cheap-chicken/.

78. Heather Long, "Trump Makes Controversial Change to Allow Chicken Plants to Operate at Faster Speeds," *Washington Post*, October 16, 2018, https://www.washingtonpost.com/business/2018/10/16/trump-team -makes-controversial-change-allow-chicken-plants-operate-faster-speeds/.

79. Oxfam America, "No Relief: Denial of Bathroom Breaks in the Poultry Industry," 2016, https://www.oxfa mamerica.org/static/media/files/No_Relief_Embargo.pdf.

80. Oxfam America, "No Relief" and Oxfam America, "Lives on the Line: The High Human Cost of Chicken," accessed November 25, 2019, https://www.oxfamamerica.org/livesontheline/#bio.

81. See "Meet Bacilio" in Oxfam America, "Lives on the Line."

82. Long, "Trump Makes Controversial Change."

83. U.S. Government Accountability Office, "Workplace Safety and Health: Better Outreach, Collaboration, and Information Needed to Help Protect Workers at Meat and Poultry Plants," GAO-18-12 (Washington, DC: GAO, November 2017), https://www.gao.gov/assets/690/688294.pdf.

84. Union of Concerned Scientists, "USDA Increases Line Speeds, Endangering Poultry Processing Plant Workers," January 9, 2019, https://www.ucsusa.org/center-science-and-democracy/attacks-on-science/usda -increases-line-speeds-endangering-poultry.

85. Based on data from twenty-nine states. Debbie Berkowitz and Hooman Hedayati, "OSHA Severe Injury Data from 29 States: 27 Workers a Day Suffer Amputation or Hospitalization; Poultry Processing among

Most Dangerous Industries," National Employment Law Project, April 2017, https://s27147.pcdn.co/wp-content/uploads/OSHA-Severe-Injury-Data-2015-2016.pdf.

86. About 125,000 people are employed in Amazon fulfillment centers in the United States. Chavie Lieber, "Suicide Attempts and Mental Breakdowns: 911 Calls from Amazon Warehouses Reveal That Some Workers Are Struggling," *Vox*, March 11, 2019, https://www.vox.com/the-goods/2019/3/11/18260472/amazon-warehouse-workers-911-calls-suicide.

87. Michael Sainato, "'We Are Not Robots': Amazon Warehouse Employees Push to Unionize," *Guardian*, January 1, 2019, https://www.theguardian.com/technology/2019/jan/01/amazon-fulfillment-center-warehouse-employees-union-new-york-minnesota. This estimate was confirmed by at least several other employees; see Greg Bensinger, "'MissionRacer': How Amazon Turned the Tedium of Warehouse Work into a Game," *Washington Post*, May 21, 2019, https://www.washingtonpost.com/technology/2019/05/21/missionracer-how-amazon-turned-tedium-warehouse-work-into-game/.

88. Alana Semuels, "What Amazon Does to Poor Cities," *Atlantic*, February 1, 2018, https://www.theatlantic.com/business/archive/2018/02/amazon-warehouses-poor-cities/552020/; and Alexia Fernandez Campbell, "The Problem with Amazon's Speedy Shipping in One Graphic," *Vox*, October 18, 2019, https://www.vox.com/identities/2019/10/18/20920717/amazon-shipping-workers-injuries.

89. Colin Lecher, "How Amazon Automatically Tracks and Fires Warehouse Workers for 'Productivity,'" *Verge*, April 25, 2019, https://www.theverge.com/2019/4/25/18516004/amazon-warehouse-fulfillment-centers-productivity-firing-terminations.

90. Shona Ghosh, "Peeing in Trash Cans, Constant Surveillance, and Asthma Attacks on the Job: Amazon Workers Tell Us Their Warehouse Horror Stories," *Business Insider*, May 5, 2018, https://www.businessinsider.com/amazon-warehouse-workers-share-their-horror-stories-2018-4.

91. Ceylan Yeginsu, "If Workers Slack Off, the Wristband Will Know (and Amazon Has a Patent for It)," *New York Times*, February 1, 2018, https://www.nytimes.com/2018/02/01/technology/amazon-wristband-tracking-privacy.html.

92. Samuel Gompers, October 4, 1904, Samuel Gompers Papers, accessed November 10, 2019, http://www.gompers.umd.edu/quotes.htm.

93. Sainato, "'We Are Not Robots.'"

94. Matthew Desmond, "In Order to Understand the Brutality of American Capitalism, You Have to Start on the Plantation," *New York Times Magazine*, August 14, 2019, https://www.nytimes.com/interactive/2019/08/14/magazine/slavery-capitalism.html.

95. Lina Khan, "Amazon's Antitrust Paradox," *Yale Law Journal* 126, no. 3 (January 2017): 564–907.

96. Annie Waldman, "How a For-Profit College Targeted the Homeless and Kids with Low Self-Esteem," *ProPublica*, March 18, 2016, https://www.propublica.org/article/how-a-for-profit-college-targeted-homeless-and-kids-with-low-self-esteem.

97. See "Exhibit 27," *Villalba et al. v. ITT ESI et al.*, January 3, 2017, https://predatorystudentlending.org/wp-content/uploads/2018/02/Exhibit-27-Description-of-how-ITT-prevented-other-opportunities-473-statements.pdf.

98. In the thirty-six states that have payday loans available, as of early 2016. Pew Charitable Trusts, "Payday Loan Facts and the CFPB's Impact," January 14, 2016, https://www.pewtrusts.org/en/research-and-analysis/fact-sheets/2016/01/payday-loan-facts-and-the-cfpbs-impact.

99. Desmond documented how landlords in poor neighborhoods refuse to make repairs even when conditions are dangerous, knowing that their tenants are desperate for cheap rent and housing stability and will be reluctant to leave. If tenants withhold rent in order to prompt the landlord to take action, oftentimes the landlord will simply evict them. The economic vulnerability of renters makes them prime targets for financial domination. Desmond found that tenant exploitation, defined as charging more than market value for a property, is highest in poor neighborhoods; landlords extract higher profits from housing units there compared with higher-income neighborhoods, contributing to the cyclical economic abuse. Matthew Desmond, *Evicted: Poverty and Profit in the American City* (New York: Crown, 2016), 69, 72, 145; Christine MacDonald, "Detroit Evictions: Mom Seeks Relief amid Rental Battles," *Detroit News*, October 5, 2017, https://www.detroitnews.com/story/news/special-reports/2017/10/05/detroit-evictions-rental-battles/106315488/; and Matthew Desmond and Nathan Wilmers, "Do the Poor Pay More for Housing? Exploitation, Profit, and Risk in Rental Markets," *American Journal of Sociology* 124, no. 4 (January 2019): 1090–124, https://doi.org/10.1086/701697.

CHAPTER SIX: ECONOMIC DIGNITY

1. The Heritage Foundation's values are "free enterprise" and "limited government." "About Heritage: Mission," Heritage Foundation, accessed November 5, 2019, https://www.heritage.org/about-heritage/mission. The Cato Institute is "dedicated to the principles of individual liberty, limited government, free markets, and peace." "About Cato," Cato Institute, accessed November 8, 2019, https://www.cato.org/about. And Americans for Tax Reform exists "to promote limited government ideals." "About Americans for Tax Reform," Americans for Tax Reform, accessed November 8, 2019, https://www.atr.org/about.

2. John Blake, "Return of the 'Welfare Queen,'" *CNN*, updated January 23, 2012, https://www.cnn.com/2012/01/23/politics/weflare-queen/index.html.

3. Arthur Delaney and Michael McAuliff, "Paul Ryan Wants 'Welfare Reform Round 2,'" *Huffington Post*, March 20, 2012, https://www.huffpost.com/entry/paul-ryan-welfare-reform_n_1368277.
4. Executive Office of the President of the United States, Council of Economic Advisers, *Expanding Work Requirements in Non-Cash Welfare Programs*, July 2018, https://www.whitehouse.gov/wp-content/uploads/2018/07/Expanding-Work-Requirements-in-Non-Cash-Welfare-Programs.pdf.
5. Executive Office of the President of the United States, Council of Economic Advisers, *Expanding Work Requirements in Non-Cash Welfare Programs*, 30, 34.
6. Phil McCausland, "Nearly 700,000 Will Lose Food Stamps with USDA Work Requirement Change," *NBC*, December 4, 2019, https://www.nbcnews.com/news/us-news/nearly-700-000-will-lose-food-stamps-usda-work-requirement-n1095726; and Alfred Lubrano, "Trump Administration Proposes Social Security Rule Changes That Could Cut Off Thousands of Disabled Recipients," *Philadelphia Inquirer*, December 12, 2019, https://www.inquirer.com/news/social-security-ssi-ssdi-trump-administration-disability-20191212.html.
7. For example, see "Lobster-Eating Food Stamp Recipient Refuses Hannity's Job Help," *Fox News Insider*, March 13, 2014, https://insider.foxnews.com/2014/03/13/welfare-surfers-saga-continues-lobster-eating-food-stamps-recipient-refuses-hannitys-help; and Liz Halloran, "Lobster Boy Looms Large in Food Stamp Debate," *NPR*, September 19, 2013, https://www.npr.org/sections/itsallpolitics/2013/09/19/223796325/lobster-boy-looms-large-in-food-stamp-debate.
8. "Among non-disabled adults participating in SNAP in a particular month in mid-2012, 52 percent worked in that month, but about 74 percent worked at some point in the year before or after that month (a period of 25 months)." Brynne Keith-Jennings and Raheem Chaudry, *Most Working-Age SNAP Participants Work, but Often in Unstable Jobs* (Washington, DC: Center on Budget and Policy Priorities, March 2018), 2, https://www.cbpp.org/research/food-assistance/most-working-age-snap-participants-work-but-often-in-unstable-jobs.
9. Dottie Rosenbaum, *The Relationship between SNAP and Work among Low-Income Households* (Washington, DC: Center on Budget and Policy Priorities, January 30, 2013), https://www.cbpp.org/research/the-relationship-between-snap-and-work-among-low-income-households. For more on SNAP and work, see Keith-Jennings and Chaudry, *Most Working-Age SNAP Participants Work*; and Stacy Dean, Ed Bolen, and Brynne Keith-Jennings, *Making SNAP Work Requirements Harsher Will Not Improve Outcomes for Low-Income People* (Washington, DC: Center on Budget and Policy Priorities, March 2018), https://www.cbpp.org/research/food-assistance/making-snap-work-requirements-harsher-will-not-improve-outcomes-for-low.
10. "Chart Book: SNAP Helps Struggling Families Put Food on the Table," Center on Budget and Policy Priorities, updated November 7, 2019, https://www.cbpp.org/research/food-assistance/chart-book-snap-helps-struggling-families-put-food-on-the-table; and Executive Office of the President of the United States, *Long-Term Benefits of the Supplemental Nutrition Assistance Program*, December 2015, 6, https://obamawhitehouse.archives.gov/sites/obamawhitehouse.archives.gov/files/documents/SNAP_report_final_nonembargo.pdf.
11. For these examples and many more, see "Testimonials: Faces of SNAP," This Is SNAP (website), accessed November 9, 2019, http://www.thisissnap.org/testimonials-faces-of-snap/.
12. "Testimonials: Faces of SNAP."
13. Pauline Leung and Alexandre Mas, "Employment Effects of the ACA Medicaid Expansions" NBER Working Paper 22540, National Bureau of Economic Research, Cambridge, MA, August 2016, 10, https://www.nber.org/papers/w22540.
14. Jeff Lagasse, "Medicaid Expansion Boosts Employment for People with Disabilities, Study Finds," *Healthcare Finance*, July 23, 2018, https://www.healthcarefinancenews.com/news/medicaid-expansion-boosts-employment-people-disabilities-study-finds.
15. See, e.g., Brynne Keith-Jennings, "More Evidence That Work Requirements Don't Work," *Off the Charts* (blog), Center on Budget and Policy Priorities, October 19, 2018, https://www.cbpp.org/blog/more-evidence-that-work-requirements-dont-work.
16. Gene B. Sperling, "The Fuzzy Claims Used to Justify Cutting Social Security Disability Insurance," *Atlantic*, May 23, 2017, https://www.theatlantic.com/business/archive/2017/05/ssdi/527802/.
17. Doug Walker, "Disability Benefits: The Numbers Tell the Story," *Social Security Matters* (blog), Social Security Administration, September 8, 2015, https://blog.ssa.gov/disability-benefits-the-numbers-tell-the-story/.
18. "Chart Book: Social Security Disability Insurance," Center on Budget and Policy Priorities, updated September 6, 2019, https://www.cbpp.org/research/social-security/chart-book-social-security-disability-insurance; and Mark Johnson, "Turned Down for Federal Disability Payments, Thousands Die Waiting for Appeals to Be Heard," *USA Today*, December 27, 2018, https://www.usatoday.com/story/news/nation/2018/12/27/thousands-die-waiting-social-security-disability-insurance-appeals/2420836002/.
19. Executive Office of the President, *The Long-Term Decline in Prime-Age Male Labor Force Participation*, June 2016, 22, https://obamawhitehouse.archives.gov/sites/default/files/page/files/20160620_cea_primeage_male_lfp.pdf.
20. David Weigel, "Rand Paul: Advocates for the Disabled Should Help Brainstorm Ways to Cut Social Security Spending," *Bloomberg News*, May 12, 2015, https://www.bloomberg.com/news/articles/2015-05-12/rand-paul-advocates-for-the-disabled-should-help-brainstorm-ways-to-cut-social-security-spending.

21. Dylan Matthews, "In Defense of Social Security Disability Insurance," *Vox*, March 8, 2018, https://www.vox.com/policy-and-politics/2018/2/6/16735966/social-security-disability-insurance.

22. "Lessons Learned from 40 Years of Subsidized Employment Programs," Georgetown Law Center on Poverty and Inequality, spring 2016, http://www.georgetownpoverty.org/issues/employment/lessons-learned-from-40-years-of-subsidized-employment-programs/.

23. Alastair Fitzpayne and Ethan Pollack, *Worker Training Tax Credit Promoting Employer Investments in the Workforce* (Washington, DC: Aspen Institute, May 2017), 2, https://www.aspeninstitute.org/publications/worker-training-tax-credit-promoting-greater-employer-investments-in-the-workforce/; and Angela Hanks and David Madland, "Better Training and Better Jobs: A New Partnership for Sectoral Training," Center for American Progress, February 22, 2018, https://www.americanprogress.org/issues/economy/reports/2018/02/22/447115/better-training-better-jobs/.

24. Alana Semuels, "What if Getting Laid Off Wasn't Something to Be Afraid Of?" *Atlantic*, October 25, 2017, https://www.theatlantic.com/business/archive/2017/10/how-to-lay-people-off/543948/.

25. OECD, *Back to Work: Sweden—Improving the Re-employment Prospects of Displaced Workers* (Paris: OECD Publishing, 2015), 28–30, https://read.oecd-ilibrary.org/employment/back-to-work-sweden_9789264246812-en.

26. U.S. Department of Labor, "Union Members Summary," news release no. USDL-19-0079, January 18, 2019, https://www.bls.gov/news.release/union2.nr0.htm.

27. Jennifer Mizrahi, "Results of New National Poll of Voters with and without Disabilities," *RespectAbility*, February 14, 2018, https://www.respectability.org/2018/02/results-new-national-poll-voters-without-disabilities/.

28. Martha Ross and Nicole Bateman, "Only Four out of Ten Working-Age Adults with Disabilities Are Employed," Brookings Institution, July 25, 2018, https://www.brookings.edu/blog/the-avenue/2018/07/25/only-four-out-of-ten-working-age-adults-with-disabilities-are-employed/.

29. See Chapter Twelve for further discussion; see also Rebecca Vallas, Shawn Fremstad, and Lisa Eckman, *A Fair Shot for Workers with Disabilities* (Washington, DC: Center for American Progress, January 2015), https://www.americanprogress.org/issues/poverty/reports/2015/01/28/105520/a-fair-shot-for-workers-with-disabilities/.

30. Gene Sperling, "If You Like Choice, Competition, and Entrepreneurship, You Should Like Obamacare," *Forbes*, March 28, 2014, https://www.forbes.com/sites/theapothecary/2014/03/28/if-you-like-choice-competition-and-entrepreneurship-you-should-like-obamacare/.

31. Linda J. Blumberg, Sabrina Corlette, and Kevin Lucia, "The Affordable Care Act: Improving Incentives for Entrepreneurship and Self-Employment," *Timely Analysis of Immediate Health Policy Issues* (Washington, DC: Urban Institute, May 2013), 1, https://www.urban.org/research/publication/affordable-care-act-improving-incentives-entrepreneurship-and-self-employment.

32. A 1.4 percentage point decline in the likelihood of starting a business out of average entrepreneurship rate of 19 percent. Karthik Krishnan and Pinshuo Wang, "The Cost of Financing Education: Can Student Debt Hinder Entrepreneurship?" *Management Science* 65, no. 10 (October 2019): 4523, https://pubsonline.informs.org/doi/pdf/10.1287/mnsc.2017.2995.

33. Krishnan and Wang, "The Cost of Financing Education," 4522.

34. Alana Semuels, "Why Does Sweden Have So Many Start-Ups?" *Atlantic*, September 28, 2017, https://www.theatlantic.com/business/archive/2017/09/sweden-startups/541413/.

35. Semuels, "Why Does Sweden Have So Many Start-ups?"

36. Government financing can also help, especially for small businesses. For example, iconic American companies like Apple, Intel, Costco, and Tesla have all at one time leveraged financing from SBA through the Small Business Investment Company program, which has channeled more than $21 billion of capital to U.S. small businesses since 2014. The Small Business Innovation Research and Small Technology Transfer Research programs support the R&D and financing of technologies, funding $42 billion since their inception, with more than 150,000 awards granted. U.S. Small Business Administration, Office of Investment and Innovation, "SBIC Overview" (PowerPoint presentation, 2019), https://www.sba.gov/sites/default/files/2019-02/2019%20SBIC%20Overview%20Presentation.pdf.

37. Dani Rodrik and Charles Sabel, "Building a Good Jobs Economy" (working paper, John F. Kennedy School of Government, Harvard University, Cambridge, MA, April 2019), 12, https://drodrik.scholar.harvard.edu/files/dani-rodrik/files/building_a_good_jobs_economy_april_2019_rev.pdf; and "Medical Milestones—Clinical Center Firsts," Research at the Clinical Center, National Institutes of Health, updated July 12, 2019, https://clinicalcenter.nih.gov/ocmr/research-discoveries.html.

38. Jonathan Gruber and Simon Johnson, "Policy Summary," *Jump-Starting America*, accessed November 10, 2019, https://www.jump-startingamerica.com/policy-summary.

39. Gruber and Johnson, "Policy Summary."

40. Lee Fleming, Hillary Greene, Guan-Cheng Li, Matt Marx, and Dennis Yao, "Government-Funded Research Increasingly Fuels Innovation," *Science* 364, no. 6446 (June 2019): 1139–41, DOI: 10.1126/science.aaw2373.

41. Rodrik and Sabel, "Building a Good Jobs Economy," 11.

42. Rodrik and Sabel, "Building a Good Jobs Economy."

43. Gene Sperling, *The Pro-Growth Progressive: An Economic Strategy for Shared Prosperity* (New York: Simon & Schuster, 2005), 171.

44. Michael Cooper, "Conservatives Sowed Idea of Health Care Mandate, Only to Spurn It Later," *New York Times*, February 14, 2012, https://www.nytimes.com/2012/02/15/health/policy/health-care-mandate-was-first-backed-by-conservatives.html.

45. Cooper, "Conservatives Sowed Idea of Health Care Mandate, Only to Spurn It Later."

46. Jonathan Gruber, "Health Care Reform Is a 'Three-Legged Stool,'" Center for American Progress, August 5, 2010, https://www.americanprogress.org/issues/healthcare/reports/2010/08/05/8226/health-care-reform-is-a-three-legged-stool/.

47. "Bold, Persistent Experimentation vs. Bold Persistence," Roosevelt Institute, May 6, 2011, https://rooseveltinstitute.org/bold-persistent-experimentation-vs-bold-persistence/.

48. John Wagner, "Howard Schultz Knocks Ocasio-Cortez, Warren and Harris for 'Extreme,' 'Punitive' and 'Not American' Policies," *Washington Post*, January 29, 2019, https://www.washingtonpost.com/politics/howard-schultz-calls-alexandria-ocasio-cortez-a-bit-misinformed-when-it-comes-to-taxing-the-wealthy/2019/01/29/b00db19e-23c5-11e9-90cd-dedb0c92dc17_story.html.

49. Tim Higginbotham, "Medicare for All Is Even Better Than You Thought," *Jacobin*, December 3, 2018, https://www.jacobinmag.com/2018/12/medicare-for-all-study-peri-sanders.

50. "Bold, Persistent Experimentation vs. Bold Persistence."

51. Barbara Corbellini Duarte and Nisha Stickles, "Exclusive: Alexandria Osasio-Cortez Explains What Democratic Socialism Means to Her," *Business Insider*, March 4, 2019, https://www.businessinsider.com/alexandria-ocasio-cortez-explains-what-democratic-socialism-means-2019-3.

52. They argue that "the state should serve as guarantor and supplier of employment, an income above deprivation levels, health insurance, high-caliber education from grade school through college, sound banking and financial services, and a birthright to a financial asset." William Darity Jr., Darrick Hamilton, and Rakeen Mabud, *Increasing Public Power to Increase Competition: A Foundation for an Inclusive Economy* (New York: Roosevelt Institute, May 2019), 3, http://rooseveltinstitute.org/wp-content/uploads/2019/04/RI_Increasing-Public-Power-to-Increase-Competition-brief-201905.pdf.

53. Darity, Hamilton, and Mabud, *Increasing Public Power to Increase Competition*.

54. The authors also note that "pure public provision on its own may not be able to stay on the cutting edge of providing the highest-quality goods and services. Just as private actors need incentives to better fulfill the quality, quantity, and access metrics when promoting the public good, we recognize that private actors innovate as well; the public benefits from private market innovation and, in many cases, a more efficient delivery of goods and services." Darity, Hamilton, and Mabud, *Increasing Public Power to Increase Competition*.

55. Joseph Stiglitz, "Public Options Are the Key to Restoring the Middle-Class Life," *Financial Times*, May 7, 2019, https://www.ft.com/content/42915ad4-6cc3-11e9-9ff9-8c855179f1c4.

56. Ganesh Sitaraman and Anne L. Alstott, *The Public Option: How to Expand Freedom, Increase Opportunity, and Promote Equality* (Cambridge, MA: Harvard University Press, 2019), 27.

57. Sitaraman and Alstott, *The Public Option*, 8.

58. Sitaraman and Alstott, *The Public Option*, 23.

59. Sitaraman and Alstott, *The Public Option*, 23.

CHAPTER SEVEN: MARKETS OF THE PEOPLE, BY THE PEOPLE, FOR THE PEOPLE

1. "Proprietary School 90/10 Revenue Percentages," School Data, Federal Student Aid (website), accessed November 12, 2019, https://studentaid.ed.gov/sa/about/data-center/school/proprietary.

2. "Average Published Charges, 2018–19 and 2019–20," College Board (website), accessed January 13, 2019, https://research.collegeboard.org/trends/college-pricing/figures-tables/average-published-charges-2018-19-and-2019-20.

3. "Trends in Student Aid: Highlights," College Board (website), accessed November 12, 2019, https://trends.collegeboard.org/student-aid/figures-tables/maximum-and-average-pell-grants-over-time.

4. Dana Goldstein, "The Troubling Appeal of Education at For-Profit Schools," *New York Times*, July 3, 2017, https://www.nytimes.com/2017/03/07/books/review/lower-ed-tressie-mcmillan-cottom.html.

5. Statistic for 2014, Adam Looney and Constantine Yannelis, "A Crisis in Student Loans? How Changes in the Characteristics of Borrowers and in the Institutions They Attended Contributed to Rising Loan Defaults," Brookings Papers on Economic Activity, Brookings Institution, 2015, 41, https://www.brookings.edu/wp-content/uploads/2016/07/PDFLooneyTextFallBPEA.pdf.

6. U.S. Senate Committee on Health, Education, Labor, and Pensions, *Executive Summary*, 2012, 5, https://www.help.senate.gov/imo/media/for_profit_report/ExecutiveSummary.pdf; and Danielle Douglas-Gabriel, "Slick For-Profit College Marketing Is Starting to Backfire," *Washington Post*, July 30, 2015, https://www.washingtonpost.com/news/wonk/wp/2015/07/30/the-slick-ways-for-profit-colleges-market-themselves-is-backfiring/.

7. U.S. Senate Committee on Health, Education, Labor, and Pensions, *Executive Summary*, 3–4.

8. "Graduation Rates," Fast Facts, National Center for Education Statistics, accessed November 12, 2019, https://nces.ed.gov/fastfacts/display.asp?id=40.

9. Chris Kirkham, "For-Profit College Recruiters Taught to Use 'Pain,' 'Fear,' Internal Documents Show," *Huffington Post*, December 6, 2017, https://www.huffpost.com/entry/for-profit-college-recruiters-documents_n_820337.

10. Kirkham, "For-Profit College Recruiters Taught to Use 'Pain,' 'Fear.'"
11. "Fact Sheet on Final Gainful Employment Regulations," Department of Education, October 30, 2014, https://www2.ed.gov/policy/highered/reg/hearulemaking/2012/gainful-employment-fact-sheet-10302014.pdf.
12. Emily Druy, "Dozens of For-Profit Colleges Could Soon Close," *Atlantic*, January 11, 2017, https://www.theatlantic.com/education/archive/2017/01/what-happens-to-students-when-for-profit-colleges-close/512831/.
13. Josh Mitchell and Gunjan Banerji, "College Stocks Soar Again," *Wall Street Journal*, March 13, 2017.
14. Erica L. Green, "DeVos Repeals Obama-Era Rule Cracking Down on For-Profit Colleges," *New York Times*, June 28, 2019, https://www.nytimes.com/2019/06/28/us/politics/betsy-devos-for-profit-colleges.html.
15. Lina M. Khan, "Amazon's Antitrust Paradox," *Yale Law Journal* 126, no. 3 (2016): 737–44, https://digitalcommons.law.yale.edu/cgi/viewcontent.cgi?article=5785&context=ylj; Zach Carter, "Meet the Man Who Is Changing Washington's Ideas about Corporate Power," *Huffington Post*, September 2, 2016, https://www.huffpost.com/entry/barry-lynn-washington-corporations_n_57c8a6a7e4b0e60d31de6433; and Tim Wu, *The Curse of Bigness: Antitrust in the New Gilded Age* (New York: Columbia Global Reports, 2018).
16. Barry C. Lynn, "Killing the Competition: How the New Monopolies Are Destroying Open Markets," *Harper's Magazine*, February 2012, https://harpers.org/archive/2012/02/killing-the-competition/.
17. Franklin D. Roosevelt, "State of the Union Message to Congress," January 11, 1944, Franklin D. Roosevelt Presidential Library and Museum, http://www.fdrlibrary.marist.edu/archives/address_text.html.
18. Wu, *The Curse of Bigness*, 72.
19. Kenny Malone, "Antitrust 1: Standard Oil," *NPR*, February 15, 2019, https://www.npr.org/templates/transcript/transcript.php?storyId=695130695.
20. Wu, *The Curse of Bigness*, 77.
21. Julia Angwin and Surya Mattu, "Amazon Says It Puts Customers First. But Its Pricing Algorithm Doesn't," *ProPublica*, September 20, 2016, https://www.propublica.org/article/amazon-says-it-puts-customers-first-but-its-pricing-algorithm-doesnt; Adam Satariano, "Amazon Faces E.U. Inquiry over Data from Independent Sellers," *New York Times*, July 17, 2019, https://www.nytimes.com/2019/07/17/technology/amazon-eu.html; and Ari Levy, "Amazon's New Refunds Policy Will 'Crush' Small Businesses, Outraged Sellers Say," *CNBC*, August 3, 2017, https://www.cnbc.com/2017/08/02/amazons-new-refunds-policy-will-crush-small-businesses-say-sellers.html.
22. *BBC News*, "Google Rivals Claim Product Search Remains Unfair," November 22, 2018, https://www.bbc.com/news/technology-46303300; and Rochelle Toplensky and Michael Acton, "Google Antitrust Remedy Delivers Few Changes for Rivals," *Financial Times*, October 27, 2017, https://www.ft.com/content/b3779ef6-b974-11e7-8c12-5661783e5589.
23. Elizabeth Dwoskin, "Facebook's Willingness to Copy Rivals' Apps Seen as Hurting Innovation," *Washington Post*, August 10, 2017, https://www.washingtonpost.com/business/economy/facebooks-willingness-to-copy-rivals-apps-seen-as-hurting-innovation/2017/08/10/ea7188ea-7df6-11e7-a669-b400c5c7e1cc_story.html; and Betsy Morris and Deepa Seetharaman, "The New Copycats: How Facebook Squashes Competition from Startups," *Wall Street Journal*, August 9, 2017, https://www.wsj.com/articles/the-new-copycats-how-facebook-squashes-competition-from-startups-1502293444.
24. Oscar Gonzales and Carrie Mihalcik, "Apple Sued by iOS Developers over App Store Fees," *CNET*, June 4, 2019, https://www.cnet.com/news/apple-sued-by-ios-developers-over-app-store-fees/; Jack Nicas and Keith Collins, "How Apple's Apps Topped Rivals in the App Store It Controls," *New York Times*, September 9, 2019, https://www.nytimes.com/interactive/2019/09/09/technology/apple-app-store-competition.html; and Tripp Mickle, "Apple Dominates App Store Search Results, Thwarting Competitors," *Wall Street Journal*, July 23, 2019, https://www.wsj.com/articles/apple-dominates-app-store-search-results-thwarting-competitors-11563897221.
25. Isaac Arnsdorf, "How a Top Chicken Company Cut Off Black Farmers, One by One," *ProPublica*, June 26, 2019, https://www.propublica.org/article/how-a-top-chicken-company-cut-off-black-farmers-one-by-one.
26. Arnsdorf, "How a Top Chicken Company Cut Off Black Farmers."
27. Arnsdorf, "How a Top Chicken Company Cut Off Black Farmers."
28. Lenore M. Palladino, "Ending Shareholder Primacy in Corporate Governance," Roosevelt Institute, February 8, 2019, https://rooseveltinstitute.org/wp-content/uploads/2019/02/RI_EndingShareholderPrimacy_workingpaper_201902-1.pdf; Lynn A. Stout, *The Shareholder Value Myth: How Putting Shareholders First Harms Investors, Corporations, and the Public* (Berrett-Koehler Publishers, Inc., 2012); and Binyamin Appelbaum, *The Economists' Hour: False Prophets, Free Markets, and the Fracture of Society* (Little, Brown, 2019).
29. "Our Commitment," Business Roundtable (website), https://opportunity.businessroundtable.org/ourcommitment/.
30. Rich Wartzman, *The End of Loyalty: The Rise and Fall of Good Jobs in America* (New York: PublicAffairs, 2017).
31. Leo E. Strine, "The Dangers of Denial: The Need for a Clear-Eyed Understanding of the Power and Accountability Structure Established by the Delaware General Corporation Law" (Institute for Law and Economics Research Paper No. 15-08, University of Pennsylvania Law School, Philadelphia, PA, March 2015): 20, https://ssrn.com/abstract=2576389.
32. eBay Domestic Holdings v. Newmark, 16 A.3d 1 (Del. Ch. 2010); Strine, "The Dangers of Denial," 18.

33. "Why Pass Benefit Corporation Legislation," Benefit Corporation, https://benefitcorp.net/policymakers /why-pass-benefit-corporation-legislation; see "About B Lab," https://bcorporation.net/about-b-lab.

34. Of course, there is also a larger literature about the negative impacts of the trend favoring stock-based executive compensation models. Many observers have noted that these compensation structures reward a relatively short-term focus on share prices, exacerbating the overall mentality of privileging shareholder wealth above all else. Addressing the composition of compensation will therefore be a necessary part of a long-term realignment toward more consideration of other stakeholders.

35. Lenore Palladino, "The Economic Argument for Stakeholder Corporations," *SSRN*, November 9, 2019, https://papers.ssrn.com/sol3/papers.cfm?abstract_id=3472051.

36. Lenore Palladino, "Worker Representation on U.S. Corporate Boards," *SSRN*, November 7, 2019, https:// papers.ssrn.com/sol3/papers.cfm?abstract_id=3476669.

37. Felix Hörisch, "The Marco-Economic Effect of Codetermination on Income Equality" (working paper, University of Mannheim, Mannheim, Germany, 2012), 15, https://www.mzes.uni-mannheim.de/publications /wp/wp-147.pdf.

38. Sigurt Vitols, *Prospects for Trade Unions in the Evolving European System of Corporate Governance* (Brussels: ETUI-REHS, November 2005), 21, http://library.fes.de/pdf-files/gurn/00299.pdf; and J. W. Mason, "Understanding Short-Termism: Questions and Consequences," Roosevelt Institute, November 6, 2015, https://rooseveltinstitute.org/understanding-short-termism-questions-and-consequences/.

39. Gabriel Zucman, "How Corporations and the Wealthy Avoid Taxes (and How to Stop Them)," *New York Times*, November 10, 2017, https://www.nytimes.com/interactive/2017/11/10/opinion/gabriel-zucman -paradise-papers-tax-evasion.html.

40. The White House and the Department of the Treasury, *The President's Framework for Business Tax Reform: An Update*, April 2016, 23, https://www.treasury.gov/resource-center/tax-policy/Documents/The-Presidents -Framework-for-Business-Tax-Reform-An-Update-04-04-2016.pdf.

41. Gene Sperling, "How the Tax Plan Will Send Jobs Overseas," *Atlantic*, December 8, 2017, https://www .theatlantic.com/business/archive/2017/12/tax-jobs-overseas/547916/; and Gene Sperling, "How Trump's Corporate-Tax Plan Could Send American Jobs Overseas," *Atlantic*, November 1, 2017, https://www.the atlantic.com/business/archive/2017/11/trump-corporate-tax-reform-jobs/544487/.

42. Recognizing the flaws in this approach, Senators Amy Klobuchar, Chris Van Hollen, and Tammy Duckworth and Congressman Peter DeFazio made a sound proposal to institute a per-country minimum tax instead. Removing Incentives for Outsourcing Act, S. 1610, 116th Cong. (2019); and "Klobuchar, Van Hollen, Duckworth Introduce Legislation to Keep Jobs in the United States," news release, May 22, 2019, https:// www.klobuchar.senate.gov/public/index.cfm/2019/5/klobuchar-van-hollen-duckworth-introduce -legislation-to-keep-jobs-in-the-united-states.

43. For example, see Sarah Holder, "The Extreme Amazon Bidder Just Got Real," *CityLab*, November 28, 2017, https://www.citylab.com/life/2017/11/the-extreme-amazon-bidder-just-got-real/546857/.

CHAPTER EIGHT: STRUCTURING CHANGE TO PROTECT ECONOMIC DIGNITY

1. Cast, "Who Lives, Who Dies, Who Tells Your Story," by Lin-Manuel Miranda, track 23 on *Original Broadway Cast of Hamilton*, August 21, 2015, compact disc.

2. Clay McShane and Joel Tarr, *The Horse in the City: Living Machines in the Nineteenth Century* (Baltimore: Johns Hopkins University Press, 2007), 38.

3. Brad Smith and Carol Ann Browne, "Today in Technology: The Day the Horse Lost Its Job," *Today in Technology* (blog), December 20, 2017, https://blogs.microsoft.com/today-in-tech/day-horse-lost-job/.

4. Smith and Browne, "Today in Technology."

5. Carl Benedikt Frey, *The Technology Trap: Capital, Labor, and Power in the Age of Automation* (Princeton, NJ: Princeton University Press, 2019), 8.

6. Frey, *The Technology Trap*, xi–xii.

7. Frey, *The Technology Trap*, 18.

8. Aaron Smith and Monica Anderson, "Americans' Attitudes toward a Future in Which Robots and Computers Can Do Many Human Jobs," Pew Research Center, October 4, 2017, https://www.pewresearch.org /internet/2017/10/04/americans-attitudes-toward-a-future-in-which-robots-and-computers-can-do -many-human-jobs/.

9. Carl Benedikt Frey and Michael Osborne, "The Future of Employment: How Susceptible Are Jobs to Computerisation?," *Technological Forecasting & Social Change* 114 (2017): 265, https://www.oxfordmartin.ox.ac .uk/downloads/academic/The_Future_of_Employment.pdf.

10. Mark Muro, Robert Maxim, and Jacob Whiton, *Automation and Artificial Intelligence: How Machines Are Affecting People and Places* (Washington, DC: Brookings Institution, 2019), 5, https://www.brookings.edu /wp-content/uploads/2019/01/2019.01_BrookingsMetro_Automation-AI_Report_Muro-Maxim-Whiton -FINAL-version.pdf.

11. Executive Office of the President, *Artificial Intelligence, Automation, and the Economy* (Washington, DC: Executive Office of the President, 2016), 17, https://obamawhitehouse.archives.gov/sites/whitehouse.gov /files/documents/Artificial-Intelligence-Automation-Economy.PDF.

12. Martin Ford, "Martin Ford: How We'll Earn Money in a Future without Jobs," Ted Talk, video, 14:38, April 2017, https://www.ted.com/talks/martin_ford_how_we_ll_earn_money_in_a_future_without_jobs.

13. Brett Milano, "The Robots Are Coming, but Relax," *Harvard Gazette*, September 22, 2017, https://news.harvard.edu/gazette/story/2017/09/as-ai-rises-youll-likely-have-a-job-analysts-say-but-it-may-be-different/; and Jason Furman and Robert Seamans, "AI and the Economy," *Innovation Policy and the Economy* 19 (2019): 162, https://www.journals.uchicago.edu/doi/pdfplus/10.1086/699936.

14. Ben Casselman, "The White-Collar Job Apocalypse That Didn't Happen," *New York Times*, September 27, 2019, https://www.nytimes.com/2019/09/27/business/economy/jobs-offshoring.html.

15. David Autor, "Why Are There Still So Many Jobs?" TEDxCambridge, YouTube video, 18:51, November 28, 2016, https://www.youtube.com/watch?v=LCxcnUrokJo.

16. Melanie Arntz, Terry Gregory, and Ulrich Zierahn, "The Risk of Automation for Jobs in OECD Countries: A Comparative Analysis," OECD Social, Employment, and Migration Working Papers No. 189 (Paris: OECD Publishing, May 14, 2016), https://www.oecd-ilibrary.org/docserver/5jlz9h56dvq7-en.pdf.

17. Michael Chui, James Manyika, and Mehdi Miremadi, "Four Fundamentals of Workplace Automation," *McKinsey Quarterly*, November 2015, https://www.mckinsey.com/business-functions/mckinsey-digital/our-insights/four-fundamentals-of-workplace-automation.

18. Abhijit V. Banerjee and Esther Duflo, *Good Economics for Hard Times* (New York: PublicAffairs, 2019), 323.

19. David Autor, David A. Mindell, and Elisabeth B. Reynolds, *The Work of the Future: Shaping Technology and Institutions* (Cambridge, MA: MIT Task Force on the Work of the Future, 2019), 20, https://workofthefuture.mit.edu/sites/default/files/2019-09/WorkoftheFuture_Report_Shaping_Technology_and_Institutions.pdf.

20. Frey, *The Technology Trap*, x.

21. Thomas Weiss, "Tourism in America before World War II," *Journal of Economic History* 64, no. 2 (June 2004), 314, www.jstor.org/stable/3874776.

22. Frey, *The Technology Trap*, 161.

23. James Bessen, "Why Automation Doesn't Mean a Robot Is Going to Take Your Job," World Economic Forum, September 26, 2016, https://www.weforum.org/agenda/2016/09/why-automation-doesnt-mean-a-robot-is-going-to-take-your-job.

24. "Automation and Anxiety: Will Smarter Machines Cause Mass Unemployment?" *Economist*, June 23, 2016, https://www.economist.com/special-report/2016/06/23/automation-and-anxiety; and James Bessen, "How Computer Automation Affects Occupations: Technology, Jobs, and Skills," *Vox*, September 22, 2016, https://voxeu.org/article/how-computer-automation-affects-occupations.

25. "Automation and Anxiety."

26. "Belgium—Unemployment," European Commission, accessed December 8, 2019, https://ec.europa.eu/social/main.jsp?catId=1102&langId=en&intPageId=4425; and "Denmark—Unemployment Benefit," European Commission, accessed December 8, 2019, https://ec.europa.eu/social/main.jsp?catId=1107&langId=en&intPageId=4496.

27. Chad Stone and William Chen, "Introduction to Unemployment Insurance," Center on Budget and Policy Priorities, July 30, 2014, https://www.cbpp.org/sites/default/files/atoms/files/12-19-02ui.pdf.

28. Stone and Chen, "Introduction to Unemployment Insurance."

29. Stone and Chen, "Introduction to Unemployment Insurance."

30. Sara R. Collins, Michelle M. Doty, Ruth Robertson, and Tracy Garber, *Realizing Health Reform's Potential—When Unemployed Means Uninsured: The Toll of Job Loss on Health Coverage, and How the Affordable Care Act Will Help* (New York: Commonwealth Fund, 2011), https://www.commonwealthfund.org/publications/issue-briefs/2011/aug/realizing-health-reforms-potential-when-unemployed-means.

31. "Fact Sheet: President Obama's Plan to Help Responsible Homeowners and Heal the Housing Market," White House Office of the Press Secretary, February 1, 2012, https://obamawhitehouse.archives.gov/the-press-office/2012/02/01/fact-sheet-president-obama-s-plan-help-responsible-homeowners-and-heal-h.

32. Referring to the "spending on active measures to help unemployed and at-risk workers, per unemployed person, as a share of per-capita economic output, 2015." Andrew Van Dam, "Is It Great to Be a Worker in the U.S.? Not Compared with the Rest of the Developed World," *Washington Post*, July 4, 2018, https://www.washingtonpost.com/news/wonk/wp/2018/07/04/is-it-great-to-be-a-worker-in-the-u-s-not-compared-to-the-rest-of-the-developed-world.

33. Katherine S. Newman, *Falling from Grace: Downward Mobility in the Age of Affluence* (Berkeley, CA: University of California Press, 1999), 174.

34. Daniel Sullivan and Till von Wachter, "Job Displacement and Mortality: An Analysis Using Administrative Data," *Quarterly Journal of Economics* 124, no. 3 (2009): 1302, http://www.econ.ucla.edu/tvwachter/papers/sullivan_vonwachter_qje.pdf.

35. Kate W. Strully, "Job Loss and Health in the U.S. Labor Market," *Demography* 46, no. 2 (2009): 233, https://link.springer.com/content/pdf/10.1353%2Fdem.0.0050.pdf.

36. Dean Baker, "Six Lies on Trade," *Truthout*, July 9, 2018, https://truthout.org/articles/six-lies-on-trade/.

37. Binyamin Appelbaum, *The Economists' Hour: False Prophets, Free Markets, and the Fracture of Society* (New York: Little, Brown, 2019), 189.

38. Cass Sunstein, *The Cost-Benefit Revolution* (Cambridge, MA: MIT Press, 2018), 68–69.

39. White House Office of the Press Secretary, "Executive Order 13563—Improving Regulation and Regulatory Review," news release, January 18, 2011, https://obamawhitehouse.archives.gov/the-press-office/2011/01/18/executive-order-13563-improving-regulation-and-regulatory-review.

40. Anton Korinek and Joseph E. Stiglitz, "Artificial Intelligence and Its Implications for Income Distribution and Unemployment," NBER Working Paper 24174, National Bureau of Economic Research, Cambridge, MA, December 2017, https://techpolicyinstitute.org/wp-content/uploads/2018/02/Kornek_AI_Inequality.pdf.

41. Gene Sperling, *The Pro-Growth Progressive: An Economic Strategy for Shared Prosperity* (New York: Simon & Schuster, 2013), 68, 71–81.

42. "Administration's FY2013 Budget Proposes Tax Policy to Boost Growth, Create Jobs and Improve Opportunity for Middle Class," U.S. Department of Treasury, February 13, 2012, https://www.treasury.gov/press-center/press-releases/Pages/tg1414.aspx; and "Fact Sheet: President Obama's Blueprint to Support U.S. Manufacturing Jobs, Discourage Outsourcing, and Encourage Insourcing," White House Office of the Press Secretary, January 25, 2012, https://obamawhitehouse.archives.gov/the-press-office/2012/01/25/fact-sheet-president-obama-s-blueprint-support-us-manufacturing-jobs-dis.

43. Peter Dizikes, "Jump-Starting the Economy with Science," *MIT News*, April 17, 2019, http://news.mit.edu/2019/public-investment-science-jump-starting-america-0417.

44. As I have long noted, manufacturing punches well above its weight in the innovation economy: "Despite representing 12 percent of U.S. GDP, manufacturing accounts for roughly 70 percent of private sector research and development, 60 percent of all US R&D employees, over 90 percent of patents issued, and the majority of all U.S. exports." And manufacturing jobs pay above average, and feed supply chains that support more than five million additional jobs. Gene Sperling, "The Case for a Manufacturing Renaissance: Prepared Remarks by Gene Sperling," Brookings Institution, July 25, 2013, 7–8, https://www.brookings.edu/wp-content/uploads/2013/07/The-Case-for-a-Manufacturing-RenaissanceGene-Sperling7252013FINALP.pdf.

45. Sperling, "The Case for a Manufacturing Renaissance," 10.

46. Sperling, "The Case for a Manufacturing Renaissance," 5.

47. Sperling, "The Case for a Manufacturing Renaissance," 6.

48. Sperling, "The Case for a Manufacturing Renaissance," 1.

49. Sarah Gardner, "Why Do U.S. Retraining Programs Fall Short?," *Marketplace*, September 1, 2017, https://www.marketplace.org/2017/09/01/globalized-world-does-retraining-actually/.

50. "Bold, Persistent Experimentation vs. Bold Persistence," Roosevelt Institute, May 6, 2011, https://rooseveltinstitute.org/bold-persistent-experimentation-vs-bold-persistence/.

51. Alana Semuels, "What If Getting Laid Off Wasn't Something to Be Afraid Of?" *Atlantic*, October 25, 2017, https://www.theatlantic.com/business/archive/2017/10/how-to-lay-people-off/543948/.

52. OECD, *Back to Work: Sweden—Improving the Re-employment Prospects of Displaced Workers* (Paris: OECD Publishing, 2015), 29–32, https://read.oecd-ilibrary.org/employment/back-to-work-sweden_9789264246812-en.

53. "Job Openings and Labor Turnover—September 2019," Bureau of Labor Statistics, November 5, 2019, https://www.bls.gov/news.release/pdf/jolts.pdf.

54. Benjamin G. Hyman, "Can Displaced Labor Be Retrained? Evidence from Quasi-Random Assignment to Trade Adjustment Assistance," University of Chicago (2018), https://papers.ssrn.com/sol3/papers.cfm?abstract_id=3155386.

55. The number of workers facing dislocation was measured during the calendar years of 2015–17. The number of dislocated workers who received TAA was measured during the fiscal years of 2015–17. *Trade Adjustment Assistance for Workers Program: FY 2018 Annual Report* (Washington, DC: Department of Labor, 2018), 15, https://www.doleta.gov/tradeact/docs/AnnualReport18.pdf; and "Displaced Workers Summary," Bureau of Labor Statistics, August 28, 2018, https://www.bls.gov/news.release/disp.nr0.htm.

56. Sperling, *The Pro-Growth Progressive*, 80–81.

57. Sperling, *The Pro-Growth Progressive*, 80.

58. "White House Outlines Plan to Help with Job Search," *New York Times*, March 12, 2012, https://www.nytimes.com/2012/03/13/business/white-house-outlines-plan-to-help-job-seekers.html.

59. Sheila Maguire, Joshua Freely, Carol Clymer, Maureen Conway, and Deena Schwartz, *Tuning In to Local Labor Markets: Findings from the Sectoral Employment Study* (Philadelphia: Public Private Ventures, 2010), vi.

60. Campbell Robertson, "In Coal Country, the Mines Shut Down, the Women Went to Work and the World Quietly Changed," *New York Times*, September 14, 2019, https://www.nytimes.com/2019/09/14/us/appalachia-coal-women-work-.html.

61. Didem Tuzemen, W. Blake Marsh, and Thao Tran, "Trends in the Labor Share Post-2000," Federal Reserve Bank of Kansas City, December 7, 2018, https://www.kansascityfed.org/en/publications/research/mb/articles/2018/trends-labor-share-post; and "A New Look at the Declining Labor Share of Income in the United States," McKinsey, May 2019, https://www.mckinsey.com/featured-insights/employment-and-growth/a-new-look-at-the-declining-labor-share-of-income-in-the-united-states.

62. Korinek and Stiglitz, "Artificial Intelligence and Its Implications for Income Distribution and Unemployment."

63. Erik Brynjolfsson and Andrew McAfee, *The Second Machine Age: Work, Progress, and Prosperity in a Time of Brilliant Technologies* (New York: W. W. Norton, 2014), 257.

64. Daron Acemoglu and Pascual Restrepo, "Artificial Intelligence, Automation and Work," NBER Working Paper 24196, National Bureau of Economic Research, Cambridge, MA, 2018, https://www.nber.org/papers/w24196.pdf.

65. Erik Brynjolfsson and Andrew McAfee, "Brynjolfsson and McAfee: The Jobs That AI Can't Replace," *BBC*, September 13, 2015, https://www.bbc.com/news/technology-34175290.
66. Erik Brynjolfsson, "Technology Is Changing the Way We Live, Learn and Work. How Can Leaders Make Sure We All Prosper?," World Economic Forum, January 4, 2017, https://www.weforum.org/agenda/2017/01/technology-is-changing-the-way-we-live-learn-and-work-how-can-leaders-make-sure-we-all-prosper/; and Andrew McAfee and Erik Brynjolfsson, *Machine, Platform, Crowd: Harnessing Our Digital Future* (New York: W. W. Norton, 2017), 124.
67. Nicole Gunasekera, "Iora Health: Redefining Primary Care Medicine," Harvard Business School (2015), https://digital.hbs.edu/platform-rctom/submission/iora-health-redefining-primary-care-medicine/.
68. Gunasekera, "Iora Health."
69. *Better Medicare Alliance: Spotlight on Innovation* (Washington, DC: Better Medical Care Alliance, 2017), 3, https://www.bettermedicarealliance.org/sites/default/files/2017-08/BMA_SPOTLIGHT_2017_07_17.pdf.
70. McAfee and Brynjolfsson, *Machine, Platform, Crowd*, 333.
71. McAfee and Brynjolfsson, *Machine, Platform, Crowd*, 333.
72. Keith Eddings, "99Degrees Simmers with a Plan to Add 350 Jobs," *Eagle-Tribune*, April 29, 2018, https://www.eagletribune.com/news/merrimack_valley/degrees-simmers-with-a-plan-to-add-jobs/article_bc3573ea-bde7-5d51-ad61-bca6331cd5b9.html.
73. Alexis C. Madrigal, "How Automation Could Worsen Racial Inequality," *Atlantic*, January 15, 2018, https://www.theatlantic.com/technology/archive/2018/01/black-workers-and-the-driverless-bus/550535/.
74. Laura Bliss, "There's a Bus Driver Shortage. And No Wonder," *CityLab*, June 28, 2018, https://www.citylab.com/transportation/2018/06/why-wont-anyone-drive-the-bus/563555/; and Madrigal, "How Automation Could Worsen Racial Inequality."
75. Bliss, "There's a Bus Driver Shortage."; and Madrigal, "How Automation Could Worsen Racial Inequality."
76. Daron Acemoglu and Pascual Restrepo, "The Wrong Kind of AI? Artificial Intelligence and the Future of Labor Demand," NBER Working Paper No. 25682, National Bureau of Economic Research, Cambridge, MA, March 2019, https://www.nber.org/papers/w25682.
77. Acemoglu and Restrepo, "The Wrong Kind of AI?"
78. Acemoglu and Restrepo, "The Wrong Kind of AI?"
79. Gene Sperling, "ConnectED: Delivering the Future of Learning," White House, September 10, 2013, https://obamawhitehouse.archives.gov/blog/2013/09/10/connected-delivering-future-learning; "Teaching Inequality: The Problem of Public School Tracking," *Harvard Law Review* 102, no. 6 (1989): 1318, https://www.jstor.org/stable/pdf/1341297.pdf.
80. Lawrence Summers, "Picking on Robots Won't Deal with Job Destruction," *Washington Post*, March 5, 2017, https://www.washingtonpost.com/opinions/picking-on-robots-wont-deal-with-job-destruction/2017/03/05/32091f08-004b-11e7-8ebe-6e0dbe4f2bca_story.html.
81. Ryan Abbott and Bret Bogenschneider, "Should Robots Pay Taxes? Tax Policy in the Age of Automation," *Harvard Law & Policy Review* 12 (2018): 145, https://papers.ssrn.com/sol3/papers.cfm?abstract_id=2932483.
82. Autor, Mindell, and Reynolds, *The Work of the Future*.
83. "About DARPA," Defense Advanced Research Projects Agency, accessed November 11, 2019, https://www.darpa.mil/about-us/about-darpa; and "A Selected History of DARPA Innovation," Defense Advanced Research Projects Agency, accessed November 11, 2019, https://www.darpa.mil/Timeline/index.html.

CHAPTER NINE: WORK AND ECONOMIC DIGNITY

1. Martin Luther King Jr., *All Labor Has Dignity*; ed. Michael K. Honey (Boston: Beacon Press, 2011), 167–76.
2. "Memphis Sanitation Workers' Strike," Martin Luther King, Jr., Research and Education Institute, Stanford University, https://kinginstitute.stanford.edu/encyclopedia/memphis-sanitation-workers-strike.
3. "Memphis Sanitation Workers' Strike."
4. King, *All Labor Has Dignity*, 170–1.
5. King, *All Labor Has Dignity*.
6. King, *All Labor Has Dignity*, 176.
7. Franklin D. Roosevelt, "'Unemployment Must Be Faced on More Than One Front'—White House Statement on a Plan for Relief, February 28, 1934," in *Public Papers of the Presidents of the United States: F.D. Roosevelt, 1934, Volume 3*, 110 (New York: Random House, 1938).
8. Cass Sunstein, *The Second Bill of Rights: FDR's Unfinished Revolution and Why We Need It More Than Ever* (New York: Basic Books, 2004), 45.
9. Frances Perkins, *The Roosevelt I Knew* (New York: Penguin Classics Reprint Edition, 2011).
10. Perkins, *The Roosevelt I Knew*.
11. "1932 Convention Address," Franklin D. Roosevelt Presidential Library and Museum Collections and Programs, https://fdrlibrary.files.wordpress.com/2012/09/1932.pdf.
12. Franklin D. Roosevelt, "A Proof of Democracy: Ours Is a Great Heritage," speech delivered before the International Teamsters Union, Washington, DC, September 11, 1940, accessed November 9, 2019, http://www.ibiblio.org/pha/policy/1940/1940-09-11a.html.
13. David M. Kennedy, *Freedom from Fear: The American People in Depression and War, 1929–1945 (Oxford History of the United States, Volume IX)* (New York: Oxford University Press, 1999), 267.

14. Dwight D. Eisenhower, "Special Message to the Congress Transmitting Proposed Changes in the Social Security Program," Social Security Presidential Statements (August 1, 1953), accessed November 9, 2019, https://www.ssa.gov/history/ikestmts.html.
15. For Gingrich welfare comments, see Rob Wells, "Tax Bill Would Deny Key Benefit to Working Poor," *Associated Press*, July 3, 1997. For "lucky duckies," see "The Non-Taxpaying Class," editorial, *Wall Street Journal*, November 20, 2002, https://www.wsj.com/articles/SB1037748678534174748; "Lucky Duckies Again," editorial, *Wall Street Journal*, January 20, 2003; and "Even Luckier Duckies," editorial, *Wall Street Journal*, June 3, 2003, https://www.wsj.com/articles/SB1037748678534174748.
16. Quoted in Steven Mufson, "Clinton's Social Safety Net: A Bigger Tax Credit," *Washington Post*, March 6, 1993, https://www.washingtonpost.com/wp-srv/politics/special/tax/stories/tax030693.htm.
17. Barack Obama: "Tonight, let's declare that in the wealthiest nation on Earth, no one who works full-time should have to live in poverty." White House Office of the Press Secretary, "Remarks by the President in the State of the Union Address," February 12, 2013, https://obamawhitehouse.archives.gov/the-press-office/2013/02/12/remarks-president-state-union-address. Bernie Sanders: "We must ensure that no full-time worker lives in poverty by increasing the minimum wage to a living wage." Bernie Sanders, Facebook, November 10, 2015, https://www.facebook.com/berniesanders/photos/a.324119347643076/927934470594891/.
18. See discussion in Cass Sunstein, *Conspiracy Theories and Other Dangerous Ideas* (New York: Simon & Schuster, 2014), 37–38.
19. For description, see David Frank, "More Caregivers for Veterans to Be Eligible for Stipends," AARP, June 6, 2018, https://www.aarp.org/home-family/voices/veterans/info-2018/veterans-caregivers-new-program.html.
20. For federal level, see "Warren and Ernst Introduce Bipartisan, Bicameral Bill to Assist Family Caregivers," May 15, 2019, https://www.warren.senate.gov/newsroom/press-releases/warren-and-ernst-introduce-biparti san-bicameral-bill-to-assist-family-caregivers. For state level, see Samantha Young, "California among States Considering Caregiver Tax Credits," *Los Angeles Times*, March 21, 2019, https://www.latimes.com/business /la-fi-caregiver-tax-credits-20190321-story.html.
21. See, for instance, the Social Security Caregiver Credit Act of 2019, sponsored by Senator Christopher Murphy (D-CT) and Representative Nita Lowey (D-NY), that would provide credit to caregivers of dependent relatives for up to five years of service when the caregiver provides care for at least eighty hours a month for a "parent, spouse, domestic partner, sibling, child, grandchild, grandparent, grandchild, aunt, or uncle." See "Murphy, Lowey Introduce Legislation to Help Caregivers with Social Security Credit," July 30, 2019, https://www .murphy.senate.gov/newsroom/press-releases/murphy-lowey-introduce-legislation-to-help-caregivers-wi th-social-security-credit.
22. Family Caregiver Alliance, "Caregiver Statistics: Work and Caregiving," accessed November 9, 2019, https:// www.caregiver.org/caregiver-statistics-work-and-caregiving.
23. Yeonjung Lee and Fengyan Tang, "More Caregiving, Less Working: Caregiving Roles and Gender Difference," *Journal of Applied Gerontology* 34, no. 4 (2013): 465–83, https://doi.org/10.1177/0733464813508649.
24. MetLife Mature Market Institute, "The MetLife Study of Caregiving Costs to Working Caregivers: Double Jeopardy for Baby Boomers Caring for Their Parents," June 2011, 14, https://www.caregiving.org/wp -content/uploads/2011/06/mmi-caregiving-costs-working-caregivers.pdf.
25. Alicia H. Munnell and Andrew D. Eschtruth, "Modernizing Social Security: Caregiver Credits," Center for Retirement Research at Boston College, August 2018 (Number 18–15), https://crr.bc.edu/wp-content /uploads/2018/08/IB_18-15.pdf.

CHAPTER TEN: THE EMPTY PROMISE OF "DIGNITY OF WORK" CONSERVATIVES

1. Arthur C. Brooks, "The Dignity Deficit," *Foreign Affairs* 96, no. 2 (March/April 2017), https://www .foreignaffairs.com/articles/united-states/2017-02-13/dignity-deficit.
2. Arthur C. Brooks, *The Conservative Heart* (New York: Broadside, 2017), 15, Kindle.
3. Ben Sasse, *Them: Why We Hate Each Other—and How to Heal* (New York: St. Martin's Press, 2018), 135; dignity is also frequently invoked in Ben Sasse, *The Vanishing American Adult* (New York: St. Martin's Press, 2017).
4. Marco Rubio, "Marco Rubio: Revive the Dignity of Work to Preserve the American Dream for Future Generations," *Sunshine State News*, November 16, 2018, http://www.sunshinestatenews.com/story/marco-rubio -revive-dignity-work-preserve-american-dream-future-generations.
5. Tunku Varadarajan, "A Conservative Economics of Dignity," *Wall Street Journal*, May 18, 2018, https:// www.wsj.com/articles/a-conservative-economics-of-dignity-1526679960.
6. Oren Cass, *The Once and Future Worker: A Vision for the Renewal of Work in America* (New York: Encounter Books, 2018).
7. Chye-Ching Huang, "Fundamentally Flawed 2017 Tax Law Largely Leaves Low- and Moderate-Income Americans Behind," Center on Budget and Policy Priorities, February 27, 2019, https://www.cbpp.org/ federal-tax/fundamentally-flawed-2017-tax-law-largely-leaves-low-and-moderate-income-americans.
8. For example, Rubio has said, "I support people making more than $9. I want people to make as much as they can. I don't think a minimum wage law works." Steve Benen, "Rubio: People 'Can't Live' on Minimum Wage, but No Increase," *MSNBC*, October 15, 2015, http://www.msnbc.com/rachel-maddow-show/rubio-people -cant-live-minimum-wage-no-increase. Brooks writes, "So governments at every level should forget about

increasing minimum wages—which is where the usual conservative argument ends. But they should also experiment with reducing minimum wages to help people trapped in long-term unemployment . . . For example, Michael Strain of the American Enterprise Institute has proposed that the federal government let employers hire long-term unemployed people at $4 per hour and then itself transfer an additional $4 per hour to each of these workers. Another promising idea is the expansion of an existing subsidy, the Earned Income Tax Credit, a refundable tax credit for low-income people who work." Brooks, "The Dignity Deficit."

9. Jeremy W. Peters, "2 Parties Place Political Focus on Inequality," *New York Times*, January 8, 2014, https:// www.nytimes.com/2014/01/09/us/politics/republicans-move-to-reclaim-poverty-fighting-mantle.html; and Benen, "Rubio: People 'Can't Live' on Minimum Wage, but No Increase."

10. Theodore Roosevelt, address before the Convention of the National Progressive Party (Chicago, August 1912), Social Security Administration, accessed November 10, 2019, https://www.ssa.gov/history/trspeech .html.

11. For example, Senator Sasse voted against an amendment that would have restored expanded TAA eligibility rules in 2015. "Senate Vote #181 in 2015 (114th Congress)," GovTrack.us, May 18, 2015, https://www .govtrack.us/congress/votes/114-2015/s181. Senator Rubio sponsored an amendment that would have eliminated TAA expansions that were enacted in the 2009 Recovery Act. Marco Rubio, "U.S. Senate Floor Speech," September 22, 2011, Washington, DC, https://www.rubio.senate.gov/public/index.cfm/fighting-for -florida?ID=8C01E831-6E8D-46E5-A694-B39A50AB0902. Senators Rubio and Sasse voted to remove TAA extension from a legislative package in 2015. "Senate Vote 190—On the Amendment," Senate Votes, *ProPublica*, May 22, 2015, https://projects.propublica.org/represent/votes/114/senate/1/190.

12. Varadarajan, "A Conservative Economics of Dignity."

13. Oren Cass, "America Should Adopt an Industrial Policy," Manhattan Institute, July 23, 2019, https://www .manhattan-institute.org/resolved-that-america-should-adopt-an-industrial-policy.

14. Senator Sasse led an effort, supported by Senator Rubio, to encourage the Department of Agriculture to tighten work requirements in the Supplemental Nutrition Assistance Program (SNAP) by limiting states' ability to waive strict limitations on benefits for able-bodied adults without children in areas of high unemployment, for example. Ben Sasse, "Sasse Praises Department of Agriculture's Proposed Rule on SNAP Work Requirements," news release, December 20, 2018, https://www.sasse.senate.gov/public/index.cfm /2018/12/sasse-praises-department-of-agriculture-s-proposed-rule-on-snap-work-requirements. After the letter, the Department of Agriculture proposed a rule that would have done so. The final rule is projected to end SNAP eligibility for nearly 700,000 people. Phil McCausland, "Nearly 700,000 Will Lose Food Stamps with USDA Work Requirement Change," *NBC*, December 4, 2019, https://www.nbcnews.com/ne ws/us-news/nearly-700-000-will-lose-food-stamps-usda-work-requirement-n1095726. Additionally, Rubio has advocated work requirements for SNAP and Social Security Disability Insurance (SSDI). Marco Rubio, "Video: Rubio Calls for Revival of the Dignity of Work," news release, November 15, 2018, https://www .rubio.senate.gov/public/index.cfm/2018/11/video-rubio-calls-for-revival-of-the-dignity-of-work.

15. Repeal of the ACA Marketplaces and subsidies would mean that children who do not have access to health care coverage through a family's employer or are ineligible for the Children's Health Insurance Program would lose coverage. In 2017, Kaiser Family Foundation estimated that repealing the ACA coverage expansions and the individual mandate (which Republicans did later in 2017) would increase the number of uninsured children by 4.4 million. Samantha Artiga and Petry Ubri, "Key Issues in Children's Health Coverage," Medicaid, Kaiser Family Foundation, February 15, 2017, https://www.kff.org/medicaid/issue-brief/key-issues -in-childrens-health-coverage/.

16. Republicans have attempted to repeal the Affordable Care Act since it was enacted in 2010, and Senators Sasse and Rubio have embraced those efforts. They have voted twice in support of major bills to largely repeal the Affordable Care Act: H.R. 3672 in December 2015 and H.R. 1628 in July 2017. "Roll Call Vote 115th Congress—1st Session," Vote Summary, United States Senate, July 28, 2017, https://www .senate.gov/legislative/LIS/roll_call_lists/roll_call_vote_cfm.cfm?congress=115&session=1&vote=00179; "Roll Call Vote 114th Congress—1st Session," Vote Summary, United States Senate, December 3, 2015, https://www.senate.gov/legislative/LIS/roll_call_lists/roll_call_vote_cfm.cfm?congress=114& session=1&vote=00329. Prior versions of the 2017 bill, without opposition from Rubio and Sasse, would have allowed states to waive Essential Health Benefits requirements. As I wrote with Michael Shapiro at the time, "These Essential Health Benefits rules require insurance companies to cover critical care, such as treatment by doctors, hospital stays, and prescription-drug costs. The guarantee of Essential Health Benefits means that no insurer can provide any health plan that excludes these critical benefits. Perhaps it goes without saying, but if these benefits are not covered, a plan is all but worthless to those with serious pre-existing conditions." Gene B. Sperling and Michael Shapiro, "How the Senate's Health-Care Bill Would Cause Financial Ruin for People with Preexisting Conditions," *Atlantic*, June 23, 2017, https://www.theatlantic.com /business/archive/2017/06/ahca-senate-bill-preexisting-conditions/531375/. This provision was stripped out of the final bill that Senators Rubio and Sasse voted for, not because of their leadership or opposition, but because Senate rules prevented the provision from being changed through the budget procedure Republicans were trying to use. Center on Budget and Policy Priorities, "Tracking the Senate Floor Debate on Health Care Repeal," *Off the Charts* (blog), updated July 27, 2017, https://www.cbpp.org/blog/tracking -the-senate-floor-debate-on-health-care-repeal.

17. Specifically, "repealing the individual mandate to have coverage or pay a penalty would immediately lead some people, many of them relatively healthy, to drop coverage or not newly enroll in it. That would destabilize the individual market by making the pool of people with coverage sicker, on average, driving up premiums and endangering the protections for people with pre-existing medical conditions over time." Center on Budget and Policy Priorities, "Tracking the Senate Floor Debate on Health Care Repeal." Similarly, the 2015 repeal bill Senators Rubio and Sasse voted for would have led to higher premiums, the collapse of the individual market, and more than 20 million people losing health insurance. Matt Broaddus and Edwin Park, "Affordable Care Act Has Produced Historic Gains in Health Coverage," Center on Budget and Policy Priorities, December 15, 2016, https://www.cbpp.org/research/health/affordable-care-act-has-produced-historic -gains-in-health-coverage.

18. Robert Pear, "Marco Rubio Quietly Undermines Affordable Care Act," New York Times, December 9, 2015, https://www.nytimes.com/2015/12/10/us/politics/marco-rubio-obamacare-affordable-care-act.html.

19. Paul Ryan famously warned that low-income workers face marginal tax rates of 80 or 90 percent from taxes and loss of benefits. Paul Ryan, "#ConfidentAmerica: Speaker Ryan's Address at the Library of Congress," streamed live December 3, 2015, YouTube video, https://www.youtube.com/watch?v=HytBikkoTyc; Isaac Shapiro et. al, "It Pays to Work: Work Incentives and the Safety Net," Center on Budget and Policy Priorities, March 3, 2016, https://www.cbpp.org/research/federal-tax/it-pays-to-work-work-incentives-and-the-safety -net; Jordan Weissmann, "It's a Trap! Paul Ryan's Theory on Poverty Is Tricksy—and Wrong," Slate, March 5, 2014, https://slate.com/business/2014/03/paul-ryan-war-on-poverty-federal-programs-are-not-a-poverty -trap.html; and "Read the House GOP's Poverty Report," Washington Post, March 2, 2014, http://apps.wash ingtonpost.com/g/page/politics/read-the-house-gops-poverty-report/850/.

20. Sharon Parrott, "Rubio Proposal to Replace EITC Would Likely Come at Expense of Working-Poor Families with Children," Off the Charts (blog), Center on Budget and Policy Priorities, January 9, 2014, https://www .cbpp.org/blog/rubio-proposal-to-replace-eitc-would-likely-come-at-expense-of-working-poor -families-with.

21. Bureau of Labor Statistics, "National Compensation Survey: Employee Benefits in the United States, March 2018," September 2018, 311, https://www.bls.gov/ncs/ebs/benefits/2018/employee-benefits-in-the-united -states-march-2018.pdf.

22. Pronita Gupta, "Senator Rubio's Paid Leave Proposal Is a Threat to Economic Security," CLASP (blog), August 6, 2018, https://www.clasp.org/blog/senator-rubios-paid-leave-proposal-threat-economic-security.

23. Huang, "Fundamentally Flawed 2017 Tax Law Largely Leaves Low- and Moderate-Income Americans Behind."

24. Marco Rubio, "What Economics Is For," First Things, August 26, 2019, https://www.firstthings.com/web -exclusives/2019/08/what-economics-is-for.

25. Marco Rubio, "America Needs to Restore Dignity of Work," Atlantic, December 13, 2018, https://www .theatlantic.com/ideas/archive/2018/12/help-working-class-voters-us-must-value-work/578032/.

26. Rubio, "America Needs to Restore Dignity of Work."

27. Cass, The Once and Future Worker, 193.

28. Cass, The Once and Future Worker, 192.

29. Cass, The Once and Future Worker, 192–93.

30. Brooks, "The Dignity Deficit"; and Arthur C. Brooks, "How Donald Trump Filled the Dignity Deficit," Wall Street Journal, updated November 9, 2016, https://www.wsj.com/articles/how-donald-trump-filled-the -dignity-deficit-1478734436.

31. Varadarajan, "A Conservative Economics of Dignity."

32. Sasse, Them, 50.

33. "Is the U.S. Labor Market for Truck Drivers Broken?" Monthly Labor Review, Bureau of Labor Statistics, United States Department of Labor, March 2019, https://www.bls.gov/opub/mlr/2019/article/is-the -us-labor-market-for-truck-drivers-broken.htm.

CHAPTER ELEVEN: AN ECONOMIC DIGNITY WAGE

1. Dennis C. Rasmussen, "The Problem with Inequality according to Adam Smith," Atlantic, June 9, 2016, https://www.theatlantic.com/business/archive/2016/06/the-problem-with-inequality-according-to-adam -smith/486071/.

2. Adam Smith, An Inquiry into the Nature and Causes of the Wealth of Nations (London: W. Strahan and T. Cadell, 1776).

3. Theodore Roosevelt, address before the Convention of the National Progressive Party (Chicago, August 1912), Social Security Administration, accessed November 10, 2019, https://www.ssa.gov/history/trspeech.html.

4. Franklin D. Roosevelt, statement on the National Industrial Recovery Act, Franklin D. Roosevelt Presidential Library and Museum, June 16, 1933, http://docs.fdrlibrary.marist.edu/odnirast.html.

5. Matthew Desmond, Evicted: Poverty and Profit in the American City (New York: Crown, 2016), 379.

6. Xavier Jaravel, "The Unequal Gains from Product Innovations: Evidence from the U.S. Retail Sector," abstract, Quarterly Journal of Economics 134, no. 2 (December 2018), https://academic.oup.com/qje/article /134/2/715/5230867.

7. Annie Lowrey, "The Inflation Gap," Atlantic, November 5, 2019, https://www.theatlantic.com/ideas /archive/2019/11/income-inequality-getting-worse/601414/.

8. George F. Will, "Prosperity amid the Gloom," *Washington Post*, October 19, 2006, https://www.washington post.com/archive/opinions/2006/10/19/prosperity-amid-the-gloom/bca7d46d-012d-4438-bafb-3c56 c79747d6/.

9. Michael Kelly, "The 1992 Campaign: The Democrats—Clinton and Bush Compete to Be Champion of Change; Democrat Fights Perceptions of Bush Gain," *New York Times*, October 31, 1992, https://www .nytimes.com/1992/10/31/us/1992-campaign-democrats-clinton-bush-compete-be-champion-change -democrat-fights.html.

10. See discussion in Chapter Two; Thomas Reed Powell, "The Oregon Minimum Wage Cases," *Political Science Quarterly* 32 (June 1917): 308, https://www.jstor.org/stable/pdf/2141734.pdf.

11. Franklin D. Roosevelt, "Radio Address of the President," Teaching American History, May 24, 1938, https:// teachingamericanhistory.org/library/document/radio-address-of-the-president/.

12. Calculation based on Congressional Budget Office data for 2016, cash wages and salaries as a share of post-tax and-transfer income. "The Distribution of Household Income, 2016," Congressional Budget Office, July 9, 2019, https://www.cbo.gov/publication/55413.

13. Jacob Hacker, "Interview: The Politics of Predistribution," interview by Ben Jackson and Martin O'Neill, *Renewal* 21, no. 2/3 (2013): 1, http://www.renewal.org.uk/articles/interview-the politics-of-predistribution/.

14. David Cooper, *Raising the Federal Minimum Wage to $15 by 2024 Would Lift Pay for Nearly 40 Million Workers* (Washington, DC: Economic Policy Institute, February 2019), 2, https://www.epi.org/publication /raising-the-federal-minimum-wage-to-15-by-2024-would-lift-pay-for-nearly-40-million-workers/.

15. David Card and Alan B. Krueger, "Minimum Wages and Employment: A Case Study of the Fast-Food Industry in New Jersey and Pennsylvania," *American Economic Review* 84, no. 4 (September 1994): 772, http:// davidcard.berkeley.edu/papers/njmin-aer.pdf.

16. Cooper, *Raising the Federal Minimum Wage*, 16. In addition, economists Paul Wolfson and Dale Belman, in a meta-analysis of thirty-seven published studies on the minimum wage and job growth, concluded there is "no support for the proposition that the minimum wage has had an important effect on U.S. employment." Paul J. Wolfson and Dale Belman, "15 Years of Research on U.S. Employment and the Minimum Wage," abstract (Tuck School of Business Working Paper no. 2705499, Tuck School of Business at Dartmouth, Hanover, NH, December 2016), https://papers.ssrn.com/sol3/papers.cfm?abstract_id=2705499.

17. Their analysis includes minimum wages of up to 55 percent of the median wage in the relevant labor market—just shy of the amount that a $15 minimum wage by 2024 would represent nationally—and they "confirm that minimum wage changes in the U.S. we study have yet to reach a level above which significant disemployment effects emerge." At the same time, the average wages of affected workers increased by 6.8 percent. Doruk Cengiz, Arindrajit Dube, Attila Lindner, and Ben Zipperer, "The Effect of Minimum Wages on Low-Wage Jobs: Evidence from the United States Using a Bunching Estimator," abstract, NBER Working Paper No. 25434, National Bureau of Economic Research, Cambridge, MA, January 2019, https://www.nber .org/papers/w25434.

18. Godoey and Reich use county-level data to isolate areas that increased their minimum wage to high levels relative to the local median wage. They find "effects on employment are small to negligible" across groups including people without college degrees and among black, Hispanic, and female workers, while household and child poverty is lower in counties with high relative minimum wages. Anna Godoey and Michael Reich, "Minimum Wage Effects in Low-Wage Areas," Institute for Research on Labor and Employment Working Paper No. 106-19, Berkeley, CA, July 2019, 21, https://irle.berkeley.edu/minimum-wage -effects-in-low-wage-areas/; and Kate Gibson, "$15 Minimum Wage: Evidence That It Won't Mean Lost Jobs," *CBS*, July 2, 2019, https://www.cbsnews.com/news/15-minimum-wage-evidence-that-it-wont-mean -lost-jobs/.

19. Arindrajit Dube analyzed seven states that increased their minimum wage to at least $10.50 by 2018 and found the "change in the overall number of low wage jobs is quite small, and statistically indistinguishable from zero," while there was a "13.8% increase in wages paid to affected workers." Arindrajit Dube, *Technical Annex A: Evidence from Seven US States on the Impact of High Minimum Wages* (Amherst: University of Massachusetts Amherst, November 2019), 8, https://assets.publishing.service.gov.uk/government/uploads /system/uploads/attachment_data/file/844755/Technical_Annex_A_Evidence_from_Seven_US_States _on_the_Impact_of_High_Minimum_Wages.pdf. Also see Jeanna Smialek, "As Push for Higher Minimum Wages Grows, New York Offers a Test Case," *New York Times*, November 13, 2019, https://www .nytimes.com/2019/11/13/business/economy/minimum-wage-new-york-pennsylvania.html; Sylvia Allegretto, Anna Godoey, Carl Nadler, and Michael Reich, *The New Wave of Local Minimum Wage Policies: Evidence from Six Cities* (Berkeley, CA: Institute for Research on Labor and Employment, September 2018), 22, https://irle.berkeley.edu/files/2018/09/The-New-Wave-of-Local-Minimum-Wage-Policies.pdf; and Lina Moe, James Parrott, and Yannet Lathrop, *New York City's $15 Minimum Wage and Restaurant Employment and Earnings* (New York: National Employment Law Project, August 2019), 1, https://www.nelp.org/publi cation/new-york-city-15-minimum-wage-restaurant-employment-earnings/.

20. David Cooper, Lawrence Mishel, and Ben Zipperer, *Bold Increases in the Minimum Wage Should Be Evaluated for the Benefits of Raising Low-Wage Workers' Total Earnings* (Washington, DC: Economic Policy Institute, April 2018), 3, https://www.epi.org/publication/bold-increases-in-the-minimum-wage-should-be -evaluated-for-the-benefits-of-raising-low-wage-workers-total-earnings-critics-who-cite-claims-of-job -loss-are-using-a-distorted-frame/.

21. Numbers are not adjusted for inflation. Estimates based on "Earned Income Tax Credit Parameters, 1975–2016," Tax Policy Center, January 5, 2016, http://www.taxpolicycenter.org/sites/default/files /legacy/taxfacts/content/PDF/historical_eitc_parameters.pdf; Margot L. Crandall-Hollick, *The Child Tax Credit: Legislative History* (Washington, DC: Congressional Research Service, 2018), 10, https://www.every crsreport.com/files/20180301_R45124_08f18f1240d9fd41057b6f4b3f183e5e778b11ca.pdf; and "2018 EITC Income Limits, Maximum Credit Amounts and Tax Law Updates," IRS, updated July 10, 2019, https://www .irs.gov/credits-deductions/individuals/earned-income-tax-credit/eitc-income-limits-maximum-credit -amounts.
22. "Policy Basics: The Earned Income Tax Credit," Center on Budget and Policy Priorities, updated June 21, 2019, https://www.cbpp.org/research/federal-tax/policy-basics-the-earned-income-tax-credit.
23. Sarah Halpern-Meekin, Kathryn Edin, Laura Tach, and Jennifer Sykes, *It's Not Like I'm Poor: How Working Families Make Ends Meet in a Post-Welfare World* (Oakland: University of California Press, 2015), 19, 98.
24. Halpern-Meekin et al., *It's Not Like I'm Poor*, 10–11.
25. Hilary W. Hoynes, "A Revolution in Poverty Policy: The Earned Income Tax Credit and the Well-Being of American Families," *Pathways*, Summer 2014, 27, http://web.stanford.edu/group/scspi/_media/pdf /pathways/summer_2014/Pathways_Summer_2014.pdf.
26. For a detailed analysis of this research, see Chuck Marr, Chye-Ching Huang, Arloc Sherman, and Brandon DeBot, *EITC and Child Tax Credit Promote Work, Reduce Poverty, and Support Children's Development, Research Finds* (Washington, DC: Center on Budget and Policy Priorities, 2015), 1, https://www.cbpp.org /research/federal-tax/eitc-and-child-tax-credit-promote-work-reduce-poverty-and-support-childrens; Hilary W. Hoynes, Douglas L. Miller, and David Simon, *Linking EITC Income to Real Health Outcomes* (Davis, CA: UC Davis Center for Poverty Research, 2013), 1, http://poverty.ucdavis.edu/research-paper /policy-brief-linking-eitc-income-real-health-outcomes; and William N. Evans and Craig L. Garthwaite, "Giving Mom a Break: The Impact of Higher EITC Payments on Maternal Health," *American Economic Journal: Economic Policy* 6, no. 2 (May 2014): 258–90.
27. Gene B. Sperling, "A Tax Proposal That Could Lift Millions Out of Poverty," *Atlantic*, October 17, 2017, https://www.theatlantic.com/business/archive/2017/10/eitc-for-all/542898/. Along with my EITC for All pro- posal, congressional Democrats like Senators Michael Bennet, Sherrod Brown, and Kamala Harris and Rep- resentative Ro Khanna have been among those to put forward ambitious proposals in this space.
28. Sperling, "A Tax Proposal That Could Lift Millions Out of Poverty."
29. For example, the poverty level for a single worker in 2019 is about $13,340, or the equivalent of working about thirty-five hours a week at the federal minimum wage of $7.25 an hour. A worker with those earnings receives an EITC of only $172, while owing about $1,135 in federal income and payroll taxes—meaning this worker's net federal tax burden of nearly $1,000 will push the individual into poverty. Chuck Marr and Yixuan Huang, *Childless Adults Are Lone Group Taxed into Poverty* (Washington, DC: Center on Bud- get and Policy Priorities, June 2019), https://www.cbpp.org/research/federal-tax/childless-adults-are-lone -group-taxed-into-poverty.
30. Chuck Marr, Brendan Duke, Yixuan Huang, Jennifer Beltrán, Vincent Palacios, and Arloc Sherman, *Work- ing Families Tax Relief Act Would Raise Incomes of 46 Million Households, Reduce Child Poverty* (Washing- ton, DC: Center on Budget and Policy Priorities, April 2019), 1, https://www.cbpp.org/research/federal-tax /working-families-tax-relief-act-would-raise-incomes-of-46-million-households.
31. "Combating Inequality: Rethinking Policies to Reduce Inequality in Advanced Economies," Peterson Insti- tute for International Economics Conference, October 17, 2019, video, 38:10, https://www.piie.com/events /combating-inequality-rethinking-policies-reduce-inequality-advanced-economies, session 4.
32. Joseph Williams, "The Other Childcare Crisis," *Economic Hardship Reporting Project*, January 16, 2019, http://economichardship.org/archive//the-other-childcare-crisis.
33. Williams, "The Other Childcare Crisis."
34. Douglas Rice, Stephanie Schmit, and Hannah Matthews, "Child Care and Housing: Big Expenses with Too Little Help Available," Center on Budget and Policy Priorities, April 2019, 4, https:///www.cbpp.org/sites /default/files/atoms/files/4-29-19hous.pdf.
35. Rice, Schmit, and Matthews, *Child Care and Housing*, 3.
36. Marybeth J. Mattingly and Christopher T. Wimer, *Child Care Expenses Push Many Families into Poverty* (Durham, NH: University of New Hampshire Carsey School of Public Policy, spring 2017), 1, https:// scholars.unh.edu/cgi/viewcontent.cgi?referer=https://www.google.com/&httpsredir=1&article=1303 &context=carsey.
37. Rasheed Malik, Katie Hamm, Leila Schochet, Cristina Novoa, Simon Workman, and Steven Jessen-Howard, "America's Child Care Deserts in 2018," Center for American Progress, December 6, 2018, https://www.ameri canprogress.org/issues/early-childhood/reports/2018/12/06/461643/americas-child-care-deserts-2018/.
38. For example, see National Women's Law Center, "Child Care Assistance for Low-Income Families Falls Short, NWLC State-by-State Report Shows," news release, November 13, 2018, https://nwlc.org/press -releases/child-care-assistance-for-low-income-families-falls-short-nwlc-state-by-state-report-shows/; Williams, "The Other Childcare Crisis"; Liz Tracy, "Trying to Find Affordable Child Care Is Not the Job I Wanted," *Refinery29*, April 2, 2019, https://www.refinery29.com/en-us/2019/04/228243/the-struggle-to -find-good-affordable-child-care; and Sarah Tenton, "Seattle Daycare Waitlists Are Now over Two Years

Long," *Local Babysitter*, March 21, 2019, https://localbabysitter.com/seattle-daycare-waitlists-continue-to-grow-over-past-five-years/.

39. Michael Madowitz, Alex Rowell, and Katie Hamm, "Calculating the Hidden Cost of Interrupting a Career for Child Care," Center for American Progress, June 21, 2016, https://www.americanprogress.org/issues/early-childhood/reports/2016/06/21/139731/calculating-the-hidden-cost-of-interrupting-a-career-for-child-care/.

40. Rice, Schmit, and Matthews, *Child Care and Housing*, 6.

41. See, e.g., Elise Gould and Jessica Schieder, "Does Trump's Tax Plan Help Families Pay for Child and Dependent Care Expenses?," Working Economics Blog, Economic Policy Institute, May 1, 2017, https://www.epi.org/blog/does-trumps-tax-plan-help-families-pay-for-child-and-dependent-care-expenses/; and Dylan Matthews, "Rich Parents Get the Biggest Child Care Tax Breaks," *Vox*, June 3, 2014, https://www.vox.com/2014/6/3/5776044/rich-parents-get-the-biggest-child-care-tax-breaks.

42. Jason Furman, "The United States and Europe: Short-Run Divergence and Long-Run Challenges" (presented at Bruegel, Brussels, Belgium, May 11, 2016), 20.

43. "Hillary Clinton's Child Care Plan," Save the Children Action Network, 2016, https://savethechildrenactionnetwork.org/wp-content/uploads/2016/04/Hillary-Clinton-childcare-plan 2016.pdf; and Anna North, "We Asked All the 2020 Democrats How They'd Fix Child Care. Here's What They Said," *Vox*, July 5, 2019, https://www.vox.com/2019/5/22/18302875/2020-election-democrats-child-care-kids-president.

44. Dayna M. Kurtz, "We Have a Child-Care Crisis in This Country. We Had the Solution 78 Years Ago," *Washington Post*, July 23, 2018, https://www.washingtonpost.com/news/posteverything/wp/2018/07/23/we-have-a-childcare-crisis-in-this-country-we-had-the-solution-78-years-ago/.

45. Elizabeth E. Davis, Deana Grobe, and Roberta B. Weber, "Rural-Urban Differences in Childcare Subsidy Use and Employment Stability," *Applied Economic Perspectives and Policies* 32, no. 1 (spring 2010): 135–53; cited in Rice, Schmit, and Matthews, *Child Care and Housing*.

46. See, e.g., Rebekah Levine Coley and Caitlin McPherran Lombardi, "Does Maternal Employment following Childbirth Support or Inhibit Low-Income Children's Long-Term Development?," *Child Development* 84 (August 2012). Results in this study were most significant for African American children; cited in Rice, Schmit, and Matthews, *Child Care and Housing*, 4.

47. Analysis based on "Budget and Economic Data," Congressional Budget Office, accessed December 6, 2019, https://www.cbo.gov/about/products/budget-economic-data#3.

48. Andy Stern, *Raising the Floor: How a Universal Basic Income Can Renew Our Economy and Rebuild the American Dream* (New York: PublicAffairs, 2016), 158; "What Is the Freedom Dividend," Yang 2020 (website), accessed December 6, 2019, https://www.yang2020.com/what-is-freedom-dividend-faq/.

49. Charles Murray, *In Our Hands* (Washington, DC: AEI Press, 2006), 7–10.

50. Eric Johnson, "Why 2020 Presidential Candidate Andrew Yang Doesn't Want to Break Up Google," *Vox*, July 19, 2019, https://www.vox.com/recode/2019/7/19/20701175/andrew-yang-2020-presidential-race-google-breakup-tech-warren-kara-swisher-recode-decode-podcast.

51. Stern, *Raising the Floor*, 186–87. Stern also cites and quotes extensively Michael Tanner, a senior fellow at the libertarian Cato Institute, about how "we've been spending more and more money developing more programs, without getting any additional benefit, for over forty years. Maybe we need to re-think the whole approach." He adds, "According to Tanner, the biggest problem with current anti-poverty programs is that they 'infantilize' the poor. 'We treat poor people like they're three years old.' . . . Tanner also says that the welfare system 'ghettoizes' the poor. 'It forces them to live in the one area of town that offers them free public housing, grocery stores that accept food stamps, and doctors who take Medicaid.'" *Raising the Floor*, 186. Also consider activist Scott Santens, who approvingly cites a misleading *Weekly Standard* piece to suggest that "basic income is entirely affordable given all the current and hugely wasteful means-tested programs full of unnecessary bureaucracy that can be consolidated into it." Scott Santens, "Why Should We Support the Idea of an Unconditional Basic Income?," *Medium*, June 2, 2014, https://medium.com/working-life/why-should-we-support-the-idea-of-an-unconditional-basic-income-8a2680c73dd3.

52. Tricia Brooks et al., *Medicaid and CHIP Eligibility, Enrollment, Renewal, and Cost* (San Francisco: Kaiser Family Foundation, January 2017), 37–40, https://www.kff.org/report-section/medicaid-and-chip-eligibility-enrollment-renewal-and-cost-sharing-policies-as-of-january-2017-medicaid-and-chip-enrollment-and-renewal-processes/.

53. Sonal Ambegaokar et al., "Opportunities to Streamline Enrollment across Public Benefit Programs," Center on Budget and Policy Priorities, November 2, 2017, https://www.cbpp.org/research/poverty-and-inequality/opportunities-to-streamline-enrollment-across-public-benefit.

54. Statement of Nancy J. Altman, Hearing on Improving Retirement Security for American Workers, United States House of Representatives Committee on Ways and Means, February 6, 2019, https://socialsecurity.news/1589-2/.

55. "Medicare and Medicaid Milestones 1937–2015," Centers for Medicare and Medicaid Services, July 2015, https://www.cms.gov/About-CMS/Agency-Information/History/Downloads/Medicare-and-Medicaid-Milestones-1937-2015.pdf; and Margot L. Crandall-Hollick, *The Earned Income Tax Credit (EITC): A Brief Legislative History* (Washington, DC: Congressional Research Service, 2018), 3, https://fas.org/sgp/crs/misc/R44825.pdf.

56. Robyn Sundlee, "Alaska's Universal Basic Income Problem," *Vox*, September 5, 2019, https://www.vox.com/future-perfect/2019/9/5/20849020/alaska-permanent-fund-universal-basic-income.

57. Elisabeth Jacobs and Jacob Hacker, *The Rising Instability of American Family Incomes, 1969–2004* (Washington, DC: Economic Policy Institute, 2008), 1, https://www.epi.org/publication/bp213/.

58. "The Risk of Losing Health Insurance over a Decade: New Findings from Longitudinal Data," U.S. Treasury Department, 2009, https://www.treasury.gov/press-center/press-releases/documents/final-hc-report09 2009.pdf.

59. Tim Dowd and John B. Horowitz, "Income Mobility and the Earned Income Tax Credit: Short-Term Safety Net or Long-Term Income Support," *Public Finance Review* 39, no. 5 (September 2011): 619–52, https://journals.sagepub.com/doi/abs/10.1177/1091142111401008.

60. For the growing concerns parents have, see Claire Cain Miller, "The Relentlessness of Modern Parenting," *New York Times*, December 25, 2018, https://www.nytimes.com/2018/12/25/upshot/the-relentlessness-of-modern-parenting.html.

CHAPTER TWELVE: A DIGNITY NET FOR ALL

1. Franklin D. Roosevelt, "State of the Union Message to Congress," January 11, 1944, Franklin D. Roosevelt Presidential Library and Museum, http://www.fdrlibrary.marist.edu/archives/address_text.html.

2. Roosevelt, "State of the Union Message to Congress.".

3. Matt Nelson, "Will Work for No Benefits: The Challenges of Being in the New Contract Workforce," interview by Yuki Noguchi, *Morning Edition*, NPR, January 23, 2018, audio, https://www.npr.org/2018/01/23/579720874/will-work-for-no-benefits-the-challenges-of-being-in-the-new-contract-workforce.

4. Jared Bernstein, "You're on Your Own vs. We're in This Together," *On the Economy*, September 6, 2012, http://jaredbernsteinblog.com/youre-on-your-own-vs-were-in-this-together/.

5. FedEx drivers have won some legal battles for classification as employees. For example, see Robert W. Wood, "FedEx Settles Independent Contractor Mislabeling Case for $228 Million," *Forbes*, June 16, 2015, https://www.forbes.com/sites/robertwood/2015/06/16/fedex-settles-driver-mislabeling-case-for-228-million/; Amy Biegelsen, "FedEx Fails to Deliver for Drivers," Center for Public Integrity, May 19, 2014, https://publicintegrity.org/federal-politics/fedex-fails-to-deliver-for-drivers/; and Lydia DePillis, "How FedEx Is Trying to Save the Business Model That Saved It Millions," *Washington Post*, October 23, 2014, https://www.washingtonpost.com/news/storyline/wp/2014/10/23/how-fedex-is-trying-to-save-the-business-model-that-saved-it-millions/.

6. Michelle R. Smith, "Why Many Employees Feel Devalued Even in Booming Job Market," *Associated Press*, August 12, 2019, https://www.apnews.com/6c9263d76e9e477da15abaec2045f6c9.

7. Smith, "Why Many Employees Feel Devalued Even in Booming Job Market."

8. Lydia DePillis, "She Thought She Was Entitled to Maternity Leave. After Asking for It, She Lost Her Job," *Washington Post*, August 14, 2015, https://www.washingtonpost.com/news/wonk/wp/2015/08/14/she-thought-she-was-entitled-to-maternity-leave-after-asking-for-it-she-lost-her-job/.

9. "California Approves Bill That Will Turn Gig Workers into Employees," *CBS News*, September 11, 2019, https://www.cbsnews.com/news/ab5-bill-passes-california-approves-ab5-bill-that-will-turn-uber-lyft-gig-workers-into-employees/.

10. The goal here is not to create a middle or "hybrid" new worker classification as some have called for, but rather to work toward a day when work—however it is done—carries with it the same basic economic dignity net.

11. Nick Hanauer and David Rolf, "Shared Security, Shared Growth," *Democracy: A Journal of Ideas*, no. 37 (summer 2015), https://democracyjournal.org/magazine/37/shared-security-shared-growth/.

12. Hanauer and Rolf, "Shared Security, Shared Growth."

13. "How Tierra del Sol Empowers Individuals in Their Community," Included Supported Empowered (website), November 21, 2019, http://wehaveastake.org/2019/11/how-tierra-del-sol-empowers-individuals-in-their-community/.

14. Madeline Twomey, *State Options for Making Wise Investments in the Direct Care Workforce* (Washington, DC: Center for American Progress, April 2019), https://www.americanprogress.org/issues/healthcare/reports/2019/04/10/468290/state-options-making-wise-investments-direct-care-workforce/. Though Medicaid is required to provide institutional care, states may choose whether to provide home- and community-based services. Judith Solomon, *Existing Medicaid Flexibility Has Broadened Reach of Home- and Community-Based Services* (Washington, DC: Center on Budget and Policy Priorities, February 2017), 2, https://www.cbpp.org/health/existing-medicaid-flexibility-has-broadened-reach-of-home-and-community-based-services.

15. MaryBeth Musumeci, Priya Chidambaram, and Molly O'Malley Watts, *Key Questions about Medicaid Home and Community-Based Services Waiver Waiting List* (San Francisco: Kaiser Family Foundation, April 2019), 2, https://www.kff.org/medicaid/issue-brief/key-questions-about-medicaid-home-and-community-based-services-waiver-waiting-lists/.

16. Researchers write, "The problem is that people with disabilities have extra costs of living that people without disabilities do not have. They have higher medical expenses and may need personal assistance or assistive devices, such as wheelchairs or hearing aids. They may need to spend more on transportation or modified housing, or be restricted in what neighborhoods they can live in to be closer to work or accessible services."

Sophie Mitra et. al, "The Hidden Extra Costs of Living with a Disability," *Conversation*, July 25, 2017, https://theconversation.com/the-hidden-extra-costs-of-living-with-a-disability-78001.

17. Ron Fournier, *Love That Boy: What Two Presidents, Eight Road Trips, and My Son Taught Me about a Parent's Expectations* (New York: Harmony, 2016), 219.

18. Brian Field, "Parenting and the High Cost of Autism," Autism Support Network, accessed October 30, 2019, http://www.autismsupportnetwork.com/news/parenting-and-high-cost-autism; see also Ariane V. S. Buescher, Zuleyha Cidav, Martin Knapp, and David S. Mandell, "Costs of Autism Spectrum Disorders in the United Kingdom and United States," *Journal of the American Medical Association Pediatrics* 168, no. 8 (August 2014): 721, https://jamanetwork.com/journals/jamapediatrics/fullarticle/1879723; and "The Financial Impact of an Autism Diagnosis," Autism Spectrum Disorder Foundation, accessed October 30, 2019, https://myasdf.org/media-center/articles/the-financial-impact-of-an-autism-diagnosis/.

19. "A Discussion with Judy Heumann on Independent Living," Disabled in Action (website), accessed December 9, 2019, http://www.disabledinaction.org/heumann.html.

20. "Judith Heumann," Disability Action Center, accessed December 9, 2019, https://actionctr.org/resources/profiles-in-courage/judith-heumann/.

21. Julia Bascom, "Addressing Diverse Disabilities: A Conversation with the Autistic Self Advocacy Network's Julia Bascom," interview by Partnership on Employment and Accessible Technology, accessed December 9, 2019, https://www.peatworks.org/content/addressing-diverse-disabilities-conversation-autistic-self-advocacy-network%E2%80%99s-julia-bascom.

22. Rebecca Cokley, "Reflections from an ADA Generation," TEDxUniversityofRochester, video, 7:30, April 2017, https://www.ted.com/talks/rebecca_cokley_reflections_from_an_ada_generation.

23. Rebecca Vallas, Shawn Fremstad, and Lisa Eckman, *A Fair Shot for Workers with Disabilities* (Washington, DC: Center for American Progress, January 2015), https://www.americanprogress.org/issues/poverty/reports/2015/01/28/105520/a-fair-shot for-workers-with-disabilities/.

24. Bascom, "Addressing Diverse Disabilities."

25. Association of Assistive Technology Act Programs, *Small Federal Investment—Large Benefits in Return*, 2018, https://www.ataporg.org/Content/EOCONTENTMEDIACENTER/documents/ATAP_FFY2018_Accessi bleKO_lp.pdf.

26. For example, see Allan Hoffman, "Innovations for People with Disabilities in the Workplace," *Monster*, accessed November 12, 2019, https://www.monster.com/career-advice/article/adaptive-technology-at-work; and Dave Zielinski, "New Assistive Technologies Aid Employees with Disabilities," Society for Human Resource Management, December 20, 2016, https://www.shrm.org/resourcesandtools/hr-topics/technology/pages/new-assistive-technologies-aid-employees-with-disabilities.aspx.

27. Jerry Carino, "NJ Forces Disabled Howell Student to Make Brutal Choice: Internship or Health Aide Money," *APP*, May 21, 2018, https://www.app.com/story/news/local/values/2018/05/21/disabled-howell-student-nj-forces-choice-internship-health-aide/610909002/.

28. Anna Landre, "America's Medicaid Trap," *Disability Visibility Project* (blog), November 18, 2019, https://disabilityvisibilityproject.com/2019/11/19/americas-medicaid-trap-essay-by-anna-landre/.

29. Azza Altiraifi, "Advancing Economic Security for People with Disabilities," Center for American Progress, July 26, 2019, https://www.americanprogress.org/issues/disability/reports/2019/07/26/472686/advancing-economic-security-people-disabilities/.

30. Of course, we should have targeted efforts to address the rare actual—and especially systematic—fraud. As I wrote in 2017, "In a program as large as Social Security Disability Insurance, are there ever serious or systemic cases of fraud? Certainly. But as with Medicare, the right way to do it is to target those engaged in major fraud through enforcement—not by cutting benefits or stigmatizing the millions of people who, due to pain and disability, are forced to live at times on a sub-poverty level payment of an average of $1,171 a month. The Bipartisan Budget Act of 2015 already stiffened penalties for conspiracy to commit Social Security Disability Insurance fraud, while expanding nationwide investigations." Gene Sperling, "The Fuzzy Claims Used to Justify Cutting Social Security Disability Insurance," *Atlantic*, May 23, 2017, https://www.theatlantic.com/business/archive/2017/05/ssdi/527802/.

31. Sperling, "The Fuzzy Claims Used to Justify Cutting Social Security Disability Insurance."

32. "Policy Basics: Social Security Disability Insurance," Center on Budget and Policy Priorities, updated July 30, 2019, https://www.cbpp.org/research/retirement-security/policy-basics-social-security-disability-insurance.

33. Lydia DePillis, "We've Tried to Smooth Disabled People's Path Back to Work. Why Isn't It Helping?" *Washington Post*, October 23, 2015, https://www.washingtonpost.com/news/wonk/wp/2015/10/23/after-years-of-trying-to-make-it-easier-for-disabled-people-to-go-back-to-work-its-as-hard-as-ever/.

34. DePillis, "We've Tried to Smooth Disabled People's Path Back to Work."

35. "Policy Basics."

36. "Employment," Position Statements, The Arc (website), accessed December 9, 2019, https://thearc.org/position-statements/employment/.

37. "Policy Basics."

38. Reforms adopted in the 1990s allowing workers with disabilities to "buy in" to Medicaid try to take the right approach by creating an affordable pathway for workers with disabilities to maintain critical health insurance even if they take a risk and enter the labor force or increase earnings. But the program depends on

state administration, and many states maintain relatively low income limits—most below $30,000 a year—and asset limits—about half of states have asset limits below $10,000 for an individual—to be eligible. "Medicaid Eligibility through Buy-In Programs for Working People with Disabilities," State Health Facts, Kaiser Family Foundation, accessed October 31, 2019, https://www.kff.org/other/state-indicator/medicaid-eligibility-through-buy-in-programs-for-working-people-with-disabilities/. As a result, as of 2011 fewer than 200,000 of more than 15 million working-age Americans with a disability deployed it because of low income and asset limits in most states. Matthew Kehn, *Enrollment, Employment, and Earnings in the Medicaid Buy-In Program, 2011* (Princeton, NJ: Mathematica Policy Research, May 2013), 20, https://www.mathematica-mpr.com/~/media/publications/PDFs/health/medicaid_buyin_enrollment.pdf; and U.S. Department of Labor, "Persons with a Disability: Labor Force Characteristics," news release no. USDL-12-1125, June 8, 2012, https://www.bls.gov/news.release/archives/disabl_06082012.htm.

39. And we must also do more to support people who are not eligible for SSDI because of limited work history and to support people with disabilities before their conditions worsen enough to apply for SSDI. This can include income support, ensuring access to medical care, funding quality educational programming, enforcing mandates for supportive workplaces, and providing wraparound skills training and services.

40. For example, I wrote in 2005 that Social Security "has always been distinguished as the only guaranteed, risk-free leg. While a failure to save, poor choices, bad luck, or a weak economy can undercut the first two legs, Social Security was designed to be the leg that ensures a modicum of economic dignity during retirement even if everything else goes wrong." Gene Sperling, *The Pro-Growth Progressive: An Economic Strategy for Shared Prosperity* (New York: Simon & Schuster, 2005), 272.

41. "Policy Basics: Top Ten Facts about Social Security," Center on Budget and Policy Priorities, updated August 14, 2019, https://www.cbpp.org/research/social-security/policy-basics-top-ten-facts-about-social-security.

42. Bureau of Labor Statistics, "51 Percent of Private Industry Workers Had Access to Only Defined Contribution Retirement Plans," *TED: The Economics Daily*, U.S. Department of Labor, October 2, 2018, https://www.bls.gov/opub/ted/2018/51-percent-of-private-industry-workers-had-access-to-only-defined-contribution-retirement-plans-march-2018.htm.

43. Jennifer Erin Brown, Joelle Saad-Lessler, and Diane Oakley, "Retirement in America: Out of Reach for Working Americans?," National Institute on Retirement Security, September 2018, 10, https://www.nirsonline.org/wp-content/uploads/2018/09/SavingsCrisis_Final.pdf.

44. Not including home equity. Transamerica Center for Retirement Studies, *A Precarious Existence: How Today's Retirees Are Financially Faring in Retirement*, December 2018, 95, https://www.transamericacenter.org/docs/default-source/retirees-survey/tcrs2018_sr_retirees_survey_financially_faring.pdf.

45. U.S. Social Security Administration, *Monthly Statistical Snapshot, September 2019*, October 2019, https://www.ssa.gov/policy/docs/quickfacts/stat_snapshot/2019-09.html.

46. As discussed earlier, we must also recognize broader forms of contribution by giving caregivers "credit" toward future Social Security benefits for time they take off to care for children, parents, or other loved ones, which will help reduce gender disparities in benefits.

47. For example, see Katelin P. Isaacs and Sharmila Choudhury, *The Growing Gap in Life Expectancy by Income: Recent Evidence and Implications for the Social Security Retirement Age* (Washington, DC: Congressional Research Service, 2018), 28, https://fas.org/sgp/crs/misc/R44846.pdf; and Timothy J. Cunningham et al., "Vital Signs: Racial Disparities in Age-Specific Mortality Rates among Blacks or African Americans—United States, 1999–2015," *CDC Morbidity and Mortality Weekly Report* 66, no. 16 (May 5, 2017), https://www.cdc.gov/mmwr/volumes/66/wr/mm6617e1.htm.

48. For a general discussion, see Ai-jen Poo, *The Age of Dignity: Preparing for the Elder Boom in a Changing America* (New York: New Press, 2015).

49. Eduardo Porter, "Why Aren't More Women Working? They're Caring for Parents," *New York Times*, August 29, 2019, https://www.nytimes.com/2019/08/29/business/economy/labor-family-care.html.

50. Ron Lieber, "New Tax Will Help Washington Residents Pay for Long-Term Care," *New York Times*, May 13, 2019, https://www.nytimes.com/2019/05/13/business/washington-long-term-care.html.

51. As I noted when Elizabeth Warren released her wealth tax proposal, "the incidence of extreme wealth inequality—as well as the magnitude of never-taxed wealth—is just so obscene at this point in our nation that I think there is simply no choice but to explore a wealth tax like this." Jim Tankersley, "Warren's Plan Is Latest Push by Democrats to Raise Taxes on the Rich," *New York Times*, January 24, 2019, https://www.nytimes.com/2019/01/24/us/politics/wealth-tax-democrats.html.

52. Angela Hanks, Danyelle Solomon, and Christian E. Weller, "Systematic Inequality: How America's Structural Racism Helped Create the Black-White Wealth Gap," Center for American Progress, February 21, 2018, https://www.americanprogress.org/issues/race/reports/2018/02/21/447051/systematic-inequality/.

53. Michelle Singletary, "Black Homeownership Is as Low as It Was When Housing Discrimination Was Legal," *Washington Post*, April 5, 2018, https://www.washingtonpost.com/news/get-there/wp/2018/04/05/black-homeownership-is-as-low-as-it-was-when-housing-discrimination-was-legal/.

54. Carmel Ford, "Homeownership Rates by Race and Ethnicity," Eye on Housing, National Association of Home Builders, March 13, 2019, http://eyeonhousing.org/2019/03/homeownership-rates-by-race-and-ethnicity/.

55. Gene B. Sperling, "A 401(k) for All," *New York Times*, July 24, 2014, https://www.nytimes.com/2014/07/23/opinion/a-401-k-for-all.html.

56. See, for example, discussions in my prior writings: Sperling, "A 401(k) for All"; and Gene Sperling, "No Pain, No Savings," *New York Times,* January 5, 2005, https://www.nytimes.com/2005/01/05/opinion/no-pain-no -savings.html.

CHAPTER THIRTEEN: DOUBLE-DIGNITY JOBS

1. See discussion of a full UBI in Chapter Eleven.
2. See discussion in Eduardo Porter, "Tech Is Splitting the U.S. Work Force in Two," *New York Times,* February 4, 2019, https://www.nytimes.com/2019/02/04/business/economy/productivity-inequality-wages.html; and David Autor, Lawrence Katz, and Melissa Kearney, "The Polarization of the U.S. Labor Market," NBER Working Paper 11986, National Bureau of Economic Research, Cambridge, MA, January 2006, https:// www.nber.org/papers/w11986.
3. U.S. Congress, House Committee on Armed Services, Subcommittee on Military Personnel and Compensation, Child Care Programs, 100th Cong., 2nd sess., 1988, H.A.S.C. No. 100-120, 30. Cited in Kristy N. Kamarck, "Military Child Development Program: Background Issues," Congressional Research Service, August 10, 2018, 2, https://fas.org/sgp/crs/natsec/R45288.pdf
4. Bryce Covert, "The U.S. Already Has a High-Quality, Universal Childcare Program -in the Military," *Think Progress,* June 16, 2017, https://thinkprogress.org/universal-military-childcare-9bb2b54bd154/.
5. Latosha Floyd and Deborah A. Phillips, "Child Care and Other Support Programs," Military Children and Families, *Future of Children* 23, no. 2 (fall 2013).
6. See David Ellwood presentation in "Combating Inequality Conference: Labor Market Tools," Peterson Institute for International Economics, October 17, 2019, https://www.piie.com/events/combating-inequality -rethinking-policies-reduce-inequality-advanced-economies.
7. See Chapter Sixteen for a discussion of the returns to society and gains from quality early childhood education and the issue of low public expenditure, resulting in limited access to early care and education supports. James J. Heckman, Seong Hyeok Moon, Rodrigo Pinto, Peter A. Savelyev, and Adam Yavitz, "The Rate of Return to the High/Scope Perry Preschool Program," *Journal of Public Economics* 94, no. 1 (2010): 114–28; Greg J. Duncan and Katherine Magnuson, "Investing in Preschool Programs," *Journal of Economic Perspectives* 27, no. 2 (spring 2013): 109–32; and Elizabeth U. Cascio and Diane Whitmore Schanzenbach, "Impacts of Expanding Access to High Quality Preschool Education," Brookings Papers on Economic Activity, Brookings Institution, 2013, 127–92.
8. Julie Kashen, Halley Potter, and Andrew Stettner, "Quality Jobs, Quality Child Care," Century Foundation, June 13, 2016, 3, https://tcf.org/content/report/quality-jobs-quality-child-care/.
9. Elise Gould, "Child Care Workers Aren't Paid Enough to Make Ends Meet," Economic Policy Institute, November 5, 2015, https://www.epi.org/publication/child-care-workers-arent-paid-enough-to-make-ends -meet/#can-child-care-workers-afford-child-care?/.
10. Gould, "Child Care Workers Aren't Paid Enough to Make Ends Meet."
11. Based on the median for preschool teachers with a bachelor's degree compared to the median kindergarten teacher salary. Kashen, Potter, and Stettner, "Quality Jobs, Quality Child Care," 3.
12. See discussion in Marnie Kaplan and Sara Mead, "The Best Teachers for Our Littlest Learners? Lessons from Head Start's Last Decade," Bellwether Education Partners, February 2017, https://bellwethereducation .org/sites/default/files/Bellwether_HeadStartWorkforce.pdf.
13. Scott Jaschik, "Wealth and Admissions: A Look at Some of the Many Ways That Affluent Applicants Have an Edge—without Bribery," *Inside Higher Ed,* March 18, 2019, https://www.insidehighered.com /admissions/article/2019/03/18/look-many-legal-ways-wealthy-applicants-have-edge-admissions.
14. For instance, scholars found that at public universities, there is "a strong, highly consistent relationship between a student's socioeconomic background and his or her probability of graduating." William G. Bowen, Matthew M. Chingos, and Michael S. McPherson, *Crossing the Finish Line: Completing College at America's Public Universities* (Princeton, NJ: Princeton University Press, 2009), 37.
15. Douglas J. Gagnon and Marybeth J. Mattingly, "Most U.S. School Districts Have Low Access to School Counselors," Carsey School of Public Policy, fall 2016, https://scholars.unh.edu/cgi/viewcontent.cgi? article=1285&context=carsey.
16. Clare Lombardo, "With Hundreds of Students, School Counselors Just Try to 'Stay Afloat,'" NPR, February 26, 2018, https://www.npr.org/sections/ed/2018/02/26/587377711/with-hundreds-of-students-school -counselors-just-try-to-stay-afloat.
17. Christopher Avery, Jessica S. Howell, and Lindsay Page, "A Review of the Role of College Counseling, Coaching, and Mentoring on Students' Postsecondary Outcomes," College Board Research, October 2014, 3, https://files.eric.ed.gov/fulltext/ED556468.pdf.
18. Jaschik, "Wealth and Admissions."
19. Michael Hurwitz and Jessica Howell, "Estimating Causal Impacts of School Counselors with Regression Discontinuity Designs," *Journal of Counseling & Development* 92, no. 3 (June 2014), https://doi.org/10.1002 /j.1556-6676.2014.00159.x.
20. College Advising Corps, "Impact Summary," accessed November 10, 2019, https://advisingcorps.org /our-impact/impact-summary/; and Advising Corps, "Where We Work," accessed December 4, 2019, https://advisingcorps.org/our-work/where-we-work/.

21. Susan Scrivener, Michael J. Weiss, Alyssa Ratledge, Timothy Rudd, Colleen Sommo, and Hannah Fresques, "Doubling Graduation Rates: Three-Year Effects of CUNY's Accelerated Study in Associate Programs (ASAP) for Developmental Education Students," MDRC, February 2015, https://www.mdrc.org/publication /doubling-graduation-rates.

22. Kit Peterson, "Why I Advocate for Direct Support Professionals," Autism Speaks, September 17, 2018, https://www.autismspeaks.org/blog/why-i-advocate-direct-support-professionals.

23. Gregory Miller, "We Must Increase Pay for Those Who Care for People with Intellectual Disabilities in Pa," York Daily Record, December 4, 2019, https://www.ydr.com/story/opinion/2019/12/04/we-must-increase -pay-direct-service-professionals-pa/2609477001/.

24. Nicole Jorwic, "Congressional Testimony: The Direct Care Crisis," The Arc, November 1, 2019, https:// thearc.org/congressional-testimony-the-direct-care-crisis/.

25. Jorwic, "Congressional Testimony."

26. Jorwic, "Congressional Testimony."

27. Jorwic, "Congressional Testimony."

28. Michael Ollove, "Children with Autism Left Behind by Low Medicaid Rates," Pew Charitable Trusts, Stateline, June 12, 2018, https://www.pewtrusts.org/en/research-and-analysis/blogs/stateline/2018/06/12 /children-with-autism-left-behind-by-low-medicaid-rates.

29. See Blythe Bernhard, "Autism Insurance Coverage Now Required in All 50 States," Disability Scoop, October 1, 2019, https://www.disabilityscoop.com/2019/10/01/autism-insurance-coverage-now-required-50 -states/27223/; and Jen Fifield, "Coverage for Autism Treatment Varies by State," Pew Charitable Trusts, Stateline, February 19, 2016, https://www.pewtrusts.org/en/research-and-analysis/blogs/stateline/2016/02 /19/coverage-for-autism-treatment-varies-by-state.

30. Tim Smith, "'We've Got to Have Some Help': Parents of Children with Autism in SC Plead for Therapy," Greenville News, November 26, 2018, https://www.greenvilleonline.com/story/news/local/south-carolina /2018/11/26/parents-autistic-children-south-carolina-medicaid-rates-plea-help/1941335002/.

31. Jeremy Hsu, "Why Are There So Few Autism Specialists?" Spectrum, November 27, 2018, https://www .scientificamerican.com/article/why-are-there-so-few-autism-specialists/.

32. Eliza Gordon-Lipkin, Jessica Foster, and Georgina Peacock, "Whittling Down the Wait Time: Exploring Models to Minimize the Delay from Initial Concern to Diagnosis and Treatment of Autism Spectrum Disorder," Pediatric Clinics of North America 63, no. 5 (October 2016): 851–59, https://www.ncbi.nlm.nih.gov /pmc/articles/PMC5583718/.

33. Leib Sutcher, Linda Darling-Hammond, and Desiree Carver-Thomas, "A Coming Crisis in Teaching? Teacher Supply, Demand, and Shortages in the U.S.," Learning Policy Institute, September 2016, 5, https:// learningpolicyinstitute.org/sites/default/files/product-files/A_Coming_Crisis_in_Teaching_REPORT.pdf.

34. Martha Ross and Nicole Bateman, "Only Four out of Ten Working-Age Adults with Disabilities Are Employed," Brookings Institution, July 25, 2018, https://www.brookings.edu/blog/the-avenue/2018/07/25 /only-four-out-of-ten-working-age-adults-with-disabilities-are-employed/.

35. U.S. Department of Justice, "Prisoners and Prison Reentry," accessed November 10, 2019, https://www .justice.gov/archive/fbci/progmenu_reentry.html.

36. Author's estimate based on Bureau of Labor Statistics news release, "Worker Displacement: 2015–2017," August 28, 2018, https://www.bls.gov/news.release/disp.nr0.htm.

37. I use the phrase "navigator" because I think it best describes the jobs where people serve as intermediaries between employers and people struggling to connect—or reconnect—to employment and careers. Other names for such jobs are "job development specialist," "employment specialist," "job coach," "counselor," "adviser," etc. The precise roles may not be the same everywhere, but the point is that these are jobs that focus on assisting job seekers during at major steps in the job search process and closing trust gaps that might keep employers from giving potential workers the chance they deserve because of a perceived barrier. The work of such navigators can include not only the intermediary role with employers but also anything from helping people seeking employment decide on a target area for jobs and skills training, to accessing child care or transportation supports, to preparing for applications through mock interviews, to seeking treatment for mental and physical health conditions that can be barriers to employment, to filling out applications, to building connections with employers to place qualified job candidates, to having some necessary accommodations.

38. Skills for Chicagoland's Future, "2018 Impact Report: Bridging the Access Gap to Jobs," March 2019, https:// www.skillsforchicagolandsfuture.com/wp-content/uploads/2019/05/2018-Impact-Report-Skills _Updated_2-2.pdf.

39. New Growth Group, "Skills for Chicagoland's Future Evaluation Project 2017: Evaluation of a Demand Driven Workforce Solution," August 2017, http://www.newgrowthgroup.com/wp-content/uploads/2017/10 /1693-NGG-Chicagoland-Report-100317-1.pdf.

40. Elaine S. Povich, "States Focus on Long-Term Unemployed," Pew Charitable Trusts, Stateline, November 18, 2014, https://www.pewtrusts.org/en/research-and-analysis/blogs/stateline/2014/11/18/states-focus-on-long -term-unemployed.

41. SEDL (Southeast Educational Development Laboratory), "Guide to Effective Employment Programs: Vocational Rehabilitation Service Models for Individuals with Autism Spectrum Disorders," 2013, https://files .eric.ed.gov/fulltext/ED593042.pdf; and Triumph Services, "Work," accessed November 11, 2019, https:// triumphservices.org/programs/work/.

42. Brian Whitehead, "How the Center for Employment Opportunities in San Bernardino Gives Those on Probation or Parole a Second Shot," *San Bernardino Sun*, December 26, 2017, https://www.sbsun.com/2017/12/26/how-the-center-for-employment-opportunities-in-san-bernardino-gives-those-on-probation-or-parole-a-second-shot/.

43. Joseph Broadus, Sara Muller-Ravett, Arielle Sherman, and Cindy Redcross, "A Successful Prisoner Reentry Program Expands: Lessons from the Replication of the Center for Employment Opportunities," MDRC, January 2016, https://www.mdrc.org/sites/default/files/CEO-PrisonerReentryReport.pdf.

44. Whitehead, "How the Center for Employment Opportunities in San Bernardino Gives Those on Probation or Parole a Second Shot."

45. Gary W. Evans, Jeanne Brooks-Gunn, and Pamela Kato Klebanov, "Stressing Out the Poor: Chronic Physiological Stress and the Income-Achievement Gap," *Pathways*, winter 2011, https://inequality.stanford.edu/sites/default/files/PathwaysWinter11_Evans.pdf.

46. Elizabeth Caucutt, "The Real Reason Why Poor Kids Perform Worse in School—and in Life," *Washington Post*, April 28, 2015, https://www.washingtonpost.com/posteverything/wp/2015/04/28/the-real-reason-why-poor-kids-perform-worse-in-school-and-in-life/.

47. Lombardo, "With Hundreds of Students, School Counselors Just Try to 'Stay Afloat.'"

48. "School Psychology," American Psychological Association, accessed October 25, 2019, https://www.apa.org/ed/graduate/specialize/school.

49. Dana Goldstein, "It's More Than Pay: Striking Teachers Demand Counselors and Nurses," *New York Times*, October 24, 2019, https://www.nytimes.com/2019/10/24/us/chicago-strike-support-staff.html.

50. Edwin Rios, "The Teachers Striking in LA Won a Big Concession: More Nurses, Counselors, and Librarians," *Mother Jones*, January 22, 2019, https://www.motherjones.com/politics/2019/01/the-teachers-striking-in-la-won-a-big-concession-more-nurses-counselors-and-librarians/.

51. See Family Learning Institute, *Annual Report 2017–2018*, http://familylearninginstitute.org/wordpress/wp-content/uploads/2019/01/Annual-report-2017-18-final.pdf.

52. Elizabeth Birr Moje and Nicole Tysvaer, "Adolescent Literacy Development in Out-of-School Time: A Practitioner's Guidebook," Carnegie Corporation of New York's Council on Advancing Adolescent Literacy, 2010, https://production-carnegie.s3.amazonaws.com/filer_public/97/16/97164f61-a2c1-487c-b5fd-46a072a06c63/ccny_report_2010_tta_moje.pdf.

53. Alyson Klein, "Trump Wants to Ax After-School Funding. What Would Be Lost?" *Education Week*, May 15, 2018, https://www.edweek.org/ew/articles/2018/05/16/after-school-funding-remains-on-thin-ice.html.

54. Paul Osterman, *Who Will Care for Us?: Long-Term Care and the Long-Term Workforce* (New York: Russell Sage Foundation, 2017), 3.

55. Erica L. Reaves and MaryBeth Musumeci, "Medicaid and Long-Term Services and Supports: A Primer," Kaiser Family Foundation, December 15, 2015, https://www.kff.org/medicaid/report/medicaid-and-long-term-services-and-supports-a-primer/.

56. AARP, "Caregiving in the U.S. 2015 Report," June 2015, https://www.aarp.org/content/dam/aarp/ppi/2015/caregiving-in-the-united-states-2015-report-revised.pdf.

57. The direct care workers that provide long-term care services in homes, also known as the home care workforce, doubled in size over the past decade. Stephen Campbell, "U.S. Home Care Workers: Key Facts (2018)," PHI, August 31, 2018, https://phinational.org/resource/u-s-home-care-workers-key-facts-2018/; and Stephen Campbell, "New Research: 7.8 Million Direct Care Jobs Will Need to Be Filled by 2026," PHI, January 24, 2019, https://phinational.org/news/new-research-7-8-million-direct-care-jobs-will-need-to-be-filled-by-2026/.

58. Ai-jen Poo, *The Age of Dignity: Preparing for the Elder Boom in a Changing America* (New York: New Press, 2015), 5.

59. Steven L. Dawson, "The Direct Care Workforce—Raising the Floor of Job Quality," American Society on Aging, spring 2016, https://www.asaging.org/blog/direct-care-workforce-raising-floor-job-quality.

60. Angelina Drake, "How 'Upskilling' Can Maximize Home Care Workers' Contributions and Improve Serious Illness Care," *Health Affairs* (blog), March 4, 2019, https://www.healthaffairs.org/do/10.1377/hblog20190227.420595/full/.

61. Allison Cook, "Home Care Worker Training and People with Alzheimer's Disease and Related Dementias: Ideas for State Policymakers," PHI, November 2017, 3, https://phinational.org/wp-content/uploads/2017/11/Home-Care-Workers-and-Alzheimers-PHI-Nov-2017.pdf.

62. As of 2015. Cook, "Home Care Worker Training and People with Alzheimer's Disease and Related Dementias."

63. Drake, "How 'Upskilling' Can Maximize Home Care Workers' Contributions and Improve Serious Illness Care"; and Robert Holly, "Home Care Industry Turnover Reaches All-Time High of 82%," *Home Health Care News*, May 8, 2019, https://homehealthcarenews.com/2019/05/home-care-industry-turnover-reaches-all-time-high-of-82/.

64. California Long-Term Care Education Center (CLTCEC), "Care Team Integration and Training of Home Care Workers—Impact Study," May 2016, https://cltcec.org/wp-content/uploads/2019/02/CLTCEC-Home-Care-Integration-Training-Project-Brief.pdf.

65. CLTCEC, "Care Team Integration and Training of Home Care Workers."

66. Kezia Scales, "Success across Settings: Six Best Practices in Promoting Quality Care through Quality Jobs," PHI, August 21, 2017, https://phinational.org/wp-content/uploads/2017/09/evaluation_brief_final.pdf.

67. Drake, "How 'Upskilling' Can Maximize Home Care Workers' Contributions and Improve Serious Illness Care."

68. Lawrence H. Summers, "The Risk to Our Economy from Secular Stagnation," *Washington Post*, March 7, 2019, https://www.washingtonpost.com/opinions/2019/03/07/risk-our-economy-secular-stagnation/; and Lawrence Summers, "The Next President Should Make Infrastructure Spending a Priority," *Washington Post*, September 11, 2016, https://www.washingtonpost.com/opinions/whoever-wins-the-presidential-elec tion-must-make-infrastructure-spending-a-priority/2016/09/11/406ef0ee-76c2-11e6-b786-19d0cb1ed06c _story.html

69. For instance, see proposal from Senators Chris Van Hollen (D-MD.) and Ron Wyden (R-OR) to provide supports and subsidized employment (generally for one year) for the long-term unemployed. "Long-Term Unemployment Elimination Act," https://www.vanhollen.senate.gov/imo/media/doc/Van_Hollen_Long _Term_Unemployment_Pen_and_Pad.pdf.

70. Anne Roder and Mark Elliott, "Stimulating Opportunity: An Evaluation of ARRA-Funded Subsidized Employment Programs," Economic Mobility Corporation, September 2013, https://economicmobilitycorp.org /wp-content/uploads/2018/01/Stimulating-Opportunity-Report.pdf.

71. Indivar Dutta-Gupta, Kali Grant, Matthew Eckel, and Peter Edelman, "Lessons Learned from 40 Years of Subsidized Employment Programs," Georgetown Law Center on Poverty and Inequality, spring 2016, https://www.georgetownpoverty.org/wp-content/uploads/2016/07/GCPI-Subsidized-Employment-Paper -20160413.pdf.

CHAPTER FOURTEEN: CAN ALL WORK HAVE MEANING?

1. Studs Terkel, *Working: People Talk about What They Do All Day and How They Feel about What They Do* (New York: Ballantine, 1989), xiii.

2. P. R. Lockhart, "'A Man of Noble and Good Heart': Read Barack Obama's Eulogy for Elijah Cummings," *Vox*, October 25, 2019, https://www.vox.com/policy-and-politics/2019/10/25/20932171/elijah-cummings -funeral-barack-obama-eulogy-transcript.

3. Nozick defines meaningful work as work that includes "(1) an opportunity to exercise one's talents and capacities, to face challenges and situations that require independent initiative and self-direction (and which therefore is not boring and repetitive work); (2) in an activity thought to be of worth by the individual involved; (3) in which he understands the role his activity plays in the achievement of some overall goal; and (4) such that sometimes, in deciding upon his activity, he has to take into account something about the larger process in which he acts." Robert Nozick, *Anarchy, State, and Utopia* (New York: Basic Books, 1974), 247.

4. Nozick, *Anarchy, State, and Utopia*, 248.

5. Christopher Michaelson, Michael G. Pratt, Adam M. Grant, and Craig P. Dunn, "Meaningful Work: Connecting Business Ethics and Organizational Studies," *Journal of Business Ethics* 121, no. 1 (2014): 82, https:// faculty.wharton.upenn.edu/wp-content/uploads/2014/04/MichaelsonPrattGrantDunn_JBE2014.pdf?_ga= 2.149538228.348110159.1570997910-880676384.1570997910.

6. John Rawls, *A Theory of Justice* (Cambridge, MA: Harvard University Press, 1971), 529.

7. Norman Bowie, "A Kantian Theory of Meaningful Work," *Journal of Business Ethics* 17, no. 9/10 (1998): 1083, https://www.jstor.org/stable/25073937.

8. Arne L. Kalleberg and Peter V. Marsden, "Changing Work Values in the United States, 1973–2006," *Social Science Research* 42, no. 2 (2013): 263, https://reader.elsevier.com/reader/sd/pii/S0049089X12002153.

9. "How Much Meaning and Fulfillment Does Each of the Following Provide You?" Pew Research Center (table), July 11, 2018, https://www.pewforum.org/wp-content/uploads/sites/7/2018/11/Detailed-Tables-FOR -WEB.pdf.

10. Greg Kaplan and Sam Schulhofer-Wohl, "The Changing Dis-utility of Work," NBER Working Paper 24738, National Bureau of Economic Research, Cambridge, MA, June 2018, http://papers.nber.org/tmp/9013 -w24738.pdf.

11. Jim Harter, "Employee Engagement on the Rise in the U.S.," Gallup, August 26, 2018, https://news.gallup .com/poll/241649/employee-engagement-rise.aspx.

12. "How Americans View Their Jobs," Pew Research Center, October 6, 2016, https://www.pewsocialtrends .org/2016/10/06/3-how-americans-view-their-jobs/.

13. "How Americans View Their Jobs."

14. "How Americans View Their Jobs."

15. Nicole Maestas, Kathleen J. Mullen, David Powell, Till von Wachter, and Jeffrey B. Wenger, *Working Conditions in the United States: Results of the 2015 American Working Conditions Survey* (Santa Monica, CA: RAND Corporation, 2017), 46.

16. Michaelson et al., "Meaningful Work," 80.

17. Catherine Bailey and Adrian Madden, "What Makes Work Meaningful—or Meaningless," *MIT Sloane Management Review* (2016), accessed November 8, 2019, https://sloanreview.mit.edu/article/what-makes -work-meaningful-or-meaningless/.

18. Amy Wrzesniewski and Jane E. Dutton, "Crafting a Job: Revisioning Employees as Active Crafters of Their Work," *Academy of Management Review* 26, no. 2 (2001): 179, https://www.jstor.org/stable/pdf/259118.pdf.

19. Wrzesniewski and Dutton, "Crafting a Job," 193.

20. Amy Wrzesniewski, "How to Build a Better Job," interview by Shankar Vedantam, March 29, 2016, in *Hidden Brain*, podcast, 21:40, https://www.npr.org/templates/transcript/transcript.php?storyId=471859161.
21. Wrzesniewski, "How to Build a Better Job."
22. Wrzesniewski and Dutton, "Crafting a Job," 191, 193. Building on this work, Wrzesniewski and her coauthors later conducted a review of the existing literature on the meaning of work and identified seven categories of mechanisms that allow people to find meaning at work. The mechanisms include "authenticity," which occurs when work enables people to act consistently in accordance with their interests and values, self-efficacy, self-esteem, furthering a sense of purpose in life, having a sense of belongingness among others, and fostering "transcendence," which means subordinating the self to a larger group or entity. Brent D. Rosso, Kathryn H. Dekas, and Amy Wrzesniewski, "On the Meaning of Work: A Theoretical Integration and Review," *Research in Organizational Behavior* 30 (2010): 91–127, https://www.sciencedirect.com/science/article/abs/pii/S0191308510000067?via%3Dihub.
23. Terkel, *Working*, 225.
24. Charles Duhigg and Keith Bradsher, "How U.S. Lost Out on iPhone Work," *New York Times*, January 22, 2012, https://www.pulitzer.org/files/2013/explanatory-reporting/01ieconomy1-22.pdf.
25. Daisuke Wakabayashi, "Google's Shadow Work Force: Temps Who Outnumber Full-Time Employees," *New York Times*, May 28, 2019, https://www.nytimes.com/2019/05/28/technology/google-temp-workers.html.
26. Alexia Fernández Campbell, "Google's Contractors Accuse CEO of Creating Unequal Workforce," *Vox*, December 7, 2018, https://www.vox.com/2018/12/7/18128922/google-contract-workers-ceo-sundar-pichai; and Wakabayashi, "Google's Shadow Work Force."
27. David Weil, *The Fissured Workplace* (Cambridge, MA: Harvard University Press, 2014), 14.
28. Weil, *The Fissured Workplace*, 76.
29. Weil, *The Fissured Workplace*, 115.
30. Eduardo Porter, "Shaky Jobs, Sluggish Wages: Reasons Are at Home," *New York Times*, February 28, 2017, https://www.nytimes.com/2017/02/28/business/economy/economy-labor-wages-subcontracting.html.
31. Neil Irwin, "To Understand Rising Inequality, Consider the Janitors at Two Top Companies, Then and Now," *New York Times*, September 3, 2017, https://www.nytimes.com/2017/09/03/upshot/to-understand-rising-inequality-consider-the-janitors-at-two-top-companies-then-and-now.html.
32. Irwin, "To Understand Rising Inequality, Consider the Janitors at Two Top Companies."
33. Irwin, "To Understand Rising Inequality, Consider the Janitors at Two Top Companies."
34. David Weil, interview with Matthew Bidwell and Lauren Weber, "Is the Rise of Contract Workers Killing Upward Mobility?" *Knowledge@Wharton*, Wharton School of the University of Pennsylvania, podcast audio, October 2, 2017, https://knowledge.wharton.upenn.edu/article/the-perils-of-contract-workers/.
35. Áine Cain, "6 Incredible Perks for Apple Employees," *Inc.*, accessed November 8, 2019, https://www.inc.com/business-insider/apple-employee-benefits-perks-glassdoor.html.
36. Julia Carrie Wong, "Revealed: Google's 'Two-Tier' Workforce Training Document," *Guardian*, December 12, 2018, https://www.theguardian.com/technology/2018/dec/11/google-tvc-full-time-employees-training-document; and Lauren Weber, "The Second-Class Office Workers," *Wall Street Journal*, September 14, 2017, https://www.wsj.com/articles/the-contractors-life-overlooked-ground-down-and-stuck-1505400087.
37. Irwin, "To Understand Rising Inequality, Consider the Janitors at Two Top Companies."
38. Julia Carrie Wong, "Facebook Worker Living in Garage to Zuckerberg: Challenges Are Right Outside Your Door," *Guardian*, July 24, 2017, https://www.theguardian.com/technology/2017/jul/24/facebook-cafeteria-workers-wages-zuckerberg-challenges.
39. Weber, "The Second-Class Office Workers."
40. Robert D. Putnam, "*E Pluribus Unum*: Diversity and Community in the Twenty-First Century; the 2006 Johan Skytte Prize Lecture," *Scandinavian Political Studies* 30, no. 2 (2007): 137–38, http://www.puttingourdifferencestowork.com/pdf/j.1467-9477.2007.00176%20Putnam%20Diversity.pdf.
41. 26 U.S.C. § 401(a)(4); and Daniel Halperin and Alvin C. Warren, "Understanding Income Tax Deferral," *Tax Law Review* 317 (2014): 327–29, https://dash.harvard.edu/bitstream/handle/1/31740606/67TaxLRev317.pdf.
42. Weil, *The Fissured Workplace*, 193.
43. Emily Guendelsberger, *On the Clock: What Low-Wage Work Did to Me and How It Drives America Insane* (New York: Little, Brown, 2019), 11.
44. Guendelsberger, *On the Clock*, 7–8.
45. Guendelsberger, *On the Clock*, 6–7.
46. Michael Sainato, "'We Are Not Robots': Amazon Warehouse Employees Push to Unionize," *Guardian*, January 1, 2019, https://www.theguardian.com/technology/2019/jan/01/amazon-fulfillment-center-warehouse-employees-union-new-york-minnesota; and Noam Scheiber, "Inside an Amazon Warehouse, Robots' Ways Rub Off on Humans," *New York Times*, July 3, 2019, https://www.nytimes.com/2019/07/03/business/economy/amazon-warehouse-labor-robots.html.
47. Matthew Desmond, "American Capitalism Is Brutal; You Can Trace That to Slavery," *New York Times*, August 14, 2019, https://www.nytimes.com/interactive/2019/08/14/magazine/slavery-capitalism.html.
48. Studs Terkel and Gary Bryner, "'Working' Then and Now: 'I Didn't Plan to Be a Union Guy,'" *All Things Considered*, NPR, September 29, 2016, audio, https://www.npr.org/templates/transcript/transcript.php?storyId=495916035.

49. Lane Filler, "Minimum Wage: Henry Ford Didn't Pay $5 a Day Just to Be Nice," *Seattle Times*, December 20, 2013, https://www.seattletimes.com/opinion/minimum-wage-henry-ford-didnrsquot-pay-5-a-day-just-to-be-nice/.
50. Maria Godoy, "Dolores Huerta: The Civil Rights Icon Who Showed Farmworkers 'Sí Se Puede,'" *NPR*, September 17, 2017, https://www.npr.org/sections/thesalt/2017/09/17/551490281/dolores-huerta-the-civil-rights-icon-who-showed-farmworkers-si-se-puede.
51. John Oliver, "Warehouses," *Last Week Tonight with John Oliver*, YouTube video, 21:17, July 1, 2019, https://www.youtube.com/watch?v=d9m7d07k22A.
52. Oliver, "Warehouses."
53. Anne Helen Petersen, Twitter post, September 12, 2019, 10:13 a.m., https://twitter.com/annehelen/status/1172151182225096704.
54. "The Fairtrade Marks," Fairtrade International, accessed December 8, 2019, https://info.fairtrade.net/what/the-fairtrade-marks.
55. Robert Mayer, "Robert Dahl and the Right to Workplace Democracy," *Review of Politics* 63, no. 2 (2001): 231.
56. Khim L. Sim, Anthony J. Curatola, and Avijit Banerjee, "Lean Production Systems and Worker Satisfaction: A Field Study," *Advances in Business Research* 6 (2015): 80, http://journals.sfu.ca/abr/index.php/abr/article/viewFile/127/103.
57. Wrzesniewski, "How to Build a Better Job."

CHAPTER FIFTEEN: WORKER POWER

1. Joel Whitburn, *Hot Country Songs 1944 to 2008* (Record Research, 2009), 319.
2. Elizabeth Anderson, *Private Government: How Employers Rule Our Lives (and Why We Don't Talk about It)* (Princeton, NJ: Princeton University Press, 2017), 63.
3. "2007 Electronic Monitoring & Surveillance Survey," ePolicy Institute, February 28, 2008, http://www.epolicyinstitute.com/2007-survey-results.
4. Dan Levine, "Apple Defeats U.S. Class Action Lawsuit over Bag Searches," *Reuters*, November 7, 2015, https://www.reuters.com/article/us-apple-bags-ruling/apple-defeats-u-s-class-action-lawsuit-over-bag-searches-idUSKCN0SX03L20151108.
5. Anderson, *Private Government*, 63.
6. Anderson, *Private Government*, 49.
7. Gene B. Sperling, "Judicial Right Declaration and Entrenched Discrimination," *Yale Law Journal* 94, no. 7 (1985), https://digitalcommons.law.yale.edu/ylj/vol94/iss7/9; and Gene Sperling, "Does the Supreme Court Matter?" *American Prospect*, December 5, 2000, https://prospect.org/justice/supreme-court-matter/.
8. "The Gender Pay Gap by the Numbers," Lean In, accessed January 19, 2020, https://leanin.org/equal-pay-data-about-the-gender-pay-gap#endnote3.
9. "The Wage Gap for Black Women: Working Longer and Making Less," National Women's Law Center, August 19, 2019, https://nwlc.org/resources/the-wage-gap-for-black-women-working-longer-and-making-less; and "Equal Pay for Latinas," National Women's Law Center, November 13, 2019, https://nwlc.org/resources/equal-pay-for-latinas.
10. *Meritor Savings Bank v. Vinson*, 477 U.S. 57 (1986).
11. Augustus B. Cochran, *Sexual Harassment and the Law: The Mechelle Vinson Case* (Lawrence: University Press of Kansas, 2004), 168.
12. "60% of U.S. Women Say They've Been Sexually Harassed Quinnipiac University National Poll Finds; Trump Job Approval Still Stuck Below 40%," Quinnipiac University, November 21, 2017, https://poll.qu.edu/national/release-detail?ReleaseID=2502.
13. Catharine A. MacKinnon, "#MeToo Has Done What the Law Could Not," *New York Times*, February 4, 2018, https://www.nytimes.com/2018/02/04/opinion/metoo-law-legal-system.html.
14. Frederick Douglass, *Life and Times of Frederick Douglass* (Boston: De Wolfe, Fiske, 1895), 667.
15. Adam Liptak, "Supreme Court to Decide Whether Landmark Civil Rights Law Applies to Gay and Transgender Workers," *New York Times*, April 22, 2019, https://www.nytimes.com/2019/04/22/us/politics/supreme-court-gay-transgender-employees.html.
16. 42 U.S.C. § 2000e(b).
17. *Adair v. United States*, 208 U. S. 161, 174 (1908).
18. Elizabeth Tandy Shermer, "The Right to Work Really Means the Right to Work for Less," *Washington Post*, April 24, 2018, https://www.washingtonpost.com/news/made-by-history/wp/2018/04/24/the-right-to-work-really-means-the-right-to-work-for-less.
19. Joseph Stiglitz, "Inequality, Stagnation, and Market Power: The Need for a New Progressive Era" (working paper, Roosevelt Institute, Washington, DC, November 2017), https://rooseveltinstitute.org/wp-content/uploads/2018/01/Inequality-Stagnation-and-Market-Power.pdf; and Jason Furman and Peter Orszag, "A Firm-Level Perspective on the Role of Rents in the Rise in Inequality," (presentation, "A Just Society," Centennial Event in Honor of Joseph Stiglitz, Columbia University, New York, October 16, 2015), http://tankona.free.fr/furmanorszag15.pdf.
20. Council of Economic Advisers, "Labor Market Monopsony: Trends, Consequences, and Policy Reponses," October 2016, https://obamawhitehouse.archives.gov/sites/default/files/page/files/20161025_monopsony

_labor_mrkt_cea.pdf; and Jason Furman, "Beyond Antitrust: The Role of Competition Policy in Promoting Inclusive Growth," (remarks, Searle Center Conference on Antitrust Economics and Competition Policy, Chicago, September 16, 2016), https://obamawhitehouse.archives.gov/sites/default/files/page/files/20160916_searle_conference_competition_furman_cea.pdf.

21. Joseph Stiglitz, "Competition and Consumer Protection in the 21st Century: Opening Address," Federal Trade Commission, September 21, 2018, 30, https://www.ftc.gov/system/files/documents/public_events/1408208/ftc_hearings_session_2_transcript_9-21-18_0.pdf.

22. *Epic Systems Corp. v. Lewis*, 584 U.S. ___ (2018), slip op. at 15 (Ginsburg, J., dissenting).

23. "Union Members Summary," Bureau of Labor Statistics, January 18, 2019, https://www.bls.gov/news.release/union2.nr0.htm.

24. OECD, *OECD Employment Outlook 2018* (Paris: OECD Publishing, 2018), 101.

25. "No Relief: Denial of Bathroom Breaks in the Poultry Industry," Oxfam America, May 9, 2016, https://www.oxfamamerica.org/static/media/files/No_Relief_Embargo.pdf.

26. Gerald Mayer, *Union Membership Trends in the United States*, CRS Report RL32553 (Washington, DC: Congressional Research Service, August 31, 2004), 12.

27. "Union Members Summary."

28. Bruce Western and Jake Rosenfeld, "Unions, Norms, and the Rise in U.S. Wage Inequality," *American Sociological Review* 76, no. 4 (2011): 513–37.

29. "Employer/Union Rights and Obligations," National Labor Relations Board, accessed November 10, 2019, https://www.nlrb.gov/rights-we-protect/rights/employer-union-rights-and-obligations.

30. Kate Bronfenbrenner, "No Holds Barred: The Intensification of Employer Opposition to Organizing," Economic Policy Institute, May 20, 2009, https://www.epi.org/files/page/-/pdf/bp235.pdf.

31. Department of Labor, Office of Labor-Management Standards, "Labor-Management Reporting and Disclosure Act; Interpretation of the 'Advice' Exemption," *Federal Register* 76, no. 119 (June 21, 2011): 36186.

32. Josh Eidelson, "Boeing Workers' Vote Wednesday Could Be an 'Earthquake in the South,'" *Bloomberg News*, February 14, 2017, https://www.bloomberg.com/news/articles/2017-02-14/boeing-floods-airwaves-in-south-carolina-union-grudge-match.

33. In the more serious works council structures in Germany, the employer must either agree with the works council or convince a neutral tribunal to accept the recommendation. David Rolf, *A Roadmap to Rebuilding Worker Power* (Century Foundation, 2018), 47, https://production-tcf.imgix.net/app/uploads/2018/07/08103822/DavidRolf_All.pdf.

34. Because existing law imagines a more combative relationship between management and labor, changes to federal labor law may be required to institute widespread works councils in the U.S. The NLRA makes it illegal for an employer to "dominate or interfere with the formation or administration of any labor organization or contribute financial or other support to it." 29 U.S.C. § 158(a)(2). The goal of this restriction is to avoid employers taking advantage of workers by exerting undue influence over the union. However, this restriction also means collaborative efforts such as works councils would need to be part of a collective-bargaining agreement between an employer and a union.

35. Lydia DePillis, "Why Volkswagen Is Helping a Union Organize Its Own Plant," *Washington Post*, February 10, 2014, https://www.washingtonpost.com/news/wonk/wp/2014/02/10/why-volkswagen-is-helping-a-union-organize-its-own-plant/; and Mica Rosenberg, "UAW Wants Works Council with 'Tennessee Flavor' at VW Plant," *Reuters*, December 9, 2014, https://www.reuters.com/article/us-autos-volkswagen-uaw/uaw-wants-works-council-with-tennessee-flavor-at-vw-plant-idUSKBN0JN29H20141209.

36. Justin King, "King: Having a Voice—VW Worker Supports UAW," *Chattanooga Times Free Press*, February 11, 2014, https://www.timesfreepress.com/news/opinion/columns/story/2014/feb/11/king-having-voice-vw-worker-supports-uaw/131415.

37. Bill Chappell, "Tenn. VW Workers Reject Move to Join Union," *NPR*, February 14, 2014, https://www.npr.org/sections/thetwo-way/2014/02/14/277105945/tenn-vw-workers-reject-move-to-join-union.

38. Chris Brooks, "Why the UAW Lost Another Election in Tennessee," *Nation*, June 19, 2019, https://www.thenation.com/article/uaw-works-council-tennessee-union-volkswagen; Chris Brooks, "Volkswagen Declares War against Works Council and German Union," *Labor Notes*, June 12, 2019, https://www.labornotes.org/blogs/2019/06/volkswagen-declares-war-against-works-council-and-german-union; and Noam Schreiber, "Volkswagen Factory Workers in Tennessee Reject Union," *New York Times*, June 14, 2019, https://www.nytimes.com/2019/06/14/business/economy/volkswagen-chattanooga-uaw-union.html.

39. Jeffrey M. Jones, "As Labor Day Turns 125, Union Approval Near 50-Year High," Gallup, August 28, 2019, https://news.gallup.com/poll/265916/labor-day-turns-125-union-approval-near-year-high.aspx.

40. Shiva Maniam, "Most Americans See Labor Unions, Corporations Favorably," Pew Research Center, January 30, 2017, https://www.pewresearch.org/fact-tank/2017/01/30/most-americans-see-labor-unions-corporations-favorably/.

41. "A Growing Number of Americans Want to Join a Union," *PBS NewsHour*, September 3, 2018, https://www.pbs.org/newshour/nation/a-growing-number-of-americans-want-to-join-a-union.

42. Christine Hauser, "West Virginia Teachers, Protesting Low Pay, Walk Out," *New York Times*, February 23, 2018, https://www.nytimes.com/2018/02/23/us/west-virginia-teachers-strike.html.

43. Ryan Quinn, "Thousands of School Employees Converge on Capitol amid Work Stoppage," *Charleston Gazette-Mail*, February 22, 2018, https://www.wvgazettemail.com/news/education/teachers-walk-out -across-west-virginia-over-pay-benefits/article_b98c221e-5eb0-5dea-8a8a-152e24138634.html.

44. Dana Goldstein, "West Virginia Teachers Walk Out (Again) and Score a Win in Hours," *New York Times*, February 19, 2018, https://www.nytimes.com/2019/02/19/us/teachers-strikes.html.

45. Samantha Winslow, "Marriott Hotel Strikers Set a New Industry Standard," *Labor Notes*, December 20, 2018, https://labornotes.org/2018/12/marriott-hotel-strikers-set-new-industry-standard.

46. Richard L. Trumka, "Trumka on New NAFTA at Maryland/DC AFL-CIO Convention: We Are Not There Yet," AFL-CIO, November 18, 2019, https://aflcio.org/speeches/trumka-new-nafta-marylanddc-afl-cio -convention-we-are-not-there-yet.

47. "H.R.2474—Protecting the Right to Organize Act of 2019," Congress.gov, accessed December 8, 2019, https://www.congress.gov/bill/116th-congress/house-bill/2474/cosponsors.

48. Leo Gerard, "The PRO Act: Pathway to Power for Workers," *Common Dreams*, May 15, 2019, https://www .commondreams.org/views/2019/05/15/pro-act-pathway-power-workers.

49. Lehigh Valley Coal Co. v. Yensavage, 218 F. 547, 552 (2d Cir. 1914).

50. Kate Holton and Jane Lanhee Lee, "Uber Drivers Go on Strike in London and U.S. Ahead of IPO, Early Protests Sparse," *Reuters*, May 8, 2019, https://www.reuters.com/article/us-uber-ipo-strike/uber-drivers -go-on-strike-in-london-and-u-s-ahead-of-ipo-early-protests-sparse-idUSKCN1SE0A5.

51. Alejandro Lazo, "California Enacts Law to Classify Some Gig Workers as Employees," *Wall Street Journal*, updated September 18, 2019, https://www.wsj.com/articles/california-enacts-law-to-classify -some-gig-workers-as-employees-11568831719.

52. Lazo, "California Enacts Law to Classify Some Gig Workers as Employees."

53. Quentin R. Skrabec Jr., *The 100 Most Significant Events in American Business: An Encyclopedia* (Santa Barbara, CA: Greenwood, 2012), 206.

54. Mark Barenberg, "Widening the Scope of Worker Organizing: Legal Reforms to Facilitate Multi-employer Organizing, Bargaining, and Striking," Roosevelt Institute, October 7, 2015, 1, 3, http://rooseveltinstitute .org/wp-content/uploads/2015/10/Widening-the-Scope-of-Worker-Organizing.pdf.

55. *Artcraft Displays, Inc.*, 262 N.L.R.B. 1233 (1982), clarified by 263 N.L.R.B. 804 (1982).

56. 29 U.S.C. § 158(b)(4); *Kroger Co.*, 148 N.L.R.B. 569 (1964). Recently, there has been hope of evolution: in a 2015 decision, the NLRB held that "two or more statutory employers are joint employers of the same statutory employees if they 'share or codetermine those matters governing the essential terms and conditions of employment.'" *Browning-Ferris*, 362 N.L.R.B. No. 186, at 2, 15 (quoting *NLRB v. Browning-Ferris Indus. of Pa., Inc.*, 691 F.2d 1117, 1123 [3d Cir. 1982]). This more worker-friendly standard allows the indirect employer to be a "joint employer" if it has the right to control the workers or exercises control indirectly. However, this advance is under threat: in 2018, the Trump administration proposed a new regulation that would override the *Browning-Ferris* decision. National Labor Relations Board, "The Standard for Determining Joint-Employer Status," *Federal Register* 83, no. 179 (September 14, 2018): 46681–97.

57. Christopher L. Erickson, "A Re-interpretation of Pattern Bargaining," *Industrial and Labor Relations Review* 49, no. 4 (1996): 615–34.

58. Kim Moody, "A Pattern of Retreat: The Decline of Pattern Bargaining," *Labor Notes*, February 16, 2010, https://labornotes.org/2010/02/pattern-retreat-decline-pattern-bargaining.

59. Neal E. Boudette, "G.M. and U.A.W. Reach Deal That Could End Strike," *New York Times*, October 16, 2019, https://www.nytimes.com/2019/10/16/business/gm-uaw-strike.html.

60. Nathaniel Meyersohn, "Why 47,000 Grocery Workers in California May Go on Strike," *CNN Business*, September 5, 2019, https://www.cnn.com/2019/09/05/business/ralphs-albertsons-vons-california-grocery -workers-ufcw/index.html.

61. Meyersohn, "Why 47,000 Grocery Workers in California May Go on Strike"; and Michael Arria, "The Next Wave of Labor Unrest Could Be in Grocery Stores," *Salon*, September 15, 2019, https://www.salon.com /2019/09/15/the-next-wave-of-labor-unrest-could-be-in-grocery-stores_partner.

62. L. Fulton, "Collective Bargaining," *Worker Representation in Europe*, Labour Research Department and ETUI, 2013,http://www.worker-participation.eu/National-Industrial-Relations/Countries/Sweden/Collective -Bargaining.

63. Kalena Thomhave, "Fighting for $15—and a Union," *American Prospect*, October 16, 2018, https://prospect .org/article/fighting-15-and-union; and Steven Greenhouse, "In Drive to Unionize, Fast-Food Workers Walk Off the Job," *New York Times*, November 28, 2012, https://www.nytimes.com/2012/11/29/nyregion /drive-to-unionize-fast-food-workers-opens-in-ny.html.

64. Arun Gupta, "Fight for 15 Confidential: How Did the Biggest-Ever Mobilization of Fast-Food Workers Come About, and What Is Its Endgame?" *In These Times*, November 11, 2013, http://inthesetimes.com /article/15826/fight_for_15_confidential.

65. Alexia Elejalde-Ruiz, "'This Is an Ongoing Battle.' Workers at the Forefront of the Fight for $15 Relish Minimum Wage Victory, Press On for Union Rights," *Chicago Tribune*, February 22, 2019, https://www.chica gotribune.com/business/ct-biz-fight-for-15-victory-illinois-20190221-story.html.

66. Steven Greenhouse, "With Day of Protests, Fast-Food Workers Seek More Pay," *New York Times*, November 29, 2012, http://www.nytimes.com/2012/11/30/nyregion/fast-food-workers-in-new-york-city-rally-for -higher-wages.html.

67. Greenhouse, "With Day of Protests."
68. Erika Eichelberger, "How Those Fast-Food Strikes Got Started," *Mother Jones*, December 5, 2013, http://www.motherjones.com/politics/2013/12/how-fast-food-strikes-started.
69. Lydia DePillis, "It's Not Just Fast Food: The Fight for $15 Is for Everyone Now," *Washington Post*, December 4, 2014, https://www.washingtonpost.com/news/storyline/wp/2014/12/04/its-not-just-fast-food-the-fight-for-15-is-for-everyone-now.
70. Laura Shin, "Fight for a $15 Minimum Wage Spreads to New Industries, 190 Cities," *Forbes*, December 4, 2014, https://www.forbes.com/sites/laurashin/2014/12/04/fight-for-a-15-minimum-wage-spreads-to-new-industries-190-cities.
71. Chris Marr, "States with $15 Minimum Wage Laws Doubled This Year," *Bloomberg Law*, May 23, 2019, https://news.bloomberglaw.com/daily-labor-report/states-with-15-minimum-wage-laws-doubled-this-year.
72. Adam Janos, "When Millions of Americans Stopped Eating Grapes in Support of Farm Workers," History (website), last modified May 8, 2019, https://www.history.com/news/delano-grape-strike-united-farm-workers-filipinos.
73. Steven V. Roberts, "26 Grape Growers Sign Union Accord; Boycott Nears End," *New York Times*, July 30, 1970, https://www.nytimes.com/1970/07/30/archives/26-grape-growers-sign-union-accord-boycott-nears-end-26-grape.html.
74. Maureen Pao, "Cesar Chavez: The Life behind a Legacy of Farm Labor Rights," *NPR*, August 12, 2016, https://www.npr.org/2016/08/02/488428577/cesar-chavez-the-life-behind-a-legacy-of-farm-labor-rights.
75. "Union Affiliation of Employed Wage and Salary Workers by Occupation and Industry," Bureau of Labor Statistics, table 3, last modified January 18, 2019, https://www.bls.gov/news.release/union2.t03.htm.
76. Gosia Wozniacka, "Less Than 1 Percent of US Farmworkers Belong to a Union. Here's Why," *Civil Eats*, May 7, 2019, https://civileats.com/2019/05/07/less-than-1-percent-of-us-farmworkers-belong-to-a-union-heres-why.
77. "Worker-Driven Social Responsibility (WSR): A New Idea for a New Century," Coalition of Immokalee Workers, June 16, 2014, https://ciw-online.org/blog/2014/06/wsr.
78. Steven Greenhouse, *Beaten Down, Worked Up: The Past, Present, and Future of American Labor* (New York: Alfred A. Knopf, 2019), 262–64.
79. "New York," National Domestic Workers Alliance, accessed November 10, 2019, https://www.domesticworkers.org/bill-of-rights/new-york.
80. Alexia Fernández Campbell, "Kamala Harris Just Introduced a Bill to Give Housekeepers Overtime Pay and Meal Breaks," *Vox*, July 15, 2019, https://www.vox.com/2019/7/15/20694610/kamala-harris-domestic-workers-bill-of-rights-act.
81. Rebecca Smith, "Seattle Passes Historic Domestic Worker Bill of Rights," National Employment Law Project, July 26, 2018, https://www.nelp.org/blog/seattle-passes-historic-domestic-worker-bill-of-rights.
82. Roselyn Miller, "Seattle Considers a Domestic Workers Bill of Rights," *Slate*, June 29, 2018, https://slate.com/human-interest/2018/06/domestic-workers-bill-of-rights-in-seattle-is-most-progressive-attempt-at-protection-yet.html.
83. Anna Orso, "Philly to Expand Rights for Housekeepers and Nannies, Including Requiring a Contract and Paid Leave," *Philadelphia Inquirer*, October 31, 2019, https://www.inquirer.com/news/philadelphia-city-council-approves-domestic-worker-bill-of-rights-house-cleaners-nannies-20191031.html.
84. Lynn Thompson and Amy Martinez, "Seattle City Council Approves Historic $15 Minimum Wage," *Seattle Times*, published June 2, 2014, updated January 25, 2016, https://www.seattletimes.com/seattle-news/seattle-city-council-approves-historic-15-minimum-wage.
85. Kate Andrias, "The New Labor Law," *Yale Law Journal* 126, no. 1 (2016): 68.
86. Kate Andrias and Brishen Rogers, "Rebuilding Worker Voice in Today's Economy," Roosevelt Institute, August 2018, https://rooseveltinstitute.org/wp-content/uploads/2018/07/Rebuilding-Worker-Voices-final-2.pdf.
87. "Welcome," Alliance of Motion Picture and Television Producers, accessed November 10, 2019, https://www.amptp.org/index.html.
88. Federal Rules of Civil Procedure 23.
89. Kate Conger, "Sexual Harassment Lawsuit against Google Might Proceed as Class Action," *Gizmodo*, March 27, 2018, https://gizmodo.com/sexual-harassment-lawsuit-against-google-might-proceed-1824132680.
90. Katherine V. W. Stone and Alexander J. S. Colvin, "The Arbitration Epidemic," Economic Policy Institute, December 7, 2015, https://www.epi.org/publication/the-arbitration-epidemic.
91. Conger, "Sexual Harassment Lawsuit against Google Might Proceed as Class Action."
92. Alexander J. S. Colvin, "The Growing Use of Mandatory Arbitration," Economic Policy Institute, April 6, 2018, https://www.epi.org/publication/the-growing-use-of-mandatory-arbitration-access-to-the-courts-is-now-barred-for-more-than-60-million-american-workers.
93. Jon O. Shimabukuro and Jennifer A. Staman, *Mandatory Arbitration and the Federal Arbitration Act*, CRS Report R44960 (Washington, DC: Congressional Research Service, September 20, 2017), 1.
94. *Gilmer v. Interstate/Johnson Lane Corp.*, 500 U.S. 20 (1991).
95. *American Express Co. v. Italian Colors Restaurant*, 570 U.S. 228 (2013); and *AT&T Mobility LLC v. Concepcion*, 563 U.S. 333 (2011).

96. *Epic Systems Corp. v. Lewis*, 584 U.S. ___ (2018). At issue was the enforceability of class-action waivers in mandatory employer arbitration agreements. Workers at multiple companies claimed that enforcing arbitration clauses that barred class-actions was a violation of Section 7 of the NLRA, which guarantees workers "the right to self-organization, to form, join, or assist labor organizations, to bargain collectively through representatives of their own choosing, and to engage in concerted activities for the purpose of collective bargaining or other mutual aid or protection." 29 U.S.C. § 157. The workers argued that "concerted activities" includes joining together claims in arbitration or in court.

97. *Epic Systems Corp. v. Lewis*, 584 U.S. ___ (2018), slip op. at 17 (Ginsburg, J., dissenting).

98. *Pollock v. Williams*, 322 U.S. 4, 17–18 (1944).

99. 8 U.S.C. § 1101(a)(15)(H)(ii)(a).

100. 20 C.F.R. § 655.1310(b).

101. Gosia Wozniacka, "The H-2A Guest Worker Program Has Ballooned in Size, but Both Farmers and Workers Want It Fixed," *Civil Eats*, July 16, 2019, https://civileats.com/2019/07/16/the-h-2a-guest-worker-program-has-ballooned-in-size-but-both-farmers-and-workers-want-it-fixed.

102. U.S. Government Accountability Office, *H-2A and H-2B Visa Programs: Increased Protections Needed for Foreign Workers*, GAO-15-154 (Washington, DC: GAO, March 2015), 37–38, https://www.gao.gov/assets/690/684985.pdf.

103. Jennifer J. Lee and Kyle Endres, "Overworked and Underpaid: H-2A Herders in Colorado," Colorado Legal Services, January 14, 2010, https://humantraffickinghotline.org/sites/default/files/Overworked%20and%20Underpaid%20-%20CLS.pdf.

104. Jacob Ripple-Carpenter, "The Resolute Shepherd," *Denver Voice*, January 1, 2010, https://www.denvervoice.org/archive/2010/1/1/feature-the-resolute-shepherd.html.

105. Daniel Costa, "H-1B Visa Needs Reform to Make It Fairer to Migrant and American Workers," Economic Policy Institute, April 5, 2017, https://www.epi.org/publication/h-1b-visa-needs-reform-to-make-it-fairer-to-migrant-and-american-workers.

106. Farah Stockman, "Teacher Trafficking: The Strange Saga of Filipino Workers, American Schools, and H-1B Visas," *Boston Globe*, June 12, 2013, https://www.bostonglobe.com/editorials/2013/06/11/your-child-teacher-victim-human-trafficking/dQz2fYPwg6Xkgt1aV6HaiL/story.html.

107. Stockman, "Teacher Trafficking."

108. U.S. Department of Labor, "U.S. Department of Labor Investigation Recovers $173,044 in Wages for 12 Technology Employees Due to Violations of the H-1B Visa Program," news release, May 1, 2018, https://www.dol.gov/newsroom/releases/whd/whd20180501-2.

109. Maria L. Ontiveros, "H-1B Visas, Outsourcing and Body Shops: A Continuum of Exploitation for High Tech Workers," *Berkeley Journal of Employment & Labor Law* 38, no. 1 (March 2017): 43–44.

110. Matt Marx, "The Firm Strikes Back: Non-compete Agreements and the Mobility of Technical Professionals," *American Sociological Review* 76, no. 5 (October 2011): 695–712.

111. Dave Jamieson, "Jimmy John's Makes Low-Wage Workers Sign 'Oppressive' Noncompete Agreements," *Huffington Post*, October 13, 2014, https://www.huffpost.com/entry/jimmy-johns-non-compete_n_5978180?1413230622.

112. Sarah Whitten, "Jimmy John's Drops Noncompete Clauses following Settlement," *CNBC*, June 22, 2016, https://www.cnbc.com/2016/06/22/jimmy-johns-drops-non-compete-clauses-following-settlement.html.

113. Research by University of Maryland professor Evan Starr and University of Michigan professors J. J. Prescott and Norman Bishara has found 14 percent of workers without a bachelor's degree are currently covered by noncompetes. Evan Starr, J. J. Prescott, and Norman Bishara, "Noncompetes in the U.S. Labor Force," University of Michigan Law and Econ Research Paper No. 18-013, University of Michigan Law School, Ann Arbor, MI, August 30, 2019, last modified September 2, 2019, https://papers.ssrn.com/sol3/papers.cfm?abstract_id=2625714. A study by the *Wall Street Journal* found that the number of workers sued by employers for a breach of a noncompete increased 61 percent between 2002 and 2013. Ruth Simon and Angus Loten, "Litigation over Noncompete Clauses Is Rising," *Wall Street Journal*, August 14, 2013, https://www.wsj.com/articles/litigation-over-noncompete-clauses-is-rising-does-entrepreneurship-suffer-1376520622. While courts have traditionally taken the view that noncompetes are enforceable only if they are "reasonable"—because many workers are not aware of their legal rights and cannot afford a lawyer to defend themselves—the threat of litigation alone can have a chilling effect. Courts therefore do not always enforce noncompete clauses that cover too long a time period, too broad a geographic region, or are too expansive in their definition of what counts as a competitor. Alan B. Krueger and Eric A. Posner, "A Proposal for Protecting Low-Income Workers from Monopsony and Collusion," Hamilton Project, February 2018, 10, https://www.hamiltonproject.org/assets/files/protecting_low_income_workers_from_monopsony_collusion_krueger_posner_pp.pdf. Differences in legal rights can have an outsize impact on wages. A 2016 study by the U.S. Department of Treasury found that states with strict enforcement of noncompete agreements typically have lower wages than states with lenient enforcement, which translates to a 5 percent reduction in pay for a twenty-five-year-old worker and a 10 percent reduction for a typical fifty-year-old worker. U.S. Department of Treasury, Office of Economic Policy, *Non-compete Contracts: Economic Effects and Policy Implications*, March 2016, 20, https://www.treasury.gov/resource-center/economic-policy/Documents/UST%20Non-competes%20Report.pdf.

114. Alan B. Krueger and Eric Posner, "Corporate America Is Suppressing Wages for Many Workers," *New York Times*, February 28, 2018, https://www.nytimes.com/2018/02/28/opinion/corporate-america-suppressing -wages.html.

115. 29 C.F.R. § 531.52.

116. Dana Hatic, "How Restaurants Get Away with Stealing Millions from Workers Every Year," *Eater*, September 25, 2018, https://www.eater.com/2018/9/25/17886990/how-restaurants-steal-from-workers-wage -theft.

117. Annette Bernhardt, Ruth Milkman, and Nik Theodore, "Broken Laws, Unprotected Workers: Violations of Employment and Labor Laws in America's Cities," National Employment Law Project, September 21, 2009, https://www.nelp.org/publication/broken-laws-unprotected-workers-violations-of-employment -and-labor-laws-in-americas-cities.

118. Heidi Shierholz, "Combating Inequality Conference: Labor Market Tools," filmed October 18, 2019 at Combating Inequality: Rethinking Policies to Reduce Inequality in Advanced Economies, Washington, DC, video, 36:32, https://www.youtube.com/watch?v=UbVuopuFJkw.

119. When deciding whether to raise rates, the Fed should consider the potential costs of a mistake in either direction. Gene B. Sperling, "Fed, Don't Raise Rates Yet!," *Politico*, September 9, 2015, https://www.politico .com/magazine/story/2015/09/federal-reserve-interest-rate-213132.

120. Jason Furman, "The Fifth Anniversary of the American Recovery and Reinvestment Act," Obama White House (blog), February 7, 2014, https://obamawhitehouse.archives.gov/blog/2014/02/17/fifth-anniversary -american-recovery-and-reinvestment-act.

121. Dean Baker and Jared Bernstein, *Getting Back to Full Employment: A Better Bargain for Working People* (Washington, DC: Center for Economic and Policy Research, 2013), 56, http://cepr.net/documents/Getting -Back-to-Full-Employment_20131118.pdf. Additionally, a recent study by Josh Bivens and Ben Zipperer of the Economic Policy Institute finds that a 1 percentage point decline in unemployment raises 10th percentile real wages by about 0.5 percent, median real wages by 0.4 percent, and 90th percentile wages by 0.3 percent. A percentage point decline in unemployment raises annual hours by 2.7 percent for African American households. Josh Bivens and Ben Zipperer, "The Importance of Locking in Full Employment for the Long Haul," Economic Policy Institute, August 21, 2018, https://www.epi.org/publication/the -importance-of-locking-in-full-employment-for-the-long haul.

122. Jared Bernstein and Keith Bentele, "The Increasing Benefits and Diminished Costs of Running a High-Pressure Labor Market," Center on Budget and Policy Priorities, May 15, 2019, https://www.cbpp.org /research/full-employment-the-increasing-benefits-and-diminished-costs-of-running-a-high-pressure. Real wages of workers in the bottom quintile grow 2.3 percent in tight labor markets but fall 3.9 percent in slack labor markets—a difference of 6.1 percentage points—with the biggest effects at the bottom of the income distribution. Even greater gains in tight labor markets are observed for low-income single mothers (13 percentage points) and low-income black households (7.9 percentage points) compared to 2.2 percentage points for low-income white households. Tight labor markets have also made significant contributions to wage growth for prime-age, non-college-educated workers, with tight labor markets accounting up to half of wage growth for men and up to one-third of wage growth for women.

123. Gene Sperling, "The US Labour Market Bears Deep Scars from the Financial Crisis," *Financial Times*, December 8, 2014, https://www.ft.com/content/9e843c48-7eb7-11e4-b83e-00144feabdc0.

124. Janet L. Yellen, "Former Fed Chair Janet Yellen on Why the Answer to the Inflation Puzzle Matters," Brookings Institution, October 3, 2019, https://www.brookings.edu/research/former-fed-chair-janet -yellen-on-why-the-answer-to-the-inflation-puzzle-matters.

125. Benjamin Stone, "Fiscal Policies and Full Employment: An Interview with Jared Bernstein," *Chicago Policy Review*, September 19, 2013, https://chicagopolicyreview.org/2013/09/19/fiscal-policies-and-full -employment-an-interview-with-jared-bernstein.

CHAPTER SIXTEEN: WORKER POTENTIAL

1. For example, Katz recently stated that "in the short run, the institutional things will have a bigger impact on inequality—taxes, regulatory, and worker power—but over the long haul, education is going to be a very big part of any solution." "Combating Inequality: Rethinking Policies to Reduce Inequality in Advanced Economies," Peterson Institute for International Economics Conference, October 17, 2019, video, 5:07:50, https://www.piie.com/events/combating-inequality-rethinking-policies-reduce-inequality-advanced -economies.

2. Paul Krugman, "Jobs and Skills Zombies," *New York Times*, March 30, 2014, https://www.nytimes.com /2014/03/31/opinion/krugman-jobs-and-skills-zombies.html.

3. Jay Shambaugh and Ryan Nunn, eds., *Revitalizing Wage Growth: Policies to Get American Workers a Raise* (Washington, DC: Hamilton Project, 2018), 26, fig. 1, https://www.brookings.edu/wp-content/uploads /2018/02/es_2272018_revitalizing_wage_growth_full_book.pdf.

4. In 2015, the unemployment rate for college graduates ages twenty-five to thirty-four was 2 percent, compared to 8.4 percent for high school graduates, for example. David Leonhardt, "College for the Masses," *New York Times*, April 24, 2015, https://www.nytimes.com/2015/04/26/upshot/college-for-the-masses.html.

5. Kevin Drum, "Chart of the Day: The College Wage Premium over Time," *Mother Jones*, August 9, 2019, https:// www.motherjones.com/kevin-drum/2019/08/chart-of-the-day-the-college-wage-premium-over-time/.

6. Census data for 2018. Note this appears to be the official poverty rate, not the Supplemental Poverty Measure. "Poverty Status in 2018," United States Census Bureau, accessed November 1, 2019, https://www.census.gov/data/tables/time-series/demo/income-poverty/cps-pov/pov-29.html#par_textimage_10.

7. "Education and Lifetime Earnings," Research, Statistics & Policy Analysis, Social Security Administration, November 2015, https://www.ssa.gov/policy/docs/research-summaries/education-earnings.html.

8. Tim Bartik and Brad Hershbein, "College Does Help the Poor," *New York Times*, May 23, 2018, https://www.nytimes.com/2018/05/23/opinion/college-does-help-the-poor.html.

9. Diane Whitmore Schanzenbach, Lauren Bauer, and Audrey Breitwieser, *Eight Economic Facts on Higher Education* (Washington, DC: Hamilton Project, April 2017), 1, https://www.brookings.edu/research/eight-economic-facts-on-higher-education/.

10. Shambaugh and Nunn, *Revitalizing Wage Growth*, 28.

11. Philip Oreopoulos and Uros Petronijevic, "Making College Worth It: A Review of the Returns to Higher Education," *The Future of Children* 23, no. 1 (spring 2013): 55, https://oreopoulos.faculty.economics.utoronto.ca/wp-content/uploads/2014/08/23_01_03.pdf.

12. Oreopoulos and Petronijevic, "Making College Worth It."

13. Lawrence Katz, interview by Douglas Clement, *The Region*, Federal Reserve Bank of Minneapolis, September 25, 2017, https://www.minneapolisfed.org/publications/the-region/interview-with-lawrence-katz.

14. Nick Hanauer, "Better Schools Won't Fix America," *Atlantic*, July 2019, https://www.theatlantic.com/magazine/archive/2019/07/education-isnt-enough/590611/.

15. Executive Office of the President, *Artificial Intelligence, Automation, and the Economy*, December 2016, https://obamawhitehouse.archives.gov/sites/whitehouse.gov/files/documents/Artificial-Intelligence-Automation-Economy.PDF.

16. "Student Debt and the Class of 2018," Institute for College Access & Success, 14th Annual Report, September 2019, https://ticas.org/wp-content/uploads/2019/09/classof2018.pdf.

17. Sibile Marcellus, "Underemployment for Recent Grads Worse Today Than in Early 2000s," *Yahoo! Finance*, May 21, 2019, https://finance.yahoo.com/news/underemployment-for-recent-grads-worse-today-than-in-early-2000-s-180429491.html.

18. A recent study by the Federal Reserve Bank of New York estimates that over one-fifth of the decline in homeownership among Americans ages twenty-four to thirty-two is due to the rise in student loan debt—representing "over 400,000 young individuals who would have owned a home in 2014 had it not been for the rise in debt." Alvaro Mezza, Daniel Ringo, and Kamila Sommer, "Can Student Loan Debt Explain Low Homeownership Rates for Young Adults?" *Consumer & Community Context* 1, no. 1 (January 2019): 5, https://www.federalreserve.gov/publications/files/consumer-community-context-201901.pdf; and Vadim Revzin and Sergei Revzin, "Student Debt Is Stopping U.S. Millennials from Becoming Entrepreneurs," *Harvard Business Review*, April 26, 2019, https://hbr.org/2019/04/student-debt-is-stopping-u-s-millennials-from-becoming-entrepreneurs.

19. Jacob S. Hacker, *The Great Risk Shift: The New Economic Insecurity and the Decline of the American Dream*, 2nd ed. (New York: Oxford University Press, 2019), 82.

20. Jaison R. Abel and Richard Deitz, "Working as a Barista after College Is Not as Common as You Might Think," *Liberty Street Economics* (blog), January 11, 2016, https://libertystreeteconomics.newyorkfed.org/2016/01/working-as-a-barista-after-college-is-not-as-common-as-you-might-think.html.

21. Clive R. Belfield and Thomas Bailey, "The Benefits of Attending Community College: A Review of the Evidence," *Community College Review* 39, no. 1 (January 2011): 49, https://journals.sagepub.com/doi/pdf/10.1177/0091552110395575.

22. Hacker, *The Great Risk Shift*, 205.

23. Doug Shapiro, Afet Dundar, Faye Huie, Phoebe Khasiala Wakhungu, Ayesha Bhimdiwala, and Sean Eric Wilson, *Completing College: A National View of Student Completion Rates—Fall 2012 Cohort* (Herndon, VA: National Student Clearinghouse Research Center, December 2018), figs. 3 and 6, https://nscresearchcenter.org/signaturereport16/.

24. Shapiro et al., *Completing College*, figs. 16 and 17.

25. "Graduation Rate from First Institution Attended for First-Time, Full-Time Bachelor's Degree-Seeking Students at 4-Year Postsecondary Institutions, by Race/Ethnicity, Time to Completion, Sex, Control of Institution, and Acceptance Rate: Selected Cohort Entry Years, 1996 through 2011," Digest of Education, National Center for Education Statistics, table 326.10, https://nces.ed.gov/programs/digest/d18/tables/dt18_326.10.asp.

26. Shambaugh and Nunn, *Revitalizing Wage Growth*, 26.

27. Ellen Ruppel Shell, "College May Not Be Worth It Anymore," *New York Times*, May 16, 2018, https://www.nytimes.com/2018/05/16/opinion/college-useful-cost-jobs.html.

28. White House Office of the Press Secretary, "President Clinton: Opening the Doors to College and Economic Opportunities for All Americans," news release, June 10, 2000, https://clintonwhitehouse3.archives.gov/WH/New/html/20000612_2.html.

29. Lionel Foster, "Investing in Education: A Conversation with Cecilia Rouse," U.S. Partnership on Mobility from Poverty, May 30, 2017, https://www.mobilitypartnership.org/blog/investing-education-conversation-cecilia-rouse.

30. Susan Scrivener, Michael J. Weiss, Alyssa Ratledge, Timothy Rudd, Colleen Sommo, and Hannah Fresques, *Doubling Graduation Rates* (New York: MDRC, February 2015), 1–3, https://www.mdrc.org/sites/default/files/doubling_graduation_rates_es.pdf/.

31. Susan Dynarski, "How to Improve Graduation Rates at Community Colleges," *New York Times*, March 11, 2015, https://www.nytimes.com/2015/03/12/upshot/how-to-improve-graduation-rates-at-community-colleges.html.

32. Scrivener et al., *Doubling Graduation Rates*, 7.

33. Three Ohio community colleges have successfully replicated this model. John Hutchins, Joseph Tirella, Tracy Green, and Jeff Robinson, "Ohio Programs Based on CUNY's Accelerated Study in Associate Programs (ASAP) More Than Double Graduation Rates," MDRC, December 2018, https://www.mdrc.org/news/press-release/ohio-programs-based-cuny-s-accelerated-study-associate-programs-asap-more-double.

34. "Posse Facts and Figures," Posse Foundation, accessed November 3, 2019, http://www.possefoundation.org/quick-facts; and Executive Office of the President, *Increasing College Opportunities for Low-Income Students*, January 2014, 7–8, https://obamawhitehouse.archives.gov/sites/default/files/docs/increasing_college_opportunity_for_low-income_students_report.pdf.

35. Raj Chetty et al., "Mobility Report Cards: The Role of Colleges in Intergenerational Mobility," National Bureau of Economic Research Working Paper No. 23618, July 2017, http://www.nber.org/papers/w23618.

36. Paul Tough, *The Years That Matter Most: How College Makes or Breaks Us* (New York: Houghton Mifflin Harcourt, 2019), 18, citing Chetty et al., "Mobility Report Cards."

37. Chetty et al., "Mobility Report Cards."

38. Chetty et al., "Mobility Report Cards"; and David Leonhardt, "America's Great Working-Class Colleges," *New York Times*, January 17, 2017, https://www.nytimes.com/2017/01/18/opinion/sunday/americas-great-working-class-colleges.html.

39. Chetty et al., "Mobility Report Cards."

40. For a thoughtful discussion of how to do so, see James Kvaal, "Colleges Can Help Students Move Up. Let's Make It Easier," *Chronicle of Higher Education*, February 19, 2017, https://www.chronicle.com/article/Colleges-Can-Help-Students/239236.

41. Leonhardt, "College for the Masses."

42. Leonhardt, "College for the Masses."

43. Seth D. Zimmerman, "The Returns to College Admission for Academically Marginal Students," *Journal of Labor Economics* 32, no. 4 (October 2014): 711, https://www.journals.uchicago.edu/doi/10.1086/676661.

44. Marshall Steinbaum, "A Brown v. Board for Higher Ed," *Boston Review*, September 1, 2017, http://bostonreview.net/education-opportunity/marshall-steinbaum-brown-v-board-higher-ed.

45. Katz, interview.

46. Katz, interview.

47. Steven Mintz, "Community Colleges and the Future of Higher Education," *Higher Ed Gamma* (blog), *Inside Higher Ed*, March 9, 2019, https://www.insidehighered.com/blogs/higher-ed-gamma/community-colleges-and-future-higher-education.

48. Elizabeth Mann Levesque, *Improving Community College Completion Rates by Addressing Structural and Motivational Barriers* (Washington, DC: Brookings Institution, October 2018), https://www.brookings.edu/research/community-college-completion-rates-structural-and-motivational-barriers/.

49. For example, Steinbaum writes that "free higher education would all but end the predatory for-profit sector." Steinbaum, "A Brown v. Board for Higher Ed."

50. Richard Feloni, "IBM Helps Run a Public School in Brooklyn That Could Change the Way We Think about Education—and It's One of the Only Things Both Trump and Obama Support," *Business Insider*, October 24, 2019, https://www.businessinsider.com/ibm-ptech-brooklyn-high-school-future-of-education.

51. Lul Tesfai, "Creating Pathways to College Degrees through Apprenticeships," New America (website), updated September 19, 2019, https://www.newamerica.org/education-policy/reports/creating-pathways-postsecondary-credentials-through-apprenticeships/.

52. Paula McAvoy, David Campbell, and Diana Hess, *The Relationship between a Liberal Arts Education and Democratic Outcomes* (New York: Andrew W. Mellon Foundation, January 2019), https://mellon.org/news-blog/articles/relationship-between-liberal-arts-education-and-democratic-outcomes/.

53. David Deming, "In the Salary Race, Engineers Sprint but English Majors Endure," *New York Times*, September 20, 2019, https://www.nytimes.com/2019/09/20/business/liberal-arts-stem-salaries.html; and Heather Long, "The World's Top Economists Just Made the Case for Why We Still Need English Majors," *Washington Post*, October 19, 2019, https://www.washingtonpost.com/business/2019/10/19/worlds-top-economists-just-made-case-why-we-still-need-english-majors/.

54. "Careers and Apprenticeships," About Us, AFL-CIO, accessed December 7, 2019, https://aflcio.org/about-us/careers-and-apprenticeships.

55. IMT began in Milwaukee, Wisconsin, and has since expanded to eight states. According to EPI, "Labor union partners include the International Association of Machinists and Aerospace Workers (IAMAW), the International Association of Sheet Metal, Air, Rail and Transportation Workers (SMART), the International Brotherhood of Electrical Workers (IBEW), the United Automobile Workers (UAW), and the United Steelworkers (USW)." Josh Bivens, Lora Engdahl, Elise Gould, Teresa Kroeger, Celine McNicholas, Lawrence Mishel, Zane Mokhiber et al., *How Today's Unions Help Working People* (Washington, DC:

Economic Policy Institute, August 2017), 17, https://www.epi.org/publication/how-todays-unions-help-working-people-giving-workers-the-power-to-improve-their-jobs-and-unrig-the-economy/.

56. See discussion in Chapter Six and Alana Semuels, "Why Does Sweden Have So Many Start-Ups?" *Atlantic*, September 28, 2017, https://www.theatlantic.com/business/archive/2017/09/sweden-startups/541413/.

57. David Fein and Jill Hamadyk, *Bridging the Opportunity Divide for Low-Income Youth: Implementation and Early Impacts of the Year Up Program*, OPRE Report #2018-65 (Washington, DC: Office of Planning, Research, and Evaluation, May 2018), 73, https://www.yearup.org/wp-content/uploads/2018/06/Year-Up-PACE-Full-Report-2018.pdf.

58. Kelsey Schaberg, *Can Sector Strategies Promote Longer-Term Effects? Three-Year Impacts from the WorkAdvance Demonstration* (New York: MDRC, September 2017), 1, 15, https://www.mdrc.org/sites/default/files/WorkAdvance_3-Year_Brief.pdf.

59. Anne Roder and Mark Elliott, *Nine Year Gains: Project QUEST's Continuing Impact* (New York: Economic Mobility Corporation, April 2019), 1–4, https://economicmobilitycorp.org/wp-content/uploads/2019/04/NineYearGains_web.pdf.

60. Chris Tomlinson, "San Antonio Program Moves Low-Skilled Workers into Middle Class," *Houston Chronicle*, April 17, 2019, https://www.houstonchronicle.com/business/columnists/tomlinson/article/San-Antonio-program-moves-low-skilled-workers-13772983.php.

61. That translates to about a $5,000 annual boost. Roder and Elliott, *Nine Year Gains*.

62. Nelson D. Schwartz, "Job Training Can Change Lives. See How San Antonio Does It," *New York Times*, August 19, 2019, https://www.nytimes.com/2019/08/19/business/economy/worker-training-project.html.

63. "Prior Initiatives," Opportunity@Work, accessed November 1, 2019, http://www.opportunityatwork.org/prior-initiatives.

64. Wilkin Sánchez, "From Fast Food Worker to IT Support Specialist—TechHired in Providence," interview by Dan Schiff, *Opportunity@Work* (blog), *Medium*, June 12, 2018, https://blog.opportunityatwork.org/wilkin sanchez-39f9973e9e8f.

65. "Real Jobs Rhode Island," Rhode Island Government (website), accessed December 9, 2019, http://www.dlt.ri.gov/realjobs/.

66. Joseph Parilla and Sifan Liu, *Talent-Driven Economic Development: A New Vision and Agenda for Regional and State Economies* (Washington, DC: Metropolitan Policy Program at Brookings Institution, October 2019), 24–25, https://www.brookings.edu/wp-content/uploads/2019/10/2019.10.15_Brookings-Metro_Talent-driven-economic-development_Parilla-Liu.pdf.

67. Nathaniel Hendren and Ben Sprung-Keyser, "A Unified Welfare Analysis of Government Policies" (working paper, Harvard University, Cambridge, MA, July 2019), 4–5, 28, https://scholar.harvard.edu/files/hendren/files/welfare_vnber.pdf.

68. Isabel V. Sawhill and Jens Ludwig, *Success by Ten: Intervening Early, Often, and Effectively in the Education of Young Children* (Washington, DC: Hamilton Project, February 2007), 2, https://www.brookings.edu/research/success-by-ten-intervening-early-often-and-effectively-in-the-education-of-young-children/. As Hamilton Project noted, researchers have "looked at programs that target home visiting, early childhood education, and those programs that maintain both a school and a home component. They find that, decades after enrollment, participants see effects on earnings. The largest gains are for the programs considered most intensive—the Perry Preschool Project (1962–67) and the Carolina Abecedarian Project (1972–85)—but for every program studied the long-term effect on earnings was positive." Shambaugh and Nunn, *Revitalizing Wage Growth*, 31.

69. Executive Office of the President of the United States, *The Economics of Early Childhood Investments*, January 2015, https://obamawhitehouse.archives.gov/sites/default/files/docs/early_childhood_report_update_final_non-embargo.pdf.

70. "PF3.1: Public Spending on Childcare and Early Education," OECD Family Database, updated February 4, 2019, https://www.oecd.org/els/soc/PF3_1_Public_spending_on_childcare_and_early_education.pdf.

71. A key reason so many young children continue to miss out on pre-K is that Head Start, the federal government's program providing pre-K to poor children, reaches less than half of eligible students due to persistent underfunding. This flies in the face of equality of opportunity and true first chances, yet the share of three- and four-year-olds enrolled in pre-K has barely budged since 2005, when I wrote in *The Pro-Growth Progressive* that we must take more seriously the idea of a "truly comprehensive 0–5 education and child care initiative that offers all children from modest and low-income families access to quality infant, toddler, and preschool programs." David Reich and Chloe Cho, "Unmet Needs and the Squeeze on Appropriations," Center on Budget and Policy Priorities, May 19, 2017, https://www.cbpp.org/research/federal-budget/unmet-needs-and-the-squeeze-on-appropriations#head_start; "Enrollment of 3-, 4-, and 5-Year-Old Children in Preprimary Programs, by Age of Child, Level of Program, Control of Program, and Attendance Status: Selected Years, 1970 through 2017," Digest of Education, National Center for Education Statistics, table 202.10, https://nces.ed.gov/programs/digest/d18/tables/dt18_202.10.asp; and Gene Sperling, *The Pro-Growth Progressive: An Economic Strategy for Shared Prosperity* (New York: Simon & Schuster, 2005), chap. 9.

72. Matt Weyer, "Pre-Kindergarten–Third Grade Literacy," National Conference of State Legislatures, May 24, 2018, http://www.ncsl.org/research/education/pre-kindergarten-third-grade-literacy.aspx.

73. Roseanna Ander, Jonathan Guryan, and Jens Ludwig, "Improving Academic Outcomes for Disadvantaged Students: Scaling Up Individualized Tutorials," Hamilton Project, March 2016, https://www.hamiltonproject.org/assets/files/improving_academic_outcomes_for_disadvantaged_students_pp.pdf.

74. Ander, Guryan, and Ludwig, "Improving Academic Outcomes for Disadvantaged Students."
75. Dana Afana, "Obama Administration Economist Reopens Ann Arbor Tutoring Center His Mother Founded," Mlive.com, October 8, 2019, https://www.mlive.com/news/ann-arbor/2019/10/obama-adminis tration-economist-reopens-ann-arbor-tutoring-center-his-mother-founded.html; for more on FLI also see "The Doris H. Sperling Blueprint for Reading Success: The History, Components, and Proven Record of Student Achievement in the Family Learning Institute," The Family Learning Institute, February 2020, http://familylearninginstitute.org/.
76. Kaisa Snellman, Jennifer M. Silva, and Robert D. Putnam, "Inequity Outside the Classroom: Growing Class Differences in Participation in Extracurricular Activities," *Voices in Urban Education* 40 (2015): 8–14, http://vue.annenberginstitute.org/issues/40/inequity-outside-classroom-growing-class-differences -participation-extracurricular; and Alia Wong, "The Activity Gap," *Atlantic*, January 30, 2015, https://www .theatlantic.com/education/archive/2015/01/the-activity-gap/384961/.
77. Snellman, Silva, and Putnam, "Inequity Outside the Classroom," 8.
78. Snellman, Silva, and Putnam, "Inequity Outside the Classroom," 8.
79. Afterschool Alliance, *America after 3PM Special Report: Afterschool in Communities of Concentrated Poverty*, August 2016, http://www.afterschoolalliance.org/aa3pm/concentrated_poverty.pdf.
80. Afterschool Alliance, *America after 3PM Special Report.*
81. Survey respondents living in communities of concentrated poverty are those who "live in a zip code that falls within a census tract that the Census Bureau has designated as a community of concentrated poverty, and live in a zip code that has poverty rate of 30 percent or above." Afterschool Alliance, *America after 3PM Special Report.*
82. For more, see "What Is CYD and Its Impact?" Creative Youth Development National Partnership, accessed January 20, 2019, https://www.creativeyouthdevelopment.org/national-action-blueprint/what-is-cyd-and -its-impact/.
83. Lorraine M. Gutiérrez and Michael S. Spencer, *Excellence on Stage and in Life: The Mosaic Model for Youth Development through the Arts* (Detroit: Mosaic Youth Theatre of Detroit, 2008), 3, https://mosaicdetroit.org /wp-content/uploads/2019/01/The-Mosaic-Model.pdf.
84. Molly E. Fifer and Alan B. Krueger, *Summer Opportunity Scholarships (SOS): A Proposal to Narrow the Skills Gap* (Washington, DC: Hamilton Project, April 2006), 7, https://www.hamiltonproject.org/assets/legacy /files/downloads_and_links/Summer_Opportunity_Scholarships_SOS_A_Proposal_to_Narrow_the _Skills_Gap.pdf; and Jason Furman and Jason E. Bordorff, eds., *Path to Prosperity* (Washington, DC: Brookings Institution, 2008), 13.
85. Catherine H. Augustine, Jennifer Sloan McCombs, John F. Pane, Heather L. Schwartz, Jonathan Schweig, Andrew McEachin, and Kyle Siler-Evans, *Learning from Summer: Effects of Voluntary Summer Learning Programs on Low-Income Urban Youth* (Santa Monica, CA: RAND Corporation, September 2016), https://www .wallacefoundation.org/knowledge-center/pages/learning-from-summer-effects-of-voluntary-summer -learning-programs-on-low-income-urban-youth.aspx; and Emma Brown, "New Evidence That Summer Programs Can Make a Difference for Poor Children," *Washington Post*, September 7, 2016, https://www .washingtonpost.com/local/education/new-evidence-that-summer-programs-can-make-a-difference-for -poor-children/2016/09/06/cfa4f52c-73cc-11e6-be4f-3f42f2e5a49e_story.html.
86. Rebecca Leung, "I Have a Dream: College Tuition," *CBS*, May 20, 2004, https://www.cbsnews.com/news /i-have-a-dream-college-tuition/.
87. Erica L. Green, "Government Watchdog Finds Racial Bias in School Discipline," *New York Times*, April 4, 2018, https://www.nytimes.com/2018/04/04/us/politics/racial-bias-school-discipline-policies.html; and Joshua Rovner, "Racial Disparities in Youth Commitments and Arrests," Sentencing Project, April 1, 2016, https://www.sentencingproject.org/publications/racial-disparities-in-youth-commitments-and-arrests/.
88. Sperling, *The Pro-Growth Progressive*, 138–39, chap. 8, n. 9.
89. "Declare a Dream," College Track (website), accessed November 3, 2019, https://collegetrack.org/high -school/.
90. See more extensive discussion in Sperling, *The Pro-Growth Progressive*, chap. 8.
91. Career Academies are small learning communities that focus curricula on a career theme and work with local employers to provide experiential, work-based learning opportunities. As rigorous evaluation by MDRC has found, Career Academies led to a significant boost in postsecondary graduation rates and an 11 percent increase in earnings per year that persisted over at least eight years. Executive Office of the President, *Increasing College Opportunities*, 32; and James J. Kemple and Cynthia J. Willner, *Career Academies: Long-Term Impacts on Labor Market Outcomes, Educational Attainment, and Transitions to Adulthood* (New York: MDRC, June 2008), 12, https://www.mdrc.org/sites/default/files/full_50.pdf. The cohort-based approaches, namely, the "I Have a Dream" Foundation, Project GRAD, and College Track, provide intensive early interventions that promote awareness of college opportunities, financial aid, mentorship, counseling, academic support, college visits, or a variety of other approaches, and each has been linked to increased high school completion and college enrollment. Executive Office of the President, *Increasing College Opportunities for Low-Income Students*, 7–8.
92. Tough, *The Years That Matter Most.*
93. Executive Office of the President, *Increasing College Opportunities for Low-Income Students*, 38.
94. Executive Office of the President, *Increasing College Opportunities for Low-Income Students*, 31.

CONCLUSION: INCLUSIVE DIGNITY OR DIVISIVE DIGNITY?

1. Diana C. Mutz, "Status Threat, Not Economic Hardship, Explains the 2016 Presidential Vote," *Proceedings of the National Academy of Sciences* 115, no. 19 (May 8, 2018), https://www.pnas.org/content/115/19/E4330.full.
2. Mutz, "Status Threat, Not Economic Hardship, Explains the 2016 Presidential Vote."
3. John Sides, Michael Tesler, and Lynn Vavreck, *Identity Crisis: The 2016 Presidential Campaign and the Battle for the Meaning of America* (Princeton, NJ: Princeton University Press, 2018).
4. See "2016 Time Series Study," American National Election Studies, https://electionstudies.org/data-cen ter/2016-time-series-study/, cited in Geoffrey Skelley, "Just How Many Obama 2012–Trump 2016 Voters Were There?" Rasmussen Reports, June 1, 2017, http://www.rasmussenreports.com/public_content/politi cal_commentary/commentary_by_geoffrey_skelley/just_how_many_obama_2012_trump_2016_voters_we re_there.
5. Eduardo Porter, "Where Were Trump's Votes? Where the Jobs Weren't," *New York Times*, December 13, 2016, https://www.nytimes.com/2016/12/13/business/economy/jobs-economy-voters.html.
6. Andrew J. Cherlin, "In the Shadow of Sparrows Point: Racialized Labor in the White and Black Working Classes," Russell Sage Foundation, October 2019, 24, https://www.russellsage.org/sites/default/files/In%20the %20Shadow%20of%20Sparrows%20Point.pdf.
7. W. E. B. Du Bois, *Black Reconstruction in America* (New York: Oxford University Press, 2007). First published 1935 by Harcourt, Brace and Howe (New York).
8. Quoted in Ta-Nehisi Coates, "The First White President," *Atlantic*, October 2017, https://www.theatlantic .com/magazine/archive/2017/10/the-first-white-president-ta-nehisi-coates/537909/.
9. Michelle Alexander, *The New Jim Crow: Mass Incarceration in the Age of Colorblindness* (New York: New Press, 2010), 34.
10. Dan Carter, "What Donald Trump Owes George Wallace," *New York Times*, January 8, 2016, https://www .nytimes.com/2016/01/10/opinion/campaign-stops/what-donald-trump-owes-george-wallace.html.
11. Fareed Zakaria, "Populism on the March: Why the West Is in Trouble," *Foreign Affairs*, November/December 2016, https://www.foreignaffairs.com/articles/united-states/2016-10-17/populism-march.
12. Jack Snyder, "The Broken Bargain: How Nationalism Came Back," *Foreign Affairs*, March/April 2019, https://www.foreignaffairs.com/articles/world/2019-02-12/broken-bargain.
13. Meagan Flynn, "Trump Picked a Fight over Greenland with an Unlikely Target: Denmark's Anti-immigration Prime Minister," *Washington Post*, August 21, 2019, https://www.washingtonpost.com/nation/2019/08/21 /trump-picked-fight-over-greenland-with-an-unlikely-target-denmarks-anti-immigration-prime-minister/; and Ellen Barry and Martin Selsoe Sorensen, "In Denmark, Harsh New Laws for Immigrant 'Ghettos,'" *New York Times*, July 1, 2018, https://www.nytimes.com/2018/07/01/world/europe/denmark-immigrant-ghettos .html.
14. Jon Stone, "Denmark Gets New Left-Wing Government with Plans to Increase Welfare Spending and Scrap Anti-immigration Measures," *Independent*, June 26, 2019, https://www.independent.co.uk/news /world/europe/denmark-new-government-left-mette-frederiksen-welfare-spending-anti-immigration-a 8975096.html; and Flynn, "Trump Picked a Fight over Greenland with an Unlikely Target."
15. See Christina Anderson and Steven Erlanger, "Sweden's Centrists Prevail Even as Far Right Has Its Best Showing Ever," *New York Times*, September 9, 2018, https://www.nytimes.com/2018/09/09/world/europe /sweden-elections.html.
16. Saskia Brechenmacher, "Comparing Democratic Distress in the United States and Europe," Carnegie Endowment for International Peace, June 21, 2018, https://carnegieendowment.org/2018/06/21/comparing -democratic-distress-in-united-states-and-europe-pub-76646.
17. See the following for related discussions: Karin Borevi, "Multiculturalism and Welfare State Integration: Swedish Model Path Dependency," *Identities: Global Studies in Culture and Power* 21, no. 6 (2014): 708–23, https://www.tandfonline.com/doi/full/10.1080/1070289X.2013.868351; and OECD, *Working Together: Skills and Labour Market Integration of Immigrants and Their Children in Sweden* (Paris: OECD Publishing, 2016).
18. Chloe Colliver, Peter Pomerantsev, Anne Applebaum, and Jonathan Birdwel, "Smearing Sweden: International Influence Campaigns in the 2018 Swedish Election," ISD and LSE Institute of Global Affairs, 2018, https://www.isdglobal.org/wp-content/uploads/2018/11/Smearing-Sweden.pdf; and Jo Becker, "The Global Machine behind the Rise of Far-Right Nationalism," *New York Times*, August 10, 2019, https://www .nytimes.com/2019/08/10/world/europe/sweden-immigration-nationalism.html.
19. Manuel Funke, Moritz Schularick, and Christoph Trebesch, "Going to Extremes: Politics after Financial Crises, 1870–2014," Center for Economic Studies and Ifo Institute Working Paper No. 5553, October 2015, https://www.ifo.de/DocDL/cesifo1_wp5553.pdf.
20. Manuel Funke, Moritz Schularick, and Christoph Trebesch, "The Financial Crisis Is Still Empowering Far-Right Populists," *Foreign Affairs*, September 2018, https://www.foreignaffairs.com/articles/2018-09-13 /financial-crisis-still-empowering-far-right-populists.
21. Funke, Schularick, and Trebesch, "The Financial Crisis Is Still Empowering Far-Right Populists."

INDEX